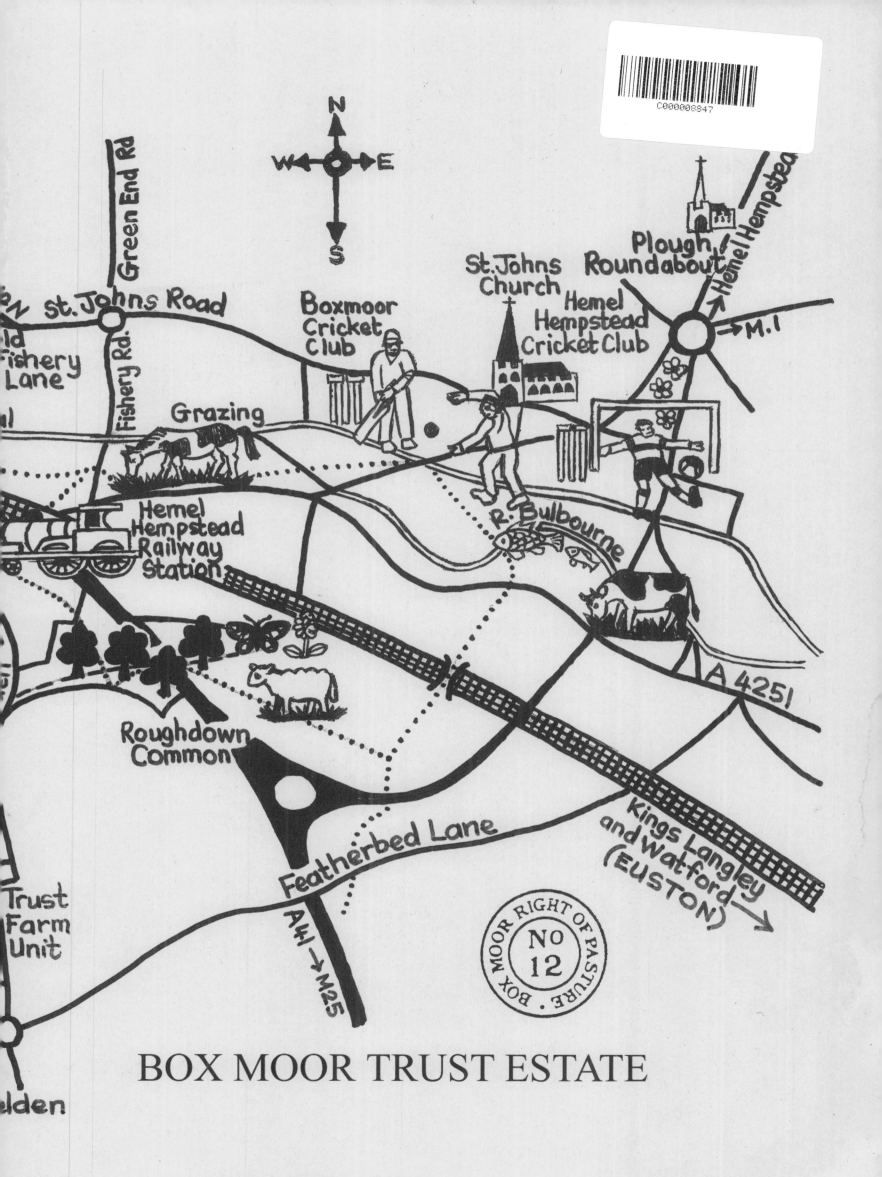

BOX MOOR TRUST ESTATE

ROYALTY TO COMMONERS

Four Hundred Years of the Box Moor Trust

1594–2004

By Joan and Roger Hands

First published in 2004 by The Box Moor Trust
London Road, Hemel Hempstead, Herts HP1 2RE

Text © Joan and Roger Hands, 2004
Production © The Box Moor Trust, 2004

ISBN: 0-9504532-2-6

A CIP catalogue record for this book is available from the British Library.
British Library Cataloguing-in-Publication Data.

This book was produced by Alpine Press Ltd for The Box Moor Trust

Design and typesetting: Alpine Press Ltd
Editorial: Mandi Gomez
Index: Hilary Bird
Repro, printing and binding: Alpine Press Ltd, Station Road, Kings Langley, Hertfordshire. Tel. 01923 269777

Cover illustrations: Spring: Riders and walkers on bridleway near Howe's Retreat.
Summer: Belted Galloways on Snoxall's Moor.
Autumn: Chestnut avenue on Blackbirds' Moor.
Winter: Winter sports on Sheethanger Common.

DEDICATION

**To the Beneficiaries of the Box Moor Trust from 1594
'for their heirs and assigns forever ...'**

Box Moor - that other England

For David and Stephen

that other England is my home –
not for me the concrete sprawl
congested roads and fouled up air.
I wake each morning to jackdaw's cry
and lofty beech with tinted leaves,
the only sound the milk float's hum,
not commuting traffic's constant drone.

that other England's a secret home
of chalkhill shrubs and ancient dells,
of harebells, Lady's Smock and bees,
where water meadows still gleam gold,
token of bounty yet to come,
of belted cattle taking their ease
on common land owned by everyone.

that other England is our home,
though children leave for urgent toil
of higher status, wilder dreams,
yet within they carry a finite bond
born of hours in Roughdown's woods
tracking their hopes in brambly dens –
until the day they'll no more roam.

Joan I. Hands

(First published in *Central England Poets*, Arrival Press, 1995)

ACKNOWLEDGEMENTS

The authors wish to express their gratitude to all those individuals, institutions and organisations that have helped in the preparation of this book.

The Box Moor Trustees, Managers and Staff, past and present, in particular colleagues on the Records Committee, namely Reg Sear, Stan Snoxall, Paul Stanbridge, Tom Williams and Jack Marshall, who deserves a special mention for his research when Administrator of the Trust. Sadly Reg, Stan, Tom and Jack have now all passed away.

The past and present members of the Dacorum Heritage Trust, especially Elizabeth Buteux, Peter Clayton, Eric Edwards and Denis Miles. Its Curator, Matt Wheeler, and Assistant Curator, Catherine Peet, have given invaluable and constant support.

Berkhamsted and District Archaeological Society, Berkhamsted Local History and Museum Society, Bovingdon Parish Council, Dacorum Borough Council, *Hemel Hempstead Gazette*, Hemel Hempstead Library, Hemel Hempstead Local History and Museum Society, Hemel Hempstead Photographic Society, Hertfordshire Archaeological Trust, Hertfordshire Archives and Local Studies, Herts. Library Service and Kings Langley Local History and Museum Society have all been willing to share their resources.

Apsley Paper Trail, Ashridge Management College, Bedford and Luton Record Office, Beverley Council, Bodleian Library, (Oxford), Bryan Donkin Trust, British Paper Company, House of Lords Record Office, Ironbridge Gorge Museum Trust, Kenfig Council, Museum of St Albans, National Portrait Gallery, (London), Lindley Library of the Royal Horticultural Society, Trustees of the Wallace Collection, (London), and Roger Bolton have all kindly supplied information and/or images for reproduction. The authors are pleased to have been allowed to include original artworks by Dennis S. Edmonds, Dennis Furnell and Peter Wagon.

The modern photographs are primarily the work of Keith Huggett, to whom the authors and Trustees are indebted for his willing involvement and professionalism. The hand-drawn maps (front and end papers) by Julie Evans are an original feature and the authors wish to thank her especially for her contribution. Copying old photographs and maps has been kindly arranged by Nigel Wickens and Edwin Blenkinsopp and the authors are indebted to them for their expert assistance.

Gerald Salisbury and Jill Saunders are to be congratulated for their comprehensive records and monitoring of the Flora on the Box Moor Estate. The authors are sure this appendix will have wider uses in the future.

David and Jean Stevens are sincerely thanked for their individual contributions, in both text and images; also, Alice Wear, for permission to use the article on 'Memories of Westbrook Hay' and Myfanwy Lee for her reminiscences.

The formatting of the extensive appendices was only achieved with the help of Michael and Margaret Stanyon and initially of Penny Pelham. Keith Davidson undertook the immense task of proof-reading and the authors are grateful for his professional guidance.

Many old and new photographs are from the authors' own collection, with extra images and/or information provided by Clive Agnew, Justin Arundale, Box Moor Trust, Sarah Brown, Jim Cannon, Barbara Chapman, David Clarke, Alistair Cowe, Cyril Collins, Dacorum Heritage Trust, Keith Davidson, Dennis Furnell, Stuart Grieve, David Harrington, Hemel Hempstead Gazette, Rachel Hemming, Eric Holland, Daphne Hughes, David Kirk, Dave Lees, John Leonhardt, P. H. Lomax, N. Mistry, Mary Nobbs, Pat Parrish, Fred Penhearow, Tom Price, Kath Radlett, Edward and Ted Sammes, David Spain, Kay Sanecki, Pauline Siddell, Frank Thompson, A. J. 'Peter' Ward, Ken Whiteley, Richard Whitmore, Alan John Willmott and Geoff and Sue Woodward.

The sports clubs on the Box Moor Estate have been very useful sources for research and special thanks are due to: Boxmoor Cricket Club, Maurice Wigmore and Stanley Gillon; Boxmoor Golf Club: Val Daley, Ted Duel, Philip Levis, John Linton, Bob Newark and Gary Newark; Hemel Hempstead (Camelot) Rugby Club: John Clapham, Air Cdre. Noel James and Jack Marshall; Hemel Hempstead Town Cricket Club: Peter Frogley and Nick Wright.

Finally, to Mandi Gomez, Hilary Bird and the Staff of Alpine Press, the authors wish to convey their appreciation.

If there are any errors or major omissions, the authors apologise but feel that they have tried their best to achieve a balanced and factually accurate view of a complex story. There is a great deal more which could have been included, save for restraints of space and time. The story continues to unfold ...

FOREWORD

I can remember playing on the open common land years before I knew about the Box Moor Trust. We used to bounce our iron hoops down the slopes into the chalk pit on Roughdown, a favourite spot for picnics. I played football for Two Waters Central School on the Moor opposite the School, without realising to whom we owed that privilege. It was not until I was elected a Trustee in 1975 that I came to appreciate the extent of the Trust's holdings and its benefit to the locality over the centuries.

The idea of a book telling the full story of the Box Moor Trust had long been an unfulfilled desire. The Trustees for many years showed interest, but the important question of who should do it was never resolved. Then, in 1991, Roger Hands, one of the Trustees, offered to put all his years of research and extensive collection of photographs to the test, in order to produce a book to mark Four Hundred Years of the Box Moor Trust. He combined his background knowledge with the literary skills of his wife, Joan, and this book is the final result. It serves as a record of the Trust up to the present. It has not been born without hours of painstaking work, but it has at last materialised and the Trust is grateful to the authors for their commitment to the task.

The Trustees hope that this book will enlighten the present generation living in the Area of Benefit as well as providing an inspiring picture for a nationwide audience, of a unique and historic Trust, showing something of what it has achieved in the past and looking forward to what it might achieve in the future.

Above all, we hope that local people will still be willing to give their time and energy to serve as Trustees, even though their efforts are entirely without remuneration. Read and enjoy the book – and then 'Go and do thou likewise!'

Reg Sear

Reg Sear

A pleasure that never wanes – fun on the rope swing beside the river Bulbourne on Harding's Moor. The formal aspects of the Box Moor Trust are balanced by the informal – the many opportunities that abound for fresh air and exercise make all the hard work and voluntary effort worthwhile.

CONTENTS

In the Beginning

1. A Bird's-Eye View

'The further backward you look the further forward you can see.'
Winston Churchill.

Prehistoric man once wandered over this ancient landscape, searching for food, fresh water and a safe resting place. The Mesolithic flint axe-head, found during excavations at the Boxmoor Trout Fishery, conjures up scenes of small tribes of hunter-gatherers roaming the river valleys and the chalky hills. The puddingstone* quern*, or corn handmill that was also found at the trout lake, was evidence of a more settled life style over 3,500 years ago.

Farming was the underlying raison d'être of this south-western corner of Hertfordshire over many centuries. By the sixteenth century wheat, barley, peas and oats were all grown locally, as well as root crops, with wheat remaining as the staple crop. The innovations and writings of William Ellis of Little Gaddesden in the first half of the eighteenth century and the interest shown by the seventh Earl of Bridgewater in new farming methods seventy years later, were part of the wider involvement in agriculture which brought employment and a modicum of comfort to the local inhabitants. The gradual rise of Hemel Hempstead to become the chief corn market in the county by the late 1700s is well documented. Straw plaiting* was a major source of income for the cottagers, especially in the villages surrounding the towns of Hemel Hempstead, Berkhamsted and Tring. The hat trade of Luton and Dunstable relied on a steady supply of intricately plaited straw and the pay was often much better than that of general farm workers.

The Saxon and Norman system of community farming, with its hierarchy of serfs*, villeins* and freemen, overseen by the Lord of the Manor*, had worked in its day but had been replaced in time by the payment of money in exchange for manorial duties. When the chance arose, in 1581, the householders of Hemel Hempstead and Bovingdon grasped it and, in the guise of a Feoffement* secured their water meadows for fishing and grazing for ever. The Conveyance of 1594 made their intentions public. The Box Moor Trust was the result.

What prompted the local community to enter into this secret purchase? It is an accepted fact that between 1600 and 1800 England achieved extraordinary growth compared to the rest of the world. Although the population tripled during this time, the area of land used for agriculture did not significantly increase. The quantity and quality of British livestock, especially the efficient use of horse power, seems to have been a major factor in these differences. The opportunity to own good pasture in perpetuity, afforded by the water meadows of Box Moor, must have been uppermost in the minds of those early Feoffes. The perceived threat of enclosure may also have been an underlying issue. Timber, furze, beech and acorn mast, were all valuable commodities, together with the fishing in clear chalk streams. Whatever their reasons, their astute foresight gave rise to the events which are illustrated in the following pages.

In 1691, copyholds* were replaced by freeholds and private enterprise became the keyword. The wide-scale enclosure of wastes and commons, the introduction of sheep in large numbers and the rise of the middle classes all had their effect on English society as a whole. Hemel Hempstead and its nearby villages slowly but surely expanded. The mills recorded in the eleventh-century Domesday register*, still utilised the local water power, but some were converted by the late 1700s to making paper instead of grinding corn or fulling* cloth.

The agricultural changes of the sixteenth and seventeenth centuries were followed in the eighteenth century by the Industrial Revolution, eras that were to prove significant in the history of the Box Moor Trust. Industrialisation of methods of production and the increasing use of steam-driven machines, which fed hungrily on coal, led to construction of the first canals. The 'Canal Duke', Francis Egerton, the third Duke of Bridgewater, inherited the family estate of Ashridge near Berkhamsted in 1759. He happened to be the proverbial right man in the right place at the right time, returning from a Grand Tour of Europe where he had seen canals put to use for industry. Utilising this knowledge, he used canal transportation on both the family estate and his coal mines in Worsley. The next seventy years saw the great age of canal building and by 1797 the Grand Junction Canal reached Boxmoor, followed in 1837 by the London and Birmingham Railway.

Both of these major transport solutions caused problems for the Trust, although some benefits did accrue from the required sale of the land. The despoliation of the Moors may have seemed a minor matter to people outside the Area of Benefit at the turn of the eighteenth century, but when the same corridor of land was compulsorily required for the 'greater good' of the public in the shape of a new motorway, tempers were again roused and a Public Inquiry was held.

'Motorway Mania' came and went, leaving a sinuous dual carriageway, by-passing prehistoric and industrial heritage sites, Roman roads and Royal routes, canal, rivers, railways, rare breeds of sheep and cattle, golf courses and sports grounds, Sites of Special Scientific Interest and of natural scenic beauty – all part of the continuing story of the Box Moor Trust.

The Box Moor Trust Area of Benefit

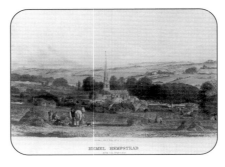

Hemel Hempstead from the North East by Lefevre Cranstone, looking towards the northern boundary of the Area of Benefit, which in the past would have been mainly agricultural.

Marchmont Farm, Piccotts End in 1948, adjacent to the northern boundary of the Area of Benefit at Water End.

Nash Mills Lock, looking towards Red Lion Lane on the eastern boundary of the Area of Benefit.

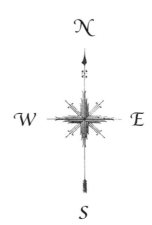

N

W   E

S

The Bourne Gutter, 2000. This flash stream flows only when the water table is high enough, which can be as infrequently as every seven years. It forms part of the western boundary of the Area of Benefit. Viewed from the A41 By-pass, it appears as a scenic silver stream, but in olden times it was believed to be a portent of war, or 'woe water'.

Today, the Box Moor Trust manages an Estate of approximately 470 acres on behalf of the inhabitants of Hemel Hempstead and Bovingdon who live within the Trust's Area of Benefit.

Shantock Hall Farmhouse, Bovingdon, by George Eyre Brooks. The farm is near the southern boundary of the Area of Benefit.

An early view of rural Boxmoor, with unfenced common land. This section of the Area of Benefit forms part of the original Box Moor, purchased in 1581 by a secret trust. In the middle distance, barely visible, are the signs of the changing times when the first railway terminus in the country was established here in 1837.

2. ELIZABETH I AND THE EARL OF LEICESTER

An oil painting on a door panel discovered in the old Manor House at Little Gaddesden in 1878. The nearby estate of Ashridge was later granted to Princess Elizabeth by her half-brother, Edward VI, following the wishes of their father, Henry VIII. Elizabeth was living at Ashridge in 1554 when she was arrested and transported to the Tower of London, on suspicion of being implicated by Wyatt's rebellion against her half-sister, Queen Mary. (By courtesy of Roger Bolton).

A gift of land in 1574 from Queen Elizabeth I to her favourite courtier, Robert Dudley, truly began the story of the Box Moor Trust. From this generous bequest, the Hertfordshire town of Hemel Hempstead and neighbouring village of Bovingdon have fortuitously benefited to the present day.

Elizabeth succeeded to the throne of England on 17 November 1558 and a whole new era of royal courtly behaviour came into its own. The young and personable Queen liked the company of virile, handsome men in her entourage and she soon found a responsive consort in Robert Dudley.

Dudley was the fifth son of the ambitious John, Duke of Northumberland, notoriously involved in the vain attempt to establish the unfortunate Lady Jane Grey as Queen of England in 1553. They had both suffered the traitor's fate at the hands of the executioner, along with Lord Guildford Dudley, to whom Lady Jane had been married against her

will in May that year. Robert's grandfather, Edmund Dudley, was beheaded by order of Henry VIII, not exactly promising antecedents for a consort of the new monarch. Dudley had also been imprisoned in the Tower of London awaiting a similar end, before being released in 1554, and thereafter distinguishing himself in France, in the army of Philip II of Spain. He was a very accomplished horseman and jouster, talents which appealed to Elizabeth.

The Queen kept Dudley bound to her throughout his life – 'her little dog' or 'her eyes' as she fondly or satirically called him, depending on her mood of the moment. She rewarded him with lucrative offices, privileges (he had virtually free access to her bedchamber, although, allegedly, she was always accompanied by her Ladies in Waiting), a sumptuous apartment next to her own at Greenwich and the substantial retainer of £1,000 per annum. He, on his part, had hopes of a royal marriage that would never come to fruition.

Dudley cut a fine figure of a man: 'almost six feet tall, attractively dark-skinned, with reddish brown hair and moustache and heavy lidded eyes'. He was often referred to by his detractors as 'the Gypsy'. He could dance and sing, much needed accomplishments at the Elizabethan court, was well read and could speak French and Italian. He had known the Queen long before she came to that high position.

Robert Dudley, Earl of Leicester *(1532–1588), by Steven van der Meulen c.1560–65. Dudley sold the land given to him by Elizabeth I which later became part of the original Box Moor Estate. (Reproduced by kind permission of the trustees of the Wallace Collection, London).*

They had played together as children, as well as sharing some similarities of fortune. The Queen once remarked that she was more attached to him than anyone else because he had helped her and given her money in her time of distress during the reign of her half-sister, Mary.

Dudley had ridden from his estates in Norfolk to Hatfield when the news of her accession was broadcast, to offer his loyalty and services; throughout most of her life Elizabeth did not forget her childhood friend. Indeed, it has often been speculated that Dudley was the only man she ever truly loved. The fact that he was already married to Amy Robsart did not diminish Elizabeth's admiration of him, much to the consternation of her ministers and court.

Yet, despite all his manly attributes, or perhaps because of them, 'bonny sweet Robin' had many enemies at court. The sudden and inexplicable death of his wife, who was found with a broken neck at the foot of the stairs at Cumnor Place near Abingdon, did nothing to add to his suitability as the future King of England and rumour added its own lurid details.

Dudley's early attempt to be elevated to the peerage failed, having previously been made Master of the Horse, Knight of the Garter, a Member of the Inner Temple of the Inns of Court and a Privy Councillor. He still held ambitions to marry Elizabeth, but the Queen took care not to commit herself to any suitor. She did, however, restore to Dudley many of the lands formerly held by his disgraced father and a licence to export woollen cloth, at that time the backbone of England's trade overseas. In 1563, Elizabeth endowed her favourite courtier with Kenilworth Castle in Warwickshire. His substantial income and privileges would have satisfied many a lesser man, but Dudley was always aiming at the greater prize and often lived beyond his means.

Dudley's ambitions were finally satisfied on at least one issue when he was eventually raised to the peerage in 1564. His new titles of Baron Denbigh and Earl of Leicester were given partly to reward his constancy and partly to make him more acceptable as a possible husband for Elizabeth's cousin, Mary, Queen of Scots. Elizabeth had been conniving to arrange this union for some time, even though it would mean losing her dearest friend to her perceived enemy. The idea was prompted by the need to find Mary a Protestant husband, who would be resolutely loyal to Elizabeth, and not a Catholic aristocrat with European affiliations. Incidentally, Francis Russell, the Earl of Bedford, was one of the commissioners for this match-making scheme. At the last minute, Elizabeth could not bear to see her gallant Robin married to her rival and changed her mind about the match. Confused, Dudley asked for the Queen's hand in marriage at Christmas, 1565, but Elizabeth by then had become practised at evasion.

However, another woman had taken the Earl's fancy – the twenty-five year old Douglas, the Dowager Lady Sheffield – and he secretly married her in May 1573. In that year, the Queen had reached the ripe age (for the time) of forty and yet her affection for Dudley was still fundamentally intact. Even the news of Douglas's deliverance of a baby son, named Robert, did not alter her unique relationship with the father. The Queen believed the child was born out of wedlock and Dudley did not correct her false impression. He denied the marriage later and persuaded Douglas to bastardise their son.

At some occasion during 1574, Elizabeth gave even more land to the dissembling Earl, including property in the vicinity of Hemel Hempstead. The gift was recorded at Gorhambury, near St Albans, the home of Sir Nicholas Bacon, Lord Keeper of the Great Seal. Dudley's response to her generosity and continuing friendship was the fantastic display at Kenilworth Castle when, in the summer of 1575, Elizabeth went on one of her fabled 'progresses' around her kingdom. Leicester was made Lord Lieutenant of Hertfordshire in 1586, continuing the link with this part of the country. He died suddenly on 4 September 1588, at Cornbury Park, near Woodstock, Oxfordshire, after the defeat of the Spanish Armada. With his demise some of the vitality went out of the Virgin Queen. At the time of his death, Dudley was bigamously married to Lettice Knollys, an acclaimed beauty of her day and a member of the royal household. He left his widow with debts of £50,000, half of which was owed to the Queen. It may have been his constant impecunious state that led him to sell some of the property given to him by Elizabeth in 1574. This act was to have far-reaching consequences for the inhabitants of Hemel Hempstead and Bovingdon.

Elizabeth I (1553–1603) by Marcus Gheeraerts the Younger c.1592. (Reproduced by courtesy of the National Portrait Gallery, London).

3. A SECRET TRUST

'These premises were granted to Robert Earl of Leicester by our Lady Queen Elizabeth by Letters Patent under the Great Seal dated at Gorhambury 5 April.'
Indenture belonging to the Box Moor Trust, St Albans, 1574.

The 'premises' mentioned above were situated in Hemel Hempstead. They did not stay for long in Leicester's keeping, since on 11 May 1574 he parted with them to Francis, Earl of Bedford and Peter Graye of Segenhoe, Bedfordshire. There was an historical link between the Earls of Leicester and Bedford. Francis Russell, born in 1527, was the second Earl of Bedford and lived nearby at Chenies Manor in Buckinghamshire. He had been involved in the tragic nine-day accession of Lady Jane Grey and had departed the country in a hurry following her execution. Robert Dudley had lost his father and an elder brother to the same cause, narrowly escaping a similar fate himself.

When the Protestant Elizabeth succeeded to the throne, Francis returned and became a loyal supporter, gaining several Offices of State in the process, including the Lord Presidency of Wales. The Queen, like her father, paid many visits to Chenies and even held Privy Council meetings there; arrangements for the imprisonment of Mary Stuart, Scotland's long-suffering Queen, were settled at one such meeting.

Peter Graye, Armiger (or Squire) is listed as the leaseholder of the manor of Brogborough in 1564 and the manor of Segenhoe in 1566, which he still held in 1576, but little else is known about him. In the Bedfordshire Visitation Records he is shown to have married Elizabeth Wood of Fulbourne, Cambridgeshire. There is no record of the amount paid by Russell and Graye to Leicester, but the Queen's chosen confidant often had cash-flow problems. Expensive presents from Robert Dudley to Elizabeth were partly to blame for this state of affairs. He had clandestinely married Douglas, Lady Sheffield, but this liaison did not prevent him from giving the Queen a fan with a golden handle engraved with 'his and her' emblems on her fortieth birthday in 1573. The imminent birth of Dudley's son (on 7 August 1574) might also have prompted the sale. A further sale was made on 23 June 1574:

'By which Francis Earl of Bedford and Peter Graye Esq. of Segenhoe (parish of Ridgmount) Bedfordshire sold part of their holdings on to Francis Combe son and heir apparent of Richard Combe Esquire of Hemel Hempstead all that grove and hereditaments appertaining*

called Lordes hartes grove (8 acres of land and wood formerly demised to William Stevans) and a little grove called Hartes hill (8 acres formerly demised to Francis Babb by copy of court roll) all of which premises are in Hemel Hempstead in the County of Hertford.'

Elizabeth had leased Ashridge, the former monastic property, in 1556 to Richard Combe of Hemel Hempstead for twenty-one years for the sum of £6 0s 10d per annum.

Peter Graye had seven children and the name of his eldest son, Richard Grey of Segenhoe, is the next to appear in the saga. By 1577 he had acquired both shares in the remaining property and once again it was soon to be sold, this time to three men from Hemel Hempstead.

Trade token belonging to William Gladman of Hemel Hempstead, undated. The obverse shows a dog and a duck on a gallows sign; its value was a halfpenny. Gladman was named in the initial secret purchase of the Trust lands in 1581, but he had died by the time of the 1594 Feoffement. In 1623, a William Gladman was elected as Bailiff for Hemel Hempstead. The Gladman family was widespread in the area, with members located in the town and districts of Estbroke, Crouchfield and Flaunden.

A Feoffement of 26 May 1581, between Richard Grey of the first part and John Rolfe, Richard Pope and William Gladman of the second part, made no mention of the uses for which the property was to be held. A Feoffement, or conveyance of freehold estate by formal transfer, was a common device of the period to avoid disclosing the true purchaser, or reasons for such purchase.

The lands were named as 'one meadow in Hemelhemsted called or known by the name of Castlemead with the appurtenances alias Haywardes Meade alias Bayley Mead alias Haybourne' and the purchase price was the princely sum of £75. The deal included at least nine houses and 25 acres of land in several parcels, as well as the all-important meadows recorded above.

As it was later discovered, John Rolfe, yeoman*, Richard Pope, shoemaker, and William Gladman, yeoman, had bought the pastures as a secret Trust on behalf of the inhabitants of Hemel Hempstead and Bovingdon for their general use in perpetuity.

The yeomen of England were legally freemen who held land worth forty shillings a year and could therefore cast a parliamentary vote. They were farmers who cultivated their own moderate estates and by that time were men who had risen in the social hierarchy of the day to become a substantial middle tier between the noblemen and landed gentry above and the labourers below: in other words, part of the burgeoning middle class of English society. The remarkable fact is that it was these kinds of people, the 'middling sort' in the vernacular of later days, who were the initiators of this fortunate scheme.

There was probably a degree of self interest in the purchase, since Richard Pope, although described as a shoemaker, was also landlord of the Cock Inn, once situated in the High Street. He subsequently acquired the freehold to the inn. John Rolfe bought a house and land, possibly in Boxted, whilst William Gladman, a farmer from Piccotts End, gained the freehold of the property in which either he or members of his family resided.

The crucial Indenture* of Feoffement of 1594 laid down the earliest rules for the maintenance of the Box Moor Trust, for the most part unchanged up to the present day. This precious document transferred the lands from Richard Pope and John Rolfe, to sixty-seven named local householders. It appears that William Gladman, one of the three original named purchasers, had died prior to this date.

The first name on the list was that of the eleven year-old Francis Combes the younger. These people then became the first Feoffes, or Trustees, of the land in question; their heirs and assigns to hold them for ever and to administer them for the common good. It is notable that there was no differentiation made between the statuses of the inhabitants, the only criteria being that they resided in the Area of Benefit. Society at the time was composed of households and only the heads of those households who were freemen, not bondmen, constituted the 'commonwealth'. Therefore, all the listed names were males, a fact that held true right up until 1979, when the first female Trustee was elected. In Tudor times, the usual place of women was to keep house and look after their families, not to meddle with matters abroad, or be part of the body politic, or to bear civil office. The fact that the sovereign was a female seemingly did not come into the equation!

It was made abundantly clear in the Deed of 26 April 1594 that part of the money with which Rolfe, Pope and Gladman bought the meadows and premises in 1581 was raised from the local population at the time of the purchase.

[It] *'was disbursed and paid at the costs and charges of divers and the most of the Inhabitants of Hemelhempstead and Bovington in performance of the said entente and purpose, videlicet*, that the said inhabitants of Hemelhempstead and Bovington might for ever hereafter have, hould and freely enjoy all the profites, commodities and benefittes of the said Meadow and Fishing as is aforesaid.'*

There were numerous legal restrictions on the conveyance of property and a direct sale to the ordinary inhabitants of the district might have caused difficulties. However, the forward-thinking inhabitants had seized their opportunity in 1581 to claim the meadows and rivers and make a deal, fronted by three prominent local men of the time. In effect, the latter had acted as the cover for them to secure their common rights* in perpetuity and to take control of their own affairs. The material gains arising from this transaction included the use of good grazing land and fishing rights in the trout streams of the Gade and Bulbourne. The water meadows were especially desirable, since their use brought forward the time that poorly fed, over-wintered stock could be let out to graze in the spring.

Trade token belonging to John Rolph, later in date to that of Gladman: 1668. The value of this token was a halfpenny; the obverse shows a bull. The family appears to have been influential in Hemel Hempstead over a long period, but the name was spelt as Rolf or Rolfe as well as Rolph. William Rolfe was Bailiff in 1619; John Rolfe in 1675; Thomas Rolph in 1855 and Edward Rolph in 1874. The Feoffes of Box Moor came largely from the area's tradesmen and men of some social standing. The various Feoffements list a wide variety of trades, such as tanners, blacksmiths, innkeepers, maltsters, husbandmen, yeomen, butchers, bakers and candle-makers as well as gentlemen. (See Appendix 2)

The list of sixty-seven Feoffes in the original document of 1594 makes interesting reading since it contains many still familiar local names. John, Jeromy, William and Zachary Rolfe, as well as John, Ralfe, Richard and Robert Pope are named; Abriell and Seth Gladman were also present. Other prominent names in the locality at the time included Axtell, Besouth, Howe and Puddiphat. There is speculation that George Washington's great-grandmother, Ann Pope, may have been related to the Hemel Hempstead branch of the Pope family. It is known that John Washington and his wife, Ann Pope, emigrated from Tring to Virginia in 1657. (See Appendix 2)

The fee for grazing the pastures was set at 7s 6d per annum and the profits were to be used to drain and improve the lands. They should all 'maintain, keep, observe, perform and fulfil all such and so many of the Orders and Bye Laws as then were or thereafter should be made, and at any time forever, by Twelve of the best of the Inhabitants of Hemelhempstead and Bovington …'

In this manner, the long years of the Box Moor Trust and its twelve Trustees, chosen to manage the day-to-day affairs of the Estate, were put into motion – some might say, into perpetual motion!

In the same Indenture it was also decided that whenever a large proportion of the Feoffes 'should depart out of this natural life, and die, then at all times after (if it be thought needful) … they should make a new Feoffement to as many and the like Number of the then Inhabitants of Hemelhempstead and Bovington aforesaid …' They cannot have had any premonition of the huge rise in the population, especially in the last century.

The Feoffements, or lists of named inhabitants, that cover the next two centuries, are virtually the only existing record of the life of the Trust at this period. No minutes have survived if, indeed, they ever existed, except for those of a meeting in 1763. (See Appendix 11)

The enterprising spirit of those former residents – mostly farmers and tradesmen – should not be underestimated. The long-term benefits that their bold plan brought to the district and the resultant formation of the Box Moor Trust are unique features in our country's history.

Heath Barn in 1989. The Heath Barn is a listed Grade II late sixteenth- or early seventeenth-century building. Lt. Col. F. S. Brereton once lived there but it is now a Music Centre for Hemel Hempstead School. The 'Haybarns' or Heath Barns was a sub-manor of Hemel Hempstead and Haywards Meade (Haybourne) was named in the 1581 Feoffment. It occupied the site of the much later Heath Park Hotel. The Box Moor Trustees purchased Haybarns Meadows in 1837.

The old Manor Farm House. The last court of Buers (Beavers) Manor was held there in 1805. The farm house stood at the corner of Featherbed Lane and London Road, Apsley; it was demolished as part of the New Town plan to industrialise Apsley.

4. OF COMMONS AND COMMONERS

'The law locks up the man or woman
who steals the goose from off the common,
but lets the greater villain loose
who steals the common from the goose!'

Anon.

Dacorum* is fortunate in enjoying an unusually large proportion of common land* compared to most other parts of the country. Whilst commons, including parts of the Box Moor Estate, are nowadays looked upon as areas to be enjoyed for 'fresh air and exercise', historically they were a major element in the agricultural lives of the local inhabitants. Even as late as 1763 the rights of 'felling, cutting down and converting the trees, bushes, furzes and other things growing on Box Moor' were still being quoted.

The commons of England and Wales date back to Saxon, Norman and medieval times; Scotland and Ireland never had commons since they did not adopt the manorial system. The soil belonged to the Lord of the Manor, although his right of property was limited by the existence of rights belonging to other people. These common rights were known as 'herbage, estovers, pannage, turbary and piscary' (or pasturage, taking of essential timber, foraging for pigs, cutting of turf or peat for fuel and fishing). The other people might be freehold tenants of the manor, or inhabitants of the manor whose rights were claimed by prescription over preceding years.

In the sixteenth and seventeenth centuries Dacorum seems to have been well endowed with common land: Sheethanger*, Dew Green, Roughdown*, Howgrove, Water Moor, Spencer's Field and Little Spencer's Field are all recorded, as are the common pastures of Ashridge, Bovingdon Green and Felden* Heath. In 1650 Two Waters Moor and Box Moor (which replaced the earlier names of Haywardes Meade, or Haybourne and Castlemead) comprised about 120 acres. However, a third part of Sheethanger (Shothanger), Dew Green (Draw Green) and Roughdown (Row Down) was enclosed in 1663. A certificate dated 11 July 1663 verifies that the inhabitants of Hemel Hempstead gave their consent to Sir Richard Combe for this act, 'for the space of seven years'.

The enclosures of the eighteenth and nineteenth centuries were the response of the agriculturalists to the growing demands of the new urban food markets. Thirteen per cent of Hertfordshire was enclosed by various Acts of Parliament during this period. Conversely, it can perhaps be argued that such enclosures caused the landless labourers to move to the burgeoning factory towns in the first place, whilst at the same time providing the food with which to feed them.

In fact, it is difficult to discuss commons without reference to enclosures, whether ancient or modern, official or unofficial. The events leading up to the 'Battle of Berkhamsted Common' and the dispute between Augustus Smith of Ashlyns and Lord Brownlow of Ashridge in 1886 are well recorded locally. This resulted in newly erected fencing being forcibly and secretly removed in the dead of night by an army of navvies brought for the very purpose by Smith on a steam train from Euston to Tring Station.

'Before the morning dawned the whole of the fence was level with the ground, and the freedom of the Common was again restored to those whose right it is.'

The jubilant locals took away sprigs of gorse as symbols of their victory!

It is not generally appreciated that most commons today are privately owned, either by Crown Estates, the National Trust, Local Authorities (who have a duty to protect 'ownerless commons') and Trustees such as the Box Moor Trust, as well as private individuals. It is also not generally known that access can, in fact, be denied to common land. Nowadays, commoners are those who hold rights as recorded under the Commons Registration Act of 1965, the register being closed in 1970. Most of the original Estate, Roughdown and Sheethanger Commons together with Dew Green, are registered as common land. The land purchased or acquired since 1965 is not registered as common land. The Act proclaimed that even though these age-old rights were no longer exercised, former wasteland* of a manor that was still unenclosed could be registered as common land. Interpretations of the Act since then have led to some lengthy legal debates. It is fortunate that the Trust had the Box Moor Act of 1809 and earlier conveyances and indentures to prove its claims to the land. Hemel Hempstead and Bovingdon between them have about 280 acres of registered land.

The Box Moor Trustees recently made the decision to fence the Moor in order to deter cattle from straying upon the increasingly busy roads. Generally, any new lines of fencing result in adverse comment, despite the good cause, a reminder of those times when the act of enclosure was seen as a threat to the ordinary folk and 'the vital open spaces of the nation'.

Postcard, c.1940, showing Northchurch Common, near Berkhamsted. Dacorum district is fortunate to have retained a large proportion of common land. Note the gypsy caravans, once a regular feature of the area.

5. THE MANORS OF HEMEL HEMPSTEAD

The manor of Hemel Hempstead was divided almost equally between the Abbot of St Albans and the Saxon kings at the time of the Norman Conquest in 1066 and was held by two brothers, both Earl Leofwin's men (the brother of King Harold). William I rewarded his nobles and bishops with lands taken from the Saxons and astutely divided them into far-separated parcels to avoid making any one of them a stronger overlord than himself. The Count of Mortain, his half brother, was given, amongst many others, the manors of Hemel Hempstead and Berkhamsted, the latter deemed to be the more important at the time. Within a short period, the old Anglo-Saxon defences at Berkhamsted had been upgraded into a wooden castle with motte-and-bailey* and, over the years, other formidable barriers to attack. The formalised manorial system and the Domesday Book, a survey of all lands and other valuable holdings in the kingdom, were both outcomes of William's somewhat ruthless methods of subjugation. The local populace of this otherwise peaceful valley must have regretted the changing order as they came under the closer scrutiny of the Crown.

At the time of the Domesday survey in 1086, Hemel Hempstead was assessed as being worth £22. There were ten hides of land (about 1,200 acres), enough land for 30 ploughs, 4 mills, 275 eels, meadow for 4 ploughs, woodland for 1,200 pigs and pasture for livestock: a prosperous sounding place. Two Frenchmen with thirteen smallholders had 20 ploughs. A whole social class, the former Anglo-Saxon aristocrats, seems to have virtually disappeared, to be replaced by William's own Norman and French supporters.

The manor remained with the Crown, together with the manor of Great Berkhamsted, until it was conferred on the College of Bonhommes, c.1283–85. The Bonhommes* were a new monastic order founded by Edmund, Earl of Cornwall, at Ashridge and the portion of land possessed by the monastery was known as the Bury or Burystead. Free warren* in Hemel Hempstead, Bovingdon, Frithsden and Gaddesden was given to the local people in 1309, formerly the privilege of the Brethren only, but Edward I reserved the Royal warren of 'Le Frith'. Edward III authorised some existing leases and licensed the formation of others in 1336 because the monks were unable to cultivate 'certain lands and waters'.

After the dissolution of the monastery on 6 November 1539, Ashridge reverted to the Crown. Elizabeth was bequeathed the estate in Henry VIII's will and she then leased Ashridge to Richard Combe, a relation of Thomas Waterhouse, the last rector. An indenture dated 23 June 1574 stated that Francis, Earl of Bedford and Peter Graye Esq of Segenhoe, Bedfordshire, sold land in Hemel Hempstead to Francis Combe. The Combe family were to feature frequently in Box Moor Trust indentures over the following decades and both they and the Waterhouses are remembered today by street names in the centre of the town.

A sketch by Peter Wagon of the remains of the old Bury in Gadebridge Park, 1988. The original building belonged to the rector and monastery at Ashridge and at the Dissolution it was let to Henry VIII's auditor, John Waterhouse and his son-in-law, Richard Combe. In December 1539 they invited the King to a grand entertainment at the Bury and loaned him some money. Hemel Hempstead was thus granted its Royal Charter, giving it the status of a Bailiwick with a weekly market, a Court of Piepowder and an annual fair. The porch is of a later date.

Following the demise of the monastery at Ashridge and St Albans Abbey, Hemel Hempstead once again became a Royal manor. At the end of the sixteenth century Richard Combe demolished the old manor house, or the Bury, at Hemel Hempstead and built himself a splendid new house of fourteen rooms, all well furnished. Today, only the porch remains, or what is often referred to erroneously as the 'Charter Tower' at the entrance to the Charter Gardens in Gadebridge Park. Bury Mill was close by and formed part of the lands granted to the monastery at Ashridge that was subsequently part of the manor held by Elizabeth I before her accession. In 1610 it was granted to Prince Henry of Wales and, after his death, to Prince Charles. In 1650 it was sold, along with other possessions of Charles I, who was beheaded the previous year.

By 1655, a portion of the manor had been bought by Richard Combes, who was later knighted. At the Restoration of the Monarchy in 1660 the whole manor once more reverted to the Crown. Richard Combes was made the Steward of the Manor in 1660. He died in the late 1670s and the manor having been bestowed on Catherine of Braganza, the wife of Charles II. The Halsey family came into the picture in 1702, when a lease was granted to Thomas Halsey. The Halseys eventually purchased the manorial rights in 1815. Their seat, Gaddesden Place, was built in the Italian style in c.1774. The architect was James Wyatt, who was also involved in the renovation of the former monastery at Ashridge.

From the earliest records the manor of Bovingdon has always been attached to that of Hemel Hempstead, when it was mainly an area of woodland and waste; in 1289 it comprised 10 acres of wood and 254 acres of waste. Queen Eleanor the wife of Edward I, her tenants of Langley and others, had Rights of Common there. The exact location of the manor house is unknown, but the sub-manor of Westbrook Hay* played a large part in the affairs of the hamlet.

Flaunden* was part of the manor of Hemel Hempstead and also included in the liberty of Berkhamsted in the Middle Ages. The sub-manor was held by Nicholas de Flaunden in the latter part of the thirteenth century. His son, Thomas, was granted the manor; improved it and named it after his father. The village grew and by 1279 it was conveyed to Sir Hugh, the Lord of the Manor of nearby Latimer. By 1540, after the Dissolution of the Monasteries, it was again under the patronage of Hemel Hempstead and remained so until the nineteenth century. In the valley of the Chess, the old village and church declined and a new church was built in 1838 higher on the hill. There is hardly a trace now of the former settlement, but Flaunden and the Church of St Mary Magdalene continue to thrive.

Other sub-manors of interest were Aignells, Buers (Beavers), Haybarnes (Eames), Mareschall, Westbrook Hay and Woodhall. Haybarnes was situated in the Heath Park* area of Boxmoor; both it and Buers in Boxhamsted (today's Manor Estate) were held by Robert Eames in the time of Elizabeth I. In 1565 the manor of Mareschall was conveyed to Thomas Penyston, thereafter going by the family name. This appears to have become annexed to Westbrook Hay and descended to the Ryder family. Aignell was also a local family name, dating from at least the twelfth century, which appears today in the guise of St Agnells Lane. Woodhall was probably on the site of the modern development at Woodhall Farm. It was merged with that of Aignells and eventually both estates were owned by the Earls of Strathmore.

Copied from an extract of the Parliamentary Survey of the Manor, 1650. In former times the Lord of the Manor and a jury of his tenants perambulated the boundaries of their land, marking them with a stone cross or 'beating' the knowledge into the participants. This was particularly important after the Black Death, when local information was wiped out with the sudden demise of so many people. The last recorded official occasion of Beating the Bounds in Hemel Hempstead took place in 1744.

Gaddesden Place, 1878, the seat of the Halseys until recent times. The manor of Hemel Hempstead was first leased to Thomas Halsey in 1702 and the manorial rights were eventually purchased by the family in 1815. They now reside at the Golden Parsonage and still farm the estate.

6. Medieval Box Moor

The river valleys and water meadows of the Gade and Bulbourne were formerly part and parcel of the assets belonging to the manor of Hemel Hempstead and were bequeathed to the College of Bonhommes at Ashridge.

Before the Dissolution of the Monasteries by Henry VIII, Ashridge had been a medieval monastery and a place of pilgrimage. It was originally founded in 1283 and endowed by Edmund, son of Richard, Earl of Cornwall, in woodlands not far from Berkhamsted. Edmund was born at Berkhamsted Castle on 26 December 1249. When he was eighteen he travelled with his father to the continent and returned to England with a phial which he believed contained a droplet of Christ's blood. To safeguard this holy relic, he gave one-third to his father's foundation at the Abbey of Hailes and for the remainder, according to Holinshed: 'he founded the abbey at Asserugge in Hertfordshire, a little [way] from the manor of Bercamsted, in which he placed the monks of the order of Bonhommes [Good Men], being the first that had ever been of that order in England'. Edmund granted his favourite religious house the manors of Ashridge, Hemel Hempstead, Little Gaddesden and Pitstone as well as rights of pasturage in the woods called Berkhamsted Frith. This endowment included the land that was to become the original Box Moor Estate.

In April 1286, Edward I confirmed Edmund's charter of 1283 to establish the College of Bonhommes. A rector and twenty brethren, thirteen of whom were obliged to be priests, were needed to follow the rule of Saint Augustine and they were to be bound by a strict daily routine of prayer, study and rest. In fact, there were only seven priests at its foundation and the means of adding to that number were not attained until much later. The first rector was Richard of Watford and the first bishop was Edmund's friend, Thomas de Cantilupe, Bishop of Hereford. When the latter was canonised, his heart was enshrined at the monastery, such was the custom of the time. By 1290 more land and privileges were granted to the monks, at Edmund's behest, including the valuable woodland of Bovingdon. Edmund himself died without an heir on 25 September 1300, at his beloved Ashridge. His heart, too, was placed in a shrine at the college.

Edward the Black Prince, eldest son of Edward III, subsequently helped to re-endow the college in 1376 and donated many precious items, as well as giving the rector and brethren free warren in 'all their demesne lands of ... Hemel Hempstead, Bovyndon, Boxhamstede ...' The lands and powers conferred on the Bonhommes by the end of the fourteenth century were substantial.

The Peasants' Revolt of 1381 had been a violent indication of the feelings of the common man of that period. The old feudal system was breaking down and the labour shortage caused by the ravages of the Black Death had brought rising prices and payments for rent instead of services to the Lord of the Manor.

The rebellion had spread to St Albans and, under the leadership of William Grindecob, the populace had managed to extract a charter from the terrified clerics which promised that they could hunt and fish and find pasture for their animals on abbey land and, more importantly, grind their own corn in the mills belonging to the abbey. A similar charter was also granted to the people of Hemel Hempstead and Berkhamsted, after the monks at Ashridge sustained considerable losses. In the event, both charters were useless, since civil order was restored; Grindecob and other ringleaders were hanged and Wat Tyler, the mainstay of the Kent and Sussex rebels, was killed.

In 1409 the tenants of the monastery tried to combine forces in an attempt to avoid their irksome manorial duties and were subjected to a visit from the justices. The monks tried hard to sustain the system of service on the land rather than money dues, but in the end could not stave off progress.

A dispute was recorded in 1499 between the rector, John Witton (Johannes Whytton), and his tenants. Their claim was for rights of pasture and free fishing in the vicinity of Box Moor. The pastures were named as 'Castlemede, Bayliemede, Roudowne, Felden Heth and Twowaters More', names which were to play a significant part in the future. They were able to secure their ancient 'customs of the manor', a privilege for which they had to pay 6s 8d. The grazing and fishing rights, as well as the right to fell trees, underwood, bushes and furzes, were thus safeguarded – but at a price.

The inhabitants of Hemel Hempstead were also a match for the next rector, John Berkhamstede, and complained in high quarters about his request for a gift of £10 on his first appointment. They managed to reduce the amount to £5, which then, in a manner peculiar to England, became one of those very 'customs of the manor'. These were not always written down and therefore were often the cause of controversy. In 1521 another case was brought against John Berkhamstede and his customary tenants in the parish of Hemel Hempstead. This resulted in a valuable record in the form of a 'Rental'* and many of the ambiguous areas were defined, such as those for land deal payments. The latter was fixed at half the annual quit rent*, rather than a variable sum decided at the whim of the rector, which had been one of the tenants' previous grievances.

Another cause of resentment was that the tenants had to take their cloth to the rector's mill to be fulled. The Bonhommes had been endowed with five mills, namely Piccotts Mill, Bury Mill, Two Waters Mill, Fulling Mill and Whelpesbourne Mill at Bourne End. Mills played a vital part in medieval manorial life, providing a substantial income for the owners.

The lessee miller was responsible for repairs, as in 1269, yet he was not even allowed to fish in his own mill dam!

'For repairing the timber at the sluice of Two Waters Mill 10d
For roofing Two Waters Mill..10d'

The monastery at Ashridge continued to feature in the lives of the local inhabitants, although the spirit of the Peasants' Revolt was still alive under an assumed mantle of compliance and Lollardism* was rife. Thomas Waterhouse, the last rector, served on a panel which led to the burning of a Lollard at Chesham, Buckinghamshire.

'The majority of people in the parish were below the rank of gentleman and above that of labourer...the great majority were farmers for at least part of their time and only a very few were entirely occupied in other trades or crafts.'

Arms of the College of Bonhommes.

Thomas Waterhouse, the last rector of the monastery at Ashridge who was buried in St Mary's, Hemel Hempstead. Waterhouse Street in Hemel Hempstead is named after his family.

Bury Mill, October 1961, prior to its demolition in 1962. One of the five mills confirmed to the monastery at Ashridge in 1290. Richard Combe leased the corn mill from the Crown after the dissolution of the monastery; in 1577 he purchased the property.

The monks' barn at the college was built at the end of the fifteenth century and is evidence of the prosperity of that period. It was completed c.1480 and the present owners, Ashridge Management College, renovated the remaining building in 2000 as part of their Millennium Project.

The Order of Bonhommes fell into more dissolute ways over the next few years. In 1509 Henry VIII ascended the throne and the omens looked promising for a long and strong reign. However, by the 1530s, following his divorce from his first wife, Catharine of Aragon, and his subsequent marriage to Anne Boleyn and birth of their daughter Elizabeth, things did not bode well for the legitimate succession. Not only in royal circles were things falling apart; landowners were trying to find more lucrative systems of farming and wool was in great demand. The manorial system was coming to its inevitable end.

Piccotts End Mill, watercolour, c. 1920. The artist is unknown but the picture is signed A. W. (Dacorum Heritage Trust Collection).

7. DISSOLUTION AND DESPOTISM

The College of Bonhommes at Ashridge did not survive into the seventeenth century, for three main reasons: the extravagant and licentious behaviour of many of the monks; the accumulated wealth of the monastic houses by that time; and as a consequence of Henry VIII's desire to marry his paramour, Anne Boleyn. Henry's obsession to father a healthy male heir had long-term consequences and inevitably changed the nature of religious practices while challenging the supremacy of the Pope and the Catholic Church in England.

Eventually, Henry's attack on the wealthy and corrupt monasteries and other religious orders, spearheaded by Thomas Cromwell his Chancellor in the 1530s, had an impact on Ashridge. The reputed bad behaviour of the monks included the frequenting of taverns, deliberate non-attendance at divine services, practising the art of physic and surgery and disobedience to the rector. There was little resistance to the new Act of Supremacy laid down by the King, with Cromwell's connivance, in 1534. This Act declared the power of the sovereign over both the Church and State in England and Vicars Bell conjectured that all seventeen monks were glad to sign on the dotted line and take their pensions. The final note records: 'in this year [1539] the noble house of Asserugge was destroyed and the brethren driven out on St Leonard's Day*'.

The monastery's treasures probably went into Henry's coffers and sacred relics, such as the heart of Saint Thomas (the Bishop of Hereford) were openly ridiculed; the once revered blood of Christ was shown to be merely 'honey coloured with saffron'. Thomas Waterhouse, the rector whom King Henry once referred to as 'our gentleman priest', was handsomely reimbursed with a pension of £100 a year, together with fifty loads of wood. He held the 'living' in Quainton, Buckinghamshire and lived for a while in Castle Street, Berkhamsted and then at the Bury in Hemel Hempstead. Soon after the monastic estates were confiscated by the Crown, Thomas's brother John rented part of the lands in Hemel Hempstead, including the old manor house. John was auditor to Henry VIII and the Royal connection did not go unrecognised.

The year 1539 proved to be an auspicious one for Hemel Hempstead, since Henry visited the town and gave it a Royal Charter. This increase in status allowed the town to elect a Bailiff*, hold an annual fair on the Feast of Corpus Christi*, a market every Thursday, and a Court of Piepowder*.

Henry had finally achieved one of his aims, when, on 25 January 1533, he secretly married Anne Boleyn. Archbishop Cranmer declared her Henry's legal wife in May and she was crowned on Whit Sunday in Westminster Hall.

Ashridge, seen here in its time as the seat of Francis, third Duke of Bridgewater, (1736–1803), prior to the extensive rebuilding by his cousin and heir, John William Egerton. Ashridge was originally a religious house, endowed by Edmund, Earl of Cornwall, in 1283 with what was believed to be a portion of Christ's blood as a sacred relic. The monks were to pray for the soul of his father, Richard, until the world's end. The monastery was finally dissolved in 1539 and the estate, including the manor of Hemel Hempstead, reverted to the Crown. (Reproduced by kind permission of The Bodleian Library, University of Oxford, Gough Maps 11, fol.62r).

Edward the Black Prince presented the College of Bonhommes with other important relics, such as a piece of the True Cross, set in a table of gold and silver enriched with rubies, sapphires, emeralds and pearls. The treasures probably found their way into the coffers of Henry VIII following the dissolution of the monastery.

Their only daughter Elizabeth was born at Greenwich on 7 September in that same year and Cranmer was her godfather. From the age of three months she was given her own household at Hatfield, Hertfordshire. After her mother's execution for alleged witchcraft, incest and adultery in May 1536, the princess spent some time at Ashridge. She was joined there in 1543 by her elder half-sister, Mary and her younger half-brother, Edward.

The end of Henry's reign came in a more ignoble fashion than its beginning. Wracked with ulcers and fevers, he passed away on 28 January 1547, in the care of his sixth wife, Catherine Parr. He was succeeded by the young Edward VI, his only legitimate son out of six royal marriages. Edward granted Ashridge to his half-sister, Elizabeth, in 1550, following the wishes of his father's will. After Edward's early death in 1553, in a precarious situation once more, Princess Elizabeth returned to Ashridge, the former College of Bonhommes. There she awaited with some misgivings the outcome of Mary's succession to the throne and the inevitable imposed reversion of her subjects to the Catholic faith.

It was from Ashridge that Elizabeth was escorted under guard in 1554, slowly, unwillingly and not at all in good health or spirits, to the infamous Tower of London. Sir Thomas Wyatt's rebellious plans, favouring Lady Jane Grey in place of Mary, had also seemed to implicate her half-sister. Elizabeth survived the intrigues and was probably a stronger person for all her adversity and insecurity. It is not surprising that she never returned to Ashridge once she, herself, became Queen.

Thomas Waterhouse also had a sister, called Agnes, who married Robert Combe of Newington, Middlesex. Their son, Richard, married Elizabeth Marshall of Edlesborough. In 1540 Richard Combe bought from the Crown the manor house of 'Hempstedbury', various meadows, Bury Mill and the watercourse and fishery attached to it. He was granted a twenty-one-year lease of the Ashridge estate in 1556 by Princess Elizabeth.

Thomas Waterhouse died on Ascension Day 1555 and was buried in St Mary's Church, Hemel Hempstead. His relations, the Combe family, local gentry of the time, were to play a leading part in the foundation of the Box Moor Trust.

Remains of old Ashridge House in 1814. Edward VI was resident for a time in the 1540s. The young Princess Elizabeth, his half-sister, was there in 1543 and again in 1544 with her governess, 'Cat' Ashley.

THE IMPACT OF ROADS, CANALS AND RAILWAYS

8. THE TURNPIKE ROAD

'The world runs on wheels with many whose parents were glad to go on foot.'
John Stow.

The Roman road known as Akeman Street passed through this district from even earlier times, sweeping in a great arc, comprising part of the ancient tracks of the Icknield Way and seeking a way through the Chilterns to Bath. Its name derives from the former name of Bath – *Acemanceaster* – or the 'way of sick men' who travelled from London to the healing spa waters of the Roman baths *(Aquae Sulis)*. Today it is only glimpsed by the existence of long established property boundaries along Chaulden Lane, Boxmoor, and Belswains Lane, Hemel Hempstead. A small part of it has been excavated at the site of the Bookseller's Retreat, in Abbots Langley. Remnants of an old Roman agger* are still distinguishable at Little Heath Lane, Bourne End*. There is also evidence for a Romanised Belgic trackway with much flint and some cobbles on its surface that once served as the main road from Aldbury to Hemel Hempstead.

The Roman roads were not properly maintained during the so-called Dark Ages that followed the demise of the Roman Empire. However, although the new raiders and settlers were not interested in underfloor heating and public baths, the road system was put to constant use. Contrary to popular belief, there is evidence of frequent movement from place to place in this period. The four 'Royal Roads' and the 'London Way' were in constant use, for many commodities such as limestone, iron, lead and salt would have been unobtainable locally. Trade relied on roads and navigable rivers for its success and in times of war or emergency, a quick route for the army was necessary.

The Saxon settlements were mostly on gravel terraces above the wettest part of the valley floor, such as the land in the district of *Haemel* granted by Offa, King of the Saxons, to the Bishop of London in 705. An early settlement in the Hemel Hempstead area was that which lay either side of a road crossing the Gade in front of Bury Mill. It was a comparatively restricted site, enclosed between meadows and chalk slopes, and remained a small central isle until expansion into a town in the sixteenth century.

By the eleventh century, roads were more 'rights-of-way' leading from one town or hamlet to the next and travellers were allowed to diverge from the main track in poor weather. Market traders, farmers, pilgrims to the monastery at Ashridge, court officials on their way to Berkhamsted Castle, soldiers, ecclesiastics, kings and commoners alike have all journeyed along these old routes and their story is linked to the present by such place names as Cold Harbour, Icknield Way and Grim's Ditch.

Akeman Street and nearby Watling Street both played an important part as communication routes in medieval England. Their use continued throughout the Tudor and Stuart periods, but the physical condition of even the major highways left a great deal to be desired. They were certainly not up to the requirements of the new coaches which became fashionable after 1555, when the Earl of Rutland had one constructed for himself.

In the same year an Act for Mending Highways was passed, and by 1563, a surveyor or 'waywarden' was appointed for each parish whose duty it was to see that every common labourer did six days unpaid road work every year. This was called 'statute labour'; the workers were meant to provide their own materials and tools. As the villagers rarely welcomed visitors, these duties were not undertaken willingly. Poor strangers were viewed with some suspicion by the villagers lest they became a burden on the parish, whilst vagrants were moved on continuously. The coaches demanded well-made roads but the roads did not keep pace with the development of coach building.

The start of the English Civil War in 1642 required rapid and efficient movement of troops and this meant that greater attention needed to be given to transport. A national road policy was mooted in Parliament in 1657 but, unfortunately, nothing came of it. The Vestry* or Parish Councils had taken over the duties of the manorial courts by that time. In 1663, the first Turnpike Act for the Old North Road through Hertfordshire was approved and the county justices were empowered to erect toll houses and levy tolls. No gates were specified at that date, but Hertfordshire, in effect, had the first turnpike in England, at Wadesmill, near Hertford.

As travelling by coach became more popular during the eighteenth century, more staging posts were needed to cope with long-distance coach services. At towns and villages on many major turnpike roads coaching inns (such as the former Bell at Two Waters) were established. Here, every ten miles or so, the passengers could relax their aching joints; teams of horses could be changed and food, drink and a night's lodging obtained if required. The road surfaces still left a lot to be desired and the coaches were often not very well-sprung. According to Jonathan Swift:

'Soon, by ev'ry hillock, rut and stone,
Into each other's face by turns we're thrown.'

This print, re-issued in 1802, is called View of Hunton Bridge Mill, near King's Langley, *but it is in fact Bushey Mill. The carriers conveyed goods to and from London as well as to the surrounding settlements. The Sparrows Herne Turnpike Road was said to be one of the worst turnpike ways to the capital.*

The Act forming the Sparrows Herne Turnpike Trust, locally known as the Turnpike Trust was passed in 1762, sponsored by some 300 of the noblemen and landed gentry who were directly affected by the traffic passing through their estates. It originally had 129 Trustees, all of whom had to qualify by holding property worth at least £1,000. The 26-mile route lay from Sparrows Herne, Bushey Heath, to Walton near Aylesbury. The Dacorum section was substantially the same as that of the present A4251, from Kings Langley to Tring. The Turnpike Trust heard: 'A proposal for making the new Road by Paul Jollage, presented by him at the meeting of the Trustees at Berkhampsted, 14 July 1762', which was followed on 2 August by his proposal for toll houses, toll gates and tools: only the part relating to the tools was agreed at that meeting. He was subsequently appointed as the surveyor, however. The first Clerk and Treasurer was William Hayton the younger, of Stocks House, Aldbury. The Turnpike Trust regularly met at the King's Arms in Berkhamsted, where the Trustees examined the half-yearly accounts and received lists of persons liable to do Statute Duty. They also ordered the number of days to be performed in such duties by each parish, as well as the number of draught horses required.

Harry Grover was appointed a Trustee of the Turnpike Trust in 1794, in place of the local attorney William Ginger. Grover was a Box Moor Trustee from 1809–35, thus linking two important local bodies at the time. He was a prominent banker and solicitor who lived at The Bury and was married to Sibylla Ehret, with whom he had fifteen children. He became the Turnpike's Clerk and Treasurer in 1806. When he resigned the Clerkship in 1826 it was taken over jointly by his son, Charles Ehret Grover, and William Smith. Grover's firm then held the Clerkship until the Turnpike Trust was wound up in 1873. Charles became the sole Clerk in 1856, on the bankruptcy of Smith. Grover's son, Walter, and his partner William Stocken, subsequently assisted in much of the Turnpike's business.

The records were kept by Messrs Grover and Son, later Grover and Smeathman, when Lovel Smeathman became the successor to C. E. Grover in 1883. Smeathman was also Clerk to the Box Moor Trust, continuing the link between those two bodies.

The Turnpike Trustees could take persons with land bordering the road before a Justice of the Peace if they did not keep their hedges and fences in repair. Where the road travelled alongside or divided Box Moor's open common land, there were no fences until quite recently. Gravel and stones for roads feature in the Box Moor Trust minutes of the period, but there were no direct references to the Turnpike Trust. The surveyors of highways did get an occasional mention, usually because of some minor infringement, such as taking gravel from the pits opposite Heath Farm and leaving them in a dangerous state. John Brooks the younger was listed in the 1757 Feoffement; he had complained about damage done to his corn.

For over 100 years, the Sparrows Herne Turnpike Trustees battled with the weather, reluctant labourers, the shortage of suitable stones and the vagaries of the economy in order to keep the road under good repair. James McAdam, the son of John Loudon McAdam, inventor of the 'macadamizing' system of road-making, improved both the state of the road and the Turnpike Trust's management when he became its general surveyor in 1821. McAdam took his duties seriously and attended all general meetings. He also formed the specifications of all contracts and made himself familiar with the materials, carriage and labour of each district. The turnpike road competed with the canal for carrying cargo, a service that somehow survived for a time, despite the brief economic advantages of water-borne conveyance of goods. The tables were turned in the twentieth century, when road transport again claimed the ascendancy.

The railway, however, posed a bigger problem; it could carry people, agricultural produce and the Royal Mail relatively quickly. The Turnpike Trust joined forces with the Landowners' Committee in 1832 to throw out the London and Birmingham Railway Bill from the Lords, but they could not, in the end, halt the desire for speedier, cleaner and safer travel and movement of goods. The Railway Bill was passed in 1833 and road-bound mail coaches gradually disappeared. The Turnpike Trust's final demise in the 1870s coincided with the 'railway mania' that was sweeping the country.

The powers of the Turnpike Trust in respect of tolls and road maintenance ceased on 1 November 1873, thereafter the responsibility for maintenance in this area was divided between the Highway Boards of the Hemel Hempstead and Watford Districts.

The Bell at Two Waters was once a coaching inn. It survived as a hostelry until the very end of the twentieth century. The Box Moor Trust owns the cottages opposite, set at right angles to the former turnpike road.

The Swan Inn still flourishes at the junction of Box Lane and London Road. Did the highwayman James Snook really take his last drink here in 1802, on his way to be hanged at the scene of his crime on the Moor?

This photograph depicts Sparrows Herne Turnpike, or London Road, as it passed beside Trust lands on route for Bourne End and Berkhamsted. The road structure invented by John McAdam consisted of 'pieces of stone no bigger than will go into a man's mouth'. Coarse sand, rain and the iron-rimmed wheels of carts compacted the surface layer such that, before pneumatic drills, it could only be broken up with spikes and sledgehammers. The Herdsman's cottage was recently demolished to make way for a bridge when the A41 By-pass was built.

9. Box Moor's Highwayman

The name of James, Robert, or 'Robber' Snook, the locally famous highwayman, (allegedly the last highwayman in England to be hanged at the scene of his crime), still features in the district, perhaps more prominently than any of the Box Moor Trustees.

At both towns and villages on many major turnpike roads coaching inns were established. The King's Arms in Berkhamsted served this purpose and has associations with the story of James Snook, since it was also a posting-house*.

The Post Office was established in 1660. The duties of the postmasters at the designated post-houses, usually inns, were to speed the mail and deliver letters in their area. The work of the 'post-boy' was arduous, badly paid and carried out on roads that were usually poorly maintained. From the earliest times travellers of any kind, whether on foot, mounted, or in a coach or wagon, were at the mercy of highway robbers. In 1782 the incidence of mail robberies had become so acute that the Post Office advised people to send bank notes cut in half by different deliveries and it was even necessary to have military escorts in some parts of London. In earlier days, travellers were warned not to go out on Sundays, when highwaymen preferred to work, knowing that the law as it then stood would allow no redress to travellers for an assault committed on the Sabbath. For crimes committed on weekdays, the traveller could claim against the town where the crime took place, if the criminal was not caught, and therefore the victim had no difficulty in raising a hue and cry.

The memory of the exploits of Katherine Ferrers, the 'Wicked Lady'* of Markyate Cell, may have been in the mind of John Stevens, a post-boy entrusted with the mail bags from Tring to Hemel Hempstead, late one Sunday evening in May 1801. On an isolated part of Box Moor, near Bourne End, he had the misfortune to be waylaid by 'Robber' Snook. The highwayman, compelling the frightened post-boy to go to a solitary spot, then relieved him of six leather bags containing bank notes, promissory notes and letters. He told Stevens to go about his business before he rifled the mail, taking the money (£80) and leaving the unwanted bags and letters scattered over the Moor. A later account in the *London Chronicle* of 11 March 1802 stated that he left his broken saddle at the scene of the crime, a mistake which led to his identification as the culprit.

The day after the robbery, when John Page of the King's Arms, the Postmaster and High Constable of the district, began investigations, several people remembered seeing a man mending a similar broken girth-strap. Indeed, it was believed that he worked for a time as an ostler at the King's Arms himself and would, therefore, have had some knowledge of the post-boy's route. A report was printed in the *London Gazette* and a reward of an extra £200, above the £100 given by Parliament for the apprehending of highwaymen, was offered by the Postmaster-General. In the first poster printed on the day following the robbery, two men were mentioned and both a pardon and a reward were offered if either of them wished to turn the other over to the justices.

Snook was already a wanted man, in connection with a number of highway robberies between Salisbury and Bath. He had also been indicted for horse-stealing at the Old Bailey in 1799, in the name of James Blackman Snook, but was acquitted through lack of firm evidence.

Snook was born in Hungerford, Berkshire, the second of John and Mary Snook's four children; he was christened James Snook on 16 August 1761. From that date until 1799 there is no record of his life, although it is likely that he went to school in the area of his birth, since his family owned land near Hungerford. It was to be the testimony of one of his former companions, who recognised him, that led to his arrest. He was described as being between thirty and forty years of age, about five feet and ten inches tall, with light brown hair cut short and a face pitted with small-pox. He had lived in Marylebone for some five or six years and was well known in the neighbourhood of Portland Place.

The Times of 9 December 1801 reported:

'Yesterday, James Snook was brought before the sitting magistrates, charged with robbing the Tring Mail in the night of the 10th May last. William Salt, a post-boy of Hungerford, stated that he was born in the same town as the prisoner; understanding he was the same man who was advertised for robbing the Tring Mail, as he was driving a chaise and four through Marlborough Forest, in company with another chaise and four, saw the prisoner on foot, upon which he jumped off his horse with an intent to secure him; the prisoner resisted and they both fell to the ground; his brother post-boys and those that were travelling in the chaise coming to his assistance, they secured him and, on searching, two hundred pounds were found in his coat pocket.'

He also had 'a brace of very handsome pistols, loaded, in his possession', according to the *Reading Mercury* and *Oxford Gazette*. He was secured initially in the Marlborough bridewell. John Stevens was unable to identify the robber, owing to the darkness on the night of the robbery and so the case rested on a chain of circumstantial evidence.

One of the stolen bank notes was traced back to Snook's possession. It was said that he had mistakenly given a serving girl a large note to buy some cloth for a coat when he was in Southwark, after the Box Moor robbery. She returned the money to Snook, but the hue and cry was raised, only to find that he had already decamped.

He was remanded in Newgate Prison, London, and subsequently committed to Hertford Gaol on 4 March 1802 for trial five days later by Mr Justice Heath. He was found guilty. The usual punishment for highway robbery by that time was transportation, but a severe example was thought to be necessary for a crime 'of a nature so destructive to society and the commercial interests of the country' that the death sentence was passed. Thus Snook, probably no more than a petty criminal during his lifetime, came to have a lasting hold on the memories and imagination of the local populace who flocked to the Moor to see the last highwayman in England to be hanged at the scene of his crime.

Legend has it that the post-chaise carrying Snook to the fateful gallows on 11 March 1802 stopped outside a nearby public house for the traditional last drink. It may have been the Swan Inn, on the old London road, not far from the spot chosen for his hanging. Snook is reputed to have called to the crowd, 'It's no good hurrying – they can't start the fun until I get there!' Gentlemen of the road were expected to receive their just desserts with an air of bravado.

He was said to have offered his watch to an acquaintance, asking if he would carry away his remains, but the offer was declined. He was supposed to have made a highly moral and salutary speech before he was executed and his story eventually found its way into a railway guidebook of 1838.

The exact position of Robert, 'Robber' or James Snook's grave is subject to speculation. The headstone was placed on Snook's Moor in 1904 by the Box Moor Trustees as a memento of this dramatic episode in the Trust's history. A footstone was added in September 1994 during celebrations of four hundred years of the Trust.

 ## GENERAL POST-OFFICE,

Monday, May 11th, 1801.

THE Poſt Boy conveying the Mail from Tring to Hemel Hempſtead, was ſtopped near Bone End, in the Pariſh of North Church, about fifteen Minutes paſt Ten o'Clock laſt Night, by two Men, who took from him the following Bags of Letters for London, viz.

Winſlow
Wendover
Ayleſbury   } Bags for London.
Tring &
Berkhempſtead

Whoever ſhall apprehend and convict, or cauſe to be apprehended and convicted, the Perſons who committed the ſaid Robbery, will be entitled to a Reward of TWO HUNDRED POUNDS, over and above the Reward given by Act of Parliament for apprehending Highwaymen: Or if either of the Perſons concerned therein will ſurrender himſelf, and make Diſcovery, whereby the other Perſon who committed the Robbery may be apprehended and brought to Juſtice, ſuch Diſcoverer will be entitled to the ſaid Reward, and will alſo receive His Majeſty's moſt gracious Pardon.

By Command of His Majeſty's Poſtmaſter-General,

FRANCIS FREELING,
SECRETARY.

A reward of £200 over and above the reward given by the Government for apprehending highwaymen was a considerable sum and perhaps led to Snook's eventual arrest in Marlborough Forest, near his home town of Hungerford.

The report in Chamber's *Edinburgh Journal* stated starkly: 'The apparatus of death, brought from Hertford, having been previously erected, he was placed in a cart and from that launched into eternity'. According to Henry Nash's *Reminiscences*, 'This revolting scene was witnessed by thousands of people from Berkhamsted and the surrounding neighbourhood, who made it the occasion of a special holiday.' The local residents petitioned against having the body hanging in chains and, although no-one came forward with a coffin on the day of his execution, the charitable inhabitants of Hemel Hempstead did appear with a suitable one the next day. His corpse was dug up from under the gallows and unceremoniously re-buried on the Moor.

By law the execution took place on public ground nearest to the scene of the crime. However, the exact site of his grave is subject to some speculation. The headstone seen today was placed on the suitably named Snook's Moor in 1904 by the Box Moor Trustees as a memento of this dramatic part of the Trust's history. Since that date, the stone has been painted white from time to time. A footstone was added in 1994 to mark the Trust's four hundred years' anniversary. There is no record of the feelings of the Trustees at the time of the execution, but some Boxmoor folk claim that if you run round his grave at midnight and call his name three times, his ghost will appear!

10. TWO WATERS MILL

'On the Gade are numerous paper mills, which give employment to the inhabitants of Hemel Hempstead and the neighbouring populous villages of Boxmoor and Two Waters.'
Post Office Directory, 1867.

The name 'Two Waters' goes back over a thousand years, the two waters being the meeting place of the congruent rivers Gade and Bulbourne. Two Waters Moor was one of the manorial wastes of the district. One of the earliest spellings indicated that there was a mill here: Tuewatirmelne in 1290. It was situated on the Moor, at the confluence of the old courses of both rivers, later altered by the construction of the canal. The land was part of the original parcel of meadows named in the Box Moor Conveyance of 1594 as: 'The Common Mead alias Two Waters Moore'.

There were four corn mills in Dacorum mentioned in the Domesday survey of 1086, testimony to the suitability of the soil in the district for growing corn. The irregularities in the courses of the rivers, with many knickpoints*, were ideal for water mills. In 1283 the Bonhommes, the Order of monks at the monastery at Ashridge, had been endowed by Edmund, Earl of Cornwall, with five mills, namely: 'Burimilne, [Bury Mill], Follingmilne [probably Covent Mill, later called Frogmore Mill], Picotesmilne, [Piccotts End Mill], Welpesbourne, [Bourne End Mill] and Two Watermilne [Two

Waters Mill].' These must have been a valuable asset to the monastery. The rule of the manor was that all tenants used their Lord's mill, causing unrest and even revolt at times. In 1269 five men from Hemel Hempstead were fined for disobeying this principle.

In a survey carried out in the manor of Hemel Hempstead in 1650, Two Waters Mill was registered as a cloth-fulling mill and was occupied by William Hitchcocks. It had probably changed to this function in the thirteenth or fourteenth centuries when the river provided sufficient power for the work previously done by the foot-power of men treading the cloth in a trough. It was described as being:

'… on a comon called Two Waters Moore, on the west side of ye way leadinge from Hempstead to Two Waters, consisting of a hall, two rooms below stayres with three chambers over ye same with a little barne and a small gardine … Value £20 per annum.'

Two Waters grew into a sizeable settlement and it became even more important at the beginning of the nineteenth century. The Industrial Revolution increased demand for paper and the corn mills were adapted to this purpose. By 1763, Two Waters Mill was operating as part corn mill and part hand paper-making mill. Frogmore Mill, Apsley* and Nash Mills were also being used for hand paper-making by the 1770s, during which time Edward Austin was recorded in a baptismal record as a paper-maker at Frogmoorend.

Two Waters, Herts, a drawing by J. Hassell, c.1819. The upper storey was used as a drying loft for hand-made paper. First Frogmore and then Two Waters Mill were used for machine paper-making in the early nineteenth century.

In 1792 Two Waters Mill was still a hand paper-making operation, but Box Moor was about to witness the beginnings of a new development in paper-making; one that was to have worldwide implications when the occupancy of Two Waters Mill was taken over by Henry Fourdrinier, William Bloxam, Henry Fourdrinier junior and Charles Fourdrinier. Bloxam and Fourdrinier was an established and wealthy firm of wholesale stationers in the City of London.

The first person known to have made paper by using a machine was a Parisian, Nicolas Louis Robert. He left the army to become a printer's proofreader for the publishing firm of Pierre Francois Didot. He was then promoted to manage the hand paper-making mill at Essonnes in France, given by Monsieur Didot to his son, Leger Didot. To overcome the personnel difficulties of his large and sometimes recalcitrant workforce, he set about trying to find a mechanical answer to the problem. He eventually succeeded with a machine that made paper, in a wet state, about two feet wide and a few yards long. It took longer to obtain a patent for his novel idea, but the French government gave him a grant in 1798, and a patent dated 18 January 1799 was taken out for fifteen years. Leger Didot agreed to buy the patent rights from his former employee, but then upset Robert by not allowing him any association with the project. Robert took Didot to Court and regained his patent on 23 June 1801.

The on-going uncertainties of the French Revolution, as well as the bickering over the rights to the machine, meant that no real progress was made with its development until Didot sent his brother-in-law, John Gamble, to seek financial capital and a patent in England. Providentially, Gamble met Messrs Bloxam, Henry and Sealy Fourdrinier. The brothers, who were of Huguenot descent, were intrigued by the concept and on 20 October 1801 an English patent No. 2487: *Machinery for Making Paper* was granted to John Gamble. The Fourdriniers bought a one-third interest in the patent rights and undertook to find the money necessary to exploit the invention.

Henry Fourdrinier (1766–1854).

The Robert machine was brought to England, in parts, early in 1802 and sent to the works of John Hall in Dartford, Kent, to be re-assembled. Didot visited the works and spent many days there with John Gamble as the work progressed. By good fortune a former apprentice named Bryan Donkin had the necessary technical skills to improve Robert's original machine and in 1803 it was delivered to the nearby Frogmore Mill, leased by the Fourdriniers in the same year, for further trials and development. Donkin set up a bigger manufactory at Fort Place in Bermondsey, London, funded by the Fourdriniers to the tune of £3,000. Donkin, who had become John Hall's brother-in-law, then made a larger and improved machine, superior to Robert's model, in which water could be pressed out on the same machine. He later bought out the lease and took over both the business and the premises. In 1804, the Gamble patents of 1801 and 1803 were assigned to the Fourdriniers. Their later patent of 1807 incorporated many improvements and the birth of a new industry took place.

It was not born without some opposition, since the hand paper-makers felt threatened; a record of vandalism by the workers from the Chess valley who tried to destroy Two Waters Mill, fortunately to no avail, testifies to the animosity. Interestingly, Donkin supplied a paper machine to Richard Elliott of Chesham in 1810.

Expansion was evidently needed and in 1804 the Fourdriniers successfully negotiated with the existing Box Moor Feoffes to take and build upon the piece of ground adjoining the front of the mill at Two Waters, 'between the tail water of the mill and the road between the two brick bridges'. A price of £20 was agreed, with the proviso that Henry and Sealy and their heirs were to erect and keep in repair a footbridge over the spring of water running into the tail water of the mill. In 1806 a further piece of the Moor, between the house and the mill and the brick bridge leading over the road opposite, was bought for the same price and 'valuable buildings erected on it'.

Henry Fourdrinier must have become very involved in the life of the local community because he took the role of the town's Bailiff in 1815. This is surprising, since in 1810 the Fourdriniers were bankrupt, due to the expense of developing the new paper-making machines at Two Waters and Frogmore Mills, as well as one in St Neots that was managed by John Gamble. The purchase of land at Two Waters is also a strange anomaly, since the Feoffes did not normally sell land, but the additional development must have added to the Fourdriniers' financial burden. Perhaps the local inhabitants of the time could see the benefits of the new technology in spite of the loss of employment to the hand paper-makers.

The invention did not go unnoticed in the wider world and many influential people, including Sir Marc Brunel and Luke Hansard, spoke in defence of the effort and personal wealth (about £60,000) the Fourdriniers had invested in order to perfect the machines. Public compensation of £7,000 was finally awarded to them in 1840. The machine was named the

Bryan Donkin (1768–1855) was an extraordinarily versatile engineer whose genius extended from the development of the first paper-making machines to canned food, printing presses, steam engines, water wheels, the Rose engine for printing the duty stamps on banknotes and steel nibs for pens. He is remembered in this district for his involvement with the Fourdrinier brothers' paper machines at Frogmore and Two Waters Mills. He was awarded two gold medals from the Royal Society of Arts and was thought by some to be the most advanced mechanical engineer of his time.

Marchant Warrell, the first recorded paper machine-man who ran Bryan Donkin's improved Fourdrinier machine at Two Waters Mill. He is recorded as having lived in a cottage on Box Moor. Note the traditional paper-maker's hat, itself made from paper. He kept the machines running during the riots involving hand paper-makers. The Warrell family were later associated with John Dickinson's Paper Mills.

'Fourdrinier', in their honour, although it owed its existence as much to Robert and Donkin, who by 1810 had become the main manufacturer of paper machines in Europe. *The Times* helped to add further public subscriptions in 1847 and Henry lived in relative comfort at Mavesyn Ridware near Rugeley in Staffordshire until his death seven years later.

The first recorded paper-machine minder was Marchant Warrell, who served an apprenticeship at Frogmore Mill in hand paper-making and later at Two Waters Mill. He is said to have tended the first machines in 1805 at the latter mill and to have lived in an old-world timbered brick house on Box Moor. His son, Charles, followed in his father's tracks and started work at Two Waters when he was only eight years old.

Henry Fourdrinier did not renew his lease of Frogmore Mill in 1816; it was bought by the Grand Junction Canal Company in 1817. Two Waters Mill was also bought by the GJCC and various families leased it, including those of William Nash and Montague Stevens. A large fire broke out on the premises during the latter's occupancy and Hayes and Co. succeeded him. G. W. Hayes also managed Frogmore Mill and newsprint was produced at both mills. He added steam 'at ruinous expense' and built the 'tall, splendid chimney' at Two Waters Mill. George Hayes and his wife were much respected, but that did not prevent their bankruptcy in 1877, when the two sites were leased to John Dickinson's for ten years. It was then used for the preparation of 'half stuff': partly prepared pulp made from esparto grass* from Africa or Spain.

The Universal Barrel Company, owned in 1888 by T. R. Tame and Herbert S. Sanguinetti (who also founded the British Paper Company at Frogmore Mill in 1890), manufactured seamless barrels from waste paper and various other fibres at Two Waters, until the company's liquidation in July 1893. The Sanguinetti family spent some time at Two Waters Mill House, but they were nearly bankrupt by 1898. J. Harcourt Browne then set up the Boxmoor Manufacturing Company to produce paper board, but that venture only lasted until 1901. The British Paper Company continued to trade at Frogmore, and Herbert's son, Cecil, became its Managing Director and Chairman.

The end came suddenly on 19 November 1918, when there was an enormous explosion, leaving only the 130-foot chimney standing, but with the old water wheel still intact. The Patent Degreasing Company had acquired the mill and had just spent £1,000 on improving it, only to see all their hopes disappear, as it were, in a flash! They were extracting fats from wool, using carbon bisulphide, which exudes a volatile and flammable vapour. Fortunately, there were no fatalities, but the cottages opposite were wrecked. There is nothing left of Two Waters Mill today on its former forlorn site squeezed between the old and the new Two Waters Roads.

The disastrous explosion on 19 November 1918 which spelt the end of Two Waters Mill after a proud history spanning many centuries.

The river Bulbourne on its way to meet the Gade at Two Waters. It was the reason for situating a mill here in the first place, but now only the Hewden Hire buildings remain on the site.

11. THE COMING OF THE CANAL

'At two miles from Boxmoor the Moor compresses and leads between some closing hills by the village of Broadway to Bourne End. From Two Waters on the opposite side of the Grand Junction rise the hills of Crouchfield, Green End and Pinkwell with scattered cottages on their brows. There is a choice piece of scenery, looking down the navigation that traverses Box Moor ...'
John Hassell's *Tour of the Grand Junction Canal*, 1819.

The river Bulbourne winds its way through the story of the Box Moor Trust; the river Gade also plays its part, but there is yet another waterway to come into the picture. The very idea of an inland navigable waterway right on their doorstep must have come as something of a surprise to the inhabitants of this relatively secluded and non-industrial part of Hertfordshire. The impact of the new canal system was to have far reaching effects, not least upon the Feoffes of Box Moor. In the 1790s forty-eight Canal Acts were passed. The Grand Junction Canal reached Boxmoor in 1797, Berkhamsted by 1798 and Tring Summit by 1799. This was at the height of canal building in Britain. James Watt's newly invented steam engine meant that industry was no longer reliant on waterpower or manpower alone and this encouraged the movement of raw materials, especially coal, around the country. Local industries such as brick-making,

paper manufacture and timber production prospered as transport improved.

The existing water route from Birmingham to London, via the Oxford Canal, was 248 miles long with 109 locks as well as some flashlocks on the upper Thames still controlled by millers. In 1792, a proposal was made to construct a new canal, the Grand Junction, from Braunston on the Oxford Canal to Brentford on the Thames in West London. This would help to reduce the distance to 138 miles with 101 locks. The initial survey was made by James Barnes of Banbury and was financed by the Marquis of Buckingham. A committee was set up in July 1792 which had the banker, William Praed, as its Chairman. The initial capital was £350,000 made into £100 shares with a starting price of £1 per share.

This route was re-surveyed by William Jessop, who submitted his report to the shareholders' committee on 24 October 1792. The estimated cost was £372,275, a substantial sum in those days; it excluded collateral 'cuts', as the canals were termed. An Act of Parliament was secured on 30 April 1793 and work started at once at several points, with Jessop as Chief Engineer and Barnes as the full-time engineer. Work sped on and the Brentford to Uxbridge section was completed by November 1794, despite a shortage of and increase in the price of bricks brought about by the Napoleonic Wars.

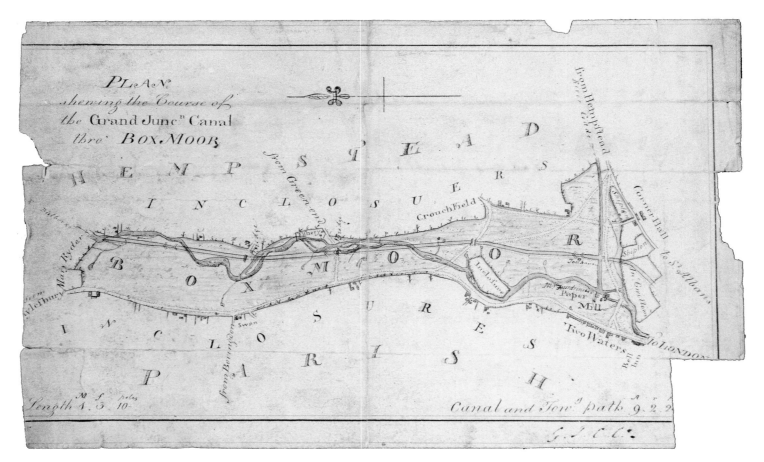

This old map shows the original course of the river Bulbourne before the canal interrupted its flow. It also clearly shows the Fourdriniers' Paper Mill at Two Waters.

The Old Mill, Boxmoor: once Aubrey's Mill, later Foster's Saw Mill. All the buildings were eventually demolished to make way for the present development known as River Park Gardens. The Mill supplied timber for buiding, fencing, joinery and even for musical instruments.

Lock 64, opposite Hemel Hempstead Town Cricket Club's ground. The Lock House has long since vanished from the scene. The land on which it was erected was compulsorily purchased by the Grand Junction Canal Company, but recently re-purchased by the Box Moor Trust.

The original plan in the Dacorum district was for a long, level stretch south from Hemel Hempstead, crossing the Gade on an embankment and an aqueduct near Kings Langley, followed by a 300-yard tunnel through high ground at Langleybury and then a flight of locks down to the river Colne north of Rickmansworth. It was decided, however, that it would be cheaper to pay a £15,000 levy to the Earl of Essex and a £5,000 one to the Earl of Clarendon, both of whom were on the Board of the Canal Company, to buy the land rights for the canal to go through Grove Park near Hunton Bridge. This change of line was allowed by an Act dated 24 December 1795, so the Board members must have been relieved and especially enjoyed their Christmas celebrations that year!

Considerable difficulties arose during the negotiations to purchase the necessary land across Box Moor. There were still about forty Feoffes in the Area of Benefit and it was an awkward task to get a collective opinion and permission for the proposed sale of land. At a meeting held with the existing Feoffes and Trustees of Box Moor and other inhabitants of the parish of Hemel Hempstead and Hamlet of Bovingdon it was resolved that:

'… a committee of Seven of the Trustees and Inhabitants aforesaid should be appointed to treat with the Company of Proprietors of the Grand Junction Canal for the Land on Box Moor through which the said canal was intended to pass … and to secure to the said Parish and Hamlet all proper and requisite Advantages and Benefits, and otherwise to transact all Matters for the Benefit of the said Moor or Inhabitants aforesaid, to the same Extent as the Trustees of the said Moor or Inhabitants could do.'

On 1 June 1797 an Indenture was signed by forty-six Feoffes whereby it was agreed to take out a covenant with John Impey, a Member of the Inner Temple in London, to raise money against the surety of the Trust lands, probably to help pay towards the expenses in dealing with the Grand Junction Canal Company (GJCC).

Thomas Squire, Samuel Collett, William Jennings, David Nicholls, Harry Grover, John Batcheldor and Charles Howe were duly appointed as the Trustees in the Deed Poll of 14 September 1799. By this time the canal was 'cut, made and formed', with its towing path alongside. A price of £45 per acre was quoted for the separated piece of land of about 6 acres and £32 per acre for the remainder. This committee was then empowered to receive any monies due from the sale of the land to the GJCC.

At a subsequent meeting, five other chief inhabitants of the parish and hamlet were added to the former committee and Thomas Collett, William Roberts, Francis Warren, Thomas Godwin and Joseph Hight were named, making twelve Trustees altogether. David Nicholls had left the area and William Collett had been proposed in his place. The Collett family was well represented at that time!

The money from the GJCC, together with that from the Fourdriniers for the purchase of land at Two Waters Mill, was used to construct a wharf on the Moor 'with all the necessary Conveniences thereto'. The rents and profits from this site went towards a workhouse in Hemel Hempstead, being three-quarters of the total Surplus due to the parish. The remaining quarter went to Bovingdon for the relief of the poor and in aid of the Poor Rates of that hamlet. This arrangement was seen at the time 'as the best that could be adopted, there being no legal Authority existing for the Application thereof by virtue of the said Trust Deeds, or otherwise'. The present-day benefits accruing from this early investment in the wharf, as will be seen, are a testament to those who proposed the idea in the eighteenth century.

A photograph by F. H. Stingemore, August 1925, showing Old Fishery Lane Bridge, which still retains its delicate ironwork, although the days of horse-drawn narrow boats have long disappeared. The horse is wearing ear-protectors, which were often elaborately decorated, to keep off the flies. (Reproduced by kind permission of Hertfordshire Archives and Local Studies).

A Fellowes, Morton and Clayton working narrow boat, with its butty boat, passing under Station Road Bridge, near Blackbirds' Moor.

Postcard by Frith of a narrow boat passing Station Moor. Note the narrow towpath, suitable for the 'lock-wheeler' to ride his bike to open the next lock gate.

12. THE BOX MOOR BILL

Notice is hereby given that a Meeting of the Committee of the Trustees of Box Moor and the Inhabitants of Hemel Hempsted and Bovingdon will be holden at the Court Loft on Thursday next the 24th. Instant for the purpose of taking into consideration the matters for which they were appointed — Dated this 17th day of September 1807.

At the beginning of the nineteenth century, the Box Moor Trust lands amounted to one large tract of open pastures collectively called Box Moor, a total of just over 177 acres. The Trust was the richer by £900 3s 10d following the sale of land to the GJCC, probably the most money it had seen as a lump sum since its inception in 1594. To this was added another £40, the proceeds of further sales of land in the vicinity of Two Waters Mill to the Fourdrinier brothers in 1804 and 1806, for their paper-making enterprise. As soon as large amounts of money are part of the equation, people become very interested and this situation was no exception to the general rule.

The existing minutes of a meeting held on 4 May 1808 record local agreement for the raising of a petition for an Act during the next session of Parliament to confirm the title of Box Moor and to regulate the same in as near a spirit to the original constitution as possible. It was hoped that the Act would '… authorize the letting of Box Moor on Terms that may render that tract of land productive and beneficial to the said Parish and Hamlet'. Many of the principal inhabitants of the town signed their names to this document, such as Christopher Thomas Tower, Thomas Collett, William Collett, Thomas Godwin and William Howard, some of whom were on the committee chosen to negotiate with the GJCC.

Another longer list of names consenting to the Bill, 'as produced and corrected at the meeting of the Inhabitants of Hemel Hempsted and Bovingdon this 10 February 1809', is also still in existence. They asked for certain provisions to be included in the Act. Firstly, that the Trustees should have the power to enclose and let those parts of the Moor that could not be viably drained or improved for pasture. The power to 'stint'* or curtail the numbers of animals grazing the land was also to be contained in the Act. The sale of land to the

Fourdriniers was mentioned and a request was made for it to be verified without any more payment.

The Trust's solicitors, Grover and Smith, then presented their suggestions in a draft Bill. The draft emphasised the uncertainties in the provision of the previous documents and the inconvenience of dealing with great numbers of Feoffes. It underlined that there were not sufficient powers to prevent encroachments, and that the land was not utilised to the inhabitant's best advantage. Furthermore, the sale of land to the GJCC was not perceived to be entirely legal, since it was initially dealt with by only seven Trustees, when the long-standing requirement was for twelve. The profits of Boxmoor Wharf, built from the proceeds of the sale, were as stated to be for the repair and improvement of the workhouse. The Bailiff was 'deemed in possession of the Moor to maintain or defend all possessory Actions'.

The properties already erected on the Moor were to be vested in the persons who constructed them for a set time at an annual rent, amounting to one shilling per pole. The revenues from the Moor were to be offset against the expenses of implementing the Act and a fence erected around the whole of the Moor; this hint at enclosure was later deleted. The income would then be committed to the draining or improving of the Moor ('planting with osiers the rushy and swampy parts' in the original). The Surplus, when it arose, was to be put to the benefit of the parish as decided by a majority of the inhabitants, who had the right of appeal to the Quarter Sessions or to Chancery. The power to raise a mortgage on the wharf in order to defray the expenses of the Act was included. Any three Trustees' sanction of Bye Laws, for example, was altered to any seven and, interestingly, the phrase 'and the value of the Rental' of the inhabitants voting on these propositions was deleted.

The twelve men already selected as the committee responsible for the sanction of Bye Laws on the Moor were to be established as the legally appointed persons, together with the standing Bailiff. The election of future Trustees was to be a matter for the inhabitants: timing for elections would be at the discretion of the existing committee and notice for elections would be posted in churches on the two preceding Sundays. If a Trustee died, moved away, or wished to discontinue, declined to act or was incapable of acting, then a Vestry meeting might substitute or appoint a new Trustee in their place. The decision of the majority in number was required and again the term 'value of the Rental' was deleted.

The whole question of what constituted an 'Inhabitant' came up in some anonymous observations recorded at the time. Every man, woman, child and pauper was deemed to have that distinction, but in the original intent of the Trust Deeds, it was conjectured that only those who contributed to the church and the Poor Rates were meant. Children, paupers and 'some coverts' (in law *feme covert* is a married woman), it was argued, could not have the means of enjoying land! They could not possibly have paid towards the purchase in 1581 and could not therefore claim to be 'Inhabitants' in the sense the writer imagined. The radical ideas continued thus: that the land could only be put to best use if it was all enclosed and put into cultivation; besides which some residents lived too far away from the Moor to enjoy it as open land; while in its open state, the Moor was subject to the intrusion of strangers and their unauthorised cattle. Damage and encroachments took place daily and the situation was altogether serious:

'the difficulty of remedying that Evil from the very unhelpful manner in which this property has been heretofore put in Trust, is so great, as to render the pursuit of it hazardous and uncertain in its result; therefore, unless some such measure is adopted, as is now proposed, it is pretty clear the whole Moor will in time become possessed and enjoyed by Individuals at their Will, as vacant property.'

The writer then contentiously proposed that the Moor should be divided up and sold to stop anyone from turning all their cattle on to it. This would bring houses and businesses to that part of the town and an increase in trade which would be a great advantage and help with local taxes. 'A very considerable improvement on this uncultivated spot' was seen to be the possible result, a foretaste of the feelings to be expressed in the 1930s. Allowances were to be made to the existing cottagers who raised geese and ducks on the Moor and the decrease in rates, it was believed, would be adequate compensation to farmers and landlords of adjacent properties. The sale of allotments of land was suggested to be for a term of ninety-nine years at a rent of £5 per annum. The writer concluded this lengthy observation with a request that Counsel's opinion should be sought and, if the measures failed to be carried into effect, the expenses should be taken from the revenues of Boxmoor Wharf.

Most of these ideas seem to have been expunged, but the question of the grazing rights and the stinting of cattle in order to keep a fair balance between householders was still a controversial one. There was some degree of opposition to the limitations of what had previously been a more lax arrangement. The point was made that in ages past the land was probably extensively wooded and as such the by-products were more easily divided up for the use of the local population. As the woods became depleted, the unproductive land was of no great interest, except to a few nearby residents who 'became permitted to acquire this exclusive enjoyment of it'. In fact they had no right by law to this exclusive use and the regular renewal and reciting of the Trust Deeds precluded them from claiming these rights. The property had always been enjoyed in the nature of a common and therefore a Stint was absolutely necessary to protect all common rights. Regulations regarding the Stint were consequently added to the Bill.

The Draft Bill was read at a public meeting in the court room on 28 April 1809, at which C. T. Tower was Chairman. There was a majority decision consenting to the Bill, subject to alterations by the legislature. The Order was presented to Parliament on 12 May 1809. On 1 June the Trustees were required in a letter from Grover and Smith to attend the House of Lords to signify their consent to the Act.

C. T. Tower, George Holloway, Harry Grover, Thomas Godwin, Francis Warren, William Collett, Thomas Collett, William Roberts, William Johnson, Joseph Hight, John Jennings and Ephraim Ware were the twelve named Trustees. In the event, William Collett was ill with a fever and could not be present on that momentous day. The Act was duly passed and the accounts from the House of Commons for expenses, amounting to £319 0s 5d, arrived in September of that year.

Generations of children have been able to enjoy the amenities of the Box Moor Estate, without realising to which historic events and personalities they owed their pleasure. The pool is opposite the Fishery Inn, a favourite stopping place for the boat people since it once had a shop and a nearby smithy, as well as stabling for their horses.

13. THE BOX MOOR TRUST ACT 1809

Notice is hereby given that a Meeting of the Trustees of Box Moor will be holden at the Court Room in Hemel Hempsted on Wednesday next the 22nd Instant at 11 o'clock precisely for the purpose of signing the Petition to Parliament for the Bill proposed to be brought in for the Regulation of Box Moor at which Meeting the Trustees are requested to attend.

Dated this 18th day of February 1809

Even before the route of the Grand Junction Canal was devised to traverse the valley of the Bulbourne and impinge on Box Moor Trust lands, there was growing concern amongst local residents about other encroachments on their common lands. As stated in the 1809 Act:

'... various Trespasses and Encroachments have from time to time been made ... by Persons who are not inhabitants of the Parish [of Hemel Hempstead] or Hamlet (of Bovingdon), by turning their Cattle thereon at times and in a manner that cannot easily be prevented. By others taking from it the Soil to the Depth of Several Inches, by others constructing Cottages and Buildings thereon, and by depositing Timber, Ashes, Digging Saw Pits, and other Purposes.'

Suggestions to counteract these nuisances ranged from the practical to the ridiculous for example the proposal to build on the common land and so defeat the trespassers' objectives. In the event, the coming of the canal gave the impetus needed to regulate practices and gave the Trustees more control over the local environment placed in their care. The people of Hemel Hempstead were worried that the canal would be too far from the centres of commerce in the town, clustered at that time around the High Street, church and market. They presented their request to the GJCC for a 'collateral cut' in 1793. The value of this branch-water highway, especially at a period when roads were in a poor state, was substantial. However, it was not to be, although the building of Boxmoor Wharf may have gone some way towards mollifying the townsfolk's feelings about their physical distance from the canal.

It was felt therefore that an Act of Parliament was needed to formalise the regulatory procedures. This eventually made its official appearance on 10 June 1809, after the actual negotiations for the canal were completed. It confirmed the sale of the Trust lands to the GJCC and acknowledged the fact that the canal now separated some of those lands; a greater price was paid for the detached parcels, perhaps to compensate for the inconvenience.

The wharf and buildings on the road to Hemel Hempstead from Two Waters were mentioned, as well as no less than twenty-six cottages or tenements previously erected on the pasture land. The list of occupiers was recorded and included Francis Axtell, Thomas Harding and the widow Rebecca Deacon. The Lock House and garden, built on Trust land by the GJCC, was also recorded in the Schedule. William Berry was the lock-keeper at that time.

The remaining land then comprised 159 acres. As the Act reminded them:

'The Inhabitants at large of the Parish of Hemel Hempstead and Hamlet of Bovingdon were the exclusive owners of a certain parcel of open Pasture ground, called Box Moor, in the Parish of Hemel Hempstead.'

In fact, the legal ownership of the Estate was vested in the elected Trustees on behalf of the said inhabitants.

The new Act empowered the Trustees 'to make Bye Laws, Orders and Regulations in respect to the said Moor'. It also allowed them to regulate and stint the quantity of cattle on the pastures, the times of use and the types of animals to be allowed to graze.

Any revenue earned by the Trust was to be used primarily for the 'draining, or otherwise improving, using, enjoying, and possessing of the Moor for the best Use and Advantage of the Inhabitants'. Any Surplus after these duties had been fulfilled was to be shared in a ratio of three-quarters to Hemel Hempstead and one-quarter to Bovingdon, to be decided at Vestry meetings in the respective places. The difference in the respective size of the population at the time accounted for this variance.

In the 1811 Census there were 3,240 people in the parish of Hemel Hempstead (excluding the chapelries), 794 in Bovingdon and 111 in the part of Flaunden that was in the Area of Benefit.

The 1809 Act tidied up some loose ends, but left a great many still to be debated at countless meetings of the Trustees over the next two centuries. The extant Box Moor Trust minutes date from this Act.

ANNO QUADRAGESIMO NONO

GEORGII III. REGIS.

Cap. 169.

An Act for vesting in Trustees a certain Tract of Open Pasture Land called *Box Moor*, in the Parish of *Hemelhempsted* in the County of *Hertford*, upon certain Trusts; applying the Produce thereof; and for better securing the Rights of the respective Parties entitled to the said Moor.

[10th *June* 1809.]

WHEREAS by Indenture of Feoffment, bearing Date on or about the Twenty-sixth Day of *April*, in the Thirty-sixth Year of the Reign of Her Majesty Queen *Elizabeth*, and expressed to be made between *John Rolfe* and *Richard Pope* of the one Part; and *Francis Combes* the younger, *Thomas Howe, Zachary Rolfe, Robert Pope, John Besouth, Sealb Gladman, John Shadde, Nathaniel Field, William Howe, William Rolfe, Michael Howe, William Younge, Richard Rolfe, John Turner, John Rogers, Christopher Besouth, James Puddevat, William Longe, Ralph Puddevat, John Knevatt, Richard Birchemore, Henry Rose, Jeromye Knight, Daniel Howe, John Pope, Matthew Glenister, Ralfe Pope, Thomas Field, William Newman, Simon Coxe* the younger, *William Colman, Edmund Howe* the younger, *John Howe, Zephaniah Besouth, Thomas Axtell, Richard Doult* the younger, *John Baker* the younger, *William Howe, John Pope, Jeromy Rolfe, John Turner, John Blisse, William Hearne* the younger, *Edmund Partridge, Roger Partridge, William Hawkins, William Rolfe, Thomas Marstone,*

[*Loc. & Per.*] 38 H *Abriell*

Front page of the Box Moor Act, 10 June 1809. (Reproduced by kind permission of the Clerk of the Records, House of Lords).

14. THE LONDON AND BIRMINGHAM RAILWAY

'... along the valley runs the Grand Junction Canal, the Railway and the old High road, in almost parallel lines, which imparts quite an air of activity to the scene as there is a constantly moving panorama ...'
Told by an 'old inhabitant', 1880.

We think of the twentieth century as the age of protest, with pressure groups being formed on every subject, from fox hunting to footpaths. Yet, when it was first proposed in 1825 that a railway should be built from the metropolis of London directly to the industrial Midlands, the outcry was as fierce and committed as anything seen in the last century. Public meetings were held in all the counties through which the line would pass and the whole idea was ridiculed, especially, and not unnaturally, by the people with vested interests in other forms of transport. The canal proprietors, trustees of turnpike roads and landowners all spurned the offers to carry people and goods more quickly, safely and economically by means of the new-fangled railroads.

Robert Stephenson, (1803–59), son of George, was the Chief Engineer on the London and Birmingham Railway.

George and Robert Stephenson were initially appointed as joint engineers for this novel undertaking; in 1825 there were only 25 miles of public railroad open in the world. Isambard Kingdom Brunel had opted for the broad gauge (7ft ¼ in) for his Great Western Railway, but Robert Stephenson preferred to follow his father's precedent and use a gauge of 4ft 8½ ins (the width of an average cart). To be sure of the best route and to find one that did not involve many gradients, Stephenson walked the whole distance over twenty times.

In the end, he decided that the most suitable route in this district lay along the Gade Valley, with a gentle gradient through Hemel Hempstead, then on to Dagnall and Leighton Buzzard. He had not reckoned with the intransigent nature of the eminent surgeon, Sir Astley Paston Cooper, whose estate at Gadebridge would have been dissected by this route. Robert Stephenson called on him:

'... in the hope of overcoming his aversion to the railway. He was one of our most inveterate and influential opponents ...We found a courtly, fine looking old gentleman, of very stately manners who received us kindly and heard all we had to say in favour of the project. But he was quite inflexible in his opposition to it ... He was opposed to railways in general and to this in particular.
"Your scheme", said he "is preposterous in the extreme ... Do you think for one moment of the destruction of property involved by it? Why, gentlemen, if this sort of thing be permitted to go on, you will in a very few years destroy the noblesse!"'

The Earl of Essex at Cassiobury and the Earl of Clarendon at Grove Park, near Watford, were equally determined that no railway should besmirch their estates. The second-choice route brought the railway into the Chiltern Gap* and the valley of the river Bulbourne. This route necessitated cutting across lands belonging to the Box Moor Trust, therefore a Special meeting was called on 20 January 1831. George Howard, tenant of Boxmoor Wharf, was particularly apprehensive and the Trustees agreed to back him and dissent from the proposed railway. The Trustees were prepared to contribute £20 to the fund being organised by the proprietors and occupiers in Berkhamsted to oppose the plans. This was all to no avail, as events transpired.

When the London and Birmingham Railway Bill eventually went before the Committee of the House of Commons in 1832, a formidable array of evidence was produced on behalf of the landed aristocracy and gentry. The Bill promised that:

'... a Railway, with proper works and conveniences ... for the carriage of passengers, goods and merchandize, from London to Birmingham, will prove of great public advantage, by opening an additional, cheap, certain, and expeditious communication between the Metropolis, the Port of London and the large manufacturing Town and neighbourhood of Birmingham and will, at the same time, facilitate the means of transit and traffic for passengers, goods, and merchandize, between those places and the adjacent districts, and the several intermediate towns and places.'

Against such logically sound principles, the opposition did not stand a chance and the Bill passed the committee and three readings in the House of Commons. However, the landowners had their revenge in the Lords and there the virulent opposition terminated the Bill with all its benefits to the workers, factory owners and business men of the day.

Undeterred, the Directors of the railway company re-presented the Bill in the next parliamentary session;

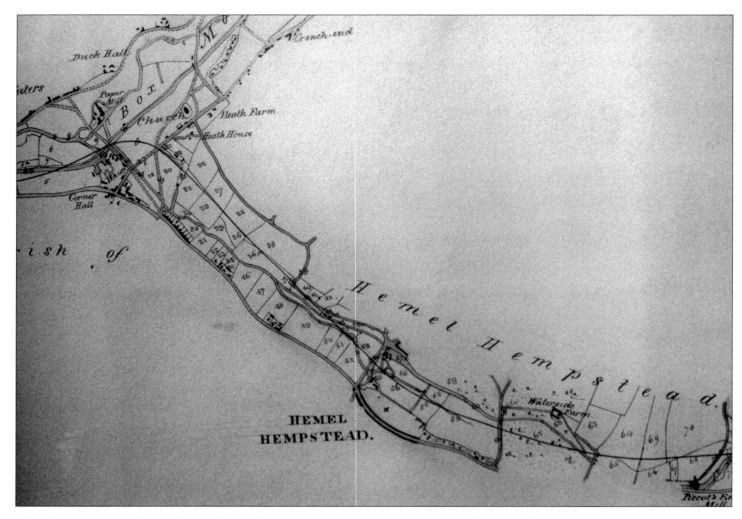

Map of the route surveyed in 1830 by Robert Stephenson. It went towards Leighton Buzzard along the valley of the river Gade. Whatever route the new railway took, it was destined to pass through Box Moor Trust land.

the Gade route was now abandoned in favour of the Berkhamsted to Bulbourne option which cut right through the Box Moor Estate and, miraculously, it passed all stages almost without protest. The astute action of doubling the prices offered to the landowners may have had something to do with this change of heart. Unfortunately, no such compensation was given to William Fensom and Henry Sibley, whose rented cottages lay on the line of the railroad on Trust land in 1833. These were unceremoniously pulled down to make way for the great undertaking.

Robert Stephenson was, with his father's blessing, then made sole engineer and the work was in progress by 1834. The only major gradient was from Chalk Farm, where the engine sheds were sited at the Roundhouse, down to the terminal at Euston. The problem of laying the rails, the 'permanent way', on a level course was overcome by using solid stone blocks as sleepers. These were dressed by hand to a regular two feet square by one foot thick and were very costly to produce. When the railway started to run on this track, the ride proved to be extremely uncomfortable and a different solution had to be found. The track had to be made more resilient and so the system of wooden cross timbers on a gravel base was adopted which avoided the rails moving apart. The redundant stone blocks were, ironically, sold to the Grand Junction Canal

Company for locks and bridges. In this area, one can still discover them being utilised for all manner of purposes.

There were more difficulties than this to resolve; tunnels and cuttings, bridges, embankments and stations all had to be designed and made to work, when there was little expertise about such major undertakings. The Tring cutting alone exemplifies the extent of this exercise and the skew bridge at Boxmoor became one of the wonders of the day.

Boxmoor Embankment, *a sketch by J. C. Bourne, c.1857. Many accidents resulted from this dangerous work. The land in the foreground became the watercress beds in Old Fishery Lane.*

A rarely seen sketch by J. C. Bourne, c.1837 of the famous Boxmoor skew bridge. 'The perfect manner in which the whole of the stone work, and the spiral courses of the bricks are executed, reflects great credit upon the builders.' During its construction, the turnpike road was diverted through the adjacent accommodation bridge which was later used by the Trust to shelter cattle. (Reproduced by kind permission of the Ironbridge Gorge Museum Trust).

A letter, the original of which is still in the archives, was received in January 1834 by the Box Moor Trustees asking for permission to survey the land. Some landowners had refused to give permission and subterfuges had to be evolved to ensure that the work progressed. The Trustees did not know how to proceed with the question of replacement land and needed to pay for professional advice on this matter. The Bill gave the railway company rights of compulsory purchase, but the Trustees were unable to sell land according to their code of conduct.

Sir William Cubitt (1785–1861), who, with his brother Lewis, was responsible for the construction of three sections of the line running from Kings Langley to beyond Northchurch Tunnel.

The local population, not only the aristocratic landowners, also objected violently to the idea of a railroad, as is evidenced by the 'memorial' which was sent to the Box Moor Trustees in October 1835. This petition was signed by 110 protesters, several of whom could only mark their names with a cross.

[They viewed] '... with extreme concern and regret that you have been called upon by the Legislature to part with so much of the Moor for the purposes of the Birmingham Railway, (in addition to upwards of sixty acres which have been previously taken from us for the purposes of the Grand Junction Canal and for Leases as presently noticed), [We] beg to express our earnest hope that they may not obtain from you one particle more than by their Act of Parliament they can strictly claim of you. The great object of this memorial is to express our hope that you will use your utmost exertion in securing an investment of the Money about to be received from the Railway Company in the purchase of Land as contiguous to the Moor and as nearly calculated to answer the objects of the Trust of it, as possible.' (See Appendix 12)

They were equally concerned about the impact of the railway on Boxmoor Wharf, with its links to the canal carrying trade and the profits that accrued from this wharf for the benefit of the inhabitants. However, none of these local problems were going to stop the onward progress of the railway. The subsequent notice from the railway company, dated 24 August 1835, stated that the line would pass through 'a Common known by the name of Box Moor Common'; it would require about 11 acres. The negotiations went ahead and on 20 November 1835 a letter from the Trust's solicitors, Smith and Grover, informed the Trustees that £992, being the price paid for the required section of the Moor, had been paid into the Court of the Exchequer. This money could be applied in redemption of land tax, or other debt or encumbrance, or in the acquisition of other lands. In the meantime it could be invested in Consols or various Government or 'real' securities. The final price was £85 per acre, against the £130 that the Trustees had originally sought.

In the initial stages, human and horse power were the only labour employed and then, in 1835 the first steam locomotive, the *'Harvey Coombe'*, arrived in sections by canal and was re-assembled in a barn at Pix Farm. This engine drew trucks of earth and chalk from cuttings to embankments and was the first railway engine to be seen operating in the county, much to the delight of the district's youth. Messrs Cubitts were the contractors for this section and the resident engineer was George Buck. The fine terrace of houses in Roughdown Villas Road was built for the railway engineers and managers who needed to be on site for the duration of the construction. The workers, many of them 'navvies'*, or builders of the canal 'navigations', camped in the vicinity; they came from multifarious backgrounds and there was often trouble within their own ranks or with the neighbouring community.

On 20 February 1836, a further letter was sent to the Trustees from the committee which had produced the 'memorial'. This accused the Trustees of parting with more land than was necessary, contrary to the promises made after the petition had been received. These incidents reflect the importance and high esteem in which the inhabitants held their Trust lands. The negotiations went ahead, however, and finally, after all the dissension and debate, 'on 6 July 1837 the first portion of the line was opened from London to Boxmoor. This event was celebrated with great rejoicing, and thousands of people assembled to witness the arrival of the first train that had made the journey from London at the rate of thirty miles an hour'.

On the official opening day, 13 July 1837, two trains containing the directors, friends and supporters of the London and Birmingham Railway Company (L&BRC) left Euston to arrive later at the Terminus at Boxmoor where they were entertained to a sumptuous celebration paid for by the company. Sadly, their triumphal return was marred by an accident, when one of the trains failed to stop at the buffers at Euston, causing injuries to some of the privileged passengers. The original passenger carriages were open to the weather and little better than goods trucks.

Newspapers around the world carried articles about the opening of the railway to Boxmoor and of the technical wonders to be seen thereabouts. The directors continued to run special trains for the first week until 20 July 1837, when the line was finally opened to fare-paying passengers.

The sound of steam engines puffing along the Boxmoor Embankment towards Berkhamsted became a part of everyday life as the construction of the line surged ahead to Tring. Though some contractors went bankrupt and many workers were injured or even killed, the railway survived these disasters and on 16 October 1837 a special directors' train left Euston to reach Tring Station one hour seven minutes later. 'In September of the following year the first train ran through from London to Birmingham in four hours and a quarter, thus placing the crowning point on the grandest engineering achievement the world had then seen.'

The railway was proclaimed a success; in the first month the daily number of passengers was 1,423 and receipts averaged £153 a day. Excursions were run from London to Boxmoor Station and a large marquee erected on Roughdown Common where passengers could obtain refreshments. The quiet existence that the area had enjoyed since Roman times was about to be overturned as the railway impacted on the overall development of the locality.

Navvies at Work, *Sketches by J. C. Bourne, c.1837. These men were not general labourers, but experienced builders of the fens, sea-walls, roads and canals. They worked in a butty of ten men, slept in their clothes, drank profusely and lived in earth huts near the building sites.*

The 'Harvey Coombe' from a print by J. C. Bourne, 1838. In 1835 the very first steam locomotive to work on this line arrived in sections by canal and was assembled in a barn at Pix Farm, Bourne End. It was named after the son of one of the directors of the railway company. This print shows the engine at work on the building of Gravel Path Bridge, Berkhamsted, in 1837. The driver was Henry Weatherburn, a friend of Robert Stephenson. He gave many local men and boys their first taste of rail travel as the engine drew truck loads of chalk from cuttings to embankments.

In this print by G. Dodgson, c.1838, a group of gypsies gather near their bender tent on Roughdown. The railway can clearly be seen in the distance. Substantial houses for the engineers were built in Roughdown Villas Road, whilst some of the navvies occupied bell tents in the adjoining fields.

'View of Boxmoor, the furthest point from the Metropolis finished, of the London and Birminham Railway, taken from Rowdown looking northwards.' This was the scene at the opening of the railway in 1837. The gate across the track shows the line not yet completed beyond Boxmoor.

The station was always two stories high, with waiting rooms and departure yard on the level of the railway, and the booking office below. It has undergone many changes of name: Boxmoor Station, 13 July 1837; Boxmoor and Hemel Hempstead Station, 17 December 1912; Hemel Hempstead and Boxmoor Station, 1 July 1930 and Hemel Hempstead Station, 15 June 1964. Silver Link trains now operate this service.

15. The Hemel Hempstead to Harpenden Railway

The first two major transport links between London and the Midlands since the Romans were the canal and railway, which cut through the Chiltern Gap and traversed the valley of the Bulbourne. As is so often the case, the Trust was looking at a double-edged sword, for although land historically belonging to the Box Moor Trust was irreversibly affected by both canal and railway, the money the Trust received from the London and Birmingham Railway Company meant that it could purchase further land. Blackbirds' Moor, bought from Norris and Pedley in 1844, proved to be a vital addition to the Estate, in the heart of what was to become Boxmoor village, in the area previously called Crouchfield*. This purchase went some way towards compensating for the loss of land due to the construction of the railway. By 1846, the London and Birmingham Railway had been re-named the London and North Western Railway (LNWR) and a new line was added to the original 'one up, one down' track in 1857–9, as well as a fourth line in 1875, seemingly without too much disruption or purchase of more Trust land.

Unfortunately, the town of Hemel Hempstead had been by-passed by both canal and railway and for the bulk of the population the railway was some distance away. To rectify this, a plan was put forward in 1862 by John William Grover (nephew of C. E. Grover) for a line running from Boxmoor Station to the The Bury in Hemel Hempstead, with an estimated start-up capital of £20,000. Almost immediately after this plan was filed, another scheme emerged, the brainchild of Samuel Stallon, Chief Clerk to Grover's Solicitors. A public meeting on 27 March 1862 heard the merits of both plans debated. The Act of 13 July 1863 eventually gave permission for John Grover's suggestion of a new railway line to run from the LNWR at Boxmoor to Hemel Hempstead. The Box Moor Trustees were generally in favour of the idea, so long as it allowed for a spur to Boxmoor Wharf. There were concerns that the railway might depreciate the value of the wharf, as there had been at the outset of the planning for the London and Birmingham Railway. The Act itself showed more concern for the flow of water to the canal and the areas of land belonging to the LNWR than it did to the Moor itself, which was once again due to be dissected.

A very early photograph of the Hemel Hempstead to Harpenden Railway line across the Moor to the Gas Works. Boxmoor Hall and Heath Park Hotel can be seen in the middle distance, some years before Heath Park Halt was constructed.

There was local objection to this further encroachment on the pastures and the railway company was duly asked to pacify the graziers with the provision of cattle arches in the embankment.

There were several objections to the proposals from those with vested interests: the GJCC objected, foreseeing partial loss of their carrying trade; the LNWR's directors were not too pleased either and, after two years' negotiations, the line was no nearer settlement. A second plan was put forward in 1865, linking Hemel Hempstead to Harpenden, with possible connections to both the Midland and the Great Northern Railways. This scheme, bearing some aspects of Stallon's original ideas, was not accepted by Parliament, due to pressure from landowners in Harpenden and the high cost of the necessary tunnelling.

The Hemel Hempstead Railway Company pressed on regardless. They were only prepared to pay the Trust grazing land prices for the acreage needed and a dispute arose over the asking price. The Trust asked for £400 per acre but the company was only willing to pay £250 per acre and in the meantime had already taken possession of some Trust land. They even served a notice to the Trust on 12 June 1865 to purchase over an acre of additional land. The final figure of £300 was not accepted by both parties until November 1865.

A third attempt to agree a workable scheme finally received Parliamentary approval on 16 July 1866, the line taking the route from Boxmoor to Harpenden but without a link to the town at Bury Mill End. The negotiations progressed extremely slowly, the Trust at length receiving from The Hemel Hempstead Railway Company a sum of just over £2,000 in 1870 for land given up. The company, however, was experiencing financial difficulties and confidence in it seems to have waned. Protracted correspondence arose out of the complicated relations in 1871, when the Trust found that more land than was specified had been taken and a further sum of £15 15s 9d was requested.

The scheme to extend this line to Chesham certainly did not meet with the Trust's approval and neither the spur to Boxmoor Wharf nor the arches in the embankment were ever built. The Midland Railway Company eventually undertook the day-to-day running of the line. The first train to leave Hemel Hempstead made the news on 16 July 1877 and journeyed to Luton via Redbourn, Harpenden Junction and Chiltern Green, amid much civic festivity.

Better means of transporting the straw plait from the Hemel market to Luton were a main objective at the outset of the plan, but by the time the railway was up and running, the trade in home-produced straw plait was in decline. The line was noted for its steep gradients, which led to the affectionate name for the engine locally of 'Puffing Annie'. In Harpenden the line was known familiarly as the 'Nickey' or 'Nicky Line'. The origins of the name have caused some debate over the years, some believing it to be a compression of the word 'funicular', since the gradients were so steep, or a reference to the knickerbockers worn by the navvies who built the track. Others believe it could be a reference to the parish of St Nicholas in Harpenden.

A short track was built across the Moor at Two Waters to supply coal for the Boxmoor Gas Works. Although connection for passenger service was possible at one time, it was never put into practice and so no paying passengers ever rode across the Moor to join with the LNWR at Boxmoor Station.

In 1906, Heath Park Halt was opened, opposite the former Heath Park Hotel at Moor End. Adjacent to this 'mini station' were the coal sidings in Cotterells. Farm produce, fruit and watercress were carried from Hemel Hempstead and Redbourn, as well as coal. The station proper was sited in Midland Road, opposite the Midland Hotel. In its last days the line was curtailed at Cupid Green and leased by Hemelite, manufacturers of building blocks.

The passenger service was 'temporarily withdrawn' in 1947 and the impressive viaduct over the southern end of Marlowes was demolished in July 1960. The last special passenger train ran on 6 September 1979, marking the end of the brief but nostalgic existence of the Hemel Hempstead to Harpenden Railway. The only visible signs of its existence today are the embankments over the Moor towards the Gas Works and the high brick arch bridge over Queensway in Hemel Hempstead. A critical eye might also notice the narrowing of the canal adjacent to the locks where a bridge previously spanned the waterway. The old tracks from Queensway have been renovated into a pedestrian and cycle trail. It will soon become a link in a long-distance cycle route between Oxford and Welwyn Garden City, part of the National Cycle Network co-ordinated by the charity, Sustrans. The old 'Nickey Line' has been revitalised, fresh air and exercise replacing steam and engine power.

The Midland Railway was incorporated on 10 May 1844 by amalgamation of the North Midland, Midland Counties and Birmingham and Derby Junction Railways. It absorbed the Hemel Hempstead Line in 1886.

Heath Park Halt, the passenger terminus, 1906. Passenger services were operated by the Midland Railway Company until 1947. 'Puffing Annie' prepares for its steep climb to Harpenden, where it was known as the 'Nickey Line'.

Bridge over the London Road (A41, now A4251), summer 1948. Railway bridges are still seen as prime locations for advertising!

Crossing the Grand Union Canal at Two Waters, on the way to the Boxmoor Gas Works. The lock was referred to as 'Jefferys Lock' in the Trust minutes of 1904.

Daily coal train on Heath Park Bridge, June 1952. The 307 bus from Harpenden to Boxmoor Station was used by commuters after the closure of rail passenger services in 1947. The engine is a Midland Class 3F 0-6-0, tender locomotive No. 43245.

Postcard reproduced by Hemel Hempstead Library Service, showing the viaduct over Lower Marlowes, c.1940.

A nostalgic view of No. 43245 seen at the sidings in Cotterells, 11 May 1957, on the occasion of a special excursion organised by the Locomotive Club of Great Britain. The land once belonged to the Box Moor Trust.

16. TRAVEL BY TRAMWAY

The Chesham, Boxmoor and Hemel Hempstead Steam Tramway, was a relatively unknown project, part of dreams that were never realised. The increasing development of steam as a motive power provided a cheaper alternative to man or horsepower. The Tramways Act of 1870 encouraged many innovative transport plans to be proposed for the Dacorum district, none of which ever came to fruition.

The brainchild of an engineer named S. P. W. Sellon, the plan comprised a 12-mile route on a 3ft 6in-gauge tramway which started at the Hemel Hempstead Midland Station, down Marlowes, then across the Moor to Boxmoor Station and via the former A41 to Bourne End. To reach Chesham, it would have spoilt the secluded, pastoral valley of the Bourne Gutter as well as the Moor. A later modification of the line, designed to avoid Stephenson's skew bridge over the main London Road, cut across the Moor towards the canal and then through a cattle arch in the railway embankment. A second branch was planned to go from the end of Marlowes to Dickinson's Paper Mills at Apsley and then to a terminus at the Red Lion bridge.

On 11 January 1888 notice was received from the Chesham Boxmoor and Hemel Hempstead Steam Tramway Company for the Trustees of Box Moor to 'declare themselves' regarding this ambitious project. Like the reigning monarch of the time, they were not amused and declared themselves neutral to the proposition. By April, they had discussed the matter sufficiently to stipulate a fee of £600 per acre if Trust land was required and in June they agreed to the plans submitted at that price. However, the scheme was never to come to anything more substantial than these diagrams on paper.

Steam was abandoned in favour of electricity at the end of the nineteenth century. The *Hemel Hempstead Gazette* received letters from two prospective tramway operators in 1899. One, a Mr Baker, wanted a service to connect the Midland Station with Boxmoor Station by means of battery operated trams, whereas D. Balfour and Sons proposed that the tram cars should receive their power from overhead lines but did not specify the route. Subsequently, the idea of an electric tramway, with an accompanying generating station near Two Waters Mill, was put forward. The plans were drawn up by V. B. D. Cooper for Hertfordshire County Council as part of their policy for improving communications within and to the county. The whole project seems to have been quashed by the local community's lack of enthusiasm, by the arrival on the scene of the petrol engine and by insular comments such as Sir A. P. Paston-Cooper's, that he had never wanted to go to Chesham and he did not see why anyone else should want to either! He was a true successor to the man who opposed the London and Birmingham Railway.

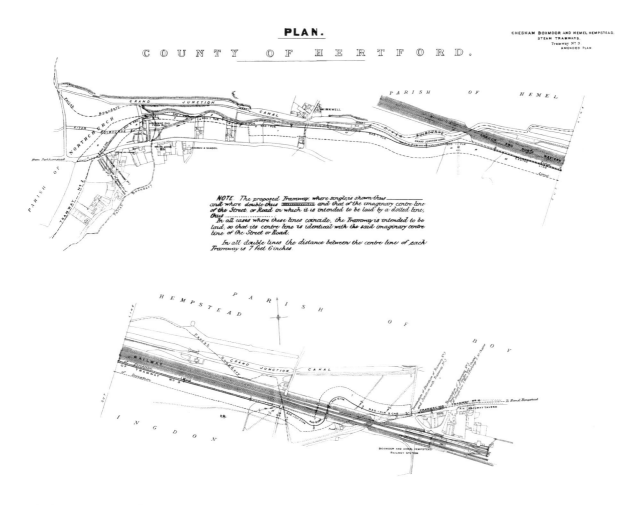

Chesham, Boxmoor and Hemel Hempstead Steam Tramway No. 3, 1888.

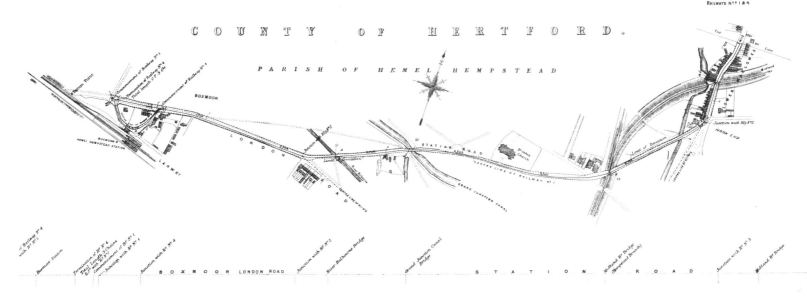

C O U N T Y   O F   H E R T F O R D.

PARISH   OF   HEMEL   HEMPSTEAD

Railway schemes proliferated. This plan of a light railway to join Hemel Hempstead and Chesham, linking with the LNWR at Boxmoor Station, is of curiosity value. It originated near Bury Mill End, crossed over the main line and swung off to the south towards Chesham. If built, it would have dissected Sheethanger and Roughdown Commons. At the time this was planned, in 1862, there was not yet a scheme to link Hemel Hempstead with Luton or Harpenden.

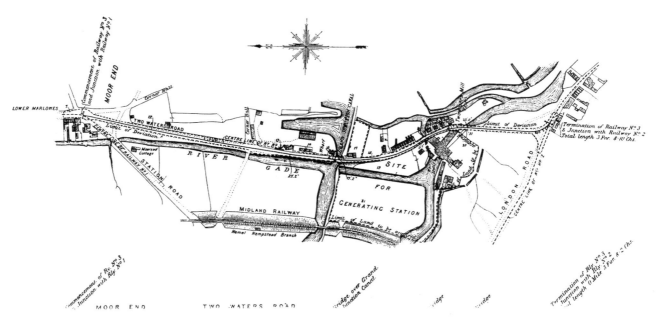

C O U N T Y   O F   H E R T F O R D.

PARISH   OF   HEMEL   HEMPSTEAD

The generating station for Railway No. 5 (County of Hertford Light Railways) would have been sited near Two Waters Mill, but, like the proposed steam tramways, it never came to pass.

THE BOX MOOR ESTATE

17. BEGINNINGS OF BOXMOOR WHARF

The Trust's own properties have had a significant part to play over the last four hundred years, none more so than the Boxmoor Wharf. It is believed to have originated as a working basin when the Grand Junction Canal was constructed in 1797. The money received from the GJCC for Trust land helped to turn it into a commercial centre based on the new waterway, with direct access for the first time to the London Docks. It became the main coal wharf for the growing town of Hemel Hempstead and its environs, although the site quickly also became associated with wines and spirits. The area encompassed the ground between the canal, Two Waters Road and Corner Hall. Today, it is still called Boxmoor Wharf and is leased to the DIY retailers B&Q.

William Howard paid £45 in rent for the year 1800, but by 1811, two years after the Box Moor Act, it had increased to £210 per annum. A 'To Let' poster of June 1815 advertised: 'A capital Wharf in full business in the iron, coal, timber, stone, soot and ashes and other trades', it was still occupied by Messrs Howard and Son. On 6 July 1815 the Trustees met to consider the tenders for the wharf and assigned the lease again to Howard and Son for twelve years. Early directories of the period named George Howard as a coal, corn, wine and spirit merchant and gave his home address as The Elms, Hemel Hempstead. The following year, it was reported by Messrs Howard and Deacon that 'various persons make a practice of landing boats and other merchandizes on the Moor to the injury of the trade of the Wharf'. It was then ordered that notices should be posted forbidding such practices on pain of prosecution. This did not deter people, for in May 1820 there were again reports that 'divers persons do unload coals and other merchandizes at a certain place adjoining the swing bridge at the bottom of the lane leading to Green End over the canal and Box Moor to the road leading from London to Aylesbury'. This spot, next to Fishery Road bridge, was later used as a wharf by Lavers the timber merchants and did not, in fact, ever belong to the Trust. Lavers also occupied Corner Hall Wharf.

In 1827, George Howard renewed the lease on the wharf, this time for a further twenty-one years. There were obviously difficulties in obtaining the rents, for in 1829 the Trust called upon Howard to pay the rent due the previous mid-summer. It was at this point the Trustees decided that, in future, all rents should be paid half-yearly. There were occasionally problems with the management of the water, as in 1833 when there was an overflow caused by the 'Tumbling Bay fixed in the Wharf Yard – from the weeds in the river above Two Waters Mill being suffered to grow and impede the course of the water'.

Repairs to the wharf itself were needed from time to time, as in 1818 when an estimate of £126 was received; the lessee paid £50 towards this bill. The Trustees accepted the suggestion by Howard to build an additional warehouse and cottage at the wharf, for which he agreed to pay £5 a year extra rent. An invoice for £162 3s 3d was subsequently paid by the Trust, with Howard agreeing to pay five per cent per annum of this charge, on the understanding that the properties would then remain in the Trust's ownership.

Problems with the crane at the wharf materialised in 1839, when it fell down from decay. This was finally resolved in 1840 at a cost of £210 to the Trust and an annual rent of fourteen guineas to Howard.

The record for November 1841 does not give any indication of the antecedents, but it was resolved that any lessee of the wharf or other properties was prohibited from 'erecting any Lime Kiln, Coke Oven, Steam Engine or any building for the purpose of carrying on any obnoxious or offensive trade, business or calling'.

A special meeting of the Trust was called at George Howard's Counting House on the afternoon of 17 November 1841. The Trustees decided to offer to purchase the beneficial part of his lease with all rights and interest in the buildings, in order that in the future no buildings could be erected on Trust lands which were not the Trust's own property.

Boxmoor Wharf: canal basin, part of the original construction when a large 'winding hole' was needed for many boats to turn round after delivering materials for the canal extension to Tring. Lavers (timber merchants) now occupy the woodyard on the left, where a timber business has been in existence for many years. The dock on the left was filled in c.1931. William Henry Lavers started his business in 1868 in London, moving to Fishery Wharf, Boxmoor, in 1869. He leased Corner Hall Wharf the following year and found the large basin useful for his horse-drawn barges and their cargo of timber.

PARTICULARS

OF A CAPITAL

WHARF,

IN FULL BUSINESS,

In the Iron, Coal, Timber, Stone, Soot, Ashes,

AND OTHER TRADES,

CALLED

BOX MOOR WHARF,

Now in the Occupation of Messrs. Howard and Son,

SITUATE AT

BOX MOOR,

IN THE PARISH OF HEMEL HEMPSTED, HERTS.

Which by order of the Trustees of Box Moor is to be Let by Tender,

In three Divisions,

For the Term of Twelve Years to commence at Christmas next.

———

The above Wharf is furnished with a large Dock, branching out of the Grand Junction Canal, capable of holding Ten or Twelve Barges, and is adjoining the Road from Hemel Hempsted to London, about one Mile from Hemel Hempsted, and twenty-two from London.

DIVISIONS 1 and 2, have a spacious Warehouse erected on them, 32 feet 8 in. by 52 feet 9in. consisting of a Ground and Upper Floor strongly supported, with a Crane in front of the Warehouse, for raising Goods out of the Barges, also a Shed next the Water 10 feet wide, the whole length of the Warehouse.

DIVISION 3, has a strong Crane fit for loading large Timber, erected advantageously on a large piece of Ground, adapted for laying Timber, Deals &c.

Each Division is to be marked out, and allotted to the respective Renters, and may be viewed any Time by applying on the Premises.

The Renters are to have Possession from Christmas next, on giving the Security, and entering into the Lease required by the Conditions.

TENDERS in writing to be delivered on or before the 24th of June next, sealed up and directed, (post paid,) to *"The Clerk of the Trustees of Box Moor, Hemel Hempstead, Herts."* within one Month of which time, those Persons whose Tenders are accepted will have Notice thereof.

The house and premises on the right of The Lawn at Corner Hall were occupied by Charles Howard. 'He carried on a large timber business with wood for building already sawn in lengths. Boatloads of this came into his dock from the canal. I remember a grand display by some gun cotton mines at the bottom of the dock … when the mines exploded a great mass of water rose some 20 feet, as broad as an ordinary cart. My word! We boys were delighted. As the intention had been given notice, some hundreds of people had assembled in the dock yards and delight was general.' (George Eyles, [prior to 1861], Hemel Hempstead Gazette, *26 March 1927).*

18. BALDERSON AND SON AT BOXMOOR WHARF

The continuing story of Boxmoor Wharf is dominated by one man – Henry Balderson. His association with the wharf started in 1843, when he was apprenticed there for three years without salary. By 1849 the wharf was leased to George and Samuel Haydon at the lower rent of £175. The local directory quotes them as wine, brandy and coal merchants, wharfingers and agents for Guinness's Dublin Stout and Bass and Company's Pale Ale. In the meantime, Henry had been to Brussels to try to persuade a company there to export German wines into England for the benefit of the 'working man' in an attempt to change a popular preference from strong beer. Henry returned without success in his mission, but by 1856 he had become a partner and taken over the lease of the wharf. The business was subsequently listed as Haydon and Balderson, at least until 1862. He must have enjoyed some other successes because he was able to purchase the adjacent tan yard at Corner Hall (previously owned by the Deacon family) and lived in the house attached to it.

In October 1859, he went to the London Coal Exchange, bought a shipload of 500 tons of coal and sold it to the Gas Works at St Albans. Henry was soon joined in his business ventures by his son Robert and the company went from strength to strength. Their interest in the tannery at Corner Hall is mentioned in the local directory in 1869. The large bark shed at the end of the tan yard was built by Henry. The Baldersons appear to have used their business acumen in reducing the rent payable to the Trust on a regular basis. By 1890 it was down to £100 per annum, even though repairs and extensions to buildings were an on-going feature. Henry became a Box Moor Trustee in 1871 and the fact that he voted on his own lease did not go unnoticed in the Trust minutes of 7 May 1884.

Messrs. Balderson were noted for their fine ports and were the proprietors of 'Ye Olde Stone Jar' Scotch whisky and the 'Tortoise' brand of sloe gin. The port came directly from Oporto in Portugal in great barrels carried by narrow boats and then bottled at the wharf.

A letter to the Trustees was read on 15 June 1905 indicating the retirement of Henry in favour of his son, Robert. The lease was transferred to the latter, but he insisted that the Trustees inspect the premises. They saw the stables, harness room, cart shed, landing stage, manager's cottage and offices – and asked Robert what he proposed should be done with them. He replied that the manager's house was unfit for habitation as the water came up above the floor and asked the Trustees if they could erect a new house. If they reduced his rent he would also build a cart shed and add a warehouse to the cottage. A certain Mr Mead considered it would be best to build new offices near the entrance gate and convert the existing offices into a manager's house.

Before his death in 1908, aged seventy-seven, Henry Balderson had been the High Bailiff and Mayor of Hemel Hempstead, a director of both the Gas and Water Companies, a member of the Highway and Burial Boards, a Churchwarden of St John's Church and a Senior Trustee of the Old Manor Lodge of Odd Fellows. He helped in the formation of the Hemel Hempstead Horticultural Society and the Rifle Volunteer Corps, as well as serving as a Box Moor Trustee. Henry was also a Fellow of the Royal Horticultural Society and even found time to serve on its Fruit Committee. They don't make them like that any more! Robert Balderson died only ten years after his father, at the age of sixty-one. There is no further record of the firm's name after about 1927, when it is believed the business went into liquidation.

These fine examples of a Balderson's stoneware whisky bottle and barrel are part of the Dacorum Heritage Trust Collection.

Postcard depicting a busy scene at Boxmoor Wharf. Note the basin leading off the Grand Junction Canal and the use of barges and narrow boats. The Trust leased the wharf to Henry Balderson and then to his son, Robert. The site is now leased to the DIY retailers, B & Q.

ANOTHER firm that occupies an influential position in the commercial circles of Hemel Hempstead is that of Messrs Balderson & Son, whose dealings in coals, artificial manures, linseed and other feeding cakes, and also in wines and spirits, are very extensive; and though being concerned with articles so widely different as those named, yet the success of this firm is beyond all doubt, the present senior partner having been connected with the business forty-seven years. The very extensive yards used for the storage of coals, timber &c. are at Boxmoor Wharf and are most conveniently situated on the Grand Junction Canal, while on the other side of the street this firm also possess large premises and pits for tanning purposes. In the other branch of their business, that of importers, shippers and bonders of foreign wines and spirits, Messrs Balderson occupy premises known as The County Wine and Spirit Stores and here the cellarage area is no less than seven thousand square feet, while the stocks on hand are immense and include the choicest brands.

Advertisement from a local trade paper c.1890.

19. LATER DAYS OF BOXMOOR WHARF

The wharf premises fronted Two Waters Road, opposite the river Gade. The tall chimney in the background belonged to Two Waters Mill. This is one of few pictures showing the old swing bridge that once carried the canal towpath over the Gade on its earlier course to Two Waters.

A new lease was signed for Boxmoor Wharf on 25 March 1929 by William Durant Wells, a builder from Piccotts End. According to a trade paper:

'Mr W. Durant Wells succeeded Mr S. C. Smith in an old established business at Piccotts End in 1912. He has had some of the best possible experience in the building trade ... Mr Wells is a Londoner by birth and was engaged with the noted firm of Messrs Holloway Bros. as an estimator and surveyor ... Both locally and at Watford and St Albans he has done much War Office Contract work, also factory and general work at Apsley and Nash Mills ... Mr Wells is a member of the Volunteer Training Corps and fond of motoring, though most of his motor journeys are naturally more closely connected with business than with relaxation.'

Wells died in 1945 and his lease was surrendered in the following year; part of the premises was then used until 1967 by the Victoria Wine Company, thus continuing the links with wines and spirits developed by the earlier lessees.

Another link occurred when the firm of L. Rose and Co. of St Albans took out a twenty-one-year lease from 1 August 1946 at an annual rent of £150, which was increased substantially to £450 in 1955. In their booklet *Green Gold*, published in 1959, the story of the lime juice for which they were renowned is revealed:

'For the past hundred years or so this distinguished member of the citrus family has been cultivated on West Indian plantations for the production of bottled lime juice and other lime products in Britain. In 1893 a Scot, Mr Lauchlan Rose, acquired estates in Dominica and planted lime trees. Among the stores supplied to the ships was lime juice ... by offering bottled lime juice to the housewives of Britain, Mr Rose

made history. He introduced the first branded fruit juice drink. Transported from London by river and the Grand Union Canal*, the casks eventually reach Rose's factory at Boxmoor in Hertfordshire, where the lime juice is stored in oak vats each holding up to 12,000 gallons; there it is left to "settle". After a short time the pulp and essential oil rise to the top, leaving the clear green-gold juice beneath. The juice is drawn off, filtered and sweetened with pure sugar. Finally, at Rose's St Albans and Liverpool factories, it is bottled and labelled, the whole process from plantation to consumer being carried out under modern hygienic conditions.'

Rose's had strong connections with the canal and were one of the last companies in this area to use it for carrying cargo. Stamford and Bude were two narrow boats still working the canal in December 1972. The 'barrel run' took about twelve hours from Brentford to Boxmoor and Tom Murrell with his son Jason were the last regular boatmen. The earliest record of a local boat was No. 2217, registered to Messrs Howard and Son at Boxmoor, former lessees of the wharf, on 26 June 1818.

The lease increased in value markedly during the next twenty years; in 1975 it was set at £23,500, which was to be reviewed in 1980. During that time the old family firm of Rose's became a subsidiary of Cadbury Schweppes. The eventual demise of the long-standing connection with lime juice came in October 1984. A Deed of Surrender for £70,000 was received by the Trust from L. Rose and Co. Ltd. and Cadbury Schweppes Ltd. relating to premises at the Wharf, Boxmoor.

The part of the wharf on the corner of Two Waters Road and Corner Hall was occupied by Litco Flights and a hairdressing business from 1967 until the DIY retailers, B&Q, became lessees of the whole Boxmoor Wharf area.

A wintry scene at Boxmoor Wharf in the days of the lime cordial producers, L. Rose and Company. The severe winter of 1963, when the canal iced over, played a major part in the general demise of the working narrow boats.

Barrels of lime juice were stored at Boxmoor Wharf, allowing the liquid to settle before being bottled at St Albans.

Eric Sykes joined Harry Corbett and Ronnie Barker to star in the popular comedy film The Bargee *in 1964, which featured the Grand Union Canal and the boat people in this district.*

Narrow boats, now used mainly for leisure purposes, still tie-up at Boxmoor Wharf. The rent from the DIY retailers B&Q is a valuable source of income for the Trust today. This store is one of their most productive outlets.

The arrival of a national company of the size and prestige of B&Q marked a change in the fortunes of the wharf and of the Box Moor Trust. In 1984, when the new buildings were erected and a car park made for customers fronting the canal, the cost of the annual lease stood at £50,000. Upon review in 1995, this sum rose to £300,452. The Trust could then, at last, make progress with many outstanding long-term projects that had been hampered by a dire lack of funds. The Trustees had attempted to secure a fixed interest bank loan to underwrite the new development, without success. The final arrangement was that B&Q would be responsible for the cost of the development and the rent would reflect this in the initial stages. The building would then revert to the Box Moor Trust. It has been a very successful partnership to date.

20. A Tale of Two Rivers

'The Gade pursues its silver winding way, wood, water and verdant fields combining to form as perfect a picture as it is possible to conceive.'
J. E. Cussans, *History of Hertfordshire*, Vol. III, 1879–81.

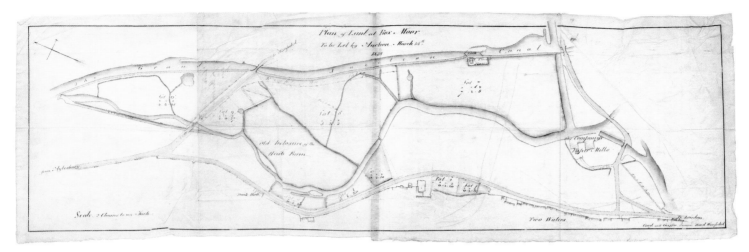

A map of 1828 by Creed and Griffin, Surveyors, of Hemel Hempstead, showing the earlier course of the river Bulbourne with its springs, shortly after the construction of the Grand Junction Canal. Since the canal was built, the rivers Gade and Bulbourne have been fundamentally altered in their course throughout Box Moor and Two Waters. They can almost now be considered man-made rather than being remnants of the glaciers that originally created the two valleys.

The Box Moor Estate lies within the valley of the Bulbourne between Bourne End and the confluence of the rivers Bulbourne with the Gade, which has afforded good fishing over many centuries. The Domesday survey of 1086 acknowledged the importance of the eel fisheries, usually sited at the mill weirs; Hemel Hempstead accounted for four mills and 275 eels.

One of the most important medieval 'Commoner's Rights' related to fishing: an early dispute recorded in 1499 between the rector of the monastery at Ashridge and the locals centred on these rights. By the sixteenth century, when the story of the Estate began, the rivers were still used to the full for angling by the locals, as well as for the replenishment of the monks' tables at Ashridge. In the original Trust Conveyance of 26 April 1594, the Meads 'together with the liberty of fishing in the Water that runneth in and through the said Meadowe and all profits commodities and advantages thereunto in any wise belonging … to the said John Rolfe and Richard Pope and one William Gladman …' were the first mentioned items. The use and enjoyment of the meadows and fishing was meant to be 'to the best commodity and benefit of all and every of the said inhabitants, their heirs and assigns being inhabitants there'.

A fascinating entry in the Ashridge records dated 16 August 1640 relates to the notes made by the Earl of Bridgewater's steward about his Lordship's waters in Hempstead. They were written in English, albeit somewhat abbreviated:

'Thomas … William Besouth, John Cato, John Dagnall, [were] prosecuted for fishing in the water by night with 2 large nets. Indicted them at Sessions - fined 10s each. Mr Williams gave me 10s towards

buying of nets. A trammell* cost me 18s, 2 shore nets cost me 8s. Williams promised to pay rest but never did it.'

Unfortunately, there was no indication of either where they were poaching, although it was probably in the Gade, or any hint at what kind of fish they caught. Another entry reveals that in 1639 at prayer time on Whit morning Peter Courteis and Jeremy Coleman's men were fishing in the river. '"I gave them warnings to come there no more." [On] 23 June – "I took them again at midnight. Jeremy, the master, gave me very ill words." Bound over to Quarter Sessions.'

The construction of the Grand Junction Canal at the end of the eighteenth century permanently altered the course of the rivers running through the Box Moor Estate. It also affected the condition and volume of the flow in the Bulbourne. Just as, in modern times, the coming of the New Town had even more diverse influences regarding water abstraction requirements and urban surface water discharge. The indigenous fish and invertebrate stocks were seriously affected by both of these human interventions.

The exact origins of the Fishery area are lost in time, but a row of cottages called Billingsgate once existed on Chaulden Meadows at the water's edge, while the piece of land that is now occupied by a private trout fishery was previously named the Fisheries. The canal-side Fishery Inn also appears to stand testimony to some old-time occupation in the vicinity.

Soon after the 1809 Box Moor Act:

'It was ordered that from and after the 3rd day of June next [1811] no inhabitants … do take, kill or destroy any fish in the canal, rivers or other waters of Box Moor with or by the means of any net or other engine except with the angler under the penalty of £5 for every offence, and that this be made a Bye Law … and it is further ordered that if any person or persons other than an inhabitant … shall take, kill or destroy the fish in the canal, river or other waters of Box Moor, or commit any trespass in attempts to do so such person or persons shall be prosecuted by the most effectual means …'

A tranquil moment on the river Gade; the canal ran under Balderson's high bridge which carried Two Waters Road. Note the swing bridge over the watercourse to Two Waters Mill. Water meadows, such as many older local residents can recall from their youth, generally no longer exist.

A dispute with Mr Stevens of Two Waters Mill over fishing in the rivers near the mill with nets met with concern in 1844 and a prosecution was considered for this infraction of the Bye Laws.

There was a wide variety of fish species noted in local waters in the nineteenth century, making it worthwhile to illegally net the rivers. Eel were still tolerably abundant, trout abounded early in the century, and stickleback, minnow, loach, millers thumb, gudgeon, bleak, dace, roach, chub, perch, ruffe, bream, tench and pike were all present.

A gentleman by the name of Pearman attended a Trust meeting of 14 July 1863 to ask for protection of the right of fishing in the waters and streams of the Moor, stating that any persons using nets were punishable under the Act relating to fishing. The Clerk was ordered to have handbills and notice boards made to inform people that they would be prosecuted for illegally taking fish by netting or snaring and a ten-shilling reward was offered to anyone giving information leading to a conviction. At a later meeting, Pearman himself offered to take out a lease for all the fishing rights at a cost of £1 for the first year, £5 the second year and £10 for the following three years. This was sanctioned by the Trustees, as far as they could

lawfully do so, but only on the understanding that Pearman paid the full expenses of the leasehold agreement.

A similar agreement was attempted in 1930 when Mr Elwes and his friends were prepared to stock with trout a length of the river Bulbourne alongside Chaulden Meadows which were being considered at that time as a Trust purchase. They then wished to rent the fishing at a nominal rent. The Trustees could not bind themselves to this until the land was definitely theirs and even then it was not certain that they could give anyone exclusive fishing rights. The matter was subsequently dropped. Thames Water Authority later introduced the requirement for all anglers to hold a fishing licence, no matter where the activity took place. The modern Bye Laws of the Trust state that no person shall bathe in any pond or stream, but no mention is made of fishing!

Ponds have also featured in the past at meetings of the Trust and the one which was once situated on Shothanger Common near the Golf Club house was referred to in the minutes of 1912, 1919 and 1928, when it needed cleaning out. The continuous problem of mud clogging up the rivers was a far more serious issue, and one to which many hours of meetings were to be devoted. In 1842 Sir John Bailey ruled that as the occupiers of the mill had the right to damn the stream, they should also clean out the mud from the Bulbourne. By 1896 the river was so full of mud the GJCC, who often undertook the cleaning up operations, could not float their dredger. One benefit of the accumulation of so much mud was the sale of 1,000 loads of it, sieved for 1s 6d a load and sold for 3s 6d in 1903. Later, in 1914 Robert Balderson was extremely irritated when mud from the Gade was put into the canal, which in turn blocked the wharf. The following year an arrangement to clear 1,150 tons from this area was made, together with 3,200 tons from Moor End Bridge to the Canal, at a cost of £138. A stretch of the Gade and Bulbourne also caused problems for the British Paper Company in 1906, from Two Waters Mill to the Bell Inn.

The river Bulbourne, having emerged from beneath the canal by way of culverts, known locally as 'The Chunks', flows peacefully towards Two Waters to join the Gade. One of three new footbridges is shown, replaced by the Trust in 1997.

The Bourne 'Brook' Gutter is a feeder of the river Bulbourne. In March 1999 it formed this large pool beside Bottom Farm.

By 1935, the list of species found locally had not altered very much from that given in 1878, except for chub. The common brown and rainbow trout, as well as golden carp, were also found in the locality.

Although the local rivers no longer feed the population, they have become an integral part of the area's natural beauty, giving pleasure in different ways to today's inhabitants. Their care and sustainable environmental development have become important subjects for the Trust because they have seriously declined in quality in recent years and contact is maintained with the Environment Agency on this account.

The Bourne Gutter joins the Bulbourne at Bourne End, just below the former mill. It only appears when the water level in the chalk sub-soil is high enough and simply flows on top of the grass. It is the only water course in the Area of Benefit that follows its own path.

The confluence of the Gade and Bulbourne at Two Waters. The river leaves the Box Moor Estate when it passes the Trust's cottages, seen in the background. Urban water run-off from the New Town and major roads has unfortunately increased the amount of pollution in the rivers.

A summer afternoon on the river Gade, near the Hemel Hempstead Town Cricket Club's junior cricket table. The popular pastime of fishing continues today, although the days of plentiful wild brown trout have passed.

21. GRAZING RIGHTS

'To the left we course the beautiful valley of Boxmoor, which presents a profusion of rural scenery … Innumerable groups of cattle are seen wandering in all parts of the valley, with sheep and horses in every direction.'
John Hassell *Tour of the Grand Junction Canal, 1819.*

Many people who regularly pass through Boxmoor today look out for, and recognise, the unusual black-and-white banded cattle that graze sedately on the lush green meadows. The Trust's herd of Belted Galloways has become identified with the area, retaining for this and future generations a closer link with the land and a sense of a shared heritage.

The rights of pasturage or grazing have been paramount over all other claims of benefit since the Trust's inception in 1594. 'The Inhabitants of Hemelhempsted … and of Bovington, their Heirs and Assigns, might and should for ever thereafter have, hold and enjoy the said Meadow …'. The words of the first Indenture, repeated in the 1809 Act, demonstrate the importance attached to this tract of open pastureland once popularly known as the Moors, but today more often called by their individual names.

The Moor opposite Boxmoor Station. Grazing has always been a major activity of the Box Moor Trust on behalf of the local inhabitants. The lush water meadows offered good-quality pasture early in the year.

Cattle were considered the most desirable of farm animals and most people kept at least one cow. The provision of 'white meats', milk, butter and cheese, the mainstay of many families, made cattle more important than horses, which were mainly used for transport, farm work and warfare. The grazing rights have been scrupulously guarded ever since and for this reason the pleasure of the general public in seeing animals feeding and breeding on the Moors in the twenty-first century is still guaranteed.

At the meeting of Feoffes in July 1763 strict conditions for grazing cattle were agreed. The locals paid six pence for the season; if they neglected to register, their cattle could be impounded and a fine was then due. 'Every person not having

right to put cattle there to pay 2s 6d for each head and the charges of impounding.' No sheep were allowed to feed on Box Moor from the first day of February until the first of November. Any miscreants would have to pay the Herdsman 2s 6d and their flock would be impounded. A notice directed at the several persons who still had sheep on the Moor insisted they remove them within fourteen days, or suffer the consequences of their animals being sent to the pound*. (See Appendix 11)

The regulation of such grazing has been part of a long and complex story. In February 1810, at the very first recorded Trust meeting, steps were taken to close the Moors from 12 February until 1 May. No geese were to be turned on it at any time from that date. This was then extended to 13 May and cattle could be impounded or proceedings taken against those who persisted in turning out geese. No stallion, bull or infectious animal was to be turned out and the stipulations about the number of shares needed for certain types of animal were written down. Geldings and mares required six shares and cows, heifers and asses needed four shares. The Moors were to be closed again on 12 November. By June in the following year it was decided to revise these arrangements and to ensure that colts also should be provided for by shares. It was not until 1827 that there was any further mention of shares, however, and then it was stated that a hog would require two shares, whereas a sow would only merit one. They had softened their approach to geese by then and the share of one 'messuage' would be sufficient. A far reaching development occurred on the 30 March 1833, when the minutes indicated that a printed or engraved and numbered ticket should be delivered annually to every person having a right of pasture on Box Moor. These could not be sold or exchanged without the knowledge of the Trust's Clerk. 'No inhabitants of houses built after the passing of the Act of 1809 were entitled to any share or rights of pasture.' If houses had been divided into different tenements, only one share could be allowed and the landlord would have to decide who received it. Impounding or prosecution would follow any infringement of these orders. These rules were repeated at various times over the next century, indicating that 'wilful trespasses' certainly did continue, despite all the Trustees' best endeavours.

Box Moor Right of Pasture Plaque.

The idea of pasture tickets was taken further on 14 September 1833 when Joseph Cranstone, the local iron founder, was asked to produce 800 plates or marks (akin to firemarks*). These were to be fixed to each property entitled to shares on Box Moor and would be necessary before anyone claimed a ticket, regardless of whether they used it or transferred it. The resulting distinctive, circular, cast iron marks were later painted a stone colour. Notices and hand bills were also ordered for the better regulation and stinting of the Moor. The plaques were not quite all in place by 21 February 1834, but it was promised that they would be affixed early in the ensuing week. It is interesting to note that few were placed in Marlowes, nowadays the main thoroughfare, rather at the 'ends' of the parish on the old cottages and farmsteads widely scattered over the area at that time.

Over one hundred years later, in 1968, the Stint was still tied to these iron plaques, as it is to this day. At that time, in order to graze an animal on the Moor (not on the Commons) the number of tickets required were: one for a goose; two for a hog; three for a donkey or heifer or steer; four for a one- to two-year-old heifer; five for an ox or steer or cow or heifer over two years old, or a yearling colt; six for a milking cow, cow in calf, mare or gelding; seven for a mare and foal, or mare in foal. The price of a ticket was thirty shillings for a horse and twenty shillings per head of cattle. It was agreed in April 1873 that the days for exchanging pasture tickets were to be moved closer to the start of the season for turning out the animals onto the Moor. By 1879 many of the original cottages had been demolished and fifty-nine right-of-pasture plaques were returned from the Cranstone family to the Trust's safe-keeping.

The purchase of Roughdown, Sheethanger and Dew Green Commons in 1886 necessitated some new Bye Laws for their management and again notice was given that no animal could be allowed to graze unlawfully. Sheep could be seen peacefully grazing under the watchful eye of their shepherd and a sheep dip was provided. 'A sheep washing brook with sluices at the usual washing place above Cangles Lane' is referred to in 1844, when fifteen shillings was charged annually for its use. The addition of a trough was agreed at the next meeting, although sheep were not strictly considered to be 'animals'.

When two houses burnt down in Bovingdon it was felt that only one share ticket, number 646, could be issued in replacement. The vicar of Bovingdon, the Revd F. P. Stevens, was also unlucky in that his request for a share for the old vicarage, which had been pulled down in the 1880s, was denied unless a new house was built on the same spot. Unfortunately, the new vicarage had already been erected at a different site.

The growth of Boxmoor village may have occasioned the thoughts at a meeting in 1887 that the Stint needed revision, due to the increase in milking cows in the district. Within living memory, local residents could still recall the days when Proctor's dairy cows ambled through the village and along St John's Road to the Moor, leaving a trail of cow pats as they progressed on their imperturbable way.

At the Public Enquiry in 1896 it was reported that there were no enclosures on the Moors, except for some fencing around the watercress beds and a railed off portion where cattle and horses were herded at night. The Commons also remained unfenced at this point in time.

William Wilson of Berkhamsted was appointed Honorary Vet by the Trust in April 1889. This office has remained an important one with regard to all the Trust's stock; Park Veterinary Practice of Watford currently provide this service. Nowadays, more horses than cows are grazed, apart from the Trust's own herd and flock. Nearly all of the former are owned by one family and they have been using the Moor for fifty years or more. The grazing system does not allow for animals to be taken from the pasture regularly and so the type of horses to be seen in the summer months are mainly breeding mares and young stock.

The demand for grazing has dramatically decreased in recent years; in the summer of 1973, the number of cattle grazed was 136 together with 22 horses. In 1991, the number of cattle had fallen to 26 but the horses remained constant at 22.

The decline in graziers led to the Trust's introduction of its own herds. The Shetland cattle were the first rare breed, later replaced by Belted Galloways. This breed can often be seen on the Moors throughout the summer.

The Trust's own Belted Galloway bull, Braveheart, in 1999. The Estate Manager often exhibits the Trust's animals at County and National Shows, as well as at local schools.

When it became obvious that the number of graziers was declining, in 1978 the Trust decided to buy some Shetland cattle. These were, and still are, a very rare breed, but proved difficult to get into calf and so Belted Galloways were selected instead. The Herdsman, Lionel Abbott and several Trustees travelled up to Scotland to sell the last of the Shetlands as a herd and buy Galloways from John Corrie in their native county instead. It has been noted that: 'Many old breeds of farm livestock do not fit into the modern economic farming system and without groups like the Trust they would become extinct'. A breeding programme was set up, to the delight of the Rare Breeds Survival Trust, and has been considerably extended over the last few years. The animals, such as Boxmoor Lace, have been shown at County Fairs and even the Royal Show at Stoneleigh. The Box Moor Trust has gradually become established as a pedigree breeder in its own right: Boxmoor Lace was awarded Supreme Champion at the South Bedfordshire Show in 1998.

One of the criteria for entering the Royal Show was that all the cattle should be certified clear of *Enzootic Bovine Lucosis* (EBL)*. In order to comply, the Trust cattle went through a series of blood tests to ensure there was no evidence of the disease. The grazing land also had to be cleared and that was one reason why the graziers' cattle never mixed with the Trust herd, kept on the EBL-free land to the west of the railway bridge. In 1999 it was announced that there were no recorded cases of the disease in the United Kingdom and the certification was lifted. In 2000 the herd comprised seventy-five head of cattle.

Roughdown Common was also in desperate need of attention and so the flock of Soay sheep, another rare breed, was bought in order to serve the environmental requisites of the Trust. On the light chalk soils of Roughdown these small yet hardy sheep were perfect for maintaining the grass without damaging the specialised flora. Unfortunately, harassment by

dogs has had its effect and the Soays are now being phased out. In their place, in 1993, the new Estate Manager, Phil Pennington, brought with him two extremely rare Norfolk Horn ewes. They were joined by two more ewes and a ram to form the nucleus of a flock which has grown prodigiously and is now enjoying all the hilly pastures at Westbrook Hay and nearby fields. The sight of so many black lambs skipping around their white-fleeced mothers, on a sunny spring morning, is one that makes all the effort seem justified.

There was, apparently, only one Norfolk Horn ram left in the whole world in 1963, but Whipsnade Zoo helped with a breeding programme and now, with the aid of organisations like the Box Moor Trust, matters are on a much more secure footing. The flock in 2000 comprised 210 sheep. The lambing barn constructed in 1998 at Snook's End is a useful development and the increased acreage for good grazing at Westbrook Hay should ensure the continuing success of this venture. The Trust's livestock is displayed at community events and schools in the locality and the policy of showing choice animals at a number of county shows, such as those in Hertfordshire, Norfolk and Suffolk, is well established.

The increase in the numbers of both the herd and flock, together with the environmental interests associated with their grazing, has meant that the Trust has added an Assistant Estate Manager to its personnel. The cattle have not been forgotten and a brand new barn has been erected for their winter quarters at Howe's Retreat. The process of 'natural service' is followed, rather than artificial insemination. This means that calves are born in the late summer and autumn rather than in the spring and the bulls are securely kept at Howe's Retreat, since the sight of a fully grown black-and-white striped bull with cows may deter anyone from venturing onto the Moor. The gestation period is nine months and calving is one of the eagerly awaited periods in the Trust's year. Some of the calves are a pale beige colour – these are called 'duns' and are a recognised form of the breed, resulting from a similarly coloured bull named Bolbec Dun Conductor. The dun cattle were primarily introduced because they were thought to have better hindquarters, therefore more valuable meat. All of these animals, as well as those of the traditional graziers, add to the overall scene of pastoral quietude, so vital an element in today's world of stressful living, and without which we would all be the poorer.

Top of following page:
A poster of 1853. Only inhabitants of houses built before the 1809 Act could claim the rights of pasture.

Bottom:
Pasture ticket poster 1853, underlining the importance of grazing in 1853 when there were two Pasture Ticket days, held at different locations.

BOX MOOR.

Notice is hereby Given,

THAT all Persons intitled to turn Cattle on the Moor, must apply for Tickets to the Clerk, Mr. DOWNING, which will be ready for Delivery on the 25th day of March next; and without such Tickets any Cattle thereon will be Impounded.

No Inhabitants of Houses built since the passing of the *Box Moor Act* in 1809, are intitled to any Share or Right of Pasturage.

The Tickets to be delivered up to the Clerk, at the *Swan* on Box Moor, on Saturday the 10th day of May next, at which time and place the Cattle must be produced, to be described and entered by the Clerk.

The Assignment of any Ticket must appear on the Back of it, and signed by the Inhabitant entitled to the Right, or Share assigned.

No such Assignment can be made to any Person inhabiting a House built since the passing of the Act as above.

Houses divided into different Tenements can have only one Share; and the Landlord is to settle to which Tenement it is to be allotted.

No Stallion, Ass, or Bull, nor any Suckling or Weaning Calves, or Glandered, Mangy, or disordered or infectious Horses or other Cattle, to be turned on the Moor.

The Cattle of all Persons which shall be turned on the Moor contrary and in opposition to the above Regulations, will be Impounded, or the Parties prosecuted, as the Trustees shall direct.

By Order of the Trustees of Box Moor,

HEMEL HEMPSTED.
December 26th, 1853.

JOHN DOWNING, their Clerk.

1853.

Notice is hereby given that the Trustees
OF

Box Moor

Will meet at the Rose & Crown Inn, Hemel Hempsted, on Tuesday, April 12th, at 9 o'Clock; and at the Swan Inn, Box Moor, on Tuesday, April 19th, at 10 o'Clock;

TO DELIVER THE

Pasture Tickets

To all the Inhabitant Householders who are entitled to a BOX MOOR SHARE.

THE FIRST DAY'S DELIVERY
Will be to all Persons who reside in the Town, at Leverstock Green, Corner Hall, Piccot's End, and Water End.

THE SECOND DAY'S DELIVERY
Will be to all Persons who reside at Bovingdon, Bourne End, Crouch Field, Two Waters, and all other parts of the Parish not specified.

On Tuesday, May 10th

The Trustees request that the Share Tickets may be returned to them at the BELL INN, TWO WATERS, where they will attend to give Cattle Tickets in exchange, and to enter the Cattle intended to be turned out on the 12th of May; and no Cattle will be allowed to be turned on the Moor until 9 o'Clock on that day, and before having been inspected by the Herdsman.

NOTE.—No Tickets will be delivered on either of the said days after 3 o'Clock in the Afternoon.

N. B. Those Parties entitled to Tickets who cannot attend personally must, previously to the day of delivery, apply to Mr. Stocken, Marlowes, or the Herdsman, for a Form to be filled up and signed by them, authorising some Person to receive the Ticket for them; and no Tickets will be delivered in such cases without such signed authority.

No Tickets will be given out except on the days of Delivery, and no Exchange Tickets issued under any circumstances after 3 o'Clock on Tuesday the 10th May.

Hemel Hempsted, March 26th, 1853.

F. MASON, PRINTER, HEMEL HEMPSTED.

A print of 1808 showing Norfolk and Hertfordshire breeds of horned sheep.

Soay sheep, a hardy, primitive breed from the Hebrides, were introduced for the environmental management of Roughdown Common. They are seen here during the summer on Fishery Moor, giving an opportunity for the rare plants to regenerate naturally.

The Brown family has for many years been a major grazier. The funeral of Charlie Brown was a special event; the horse-drawn hearse paraded around the Moor so that the horses could take their leave of their deceased owner before the service in St John's Church.

22. The Trust's Herdsmen

One of the earliest surviving documents of a meeting of the Feoffes and inhabitants of the Area of Benefit was held at the King's Arms in the High Street in July 1763. It mentions Joseph Smith of Cangles as Herdsman for one year. He was instructed to keep a book with the names of the owners and marks of the cattle pastured on the ancient meadow 'now called Boxmoore'.

Joseph Honor had the honour of being the Trust's first named choice of Herdsman on 22 June 1809, following the Box Moor Act, but within a fortnight he had declined the offer of looking after the Moor. Francis Axtell was then appointed in his place; his family name was recorded in the original list of Feoffes in 1594. The enormity of the job soon became apparent and, in August, he asked for assistance. An assistant by the name of Pooley was consequently employed to look after the upper end of the Moor. In May 1810 the mention of 'a ticket in writing' is made, which had to be shown to the Herdsman or Clerk before turning any cattle onto the pastures.

By December 1810 another name had entered the records: 'George Anstee [who] continues to be Herdsman at 12 shillings per week from this meeting to Old May Day next and on his refusal another person to be appointed'. He was still performing his duties in July 1811 and the wage continued as before from November 1811 to 1 May 1812. One of the Herdsman's main duties was to report any encroachments on the land. These were many and varied and reports were often noted in the minutes concerning the misdemeanours of their fellow men, such as John White's attempt with others to 'draw the canal river by means of a net or other engine' in 1812. Sometimes a Herdsman would attend Trust meetings to give his views in person. Strangely, the minutes for March 1816 stated that 'Francis Axtell is appointed Herdsman on the said Moor in the room of George Anstee discharged'. A sub-committee of Trustees was formed in February 1828 to give directions to the Herdsman, who in 1829 was still Francis Axtell. He remained on the payroll from 9 May 1833 at the reduced rate of four shillings a week when George Bates took over. This did not prove to be a satisfactory choice either and it was resolved on 12 August 1833 that he should be given a month's notice since 'he was not a fit person to hold the office'. Charles Johnson was the next appointee, on 6 September 1833, at a wage of ten shillings a week; one of the first tasks assigned to him was to take down a shed encroaching on the Moor. He must have impressed his new employers because they ordered a top coat for him at the cost of two guineas in November. Unfortunately, his good conduct did not last for long and he, too, was discharged for neglect of duty in December 1835.

The Herdsman's first purpose-built cottage, erected by the Trust in 1838. The nearby pound was used for drovers' strays or contagious cattle.

Ada Edwards with her family – William, Dennis and Florence, c.1908. Ada sold sweets, R. White's lemonade and even Boxmoor rock! The day trippers from London must have been grateful for her refreshments on their way to Howe's Retreat. George Edwards was Herdsman for forty-three years and his family continue to graze horses on the Moor.

The fast turnover of Herdsmen continued. Charles Bennett held the office for a short time and in February 1836 a Herdsman's cottage was on the agenda. It was to have a kitchen, a back kitchen, two bedrooms and a shed for barrows and tools. This was to be built 'at the smallest possible expense' on the nook of the Moor beyond Vyse's garden, situated on the London Road next to the railway bridge. Later, a cattle pound was added close to this building. Some consideration was given to moving the newly built Herdsman's cottage nearer to the cattle arch, but in the end it was left where it was, the expenses being drawn against the sale of gravel and paid to a Mr Groom. William Glenister was then selected as the Herdsman and took possession of the new cottage in January 1838, for a six-month trial period.

This appointment heralded a more settled chapter in the story. Glenister served until his death in office on 27 February, 1892. He outlived all the Trustees who appointed him and knew twenty-eight different Trustees. During his long service he had to deal with all the encroachments previously noted, with looking after the fences, trees, rivers and banks, with cattle that sometimes had contagious diseases, with truculent residents and even mischievous lads. He saw the coming of two railways across Trust land, the operation of the Boxmoor Baths, the purchase of the Commons and the building of St John's Church and Boxmoor Hall.

When he died, his widow was asked to vacate the cottage and given the paltry sum of £7 in lieu of a pension, for which she said she was very grateful. Her husband's post was filled by Hubert Parsons for sixteen shillings a week plus the cottage; subsequently he was found to have defective eyesight, and could not, therefore, be as vigilant as his role demanded. The next incumbent, George Wood, only stayed for four years, up until Christmas 1897.

The cottage had been subject to some modernisation, but at a meeting of October 1893 it was decided that the replacement Herdsman should not move into the Wood's cottage but that a new house should be built for the principal Herdsman at the Town end of the Moor.

Evidently the post was becoming more popular and eighteen people applied for the vacancy. Another George, this time Hawkins, was accepted and managed to retain the position until 1908, when he, too, was found to be 'unfit for work' and retired. The next round of interviewers had the choice of forty prospective employees and, in the end, yet another George was the lucky candidate.

George Edwards is a name still talked about by older Boxmoor residents. He was the 'Moorman' who terrorised the local youth and kept a keen eye on all the transgressors of the Bye Laws of both the Moor and Baths. He applied himself with vigour to his job and remained as Herdsman for forty-three years until his retirement in 1951 at the age of seventy-nine. Other assistants came and went, such as Ray and Simmonds, but on George Edwards' retirement national advertising brought five applicants, from whom Frederick Hawes was chosen. Wages had risen to £5 10s a week by then and twenty years later his assistant William (Bill) Bull took over the post. Another familiar name came on to the scene in 1975, when the independently minded Lionel Abbott was appointed. He shared in the challenge of building up the Trust's own herd and introduced Shetland cattle to the Moors and then Soay sheep to Roughdown Common. He helped to found the breeding programme for the Belted Galloways that are now such a typical sight on the Moors.

Lionel Abbott (Herdsman), Peter Willowby (Staff) and Stan Snoxall (Trustee) erecting hurdles made in the Trust's workshop at Old Fishery by Charlie Walker. Lionel Abbott was the Trust's Herdsman from 1975–89; he helped to introduce the rare Shetland cattle and Soay sheep and to found the breeding programme for the Belted Galloway cattle on the Box Moor Estate. He was the last Herdsman to live in this cottage before its demolition, prior to the construction of the A41 By-pass.

Brian Toft followed in Abbott's footsteps in 1989, but made his own contribution to the tradition of showing the Trust's cattle and won prizes at national shows. The fifteenth holder of this now historic post is Phil Pennington, but the name and duties have altered significantly since 1809. His role as Estate Manager has grown as the Estate itself has expanded in recent years. A brand new house at Snook's End, opposite Snook's Moor, was provided for the Manager and his family in 1992 following the demolition of the former Herdsman's cottage when the A41 By-pass was constructed. New lambing barns were erected in 1998 adjacent to the house to accommodate the flock of rare Norfolk Horn sheep Phil had helped develop; his two daughters take a keen interest in this and show the choicest animals at various events. Alison Shipley was employed in 1999 as Assistant Estate Manager, the Trust's first ever female Herdsperson. The Managers are currently assisted by Paul Redding and Chris Bartlett, the Estate Workers. The task of looking after the animals and the Estate continues as before, but the Trustees of 1809 would not believe the wide range of today's activities, nor the diverse skills that the Herdsmen of the twenty-first century have to display.

A splendid new residence became possible due to the building of the A41 By-pass and the Estate Manager, Phil Pennington, resides there with his wife and two daughters. It was appropriately named 'Snook's End', in memory of the local highwayman who met his end on the gallows somewhere on the opposite Moor.

Catherine and Jo-Ann Pennington show the prize-winning Norfolk Horn, Boxmoor Claire (right), awarded the Supreme Champion (Sheep) Trophy at the South Beds Show in 1999. Jo-Ann is holding the Young Handler Trophy from the Herts Show. Boxmoor Beautiful is on the left.

23. SHEETHANGER, DEW GREEN AND ROUGHDOWN COMMONS

It was on 14 April 1886 that the Box Moor Trustees formally signed the Conveyance of Shothanger, Dew Green and Roughdown Commons, thus completing the purchase from the Dean and Chapter of St Paul's, London, for the sum of £100. It was resolved at the same meeting, held in the Vestry of St Mary's Church, Hemel Hempstead, that in future the Trustees style themselves 'Trustees of Boxmoor, Shothanger, Dew Green and Roughdown Commons', a wordy title which, fortunately perhaps, quickly fell into disuse. The Trustees then felt in a position to consider making Bye Laws for the better management of the Commons.

The links between the Commons themselves and the local inhabitants had, however, already existed for a long time. It is apparent from the records that 'subsisting Common rights' had probably been established for as long as those relating to Box Moor itself.

Following the Dissolution of the Monasteries in the sixteenth century, Henry VIII granted these Commons (amongst other property) to the Dean and Chapter of St Paul's. Whilst it is likely that manorial rights existed during monastic times, all claims were later waived by the steward to the manor of Hemel Hempstead at the Court Baron*. A manorial jury in 1617 gave the verdict that these lands were severed from the manor; the records state whilst 'Shutthanger, Rowdowne, Dewgreene and Ffielden Heathe are within the Manor [of Hemel Hempstead] they are not part of it'.

Although the Commons had been used for grazing sheep, with 10 acres devoted to profitable woodland, public concern over increasing misuse, such as the building of cottages in the chalk dell on Roughdown, resulted in recommendations that the land be brought under the control of the Box Moor Trustees, and so in 1830, the Dean and Chapter leased the Commons to the Trustees for twenty-one years at the rent of five shillings a year. This lease was subsequently renewed in 1851 and again in 1872.

In 1882, however, the Dean and Chapter's agent, a Mr Clutton, informed the Trustees that the churchmen were unlikely to renew the lease, suggesting that they should make an offer to purchase the Commons instead. The Trustees replied that: 'in order to release the Chapter from the responsibility of preserving the Commons from encroachments and nuisances, the Trustees can only offer a nominal sum for the same and the sum of £30 be offered accordingly'.

As it transpired, this figure was later increased to £100 but, before the Trustees could legally proceed with the purchase, a Vestry meeting was called to sanction the proposal in accordance with the Act of 1809. Whilst the inhabitants of Hemel Hempstead passed the resolution on 20 May 1885, two days later a similar meeting for the householders of the hamlet of Bovingdon voted against. The Bovingdon residents apparently wanted to protect their rights to take chalk for agricultural purposes and to regulate what they saw as their own common land. The meeting nearly did not proceed, since several wagon loads of strangers from Hemel Hempstead tried to gatecrash the Parish Room and only dispersed when a policeman was called. That same day, undeterred, the Trustees 'resolved that by authority of the Hemel Hempstead meeting they proceed with the purchase'.

Although Trust minutes simply record the basic details of these meetings, it is not difficult to sense the strong feelings that had been aroused. Within only a few days, at a Special meeting on 15 June 1885, the Trustees were advised that an application had been made to the Ecclesiastical Commissioners to acquire the Commons by certain persons professing to represent the inhabitants of Bovingdon. The matter seemed to resolve itself very quickly, for although it was agreed that the Trustees should send a deputation to meet the Commissioners, the latter replied saying that they had already received instructions to carry out the sale to the Trustees and that such a deputation was therefore unnecessary.

Today the botanical importance of Roughdown Common cannot be underestimated and the control of the scrub hawthorn which had become a serious threat to the rich grassland and junipers has been an on-going project since 1977, with the introduction of Soay sheep helping in the overall management plan. In the nineteenth century the area was extensively quarried for chalk, but the sealed tunnels and exposed face of the chalk pit are the only reminders of the mine today. The bats that find winter hibernation quarters there, provided by the Trust, are the only remaining residents.

Dew Green is, in effect, nowadays little more than a frontage onto Felden Lane. It is adjacent to the Trust's holdings at Howe's Retreat, where improvements have recently been undertaken on the barns. In 1994 it was the scene of some interesting activity when a fresh dew pond was created by the Trust, with assistance from the pupils of Boxmoor House School.

Shothanger Common (more often known as Sheethanger today) and Dew Green are no longer grazed by sheep and at present do not possess any profitable woodland, but instead they provide for a wealth of recreational pursuits. When enjoying a pleasant stroll across the Commons, a round of golf, or perhaps a ride along a shady bridle path by horseback, one can appreciate the outstanding scenic views – without doubt amongst the finest in the district.

Exposed chalk face on Roughdown Common. Soay sheep, which closely resemble the animals kept by Neolithic farmers, were introduced to graze the Common in the late 1970s, until dogs worrying the sheep became such a problem the project was discontinued.

A Good Friday Fair c.1890 in the Chalk Pit, Roughdown. Chalk was extracted for agricultural use, to make acid soil more fertile. The remains of these pits and mines are still in evidence today. The chalk downland flora and fauna have made this a Site of Special Scientific Interest (SSSI). It is the only area of naturally regenerating junipers in Hertfordshire.

An early postcard, long before modern developments such as Beechwood Park. Sheethanger Common, which provides the course for Boxmoor Golf Club, was formerly listed as an SSSI but is today a Heritage Site. It consists of valuable chalk grassland containing orchids and other rare plants.

Dew Green, May 2004. The dew pond was created in 1994 with the help of pupils at Boxmoor House School, as part of the Trust's four hundred years' celebrations. In the 1900s there was a pond on Sheethanger Common, near the golf clubhouse.

Bridleway sign at Dew Green, 2004. In the late 1980s, in order to achieve access across Sheethanger Common by ramblers, golfers and horseriders, a separate track was established along the edge of Howes Retreat and through a copse partly owned by the Boys' Brigade and the Box Moor Trust.

24. ENCROACHMENT ON THE ESTATE

The temptations that have arisen in the past and which will undoubtedly continue to arise, to claim, change or adapt parts of the Box Moor Estate, deserve mention. They are, in principle, one of the reasons for the 1809 Box Moor Act, for since 1594 there had undoubtedly been many meetings about these constant nuisances.

The Herdsman, who was appointed in 1809, had the stated objective of looking after and reporting any encroachments on the Moor. At the same time, approaches were made to a Mr Cooper for a copy of the plan of Box Moor with accurate measurements of the ground on which each cottage then stood together with their gardens. Sheep were considered to be 'trespassers' since they were not viewed as cattle and, at the meeting of 20 July 1809, it was declared that from the beginning of August the Herdsman would be within his rights to impound any sheep trespassing on the Moor. Cattle which were not legitimately covered by grazing rights, could also be impounded at a charge of one shilling for each animal so discovered: whilst as for geese …! The owners of suckling calves feeding from cows other than their own mothers were also admonished.

Even the dung deposited on the meadows by grazing cattle was viewed as part of the Estate and could not be removed without permission. One unfortunate man, Joseph Brooks, was imprisoned for transgressing against this rule and had to sign an apology, which was then displayed in the Market Place.

It had been agreed in 1763 that no turf or earth could be privately excavated and taken on any occasion whatsoever, yet soil was carried away by the employees of the GJCC and the Trust's Clerk wrote to the company to prevent further trespass. In spite of this warning, the soil continued to be carried off and legal action was threatened.

The 1809 Act gave the Trustees something to bite with and there was a general tightening up of the Bye Laws. Arrears of rent due from the cottagers were called in to be paid immediately, or tenants would face eviction. One tenant by the name of Mead was taken to task about the works he had constructed opposite his house: his ditches needed to be drained off on that area of the Moor, since it was becoming submerged in standing water.

The Trustees often had to adjourn their meetings to view various encroachments, or even hold Special meetings on occasion. Commodities such as gravel and topsoil also provoked many disputes, such as that in October 1809, when Richard Abrook was fined five shillings. A resolution that gravel could be taken was passed by a majority vote, as long as a load of stones replaced every load of gravel, or payment of one shilling a load was made. Extractions of gravel, clay, soil, ballast and water all feature as nuisances; however, the sale of stones, gravel and sand from the Box Moor Estate actually netted about £35 in 1835.

William Howard of High Street Green was formally chastised for loading and unloading bricks, coal and hay on the Moor instead of at the wharf, in 1820. Undefined trespasses by named persons occurred from time to time and notices were eventually proposed in 1822 to forbid 'all persons from loading or unloading any kinds of merchandize'.

Likewise, the Sparrows Herne Turnpike Trustees were sometimes in trouble because their road-menders were depositing stones on the Moor. The GJCC also had their differences with the Box Moor Trustees, including disputes over clay digging and the depositing of mud (although the latter was probably beneficial to the Moor). Despite the threat of legal proceedings pieces of common land continued to be nibbled away. Even the gentry, such as Dr Davis of Boxmoor House, thought themselves above such petty Bye Laws. He dug chalk from Roughdown Common because he believed he had a right to it, but the Trustees replied that he must fill up the holes and remove the gate that opened from his field onto the Moor by the side of the railway bridge, 'as no person can be allowed to make a road over any part of the Moor'. The letter was signed by Dr Davis's neighbour, Granville Dudley Ryder, as Chairman of the Trust, but it did not appear to stop the doctor taking whatever he wanted from the Estate.

The Highway Surveyors were not exempt from censure, a fact confirmed at a meeting in February 1828 when part of the Moor opposite Heath Farm was reputedly in a dangerous state due to gravel pits situated there to mend the roads. Fences placed around properties were also deemed to be encroachments unless the land so enclosed was rented and a lease obtained for it: one leaseholder, a Mr Ward, was asked to remove his fence, or pay for it, in 1829. A Mr Harding persisted in digging up gravel and breaking the soil of the Moor in the same year and was served a notice to take out a proper lease of the cottages occupied by him. These minor infringements must have caused ill-feeling between all concerned.

The Commons were not free from 'nuisances and depreciations' either, as recorded in 1830, at the time of the Trust taking out a lease of 'Row Down and Shothanger Commons' from the Dean and Chapter of St Paul's in London. The lime kiln on John Glover's land at Duck Hall was an object of much concern in 1841, particularly as he frequently dug great quantities of chalk from Roughdown to burn in his kiln. The churches and chapels of the area were to have notices posted up 'cautioning all persons from digging or carrying away any of the soil, turf or stones'. The inhabitants were invited to a meeting at Hemel Hempstead Town Hall, on 10 November 1830 to take into consideration the best mode of managing the said Commons – a democratic way of proceeding.

Further notice boards were needed in 1833 'at each end of the Moor near the Turnpike road cautioning all persons not to trespass on the Moor or Row Down or on the waters of Box Moor'. In the following year it was felt necessary to inform all Box Moor tenants not to build or increase their buildings without the Trustees' consent. Sheds, pig sties, dung hills, heaps of mould and cut grass all constituted encroachments duly recorded over the years.

In dealing with the London and Birmingham Railway Company, one of the biggest culprits of the period, the Trustees were anxious that 'the embankment on both sides should be grassed and made as sightly as possible', thus masking the great swathe of chalk that was the result of building the line through the Moor. The drainage of the pastures was not to be obstructed, nor any wharf erected without permission. The contractors, Messrs Cubitt, did not get off lightly either, since they were using the Moor for storing materials and the Trust requested compensation for the injury caused. Further arguments ensued with regard to the railway horses crossing the Moor, a practice the Trust wanted to stop. It became a battle of wills to obtain adequate compensation for the damage done by the completion of the railway.

It might have seemed almost like a game to some persistent offenders, as in the case of a Mr Wynter who frequently drove his pigs onto the Moor but always contrived to drive them away before the Herdsman could reach the pigs to impound them. Joseph Smith even had the temerity to build a privy on the Moor. They were not very happy with a Mr Bovingdon either, who frequently rode over the Moor on horseback – in full view of the Trustees – even after their remonstrations with him. They resolved forthwith that he should be summonsed before the magistrate as a trespasser.

On a more serious note, the minutes relate that on numerous occasions warnings were not heeded and people were evicted from their houses or the houses physically removed, as in December 1839. These were often 'squatter's cottages' without proper foundations or substance. A local surveyor, George Alexander Smith, was commissioned in 1841 to produce a detailed plan of the Box Moor Estate which was to be used over the years to resolve disputes about land ownership. Complaints were made to the Trustees at this time of 'encroachments made by many parties on the Moor'. The Trust ordered a quantity of iron hurdles from the local blacksmith, Cranstone's foundry in the High Street, Hemel Hempstead, in 1843 in order to form a boundary fence on the south-west side of the field lately purchased from Norris and Pedley (now known as Blackbirds' Moor). By 1846 the Trust seems to have acted decisively and asked for a list of all the persons liable to pay for encroachments.

Pulling down fences and flint walls, demolishing squatter's houses and outbuildings, prosecuting piecemeal digging and protecting the rivers were all in a day's work for the Trustees and their staff in the nineteenth century. Although not in themselves momentous events, they underline the constant need for vigilance in safeguarding the Estate through the ages.

We the undersigned Do hereby caution and warn you not henceforth to go or trespass upon a certain Tract of Land called Box Moor in the Parish of Hemel Hempsted in the County of Hertford or any part thereof, Otherwise than on the Roads passing over the same, as on your so doing you will become and be deemed a wilful Trespasser thereon – Dated this 11th Day of December 1818
To Joseph Gape Esqre

Geo. Holloway
John Field
John Field
James Cato
T. E. Deacon
Harry Grover
John Brown
Thomas Godwin
John Bovingdon
Wm Jennings
Thomas Partridge
Wm Johnson.

Notice warning against trespass, 11 December 1818. Several similar letters were sent to men from St Albans, but there was no indication of the specific reason for this action.

Fishery Road, Boxmoor. The metal hurdles are clearly shown, continuing the tradition started in 1843.

25. PUBLIC HOUSES AND STAR COTTAGES

The Boatman. This site was part of the purchase of land by the GJCC which was recently brought back again into the Trust's ownership from British Waterways. Originally planned as toll houses, the cottages became a Lock House and beerhouse.

The Box Moor Trust once owned four public houses, none of which have survived to the present day. The Artichoke, the Boatman, the Friend at Hand and the Star once served the thirst of the local population. Various references to these establishments occur throughout the Trust's minute books.

In 1882 a right-of-way leading from the Boatman to the canal bank was opened so that Trustees would have easier access to Trust property. In a brief note of 1888, concerning the landlord Benjamin Bennett's lease expiring on 25 March 1889, it was referred to as the Jolly Boatman. Bennett, in fact, declined to make an offer for the lease and it went instead to George Luck of Catlin Street, for £10 per annum. Some years later, Luck said that he was going to give up the tenancy because the premises were damp. His wife then complained to the Clerk of the Trust, but said that if the Trust paid the rates, they would consider staying on; the Trust complied and the matter seemed to be resolved. However, by 1931, the Hemel Hempstead Corporation had decided that the old Boatman had outlived its years and a demolition notice was served on the Trust. The tenants, at that time, Mr and Mrs Bone, were offered a Council house instead, but Mr Bone kept his former garden as an allotment.

The following year, the Corporation gave another demolition order to the Trust, this time in respect of the Star Cottages. These ramshackle buildings had been in the middle of Blackbirds' Moor for a very long time; perhaps squatters' cottages, one of the 'encroachments' that were mentioned in earlier records. There had been a beerhouse* in one of them since at least 1888, when Locke and Smith of Berkhamsted offered £35 per annum for a twenty-one-year lease on the Star. It seems that the beer was not from the Star Brewery in Bury Road, surprisingly.

The beerhouse was refused a licence in 1912 and it would appear to have been no longer in use from about that date.

Certainly, the lease to Locke and Smith was withdrawn in 1913 and the tenants then paid their rent directly to the Trust. Some of the cottages were pulled down in the period 1913–16 and their right-of-pasture plaques handed back to the Trust. In 1933 all the remaining cottages (there had been as many as thirteen) were vacated and the firm of Bovis Thorne carried out the necessary demolition. The site was subsequently levelled and is hard to define today, but it was approximately in the middle of the Moor opposite the Steamcoach.

A smaller amount was accepted for a longer period when the lease of the Artichoke, on the London Road, was up for tender. Henry Wyman's offer of £25 per annum for forty years was deemed to be sufficient in 1889, but when that expired, the Trustees increased the rent to £60 per annum. The Chesham Brewery Company came into the picture in 1896, when it took over the lease. In 1905 discussions took place about extending the premises, as long as the Chesham Brewery agreed to pay a rent amounting to five per cent. Whether this ever happened the minutes do not tell, but the Licensing Justices informed the Trust that it had been referred for closing down and the licence was not renewed in 1932. The Chesham Brewery, perhaps realising that matters had gone too far, gave £30 'in respect of dilapidations under the terms of the lease'. Tenders for repairs and decorations were sent out and a woman by the name of Pipkin, possibly Lizzie Pipkin, was prepared to pay a rent of £50. In the end, she paid £60 for a seven-year lease and then, in 1940, she sold it to H. M. Ainge. The lease then changed hands several times, until in November 1962 a Mr Harper stated that he had re-opened tea rooms at these premises, but he was not allowed to advertise them with a sign on the Moor. In its latter days, the Artichoke became a pet food store until it was finally vacated and made way for several flint-faced cottages built by the Trust in 1999. The new dwellings have appropriately been named Artichoke Court.

Star Cottages on Blackbirds' Moor. The beerhouse took its name from the Star Brewery situated at 23–25, Bury Road, run at that time by William Spicer Elliott, High Bailiff in 1890. The view is from Roughdown Common, before St John's Hall and the Beechfield Estate were built. Heath Barn is on the right-hand side of St John's Road. In the middle foreground is the old cottage on Harding's Moor, next to the Station Road canal bridge.

The only extant photo which is presumed to show the Star beerhouse, in the middle of the row of cottages. The horse-drawn cart may be delivering barrels of beer.

A family group next to Star Cottages. The children attended St John's School, seen in the middle background. Mr Greene of Star Cottages supplied straw, bonnets, horse bonnets and mats as well as dealing in finished straw plait.

The Friend at Hand, an original sketch c.1930, by Ethel Salisbury, The Friend at Hand was one of four licensed premises originally owned by the Box Moor Trust.

The Friend at Hand, prior to demolition. The site on London Road, opposite Snoxall's Moor, presently stands empty.

Apart from the delightful sketch by Ethel Salisbury, a former resident of Box Lane, there does not appear to be much pictorial evidence of the existence over many years of the beer house known, equally delightfully, as the Friend at Hand. Only a rough plot exists today, fronting the London Road opposite Snoxall's Moor. In the mid 1800s there was a family by the name of Friend residing at Haxters End Farm in Bourne End, but there may not be any connection.

In 1887 the offer of a forty-year lease was made for the beerhouse and the following year Henry Wyman (late Wyman and Hall of the Anchor Brewery) agreed to pay £15 per annum if the premises were put into good repair by the Trust. He also held the lease for the Artichoke, and in 1891 the leases of both Trust properties were transferred to Thomas and John Nash of Chesham. They took over the Anchor Brewery, which had earlier connections with Thomas Elisha Deacon, and closed it down in 1891.

The landlord of the Friend at Hand was asked not to let his fowls damage the pasturage of the Moor in 1894. The Chesham Brewery, previously trading as T. J. Nash, had taken over the lease of this tenancy, as well as that of the Artichoke, by 1896. The authorities refused a licence for this establishment and compensation was paid to the Trust, to Chesham Brewery and to the tenant, a Mrs Polley, on the understanding that it would close on 31 December 1930. She was then offered the tenancy of the house for 12s 6d per week, which she duly accepted. The Fox and Hounds in nearby Bourne End closed at the same time.

A Miss Polley still lived on the premises, until she was offered alternative Trust accommodation in 1958, since it was no longer viable to repair the building. Other tenants were to follow, however, at reduced rents until the demolition order was received in June 1972. The possibility of building one or two dwellings on the site for the Herdsman or other Trust staff meant that the Trust resisted the demolition order for as long as possible, but all their hopes of erecting a building in the early 1970s came to nothing and eventually the familiar old cottage was demolished. It is still an empty plot today, but in its time it must have witnessed many a stirring scene as travellers journeyed along the old London Road.

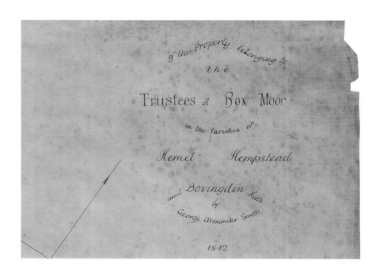

George Alexander Smith produced this fine map in 1842 at the request of the Trustees, the original of which is still in the possession of the Box Moor Trust. Smith was also associated with the surveying and production of the nationally important Hemel Hempstead Tithe Map of 1841–2, which showed other land belonging to him on the south side of Gas Works Moor. Smith lived at Marlowes House in Hemel Hempstead and a plan of his substantial copyhold estate, drawn up in 1849, depicts two houses, gardens, orchards, cottages and adjoining land. Smith was a land and architectural surveyor, auctioneer and estate agent, as well as a timber merchant, according to the *Post Office Directory* of 1850. Smith was later the actuary and secretary of the Savings Bank; his firm became Smith and Robinson in around 1870. When Smith retired, his partner, Nathaniel Wishart Robinson, continued the business, including Smith's role as the land agent for Sir John Sebright of Beechwood Park, a large estate near Markyate. He was elected a Box Moor Trustee on 28 October 1871 and served for sixteen years. At the time of his death in January 1888 the Chairman, Shadrach Godwin, proposed a Resolution of Condolence which referred to the great assistance which Smith had rendered to the Trust and to the universal respect in which he was held.

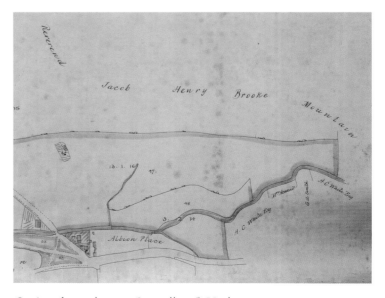

Section of map, between Cotterells and Marlowes

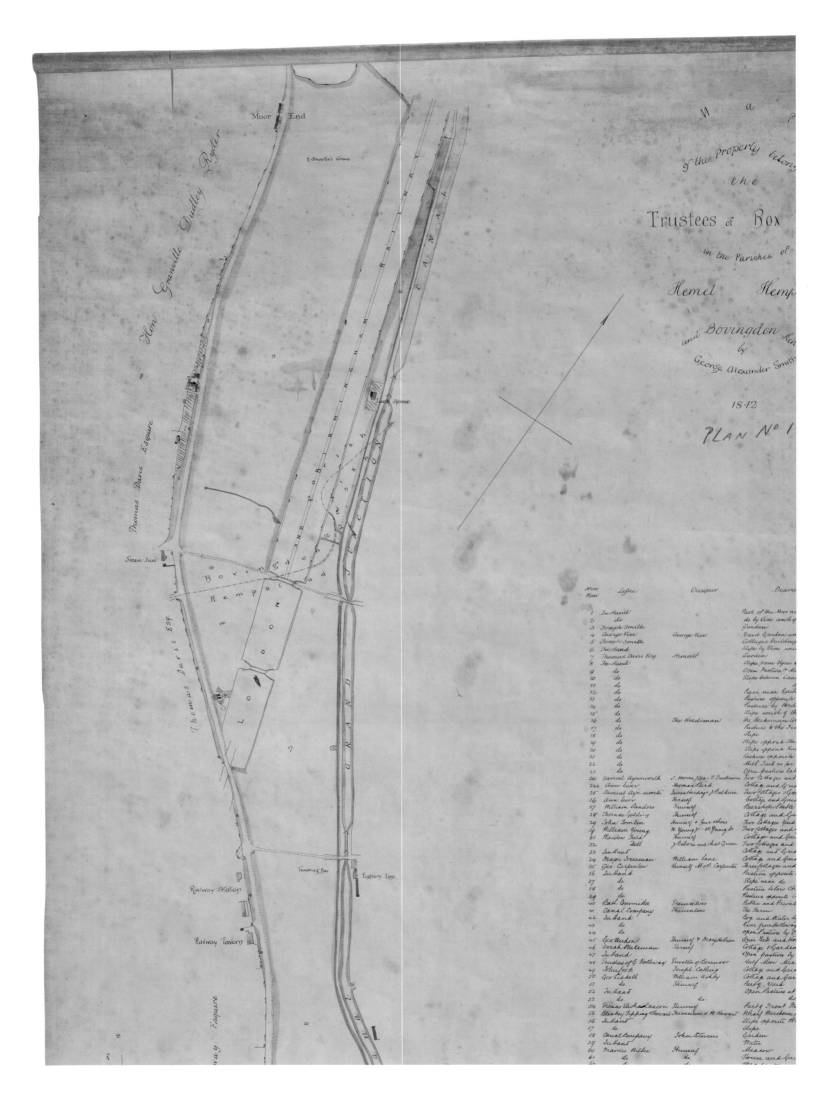

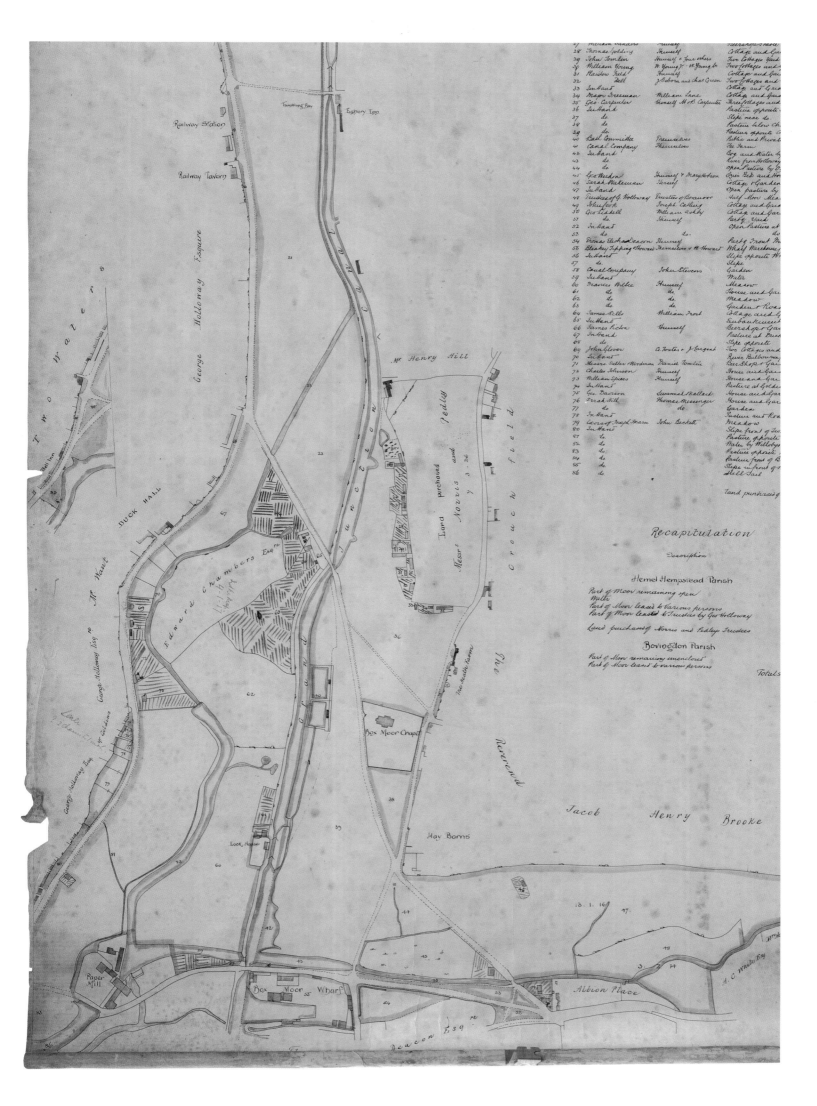

RECREATION, FRESH AIR AND EXERCISE

27. BOXMOOR BATHS

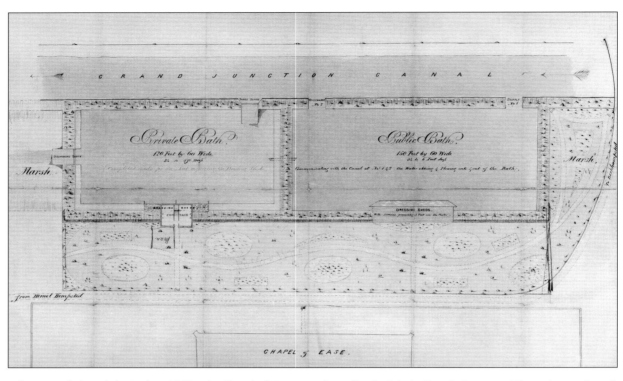

The original plan of the Baths c.1840. The Chapel-of-Ease was the earlier St John's Church, Boxmoor. The pools were formed after the extraction of clay for 'puddling' or waterproofing the canal.

Nothing remains nowadays to show that for the best part of a hundred years the inhabitants of Hemel Hempstead were fortunate in being able to enjoy a revitalising swim in open-air swimming pools on the Moor, known simply as Boxmoor Baths. One local resident, George Eyles, wrote in 1926 that it was one of the most beneficial institutions connected with the town prior to the laying down of the water mains. The first entry relating to the baths in the Box Moor Trust minutes is recorded on 15 August 1840 and the last on 30 April 1953. The intervening 113 years saw the development and the demise of both the private and public baths on the Moor, finally replaced by the Town Council's own swimming pool at the Churchill* site in St John's Road.

On 15 June 1840, the Trustees requested the Improvement Committee to ascertain whether there was any part of the Moor near the canal that contained clay. The GJCC was willing to exchange part of their existing clay pits with the Trust if they were supplied with an equivalent. At a subsequent meeting, it was stated that there was no clay in any other part of the Moor. The long-term future of these clay pits, used by the navvies for 'puddling' the bottom of the canal to keep it watertight, was assured when the following request was minuted on 15 August 1840:

'Mr. Saunders on behalf of certain inhabitants of the neighbourhood applies for permission to enclose a portion of the clay pits lately used by the Canal Company for digging clay opposite the Chapel-of-Ease ... for the purpose of constructing Baths with the necessary embankments and sheds thereon ... and for the purpose of erecting thereon such wall or other fence as may be necessary for screening the baths from the public view.'*

They were allowed to do so, on the understanding that they were tenants of the Trust, they would have to pay an annual rent of 2s 6d and would reinstate the land if they left.

The public bath was opened free of charge to males, whereas entrance to the private bath was obtained by purchasing a key. It was not until the more enlightened 1920s that mixed bathing was permitted, but even then the sexes were strictly segregated. Some daring youths would sometimes try to obtain an unauthorised free swim in the private bath, but the Trust's Moorman (Herdsman) would outwit them by switching the padlocks.

By 1846, possibly due to the ineptitude of the Baths Committee (they had lost two wheelbarrows and failed to sink a necessary drain), the Trust were asked to take over the general management. It is not certain when this happened, but by 1861 the minutes suggest it had been so decided.

An unusual event took place in 1850, as recollected by George Eyles. He was then ten years old and had been swimming in the baths since he was five, sometimes as many as ten times a week. Two men appeared one Saturday afternoon and bribed all the young lads to get out of the water with the promise of two pence each. The boys peeped through the hedge to see what was going on. Imagine their surprise when three women joined the men and were immersed, one at a time, in the murky water. It transpired that they were Latter Day Saints and had used the baths for a baptism.

The water in the baths was untreated, unheated canal water – it even included leeches and fish. Jack Dunbar, a Box Moor Trustee for many years, recalled the leaves, crayfish and wildlife in the water and, on one occasion, when competing in a swimming gala, how his cotton costume filled up with sticklebacks! His family key cost ten shillings a year and, as one of eight children, he reckoned they had their money's worth. The pools were situated end to end, parallel with the canal. A little branch was cut through from the canal and it used to overflow from the eastern end of the pool. The overflow linked into a drain which went right across the Moor and back into the canal below the locks. The changing rooms were open sheds and the baths often had to be cleared of mud.

From 1892 portions of the baths were cemented and eventually all the sides and bottom of the private bath were so treated; however, it is not certain that the public bath ever had this upgrade. Various sums were spent over the ensuing years on fencing, repairing leaks, cleaning, providing keys and caretakers. George Edwards, the Moorman, occupied this role from 1914 until 1936, on a seemingly static wage of £5 12s, which he was obliged to share with his assistant.

At a meeting of the local Education Committee in 1907 the question arose of school children using the public bath for swimming lessons. The Committee agreed to pay part of the expenses and the Trust promised to keep Saturday mornings from ten until midday free. On one occasion in 1910 a tree from the private bath fell and blocked the canal, affecting the busy traffic on the waterway. The next year Messrs W. Ward kindly offered to fell any rotten trees and repair the fence with the resulting timber.

The Hemel Hempstead Girl Guides were also given permission to use the baths in 1912 from two to four on Saturday afternoons. The Boy Scouts applied in 1920 and up to thirty boys were allowed to attend, as long as they wore their uniforms, (not, one presumes, in the water). A diving board, costing about £60, was installed by the Hemel Hempstead Engineering Company in the same year.

The first reference to the Hemel Hempstead and District Swimming and Lifesaving Society (HHDSLS) occurred in

1913, when they requested permission to use the baths and later asked for two afternoons to be set aside for ladies only. In 1919 they sought permission to erect an army hut on the eastern side as their headquarters and to build some changing rooms. The Trust had to help out with the cost, with the understanding that all keyholders could use the building. A minute of 1922 granted the HHDSLS and the George Street Schools use of the baths for swimming galas, but by then the quality of the water was causing concern, even though filters were in use.

A pump was finally installed in 1923, after the suggestion of wind power was abandoned, although the prospect of a ten-foot windmill on a thirty-foot tower must have appealed to some people. This was run by a Petter oil engine with a centrifugal pump, the bore hole going down to a depth of 80 feet. The late Stan Snoxall remembered that he did not go swimming when he heard the pump working because the water was coming straight from the chalk and it was extremely cold. The total capacity of the baths was then 570,000 gallons.

Such work was often delayed because the Trust finances were low. Vandalism sometimes added to the expenses, as in 1924 when two local lads committed damage and were summonsed. In the same year the HHDSLS informed the Trust that they were going to write to the Council for the latter to take over the baths. There was no objection by the Trustees – perhaps the constant problems were beginning to take their toll.

Swimming Gala at the Boxmoor Baths c.1920. The first Swimming Gala was held in 1914.

Swimming Gala at the Boxmoor Baths c.1920. The Boxmoor Baths finally closed in April 1937.

Objections were received, however, in 1925 at the noise from bathers during church services and it was decided to open the baths only between eight and ten on Sunday mornings.

School children had been allowed to have swimming lessons and to compete for the Schools' Cup for some time. Earl Mountbatten, when he attended Lockers Park School in 1910, is said to have learnt to swim in Boxmoor Baths. By 1933 polo matches were being played, such as the one against the Watford Club, although it was difficult, if not impossible, to see the bottom of the pool. The increasing demands on the baths gave rise to thoughts of the Council re-building the private bath. From that, it was a relatively small step to consider the idea of a totally new swimming pool.

The first suggestion for a new building was mooted in 1933–4, near the former traffic lights at Two Waters, but the Trust would not agree to this proposal. The site in Cotterells on Trust land was agreed, subject to the Charity Commissioners' approval, but nothing came of it and eventually the Council went ahead with the Churchill site in 1934. The old house was then still in existence and was later used as a Family Clinic. The large open air pool behind the house was retained until 1974, when the modern Dacorum Sports Centre with indoor swimming facilities was built. The open-air pool was still a feature of the site until the more recent re-development into a complex of indoor pools and a smaller, shallower, outdoor pool; the renamed Hemel Hempstead Sports Centre is the successor to the old baths.

The heyday of the Boxmoor Baths was over and in 1937 it became apparent that both baths had outlived their use and so in April the decision was taken to empty them. Messrs Davis and Bailey of Boxmoor Ironworks in Marlowes offered a mere £5 for the pumping engine and shed, but in the end the engine was sold for £10 to W. W. Saunders, probably the motor engineering firm in Marlowes.

Over the next ten years various organisations used the baths for the dumping of surplus soil and the chapter was closed with the sale of the remaining fencing and sheds to R. Dunn and Son of Watford for £30 in 1952; a year later, nine trees were disposed of for £55 to Messrs East and Son.

All this money went into the Trust's Baths Improvement fund and the profit was transferred to the Children's Paddling Pool and Playground fund, voted by a Vestry meeting in February 1938. Finally, the splendid sum of £16 7s 7d was paid over to the Hemel Hempstead Corporation.

One idea at the time, namely, that the baths might not be filled in, but be adapted as a model yacht pond with a surrounding ornamental garden, might have retained something of the past for today's residents, but it seems rather a tame notion after the preceding hundred years of intrepid bathing.

The woman photographed in the pool c.1930, was Mrs Woodman, who ran Woodman's Café in Marlowes, next to the railway viaduct.

28. EARLY CRICKET ON THE MOOR

'The playing field of the Borough is the Moor.'
Borough Guide, c.1900.

'The "Railway Tavern" was built after the opening of the London to Birmingham Railway in 1837. A cricket pitch was made on the Moor opposite and matches were played there. The cricketers used to wear high black hats. Some years afterwards the cricket pitch was removed to near the swimming baths and Boxmoor Church.

The bowling was always underarm, simply pitching the ball. There was no fast bowling then. On one occasion, one of the visiting players, soon after the public house on the corner [The Heath Park] was built, hit the ball right through one of the bedroom windows. The landlord was quite good tempered over it, as he seemed to think it was quite accidental.'

These memories of the town prior to 1861 were part of the reminiscences written by George Eyles and printed in the *Gazette* in 1926.

As far back as 1832, it was said that:

'The gentry in this neighbourhood have evinced a great spirit in the game of cricket this season, which has given way to the formation of a club, nearly established, consisting of tradesmen and respectable persons – no riff-raff here!'

Cricket has been played since Elizabethan times, but it was later in the eighteenth century when the then Earl of Leicester, together with his noble friends, provided the impetus for the game to thrive and become widespread over the Shires. The first recorded match involving Hertfordshire took place on 6 July 1732 in Epping Forest. The game was closely associated with gambling in those early days and substantial sums of money were at stake. There were some general rules, but there were no boundaries or over-arm bowling, the bat was curved and the players mainly wore everyday clothes, without pads or gloves.

The first recorded local match took place on 20 August 1833:

'On Tuesday, a game was played between the townsmen of Hemel Hempstead and Rickmansworth (it will be understood by the reader that the former were not connected with the "Dirty Club".) It was played with great spirits, activity and science, connected with familiarity and good conduct, and concluding with an excellent supper, good harmony and friendship at the Red Lion.

The result: a resounding win for Hemel Hempstead, suggests that their team contained some experienced cricketers. Unfortunately, no details are given of the dark deeds of the "Dirty Club".'

A letter was received by the Box Moor Trustees in September 1836 from Sidney Stevens, on behalf of his brother, to request that a piece of ground on Box Moor near the Chapel be levelled and used for cricket, with the promise that the turf would be restored and made good, at the players' expense. The request was agreed by the Trustees.

Occasional games had been played on Box Moor for many years, but the Hemel Hempstead Town Cricket Club (HHTCC) was not formally constituted until 1850, when money was raised to level a piece of land fifty yards square for cricket. In 1851 Hemel Hempstead was an important town: its population of 7,703 exceeded that of Watford and its weekly corn market was the largest in the county. Its two main industries were paper-making and straw plaiting. The Under-Bailiff for thirty-nine years and Beadle for twenty years was Solomon Willis ('Old Sol'), landlord of the Compasses public house and proprietor of a pork butcher's shop in the High Street. He also had a passion for cricket.

'Old Sol' was Captain of the team from 1860 to 1880 and his constant enthusiasm provided the foundation of the club's success. He was always ready to turn out for any team in the locality, appearing at various times for Redbourn, St Albans, Kings Langley and Abbot's Langley. When 22 of the County played 11 of England at St Albans in 1883, he batted at number 5 for the home side, but, alas, was one of the eight players who failed to score. He was regularly supported at Hemel Hempstead by the Woodman family. Auctioneer Thomas Woodman, his two sons and his brother William were all prominent players.

An Edward Sammes' photograph c.1910, taken opposite Duckhall and the Baptist Church. The team may be linked to the Oxford Club Brotherhood or Boxmoor United. Some early recollections indicate a pitch was established on Station Moor opposite the Railway Tavern, shortly after the opening of the London to Birmingham Railway in 1837. The cricketers used to wear high black hats and the bowling was always underarm, never fast. In 1857 the Trust allowed land to be levelled and a part of the Moor was enclosed with posts and rails to protect the cricket pitch. The local graziers were not amused and some even went so far as to throw pieces of fencing into the canal under the cover of darkness.

29. HEMEL HEMPSTEAD TOWN CRICKET CLUB

The millennium year was an auspicious one for the Hemel Hempstead Town Cricket Club (HHTCC) since it celebrated 150 years of its existence. The foundation date is acknowledged as 1850, when the ground adjacent to the old Boxmoor Baths and opposite St John's Chapel-of-Ease was finally prepared and it was deemed suitable for the players to become established as the HHTCC.

The Box Moor Trustees were patently in favour of the sport and, in 1867, provided two labourers for a month to carry out the work necessary to keep the levels true. The princely sum of one shilling was paid in rent in 1872 and more ground improvements took place. The club's request to have the bottom of the cricket ground next to the railway embankment drained into the canal for the benefit of the spectators in 1888

was received sympathetically. However, in 1898, the Trustees could not agree to removing turf from one section of the Moor to another for the purpose of re-surfacing the cricket pitch.

Since the latter part of the nineteenth century the club was recognised as the 'representative club of the place, receiving support from every class of the community'. This is borne out by the names of the committee members, from its President, Sir Astley Paston Cooper, Bart, to its Vice Presidents T. F. Halsey MP, the Vicar of Hemel Hempstead and the High Bailiff*, as well as lesser mortals such as the schoolmaster, F. St John Badcock, and the wine merchant, Henry Balderson.

In 1893, the club played eighteen matches of which twelve were won, three lost and one drawn; two were not played, partly owing to the dry season. Practice was organised for every evening at six throughout the season – quite a demanding schedule. The club depended on subscriptions and

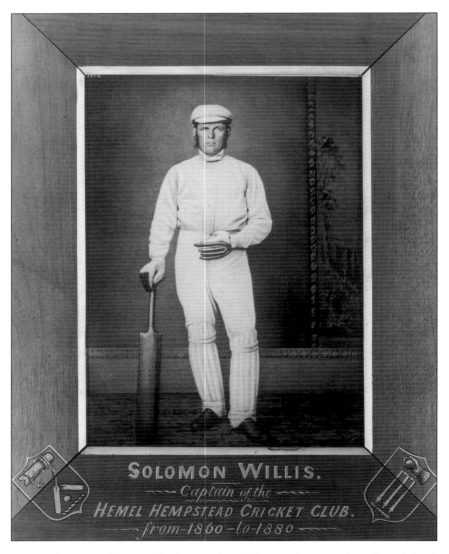

'*Presented to Mr Solomon Willis by Members of the Hemel Hempsted Cricket Club and friends in appreciation of his energetic services as Captain of the Club for upwards of ten seasons and particularly in commemoration of his excellent innings in the Match against the Beaumont Club played on Box Moor 7 June 1869, when he scored 72 NOT OUT.*'

'Old Sol' had a real passion for cricket. He was the landlord of The Compasses public house and proprietor of a pork butcher's shop in the High Street, as well as serving as the Under-Bailiff for 39 years and Town Beadle for 20 years.

if these were not up to expectations the local 'Ladies and Gentlemen kindly consented to get up a concert and dramatic entertainment in aid of the club funds'.

Percy Christopherson, Headmaster of Lockers Park School (1901–19), helped to arrange matches with Marylebone Cricket Club (MCC) which must have attracted a fair number of spectators, when England stars such as Arthur Fielder, Ted Wainwright and Harry Butt were playing. The short distance to Boxmoor Railway Station ensured visits by London clubs as well as local teams; while the nearby Heath Park Halt and the Heath Park Hotel, besides the pleasant location on common land, must also have added to the popularity of this pitch before motor transport became more accessible.

In 1900 the club complained to the Trustees that 'in consequence of Dickinson's Band playing opposite the Cricket ground, persons dance on the pitch and considerably damage it'. Further complaints of cattle roaming over the outfield and table followed in 1913, as well as unnamed 'other pastimes' encroaching upon the hallowed turf, but the Trustees felt that they had no powers to fully enclose the area. They were able to be more helpful in 1914 when earth was needed to level the outskirts of the ground. The earth was obtained from the Wood Lane widening scheme and the cemetery – the Trust paying towards the costs.

The open nature of the ground did have its drawbacks, such as the occasion when Percy Christopherson once made a great hit which struck an old roadman, but he was amply rewarded with temporary fame and the odd half crown (2s 6d), later counting his accident as a blessing. A. E. Lawton (of Derbyshire) came to reside in the area and tried to fulfil his ambition of breaking a window of the Heath Park Hotel opposite. He never realised this dream, but did manage to hit the old lock-keeper's cottage on the other side of the canal – no mean feat.

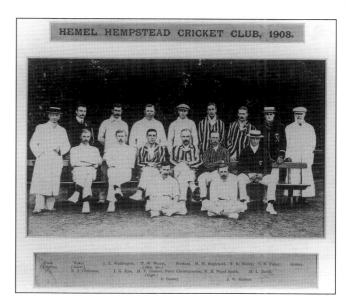

Hemel Hempstead Cricket Club, 1908, back row: Cook (Umpire), Wykes (Scorer), J. T. Waddington, T. W. Waters (Hon. Sec.), Fromant, H. W. Englefield, T. R. Stoney, F. B. Fisher, Gurney; middle row: E. J. Christmas, J. G. Eyre, H. F. Sanders (Captain), Percy Christopherson, N. B. Wood Smith, H. L. David; front row: S. Gurney, J. W. Honour.

When visitors like A. E. Lawton or D. W. Carr (who developed the 'googly') were playing, attendance was good and the club thrived. An article in the News Chronicle in the early part of the twentieth century stated that 'although Hemel Hempstead is a borough, it is to be congratulated on possessing one of the old time village greens on Boxmoor'.

The report by A. E. R. Gilligan (the former England and Sussex Captain) focused on a match between Hemel and Dunstable in which the home team were the victors by thirty-eight runs. The Hemel team included a brother of the former Worcestershire player, C.V. Tarbox, as well as an odd assortment of local tradesmen, including a hat-maker, a market gardener, an operative and a corn merchant. 'A small boy, standing on the canal bank, was aggrieved because the ball had not come his way, as he gets three pence for retrieving every ball that finds its way into the canal.' A crowd of 1,000 people watched their team, which included E. Mitchell-Innes, and they were probably relieved at the victory, since the opposing side had a brother of the Nottinghamshire player Wilfred Payton bowling for them. T. Payton took six wickets for one run on the day. Tea was served in Boxmoor Hall, the building in the immediate vicinity provided for the community by the Box Moor Trust.

By the end of the nineteenth century the club boasted a new pavilion built adjacent to the railway embankment adjoining that part of the Moor. The official opening took place in June 1899 and an appeal was made for the £300 still outstanding on the overall cost of £1,300. This served the needs of the club until 1933, when a tea room was added a short distance away. Towards the end of the Second World War, the tea room was adapted to become the main pavilion and the older building became a store.

A relaxing game of cricket – for the spectators. The tea room and pavilion can be seen in the background c.1930.

Team of 1937, back row: W. Bass (Umpire), H. Tarbox, H. Grange, R. D. Wallers, S. Capel, P. Dix, R. Mills, E. Wright (Scorer); front row: R. B. Webb, A. Atkins, R. L. Brandon (Captain), W. England, R. Purves.

A. J. Adams OBE, President of HHTCC, receiving the key of the new pavilion from G. C. Selden on behalf of the builders. In the forefront are R. J. Holliday, Secretary, and G. W. Stillman, Chairman. The official opening was performed during the interval between innings of the First XI match with St Albans on Saturday, 26 June 1949. Beverley Lyon, former Captain of Gloucestershire, was a member of the HHTCC team at the time.

HHTCC 1964, back row: J. Bickley (Umpire), R. Lamb, E. Holman, G. Ikin, R. Pratt, P. Ives, J. Winstone, B. Jackson, C. Whyman; front row: B. Capper, J. Caldicott (Captain), P. Norris, E. Stanbridge.

HHTCC, 2000, back row: Rhys Fowler, Duncan Howard, Matthew Judd, Mark Beard, Neil Morgan, Gary Thompson, Kam Akhtar and Graham Turner (Scorer); front row: Giles Berry, Michael Dale, Stewart Dunsford, Nick Wright, Richard Miller and Martin Wright.

Stewart Dunsford (President), Duncan Howard (General Secretary) and Nick Wright (Chairman) in 2000.

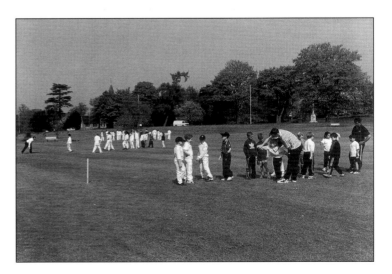

The Colts section is an important part of the Club's activities. Out-of-school coaching promotes an interest that will hopefully provide future senior team players.

In 1945 the store burnt down. The club joined forces with the Town Council in asking that the ground should be handed over to them. This followed the previous attempt by the Council to gain control of Trust lands in the 1930s, but, like the earlier approach, it faded into oblivion. The new pavilion was built by 1949 and opened by A. J. Adams, President of the club; the former tea room was sold to Bovingdon Cricket Club.

In 1963, the 'new' cricket pavilion, having lasted for fourteen years, was replaced by the present building. A permanent concrete practice wicket was agreed in 1971 and new changing rooms and showers were added in 1979. Refurbishment of the bar took place in 1994 and a brick-built score box was erected the following year. A second pitch has recently been established on Balderson's Moor, between the present clubhouse and Two Waters Road. Other grounds in the area are used to accommodate the four Saturday sides and three Sunday teams. There is also a thriving Colt's section, which is a good portent for the future.

As well as Albert Lawton, the Derbyshire Captain, who played here in 1909 and 1910, the club has witnessed the skills of Beverley Lyon, once Captain of Gloucestershire, G. R. Langdale (Somerset), C. V. Tarbox (Worcestershire) and Saliya Ahangama (Sri Lanka). Long-serving administrators have included A. J. Adams, OBE, who was a member for fifty years, during which time he served as President for twenty-five years and Treasurer for twenty-three years.

The club is a member of the Hertfordshire Cricket League and the Chess Valley League, which replaced the Home Counties League. It has had its share of honours, notably the Hertfordshire Challenge Cup in 1887 and, in more recent times, the Furnell Transport Hertfordshire Cup, 1986–8 and the Hertfordshire Championship League in 1999. The present club Chairman (2004) is Nick Wright; he has played for Hertfordshire since 1980 and his brother Martin is also a regular member of the County side.

With such a long and proud history behind it, the HHTCC looks forward with confidence. It has continued the traditions of village-green cricket and become the main cricket club of the much expanded New Town, with considerable co-operation over the years from the Box Moor Trust.

First XI 1999 – Hertfordshire League Champions, back row: Scott Mason, Duncan Howard, Jeremy Rich, Rhys Fowler, Mark Beard, Peter Waterman, Graham Turner, (Scorer); front row: Martin Wright, Giles Berry, Mike Dale, (Captain), Nick Wright, Richard Miller.

Still a relaxing scene today, in the midst of all the traffic at Moor End, courtesy of the Box Moor Trust.

Practice at the nets. A new cricket table has been provided on Balderson's Moor for the Colts and there are hopes that the pavilion will be replaced.

30. BOXMOOR CRICKET CLUB

The Boxmoor Cricket Club, as distinct from the HHTCC, acknowledges its foundation date as 1857, when the Trust allowed a piece of ground on the Moor to be 'enclosed with posts and chains from 40 to 50 yards square for the purpose of cricket'. The Trustees retained the right to remove the posts and chains at their pleasure. Thus began more than a century of the game being played in the vicinity of today's 'Boxmoor Oval', as it is affectionately called.

The levelling of the land is often referred to, as happened in 1875, when the Trustees went with the Revd Ranger to view the site and it was decided that an area of 25 square yards was to be levelled, supervised by the Managing Committee. Mr Badcock requested improvements to the ground in 1881 and by 1884 the Trustees were asking for a peppercorn rent of one shilling per annum for the use of the land.

The Trust helped towards the cost of further improving the pitch in 1920. Coaches were used for away games from 1929 and matches were played against local teams such as Abbots Langley, Kings Langley and Gorhambury. In 1930 the Stationmaster was recommended as a Vice President and, coincidentally, meetings were then held at the Railway Tavern. A horse mower was acquired, but that led to problems of hiring a horse!

The continuing popularity of the club was evidenced by their request in 1933 to erect a pavilion on the Moor, on the site of the old Star Cottages in the middle of Blackbirds' Moor. This request was not granted that year, but the following year saw the final clearance of the dilapidated Star Cottages and the general improvement of the cricket ground. A press secretary was also appointed, with a weekly column in the *Hemel Hempstead Gazette*. The Annual Dinner, at an inclusive cost of 4s 6d, was advertised – but for men only.

In 1937 there was a proposal to share the ground with the Hemel Hempstead Hockey Club. Subscriptions were raised to ten shillings a year and it was decided a new tent was needed. The onset of the Second World War had repercussions in the local cricketing world; matches were arranged for the 1940 season, but were to be reviewed if hostilities were still ongoing. The club sent gifts to their players who were by then in the armed forces and by 1941 so many young men were called up that older players had to be approached in their stead. The name of B. Carpenter, who had been presented with a gold watch in 1927 for his bowling achievement, arose again in 1941, as topping the bowling averages; he was made a life member in 1947. During the war, the first mention of the ladies making teas was recorded, but the usual Christmas Draw did not take place, due to the obvious difficulty in obtaining prizes.

After the war, the club renewed its activities. The second eleven team was revived in 1947 and a telephone was installed for the convenience of the secretary. As another sign of the changing times, the old horse mower was sold, to the Hemel Hempstead Town Football Club. The first female scorer, Miss D. Townsend, was appointed in 1950 and a match fee of just sixpence a game was introduced three years later. The club tried to stop football being played on the Moor and, more importantly, applied to the Trust to build a pavilion. The coming of the New Town in the early 1950s gave rise to many changes, including an influx of new players and the possibility of a path between the cricket pitch and the chestnut trees bordering St John's Road, at the time the Commission for the New Towns* was re-designing the St John's Road area.

Cricket has been played on Blackbirds' Moor for nearly 150 years. Note the small marquee – an early pavilion – and Star Cottages on the right.

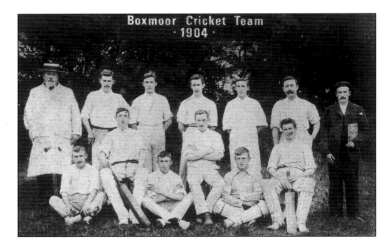

The line up for 1904 included, back row: D. Final, J. Waddington, J. Gates, S. Gurney, W. Osborne, W. Townsend and J. Cross; front row: W. Picton, H. Perry, A. Picton, W. Final (Captain), H. Kempster and C. Badcock.

The use of the ground on Sundays became an issue in 1959, and permission for this was eventually granted, providing it did not interfere with church services. The next year, after forty years of complaining about the mowers and the state of the outfield, the club secretary wrote to the council asking them to do the job. The Treasurer was very concerned about the financial state, since most of the income came from activities that were organised by non-playing members and the club was losing potential fixtures due to the poor facilities for teas. A new pavilion was still a focal point in members' minds at that time.

A turning point in the long history of the club came in 1961. The go ahead was given to Mr Selden to start the foundations for the pavilion, and not before time, since the new licensee of the nearby public house, the Steamcoach, had served them a notice to quit, the very active General Secretary had resigned, a number of players had left the area and, to cap it all, it had been a poor season on the field. The estimated cost of the pavilion was £625; it was to have a main room, kitchen, two dressing rooms and a store room. The first mention of a bar area was in 1962, but this had no connection with the water that leaked into the dressing room that season. In the same year the first Gazette Cup match was played and a Ground Committee was formed. Vandals broke into the premises in 1963, a foretaste of things to come.

Matters had improved somewhat by 1964 and a club cap was ordered in the new colours of royal blue and gold. The death of the President, A. C. Huband, in November did not add to the festive mood, nor did the act of hooligans in running off with the mower. The drive was on for more members, especially as several local clubs had disappeared and a newsletter was started in 1965 to publicise the club's activities. In 1966 an initial attempt was made to actively canvass for youngsters and, with the ground improvements completed in March, the strategy bore fruit with many fresh names on roll by May. An extension to the pavilion was contemplated. Such was the playing strength by 1968, it was agreed that any prospective member would have to play two trial games before being elected. Discussions were under way to extend and improve the pavilion and permission was eventually granted in 1969. The Colts coaching sessions were recorded as being 'overwhelmingly successful' that year. The club was accepted into the League and that necessitated a major re-arrangement of fixtures in 1970.

A loan of £1,000 was arranged to pay for the pavilion extension, but guarantors were needed; the working parties on the pavilion continued into 1971. The thought was expressed that the price of teas should go up from two shillings and sixpence to three shillings prior to decimalisation. A regular newsletter, the Oval Echo, was circulated, while the committee also sent out letters protesting about the proposed A41 Motorway. In 1980 the club won the League.

The pavilion was unfortunately gutted by fire in October 1981 and so the president, Len Hopkins, and the Chairman, Maurice Wigmore, approached the Trust for permission to replace the burnt-out shell with a brick building. A '100 Club' as well as many other activities were set up to raise funds; the club was also indebted to Dacorum Borough Council and the Playing Fields Association for loans. This fire was apparently started by vandals and, sadly, the club has suffered over the years at the hands of thoughtless people who delight in spoiling the pleasure and property of others. Club members were invited to submit ideas for the design of a pavilion and plans were sent to the Trust for approval. Julia Lowe, the first female Trustee, who was a trained architect, improved on the design by adding the veranda and the dormer feature which houses the clock, a donation by the Boxmoor Residents' Association.

In July 1982 a meeting was held between Trustees, Staff and club members Martin Cope, Maurice Wigmore and Mr Rush, the contractor. The object was to discuss ways and means of reducing the cost of moving the cricket table which was necessary because of its proximity to the road and housing. The threat of litigation from nearby residents prompted the decision. The Trust supplied some labour to help with this important project, but was unable to provide funds.

Over the last twenty years the club has seen the introduction and development of league cricket, replacing the older style inter-village competitions. Gaining points for batting, bowling and winning matches, which then decide promotion or relegation, are the main objectives. The other facilities offered by each club are also judged, so it is important to keep up to scratch. Further extensions were built in 1996, to house mowers and sight screens, with the help of a National Lottery grant. A score box was added at the same time, a requirement of the League.

The pavilion has been home to other organisations recently, such as the Munchkids and Gade Valley Harriers. Two Saturday teams and two, or occasionally three, Sunday teams take to the field nowadays, as the popularity of the sport increases again. The match ball for each league game is sponsored since local businesses as well as private individuals have become more involved with Boxmoor Cricket Club.

A wide variety of social events were planned under the guidance of the Social Secretary and current President, Stan Gillon, and the club continues making history at the start of the new century.

The latest pavilion on Blackbirds' Moor, officially opened in 1982. The previous building was wantonly destroyed by fire in 1981, when most of the old photographs were lost. The wicket was formerly at right angles to St John's Road.

Boxmoor Cricket Club, First XI 1999–2000 Season, back row: John Penfold (Scorer), Len Esterhuisen, Brook Townsend, (an unknown player), David Cope, Paul Cope, Tom Reeves; front row: Chris Marshall, John O'Donnell, Joe Sharpe, Peter Lockley, Wayne Adams. The team came in the top ten in the League.

31. THE BAT WILLOWS

The summertime sound of leather on willow is still a feature of the Moors, with the Boxmoor Cricket Club and the Hemel Hempstead Town Cricket Club both continuing to play on Trust land. In both club pavilions, and also at Bovingdon Cricket Club, there exists an even more visible link with the Trust: locally grown willow cricket bats. In 1986 three cricket bats were presented to the clubs by the Chairman, which were made from the 'bat willows' growing on the Moor.

Messrs Edgar Watts of Bungay, Suffolk, who were once major manufacturers of cricket bats, purchased Trust trees on a regular basis, from 1972 until 1990. This family-run firm had regularly turned out 2,000 'clefts' (hand-carved bat blades) a week for batsmen all over the world and also made their own bats under the trade name of Century Bats.

Following a visit to the factory, the idea of the special presentation was conceived and fortunately accomplished before the firm went into liquidation. The conditions at Box Moor are ideal for growing the special variety of willow needed in the manufacture of the traditional bat. These have been carved out of the female *Salix caerulea*, the riverbank species cultivated only in England and Kashmir, since 1840. The long grained wood is strong, light and springy – ideal for the purpose. The better wood comes from the English-bred specimens and, up until the advance of the contagious disease 'watermark', 300,000 bats a year were produced from English willow trees. Today a fifteen pence levy on every English bat sold is paying for research into finding a cure for the disease, which causes the wood to turn black and lose all its strength. The disease coincided with the severe storms of 1987 and undoubtedly caused the closure of the Edgar Watts factory.

The idea of the Trust getting involved commercially seems to have started just before the First World War. Messrs

Bartlett of Finchley bought three dead willows and suggested the land was suitable for cultivating the trees. The Trust were prepared to plant willow sets at a cost of five shillings each and so ordered one hundred whips. This price was later greatly reduced by Messrs East of Berkhamsted to three pence each and by April 1914 the Trust had planted 615 sets. An intriguing entry occurred in 1917 when 'as a result of a young man falling into the canal on a foggy night near Wharf Road, a further 150 trees were planted' – as a barrier, perhaps, for unwary pedestrians?

In January 1928 the minute book records 'Willow sets to be purchased and planted near the Plough [the former public house], Moor End'. By 1931 as many as 300 young trees were planted in the nursery adjoining the watercress beds at Two Waters; 60 inches (152 cm) was the required girth before cropping, which took about fifteen years to achieve. The willows proved to be a useful additional source of income for the Trust.

The following year the national firm of J. Lillywhite Frowd and Co. paid £78 10s for twenty-three willows and £10 was paid by W. J. Richards for twenty-two small willows from the rear of the Midland Railway Depot in Cotterells. Other sites were used over the years, such as alongside the canal from the 'High Bridge' to Foster's Saw Mills (River Park Gardens, Boxmoor). One unusual request came in 1969 when Greenhills Primary School requested some willow branches to make the framework of a coracle. There is no record that it ever floated!

Today, the rows of young trees can still be seen on the Moors and along the banks of the canal. Various other firms purchased the mature trees with their straight trunks during the twentieth century, but how long the practice will continue in the twenty-first century remains to be seen.

Young 'bat willow' trees on the Moor.

Edgar Watts' cricket bat factory at Bungay, Suffolk.

32. BOXMOOR GOLF CLUB

Lord Walter Rothschild (1868–1957), a member of Boxmoor Golf Club 1895–1907. The family were wealthy bankers who lived at Tring Park. Walter established the Natural History Museum at Tring in 1892 which became part of the British Museum in 1937.

Boxmoor Golf Club claims to be one of the oldest in the county; a hilly nine-hole course, it was inaugurated in August 1890, four years after the purchase of the Commons and following a meeting at Boxmoor Railway Station. An influential group of local businessmen who travelled to London in the same first-class carriage had been fired with enthusiasm after reading in the press about the exploits of John Ball, a member of the Royal Liverpool Golf Club, who had triumphed in the thirtieth Open Championship, held at Prestwick Links in Scotland. He was the first Englishman to succeed in the Open since its inception in 1860. They bemoaned the fact that there were so few good English courses for there to be a consistent chance of beating the Scots at their national game. Most of those were started by the cutting of a few holes on common land, for example, The Royal Wimbledon, until such time as the members could afford their own course. They then usually became private and very exclusive.

It was not long before the businessmen formed the idea of seeking permission to cut their own holes on the nearby Sheethanger Common. Thought led to action and on the return journey that same day plans were drawn up and a letter drafted to the Box Moor Trust. The minute books subsequently record that on 13 August 1890 at a meeting at Boxmoor Hall an application was received by the Trust, signed by Messrs Frank Cornwell, R. N. Byass, John F. Courtney, A. R. C. Richings, Thomas Christopher, Sam Oxenham and J. H. Clayton, for permission to play golf on Sheethanger Common, at the same time guaranteeing to make good any damage that might be done to the turf. Frank Cornwell stated persuasively that the intended new golf club would be pleased to pay £5 a year for the privilege.

The Trustees approved the idea and were about to give permission for one year when Henry Balderson proposed that permission should be for one season, 'the same to be withdrawn if the game is found in any way prejudicial to the Commoners or the convenience of the inhabitants'. The motion was carried. Thus began the story of the Boxmoor Golf Club, which is still using the common land on the original course, barely changed since those early days.

A further meeting was then speedily arranged at Boxmoor Railway Station in order to commence the business of the club itself. The first minute stated that 'A committee meeting of the Boxmoor Golf Club was held at the Boxmoor L. & N. W. Railway in August. Present: T. Christopher junior, F. Cornwell, J. Courtney, R. N. Byass, A. K. Richings'. Several members were elected and the rules of the club were agreed and passed.

The club's early minute books have their own story to tell, since they were lost for many years. In 1979, they were discovered in a loft in East Anglia. Luckily, their historical value was realised and they were returned to the landlord of the Anchor public house, who made sure that they were replaced in the club's archives.

Further committee meetings apparently took place aboard the six o' clock train from Euston, much to the other passengers' surprise, one would imagine. Although there are no minutes of these meetings, enough was achieved to lay out the course two months later and the club began to grow. The decision not to play on Sundays was an early one; today, play is permitted on Sunday afternoons in the summer months. The last meeting that year was held aboard the train on 8 December. By that time there were thirty members, but the course was only nine holes and there was a concern that it would be too crowded if all members were present. It was therefore decided to institute an entrance fee of two guineas and an annual subscription of four guineas, with a restricted membership of forty.

All proceeded as planned and in the following year the fledgling club asked if they could negotiate a yearly fee for playing on Shothanger Common (the names were often interchanged). It was decided it should be in the range of £5 to £10 per annum, depending on the financial state of the club. The balance sheet for the 1890–1 season shows that caddies and other staff were already employed, competitions organised and that the club was on a sound financial footing. In 1892 they paid the Trust £7 10s; from what had begun as no more than rough grassland and a handful of inaugural members, the club had become a thriving organisation with a membership of forty-two players.

By 1894 the club Secretary was asked to negotiate with Mr Gee of Moor End Farm about land for a club house. They seemed to have rented the cottage belonging to the club Steward, Mr Bail, at Cold Harbour for a time, but disputes arose. Money for the club to build their own pavilion was raised in £5 shares; £100 to £120 was the estimated target. A tender was accepted from Mr Humphries for a wooden pavilion for the sum of £97 10s to be erected on part of Dudley H. Ryder's land in Box Lane. It took another twenty years to pay off all the debentures raised for this worthy project.

The fact that they played on open common land did have some repercussions over the years. Sheep were grazed on the Common and lambs were sometimes injured, mainly by golf balls belonging to visitors who were not accustomed to such hazards. If the animal was killed outright, the farmer would accept payment in return for the carcass. Incidentally, during the Second World War, the club was ordered to allow sheep to graze from 1 May to 31 October.

There was no running water in the vicinity, so ponies would pull a water cart to the greens. In 1901, the owner of Box Lane Farm, Colonel L H. Bourvens, allowed the use of the well unless there was a drought. Another farmer, C. R. Oliver, allowed members to go into his fields to pick up golf balls, for a token payment of £2 a year. In general, relationships with the local farmers were good and the club tried to keep it that way.

Sadly, on Good Friday, 1910, a little girl was struck by a golf ball on the road to Bovingdon. It was deemed prudent that games should no longer take place during Bank Holidays, when more people were likely to be out taking leisurely walks.

The hilly nature of the course necessitated the use of caddies from the beginning. The 'boys' were paid four pence a round and wore special badges and caps. One of their jobs was to mound up a tee with sand – that was in the days before wooden or plastic tee pegs. They were even provided with a football for the odd moments when they were not needed on the course. By 1900 a caddy master was employed for the season at a cost of 7s 6d.

During the First World War the effect on membership was keenly felt and the club asked if the rent could be reduced. The club had supported local charities for some years, such as the poor of Bovingdon, and now it needed charity. Their rent was duly reduced to £2 10s per annum for the duration of the war.

Women were allowed to join the club from 1892, but were often treated as second-class members. On Competition Saturdays, in 1905, they were not allowed a game and on all other days they had to let 'gentlemen' pass them. The only restrictions that apply today are that they cannot play on Sunday mornings. Female members are very much part of the club scene these days with a full competition diary, including several mixed pairs' matches.

The issue of weekend play at the club has arisen continually in the past one hundred years. In 1933 play was restricted on Sunday afternoons in the summer up to 2.30pm and in the winter to 4.30pm. Rules were based on those of the St Andrew's Club from 1894, with some local allowances for the

slopes of the course. It is not for nothing that part of Sheethanger Common is called the 'Cresta Run' when it is used for tobogganing. 'The challenge to play well at Boxmoor can be daunting. Each of its nine holes is difficult if played incorrectly or if the weather is adverse.' The third hole was aced for the first time on record in 1998.

The post-war period saw a decline in membership but the advent of the New Town brought an influx of workers from London and three of the largest relocated companies, Addressograph, Alford and Alder, and Rotax, agreed to pay for twenty members per year. This was a turning point in the club's fortunes. Horses straying from bridle paths caused concern in later years, but the Trust provided two new purpose-built paths: one for equestrians and one for ramblers. A Challenge Trophy was also given by the Box Moor Trustees for the club's Centenary in 1990, as well as a presentation golf club dated 1895.

Vandalism and burglaries over the years have taken their toll, but the club has survived two World Wars and expanded. The original gold Ladysmith Medal of 1900 and wooden competition shield are lost, but, perhaps one day, like the minute books, they will reappear and once more be part of the history of an unusual and ancient golf club.

Mr Bail, aged 75, playing from the 7th tee in 1892.

Boxmoor Golf Links c.1907. J. B. Wildman and his caddie are on the right. Wildman was the first known captain of the club.

The original wooden clubhouse, sited beside Box Lane on part of Dudley Henry Ryder's Westbrook Hay Estate. This scene is unrecognisable today because many large houses have since been built on the hillside and the traffic has increased along Box Lane.

The Golf Links, looking towards Bovingdon. Box Lane was an undeveloped country lane at that time.

Plan of Boxmoor Golf Course, 1919.

View above No. 1 green, looking towards No. 9 green. The modern clubhouse in Box Lane is on the left.

Boxmoor Golf Club, 2000. Jim Newark (President in 2000), Adrian Marshall (Captain), Martin Ford (Treasurer) and Gary Newark (Secretary) with a selection of the club's trophies.

Boxmoor Golf Club's Centenary celebrations in 1990 included a special event in period costume. The Ladysmith Gold Medal, introduced to mark the Relief of Ladysmith on 29 February 1900, during the Boer War, unfortunately has long since disappeared.

Martin Ford, Graham Linton and Jim Newark dressed in style for the Club's Centenary in 1990. They became Treasurer, Head of the Course Committee and President respectively. Graham is also five-times Club champion and course record holder.

No. 2 fairway on Sheethanger Common runs parallel to Box Lane.

33. HEMEL HEMPSTEAD (CAMELOT) RUGBY FOOTBALL CLUB

In response to the rather fanciful question, 'What has Camelot to do with Box Moor?' the stranger might be perplexed to find a reply, but to the area's supporters of rugby football the answer would not be difficult. According to local legend, the tenuous link with King Arthur came about when a group of sportsmen were sitting at a round table in a pub, eating onions (the Lady of Shalott*) and someone suggested the title of Camelot for their proposed new football and social club. This was formed in 1920 and the first AGM was held in the Old House Club*, Hemel Hempstead, on 23 July 1921. The name, an alternative to Hemel Hempstead, was adopted when some old boys from Adelbert ('Adders') House of Berkhamsted School helped to form a Rugby Union Football Club. They played their first matches at Heath Brow, Heath Lane. Camelot never had a club house of its own, but for a pitch they once used Gee's Meadow, which at that time was not a part of the Trust Estate. The team generally changed at its headquarters, the Heath Park Hotel; so often, and not unnaturally, a willing publican would sponsor a local sports club. A few mementoes still exist, enough to establish its early existence, but the club amalgamated with one from Lazard's Bank and was lost to the district some time after the 1926–7 season, when its President was Sir Robert Kindersley.

The second rising of the Camelot name took place in around 1934. The paper-making firm of John Dickinson employed 4,000 people at that time and a team was raised from Home Park Mill by Sutton Curtis to play an Apsley Mill side which included Jack Marshall, one time Administrator for the Box Moor Trust. According to Jack, from this small beginning the idea of a rugby club arose. A local farmer, 'Pop' Fisher (A. G. Fisher of Wood Farm), lent the fledgling club a field and Jack's unenviable task was to go round before the game to remove what the cattle had left behind. Mrs Woodman provided tea and sandwiches, but only for the away-team.

The farmer's garage made a make-shift changing room. They even managed to get two teams running some of the time, but the outbreak of the Second World War saw over half the club, who were members of the Territorial Army, called up and by October 1939 it was deemed impossible to continue.

Phoenix-like, the club was to have a third re-birth. This occurred in 1950, at the time of the development of Hemel Hempstead as a New Town. The Development Corporation* was very keen to see sporting facilities on offer for the influx of thousands of newcomers and encouraged the idea. The club's old site at Wood Farm had been ear-marked for housing, but it was not needed in the short term. By the spring of 1951, the Corporation had indicated that they would help in finding a permanent ground if the club re-started. A cow shed was to serve them as a changing room for two more years and the players had to make it habitable. Nothing daunted, the club re-formed with Sir Thomas Halsey as President, Ray Fisher (the son of the original farmer and another ex-pupil of Berkhamsted School) as Chairman and Jack Marshall as Treasurer. In 1953 Camelot were able to move to Chaulden Meadow, where there was enough ground for three pitches.

The Box Moor Trust had had an option since 1930 to purchase this land, comprising about 31 acres, but they had never exercised this option, and in 1952 they were offered it as exchange land by the Development Corporation. It took another eight years before the deal was completed to everyone's satisfaction and by then it had become a parcel of 8.6 acres of the Trust Estate which was exchanged for the sum of £7,786 10s, along with a further 11.2 acres at Chaulden.

However, in 1953 all of Chaulden Meadows belonged to the Development Corporation. The Trustees had agreed to accept part of the land as long as it could be used for their graziers. To avoid any problems over building on Trust land, the small area nearest Old Fishery Lane was retained and leased to the rugby club. The ground was unplayable at first because it was

A team thought to be formed by boys from Berkhamsted School in 1919, some of whom later played for the Camelot rugby and football teams. The day boys who attended the school Adelbert House, or 'Adders', were associated with the formation of the original Camelot Rugby Club.

Camelot in the 1930s. Pop Fisher, E. Phillips, Winfield, Snoxall, ?, J. Phillips, Mr Marnham, Garland, Cox, Hope, J. Meyer, Mcdonald, Reynolds, Lismer, Kemp, Marshall, French, Delderfield, Collins. Mr Marnham insisted on being included as the team's only regular supporter.

Team of 1952–3, back row: J. Turner, J. B. Rowswell, A. Hudson, G. Halsey, F. Askew, P. Walker, B. Bonfield, W. Johnson, R. Norris; front row: R. Shackleford, I. Dundon, J. Reasbeck, G. Masters, J. Hancock, P. Turner.

covered in stones and flints, most of which were removed by willing members. They then set to work and started building the first proper club house. Without skilled labour and working long hours, they devised all kinds of schemes to achieve their ambition and the club house gradually came into being. This was officially opened on 14 September 1957, in the presence of Arthur Marshall, President of the Rugby Union. It consisted of a club room, changing room, kitchen and bar store; the bar counter came from the now demolished Halfway House public house. A ladies' toilet was situated within the building but the door was outside. However, a torch was thoughtfully provided at the bar to assist the ladies on dark nights. Many more extensions have taken place since 1957, testimony to the popularity of the club and its constant programme of improvements. The historical link with Berkhamsted School was re-forged in 1958 when the club offered the school use of their field and pavilion two days a week. The club is allowed to play on Chaulden Meadow for a licence fee of £5 per annum and the land is maintained in accordance with the current Licence Agreement.

Car parking became a problem and so the Charity Commission eventually agreed to allow Dacorum District Council to exchange the old railway embankment, which split Two Waters Moor, for part of Chaulden Meadows. The deeds were signed in 1980 with the Council paying all the legal expenses. The club thereby obtained its long awaited enlarged car park and Chaulden Lane was freed of parking.

By a quirk of fate, the Trust had regained land they had previously sold to the Hemel Hempstead and LNWR in the 1860s. The anomaly then was that the club stood on land belonging to three different parties: the club house on land that belonged to the Commission for New Towns; the car park on land owned by the Council and the playing areas on ground belonging to the Box Moor Trust. Fortunately, the three landlords became two in the 1990s when Dacorum Borough Council acquired the club house site in exchange for the former railway embankment at Two Waters.

But enough of land deals, when the main object is to play, enjoy and develop the game of rugby. The club runs up to five teams on a Saturday, including a Veterans side. However, the biggest recent development has been with the Youth Section. There are currently about 200 boys and girls playing in a variety of sides from age seven years upwards. The club is amongst the most successful in the county in its provision for youth rugby, even though many local schools choose soccer as their main sport.

The first match of the renewed club in 1951 was against Harpenden and Camelot won 18–0. The club achieved the County Cup in 1975 and the County Sevens three times. Probably the greatest feat to date was to beat Saracens in the Prelims of the Middlesex Sevens on their own ground and go on to appear at Twickenham.

The spirit of the former Camelot exists still, even though the club is now called the Hemel Hempstead (Camelot) Rugby Union Football Club. The old timers such as Ray Fisher, A. J. Harry, Don Hollinshead, the late Jack Marshall and Barry Rowswell (the list could go on) would be gratified to see the enthusiastic turn out at weekends and might recall the situation in 1951 when all they had was under a fiver in the kitty, one form and two duckboards, remnants of the 1930s club.

Team of 1976–7, back row: M. Welch, C. Millen, C. Knight, P. Raymond, (Capt.), John Temperley, B. Cockling, J. Bartholomew, B. Griffiths, P. Frost; front row: Jim Temperley, D. Taylor, S. East, W. Craven, J. Regan, J. English.

Opening of the Club House, 14 September 1957.

Michael Nunn and Michael Kingham (First Team Managers), 1999–2000 Season.

Peter Jeffrey training the expanding youth section, the Under-14s in 2000.

First Team match against Stevenage, 1999–2000 Season. Chaulden Meadows takes its name from the former Chaulden or Chalden House; the remains of the stable block are on the left.

First Team 1999–2000 Season, back row: Tony Impey, (Coach), Darren Perry, Damon Marii-Metuarii, Andy Minton, Richard Graham, Robert Bose, Carl McGinniss, Robert Gray, Matt Cannon, Simon Tillier; front row: Jason Bright, Tony Browett, Andy Leach, Jason Lowde (Captain), Robert Shaw, Gordon Clark, Richard Woodard, Mike Ericson.

34. Football Clubs

Football, as one of the many pastimes pursued on the Moors involving fresh air and exercise, has featured strongly over the past hundred years of the Box Moor Trust's history. The open nature of the Trust lands are ideal for this sport, with the proviso that any holes made in the ground for goal posts should always be covered when not in use.

As early as 1884 there was a team called Boxmoor United, the forerunners of Apsley End, who played on Gas Works Moor. In 1887, the latter team, which included six names from the Boxmoor side, hired the Salmon Meadow for their matches. The Trust minutes of October 1898 record a club asking for permission to play opposite the Boxmoor and National Schools. This was followed in 1902 by the Boxmoor Junior Club who wished to play on the Moor opposite the London Road Baptist Church. The number of would-be clubs proliferated over the next few years, so much so that the Trust felt it could no longer give any further exclusive rights to footballers. However, Bourne End FC was allowed to use a portion of the Moor near Moor End Farm in 1906. Boxmoor Melrose, Hammerfield, Cotterells Rovers and United, Kents (Brushworks), Riverside Rangers, Two Waters Stars and many more whose names have now been relegated to oblivion applied for permission to play. Church groups were well represented, with teams such as Apsley St Mary's, Boxmoor Baptists, Hammerfield St Francis, St John's and the Church Lads' Brigade all vying for space.

The Hertfordshire Football Association was founded in 1885 and the Apsley End team entered into the County Cup in 1889. They were also founder members of the West Herts Football Association and enthusiastically took part in its first league competition in 1891. They had been beaten the previous year in the St Mary's Cup by Hemel Hempstead United FC: the ensuing celebrations were described as 'surpassing any previous demonstration connected with football in the town'.

The first mention of Hemel Hempstead United FC in Trust records occurred in 1915, but their name does not appear in the minutes for 1920, when permission was granted to Apsley Juniors, Apsley FC, the Bourne Scouts, Boxmoor St John's, Cotterells FC and the Two Waters Wesleyan Bible Class. Grass could be cut by the clubs only under the supervision of the Herdsman.

Camelot FC, with its badge sporting a blue Excalibur on a white background, existed in the early 1920s and many of its members also played in the rugby team. Rugby was introduced at Berkhamsted School in 1915 and the gradual decline of football in the school was forecast at the time. In 1921, Camelot FC held their first AGM in the Old House Club (Hemel Hempstead Club), with Revd Houseman as President and W. Davey as Honorary Secretary. The club had been playing at Gee's Meadow, now part of the Trust Estate, and were very proud that no players had been sent off in their first season. A press report of 1922 said Sidney Hobday, previously of the Corinthians, had joined the side because they played for love of the game. Their matches were reported weekly in the West Herts League Division 2, but they appear to have ceased activities around the end of the 1927 season.

The locally famous 'Uncle's Cup' Competition took place annually in April or May, often opposite the Gas Works. This involved the John Dickinson's paper mill departments at Apsley Mill, Nash Mill and Home Park Mill, as well as other local company sides. Mr and Mrs Hawkins donated the Apsley End Charity Cup for the local competition in 1898, which then became known as the 'Uncle's Cup', during the time that 'Uncle' Hawkins was the licensee of the Salmon public house. According to a letter in the Gazette at the end of the 1800s, that name came about when a truckload of best Scottish salmon overturned on the LNWR track. To commemorate the ensuing unexpected feast, partaken at the nearby inn, the people gave it its 'immortal title'. The Salmon Meadow became the field where Apsley footballers regularly played and the publicans obviously welcomed the teams into their establishment, formerly adjacent to St Mary's Church. This charitable competition raised money for the West Herts Infirmary and produced the significant sums of £20 to £30 before the First World War.

Salmon Meadow itself once stretched from the canal arm into the Apsley Mills site up to the land facing the Apsley Club and Institute, now transformed into a large car park for Apsley Mills Shopping Centre. It often flooded, but that did not deter the players, even if the goal keeper had to use a shepherd's crook to retrieve the ball from the water that collected behind the Mill end goal! There was consternation when John Dickinson's gave the clubs notice to quit since the site was needed for development of their paper mills. The last game took place on 5 May 1928, when Sarratt carried off the Charity Cup.

The next venue was Gee's Meadow, which, strangely enough, became part of the Exchange land given to the Trust in the 1980s, but that proved to be disastrous as supporters could not be persuaded to go the extra two miles for a match. A year later, the ground was moved to Wood Lane and the association of the Apsley clubs with Trust land eventually ceased.

At the start of hostilities in 1939, London evacuees were permitted to play football in the chalk pit on Roughdown

Camelot Football Club 1922–3, taken on the Moor opposite the Swan. The Camelot name applied to both the soccer and rugby teams at that time.

St John's School Team, Boxmoor. They played on Blackbirds' Moor opposite the Victorian school, which was demolished in the 1990s.

The Sports' Club, Boxmoor St John's, 1925. The team was in the third division, West Herts League and they finished third that season.

Boxmoor Boys' Life Brigade, 1924–5; Hugh Brockman of Bargrove House helped to found the local Life Boys Group and Brockman Hall in Catlin Street was built for use by the Brigade. Their National Training Centre at Felden Lodge, Sheethanger Common, was opened in October 1949.

Common but only under the watchful eye of their schoolmaster. Troops were allowed to play on Gas Works Moor; in 1943 these were named as the 252/63 (Oxford) A/TK Battery R.A. and, later, the First Middlesex. During the war, the National Fire Services and St Ignatius' College were also granted playing space opposite Boxmoor Wharf for one afternoon a week.

Indeed, it seems that everyone in the district who ever wanted to kick a ball around with their friends inquired at some time or another whether they could play on the Moors. Boxmoor Junior School made good use of their proximity to a pitch over the years, but could not use it on Saturdays. In 1951 a local junior side was formed and affiliated to the West Herts Minor Football Association. The *Evening Echo* also ran a team, the Ember Echoes that trained on the Moor in the 1970s; this later became Leverstock Green Echoes. Hemel Lads FC requested permission in 1969 to erect a timber hut as a

changing room on a site adjacent to the Town Cricket Club. Two years later they were ambitious enough to consider floodlighting for training sessions. Leverstock Green FC, Daggs Dell United, Tornados, Emerald Vale and Hemel Aces are all names from the 1970s that must stir memories in some people's minds.

Today, the sport is still a feature of the Box Moor scene, as informal games are played all over the Estate. However, Boxmoor JMI School now has its own playing fields at its modern site in Cowper Road; Two Waters School has likewise moved elsewhere. The Boxmoor Baptist Church has amalgamated with Marlowes Baptist Church to form the Carey Baptist Church in Marlowes, and the *Evening Echo* is no more. The story of the many football teams in the Trust's Area of Benefit is a complex one and perhaps one day someone will take the time to research and record it all in more detail.

BENEFITS TO THE LOCAL COMMUNITY

35. VESTRY MEETINGS

'I never vote for anyone, I always vote against.'
W. C. Fields.

The word 'Vestry', in ecclesiastical terms, means a room in or attached to a church in which vestments and sacred vessels are kept and in which Sunday Schools and meetings are sometimes held. More specifically, in the Church of England, the word signifies a meeting of all the members of a parish, or their representatives, to transact its official and administrative business. By analogy it has come to mean the actual body of people or the Parish Council itself. All local householders could attend Vestry meetings, but, as is still the case today, only the committed few ever did, unless the debate involved issues that affected them personally. One of the roles of the Vestry until 1834 was to administer the Poor Laws; a Select Vestry, as established in Hemel Hempstead, was a limited number of male parishioners appointed annually by the Vestry.

The powers of the Select Vestry seemed to have been quite far ranging, for example in 1819, a resolution was passed that publicans would not allow common labourers to 'tipple' in public houses or stay in them after ten o' clock in the evening. Otherwise, they would be reported to the magistrates and the constables were to make every effort to enforce this mandate. This rule did not, of course, apply to gentlemen whom, it was assumed, knew better how to conduct themselves after a night's heavy drinking!

The earliest mention of the Box Moor Trust in the Vestry Order Book appears in 1736, when Richard Salter was paid £1 11s 6d for the writings that belong to Box Moor 'to be put into the Chest over the Vestry Room' and, in verification of this (according to the Churchwarden's accounts for the same year), Salter was paid 'for the deeds of the Moor'. Incidentally, this name (father and son) occurs several times in the list of Hemel Hempstead's Bailiffs.

Meetings were held annually in the Vestry Room to discuss disposal of the Surplus fund from the Box Moor Estate, or in the Town Hall if attendance demanded a larger space. The Bailiff was generally elected to the Chair, even though his civic office did not give him the right. Anyone who chose might make a proposal that a proportion of the funds be allotted to the object advocated. After the meeting, the Trustees would sign outstanding bills on production of the necessary vouchers.

Various references to Vestry meetings are made in the Trust's minutes. Any Surplus monies were divided annually between Hemel Hempstead and Bovingdon and decisions about where the money was to be used were voted on and approved at Vestry meetings attended by local householders. On 23 October 1850, £40 was applied to street lighting and £50 went towards the construction of the Town Hall. At that meeting, Mr Bontems requested that the whole of the Surplus should be divided into as many equal portions as there were householders in the parish and they would all get their share, any remaining cash not applied for was to be given to the Bailiff for street lighting. His proposal was supported by 'a number of labouring men who came to vote for the amendment in expectation of receiving a large sum'. Will Smith objected to this proposal, it being contrary to the provisions of the 1809 Act. Counsel later found that the proposed amendment was illegal and it was eventually dismissed.

The building of the Town Hall in 1852 gave rise to further extensions in 1861, when a Vestry Room was added on the north side at ground-floor level. Together with a Reading Room above, it cost £463 and it was let to the parish for £15 a year, paid for out of the parish rates. At the end of the nineteenth century, as the town gained Municipal Borough status, the need for Vestry meetings became largely obsolete and its once busy gatherings were reduced to matters mostly ecclesiastical.

The last time a Vestry meeting was held at St Mary's Church to allocate the Surplus funds from the Box Moor Trust occurred on 17 November 1964. This took place in the Vestry with only seven members of the public in attendance. In a meeting which lasted for just six minutes, £100 of the Surplus money was voted unanimously to be given to the Mayor and Bailiff's Community Appeal. On the 20 November, a similar meeting was held in the Vestry of St Lawrence Church, Bovingdon, to vote on the Trustees' proposal to allocate £25 to the Parish Council; five members of the public attended and agreed to the proposal.

The Parish Chest: this ancient chest once stored the town's charters and bailiwick records. It is still in situ, but empty now of any valuable documents. It needed three men, each with their own key, to open it at the same time, for security.

TO THE INHABITANT HOUSEHOLDERS OF THE PARISH OF

HEMEL HEMPSTED.

LADIES AND GENTLEMEN,

I hereby give you Public Notice, that although I feel convinced, in point of Law, that the Resolution which the Inhabitant Householders came to at the Meeting held on the 11th of May last in reference to the appropriation of the Surplus Rents arising from BOX MOOR, was technically correct, yet I intend to be present at the Meeting appointed by the Box Moor Trustees for Friday next the 8th instant, at Eleven o'Clock, and again to propose a Resolution, of which the following is a Copy : viz.

'That the Portion of the present Surplus of the 'Rents and Profits of the Wharf and Premises vested in 'the Box Moor Trustees, which belongs to the Parish of 'Hemel Hempsted, be invested as soon as may be either 'in the purchase of the unexpired terms of such of the 'existing Leases granted by the Trustees as can be obtain- 'ed, or of Land as contiguous to the Moor as possible, 'such unexpired Terms or Land to be vested in the pre- 'sent Trustees of the Moor upon Trust for the exclusive 'benefit of the Parish of Hemel Hempsted, and similar 'to those declared by the Box Moor Act :

'And that until such Purchases can be made, the 'portion of the present Surplus of the Rents and Profits 'belonging to the Parish of Hemel Hempsted, be invest- 'ed in the Funds in the names of the present Trustees for 'the purpose of accumulation.'

I do not consider any argument or observation neces- sary to induce you to rally round and support my Motion at the ensuing Meeting, as I feel assured that its merit alone will have this effect, and procure for it the successful result of achieving a popular, universal, and permanent, instead of a limited, individual, and temporary advantage.

I beg to subscribe myself,

LADIES and GENTLEMEN,

Your's very obediently,

Hemel Hempsted, 5th June, 1838.

FREDERICK DAY.

BUTTFIELD, PRINTER, HEMEL HEMPSTED.

The meetings that were held to decide on the application of the Trust's Surplus funds usually passed without too much controversy, but on 11 May 1858, matters took on a different complexion. An amendment was moved by Frederick Day and seconded by William Field that the Surplus should either be invested in the purchase of the unexpired terms of leases, or for the acquisition of land contiguous to the Moor. Until such purchases could be made, the proposal was that the money should be kept in the Trust's funds for the purpose of accumulation in order to achieve these ends. This challenging amendment was actually carried by a majority of twenty-two. Remember that the Act of Parliament of 1809 clearly dictated that any Surplus was to be distributed, therefore the Trustees had no choice in the matter, so they resolved that they could not legally apply the Surplus in that way and called another Vestry meeting, to 'decide upon its proper application on Friday, 8 June.

The Committee of the Bailiwick distributed leaflets for every person occupying a house in the parish to vote at that meeting; the intent was clearly stated, that the Surplus should be paid to the Bailiff and applied by him for the general benefit of the Inhabitants (women were not allowed to vote for their husbands, however). The minutes of the second meeting seem to indicate that the matter was unresolved and the Trust's subsequent note repeated their previous resolution. Mr Day was still not happy and threatened the Trustees with 'the necessary proceedings' to enforce their compliance. The Trust decided to ask Counsel's opinion and there the matter ended!

36. BENEFITS OF THE SURPLUS FUND

'Money is like muck – not good unless it be spread.'
Francis Bacon, Baron Verulam, Viscount of St Albans in his
book of Essays: *Of Seditions and Troubles.*

The Committee of the Bailiwick of Hemel Hempsted,

**Call to solicit your Attendance and Vote, at the Meeting
to be held on Friday next, the 8th of June, at 11 o'Clock
precisely, for the appropriation of the Surplus Fund of
the BOX MOOR TRUST, and that such Surplus shall be
paid to the Bailiff, and applied by him for the general
benefit of the Inhabitants.**

———————————

NOTE.---Every Person occupying a House in the Parish is entitled to one Vote,
at the said Meeting : but no Woman can Vote for her Husband.

It is necessary to define, firstly, what is meant by the frequently recurring term 'the Surplus' in relation to the Box Moor Estate. A surplus is generally taken to be an amount in excess of what is required, or an excess of total assets over total liabilities. In regard to the Charitable Trust, this translates as whatever money is left at the end of each financial year after administration, improvement and maintenance of the Estate, its lands and buildings has been accounted for, in the best manner possible for the continued use and enjoyment by the local population. These objectives have not altered over the 400 years of the Trust's history, although the focus or interpretation may have changed during that long period, just as society itself has changed.

This happy state of an excess of revenue over expenditure has been a somewhat mythical one for several periods in the Trust's history, but the present picture is far more satisfactory and this scenario will hopefully continue. Financially, the Trust is self-supporting. The Trustees receive no salary and the revenue is derived from the rents of properties, the sale of Pasture Tickets and from investments that are monitored by the Charity Commission, the approval of which still has to be obtained for major capital expenditure and investment. Otherwise the Trustees act independently of any Government or Local Authority. Over many years, however, the Trust has been able to co-operate with and assist public bodies for the welfare of the community in the Area of Benefit.

The purchase of the Moors by public subscription in a secret arrangement in 1581 was undertaken on behalf of the then inhabitants of the parish of Hemel Hempstead and the hamlet of Bovingdon. To make allowance for the difference in size of the two communities, it was agreed to allot Hemel Hempstead a three-quarter share of all 'Rents, Profits, Privileges, Commodities and Advantages' and Bovingdon the remaining one-quarter share. Thus, in the 1809 Act which followed negotiations over the sale of lands to the Grand Junction

Canal Company and the Fourdrinier brothers, the rents and profits from the resulting Boxmoor Wharf were shared out as follows:

'… have been applied as to Three Fourth Parts, the share of the said Parish of Hemelhempsted … in forming a complete House of Industry of the Workhouse belonging to the same Parish, and in repairing and improving the same from Time to Time … and the remaining One Fourth Part of such Rents and Profits, the Share of the said Hamlet of Bovingdon, hath been applied in the relief of the Poor, and in aid of the Poor Rates of the said Hamlet.'

The workhouse and relief of the poor were not, by any means, the only projects to be promoted by the Trust's Surplus. The Trust minutes detail an amazing array of items that came under this heading, from the Hemel Hempstead Recreation Ground to water for the allotments in Bovingdon. Some Surplus funds were distributed from 1817 until 1844, but from 1847 to 1907 regular yearly amounts, ranging from £60 to £400, were directed, generally in smaller sums to a wide range of worthy causes. The money was allocated by the Bailiff, after a public meeting to decide on the preferred uses of these funds.

Prior to about 1900, it would appear that Trust land and any property on it was generally leased, therefore the Trust was not responsible for maintenance. No records can be found that the Trust built any houses for general use before 1908. The income from the leases therefore exceeded the expenses of the day, allowing the Surplus to be distributed up to 1907. The Trust first decided to build two of its own houses in that year and by 1912 a further twelve houses had been erected, apparently without full permission of the Charity Commission. These were rented on a weekly or monthly basis, as were the four cottages opposite the former Bell Inn at Two Waters. The loss of income from the leases and the repayment of the loan of £4,000 from the Lands Improvement Company, together with the cost of maintaining the rented properties, would appear to have left little in the kitty thereafter for Surplus funds.

The fire brigade was a regular beneficiary of the Trust in the nineteenth century, also the Boxmoor Baths, West Herts Infirmary and Bovingdon's Parish Schools. Public lighting, lamps and wells, town and church clocks, seats and paths, all feature at some point in the records, many with regular annual mention. There were five lamps maintained in 'dangerous places in the narrow lane called Box Lane', while ten shillings was devoted to the winding of the church clock in Bovingdon: the only public clock and one that kept the time for the whole parish. The parochial schools in Bovingdon usually received the balance of any Surplus funds.

In 1850 reference was made to a 'New Town Hall' and the sum of £50 given towards its construction. This building is still standing, but is now known as the Old Town Hall, in Hemel Hempstead's historic High Street. Bovingdon Church (St Lawrence) received £30 in 1853 and the churches of

The West Herts Infirmary in Marlowes, Hemel Hempstead, built by Sir John Sebright of Beechwood Park at his own expense in 1831. It later became a nurses' home and school, then it was let to King's College Hospital as a convalescent home. A larger hospital adjacent to this site was opened in 1877 by Princess Mary, Duchess of Teck and mother of Queen Mary. The original cottage hospital in Piccotts End was started by the Royal Surgeon, Sir Astley Paston Cooper of Gadebridge, as early as 1826, one of the first in the country. It was supported by the Revd J. B. Mountain, amongst other local churchmen. This small hospital served the entire district from Bushey to Tring, St Albans and Harpenden, until it became inadequate both in size and position. Years later while being renovated for rental, a row of old cottages on the site were found to contain outstanding medieval wall paintings.

The Baptist Church, London Road, Boxmoor. The first chapel was built in 1825; the re-built and enlarged church was officially opened on 26 October 1864. The unfenced Moor opposite was often used for church events; the meeting room of the Oxford Club Brotherhood and later Sisterhood was behind the houses on the right. This organisation also helped to raise funds for local concerns in the early 1900s.

Hemel Hempstead, Apsley End and Leverstock Green were also beneficiaries.

There is an intriguing note on 'the provision of a free Reading Room for the residents of Boxmoor' in 1885, but the £50 allowance was 'not paid – divided; £25 Her Majesty's Jubilee fund; £25 Bailiwick, for Lamp Post and Fountain'. Bovingdon fared slightly better, since in 1905, £10 was given to its Reading Room. The building of the Village Memorial Hall was the objective of the grant of £25 in 1914, whilst in 1919, shortly after the First World War, the Apsley Memorial Institute, the Boxmoor Working Men's Club and the Hemel Hempstead Institute were each granted donations.

This latter foundation, inaugurated on 26 March 1839, was derived from the idea of Mechanics' Institutes and had its premises in the High Street. It later moved to Queensway and became known as the Old House Club. It has served the aspirations of local residents for many years. It is now called simply the Hemel Hempstead Club, with snooker tables and pints more in evidence than formal debates on literary or cultural matters.

The manner of deciding on the uses to which the Surplus was to be applied usually took the form of a Vestry meeting. The Surplus was given to the Vestry under the control of the Bailiff and the Vestry decided by vote how it should be allocated. Notices were relayed to inhabitant householders in the Vestry Room of the parish church for two Sundays before the meeting. In Bovingdon, they sometimes met at the Bull Inn instead. They would then: 'consider and decide on the proper application and disposal of the residue and surplus belonging to this Parish of the Rents and Profit arising from the Wharf and Premises vested in the Trustees of Box Moor'.

One of the first recorded Trust Vestry meetings on 20 January 1817 (at which twenty-three local residents were present) resolved that the Surplus for that year and subsequent years should be put towards alterations and repairs to the old Market House in the High Street. This work had commenced in 1806 at a cost of £400. The bill was not paid by the Bailiwick until 1829, and only then because of the help given by the Box Moor Trust – the original twenty-year plan, perhaps?

An extract of the minutes of the Hemel Hempstead Vestry meeting of 8 October 1828 seems to indicate an uncertainty about the position of the Vestry with regard to the Box Moor Trust funds:

'That the Trustees of Box Moor be requested to hold a meeting for the purpose of taking into consideration the propriety of assisting from the funds at their disposal in the proposed plans for erecting and endowing a Chapel of Ease and that the Vestry Clerk should address a note to them to that effect.'

This uncertainty is perhaps understandable, for this was only the third application of the Surplus after the 1809 Act and it

was not until 1847, according to the Trust minutes, that such events appear to have taken place annually.

The *Borough Guide* of *c.*1900 stated that:

'The net rents and profits of the Moor and of considerable property built upon it are handed over by the Trustees every year for the use of the respective parishes. By these grants in times past, public buildings have been erected, the fire brigade almost wholly maintained, seats provided on the Moor for the weary, and the rent of the recreation ground (in Queen Street) paid.'

The social needs of the town were seemingly well catered for by the Trust up to that time, as the following articles on the direct beneficiaries of the Surplus will illustrate.

However, the financial state of the Trust deteriorated in the twentieth century, so much so that requests for assistance from the Surplus had to be turned down, no matter how worthy the cause. The paltry total of the Trust's equipment in 1975 consisted of one very old tractor, a chain saw, an oxyacetylene welder and a few small tools. This equipment was kept at that time in the workshops at Old Fishery Cottages. It was not until after the rents were increased on the Boxmoor Wharf site in 1975 that reserves could be found to buy new equipment, bring the properties up to date and purchase suitable land as it became available, such as Howe's Retreat. It was, therefore, decided that in order to meet on-going costs reserves should be allocated whenever possible. Since then, the Trust has made sure that it operates on modern lines upon a sound financial base so that its future objectives are achieved.

Bovingdon School in 1890, by Boxmoor photographer Edward Sammes. Granville Dudley Ryder established schools at Bourne End and Bovingdon. Newman Dix was headmaster from 1885 to 1923 at the school in Chipperfield Road; its log books date from 1890 to 1927, when a new school was built in the High Street.

37. St Mary's Church

'It is a very fair and tall spire covered with lead, which is a great ornament to the town.'
Sir H. Chauncy, *The Historical Antiquities of Hertfordshire*, 1700.

The history of the Box Moor Trust is heavily intertwined with the parish of Hemel Hempstead and therefore the Parish Church of St Mary* must come into any wider picture painted of the Trust. It is situated in the old High Street overlooking Gadebridge Park and the former market place.

According to *Kelly's Railway Directory* published in the 1830s: 'The church, which is built on a cruciform plan, is of Norman origin, and has an embattled tower surmounted by a lofty octagonal spire. The interior is richly ornamented and contains a tomb of great antiquity'. The spire dates from the fourteenth century and was originally constructed in wood and covered in lead. That same spire is still a wonderful landmark and, after its recent renovation, seems set to distinguish the upper end of the town for at least another 600 years.

A later *Kelly's Directory* goes into more detail: built of flint and clunch stone* the very earliest portions of the church date from about 1150, long before the Trust existed. The arcades and the west door are fine specimens of Norman architecture and the whole building was never subjected to any kind of 'restoration' that might have deleted all signs of previous occupation.

St Mary's beautiful stained glass windows are testimony to its many benefactors in the past and there exist several monuments that are connected with Box Moor Trustees and its Clerks of former times. There are fine memorial windows to C. E. Grover, Henry Day, Lovel Smeathman and the two Smeathman boys who were killed in the First World War. The Godwin family of Grove Hill have their deserved place, since the surviving Miss Godwin contributed to the restoration of the roof of the chancel and the installation of a new west window in 1888. The Combe family memorial on the wall of the south aisle dates back even further to the very beginning of the Trust. It is recorded that the rector of Ashridge, Thomas Waterhouse, together with Francis Combe, rented the impropriation* of Hempstead shortly after the dissolution of the monastery at Ashridge and they both lived at the Bury. He died on Ascension Day 1555 and was buried in Hemel Hempstead. St Mary's was the Conventual* church of the monastery.

The Vestries date from 1897 and occupy the site of a former building that had fallen into decay. The parish Vestry meetings, which featured so heavily in the early days of the Trust, were held in the room above the modern-day Vestries. All the ancient Charters and Bailiwick records were once stored in the strong parish chest until they were conveyed into the care of the Bailiff in 1896. One Vestry Order Book for the years 1732–42 still exists. Church Registers were actually begun in 1538 by an Act of Parliament instigated by Thomas Cromwell. By 1636 they had to be written on parchment and kept together in one volume.

In 1693, during the reign of William and Mary, a dispute arose between the hamlet of Bovingdon and the Bailiwick of Hemel Hempstead regarding taxes for the upkeep of the Parish Church of Hemel Hempstead. The church, it was said, 'has fallen into certain ruins and needs divers repairs … the expenses for the upkeep of the said church ... will amount in the whole to the sum of five hundred pounds'. The people of Bovingdon claimed exemption from such an exorbitant charge, except for a list of occupiers of a certain 200 acres of land, the location of which is still uncertain. This was judged to be the time-honoured case and all charges were dropped.

The year 1594, an auspicious date for the Box Moor Trust, was a plague year in Hertfordshire as well as in London. There were thirty-two burials due to this scourge in Hemel Hempstead, from August to October 1594. The Gladman and Howe families both suffered losses, names that appeared in the Trust Feoffement of that year. Money was often bequeathed for a mass to be sung or for the altar lights to be kept burning. One of the more unusual altars at St Mary's was that of St Uncumber, apparently an ideal saint for wives who wished to be 'unencumbered' of their husbands!

There cannot be many vicars who have ordered that a public house should be built close to their church, but in 1527 John Eggerton had The Lamb erected in the Market Place to prevent ale from being consumed in St Mary's itself on market days. The original ring of five bells has long since disappeared, but the present peal of eight, dating from 1604, were re-hung by Gillett and Johnson of Croydon in 1950.

A significant portion of the Box Moor Trust's Surplus supported the church in the early days after the 1809 Act. The accounts for 1819 show that £200 was used for the proposed repairs and improvements to the church out of the Hemel Hempstead share. The churchwardens were often the recipients of quite large sums of money for the times, such as £225 in 1840. The amounts diminished over the twentieth century, but were recorded regularly. There appears to have been a standard payment of £7 10s in the early 1900s. A larger amount of £75 was subscribed in 1914 for repairs, any balance going towards the bandstand at Heath Park. A further £75 was sanctioned in 1920 but the Surplus dried up and the last time a Vestry meeting was held in the parish church to allocate Trust money was on 17 November 1964, as previously noted.

Parish Church. Hemel Hempstead.

The Parish Church of St Mary's, Hemel Hempstead, published by S. T. Greaves, High Street. The oldest parts date to c.1150 and the Norman west door is a fine example of this period, complemented by a magnificent fourteenth-century spire. This has recently been renovated after major fundraising by the Friends of St Mary's. The Tithe maps of 1843 were found to be in very poor condition and the Trustees felt able to contribute towards their expert restoration. In 1987, Essex County Council Records Office was approached for estimates, and since the St Lawrence, Bovingdon map of 1841 had also been found, both were duly restored at a cost of almost £3,000. A small brass plaque for mounting on the map cases and a set of transparencies were given to each church by the Trust. These fascinating old maps were presented to St Mary's and St Lawrence in December 1988 and March 1989, respectively.

38. Chapels and Churches

The Parish Church of St Lawrence, Bovingdon. Hardly any records remain of the original thirteenth-century church, when the hamlet of 'Buendon' or 'Bovington' was in its infancy. The church was replaced by a grander building in c.1320; the chest tomb of the anonymous knight dates from c.1370. The steeple was removed in c.1725 and the ensuing years of neglect took their toll. Granville Ryder came to the rescue and eventually just over £3,000 was raised for the rebuilding project in 1845. Two of the early bells were still in existence and a third was added in 1845. The Ryder memorials pay tribute to the family from Westbrook Hay who benefited the hamlet in many ways. Tim Marshall, the Vicar in 2000, stated in the church's Millennium commemorative booklet: 'For nearly half of the last thousand years, St Lawrence Church has been at the centre of Bovingdon to stand alongside and offer Christian service through all the ups and downs of village life'.

The separate parish of St Lawrence, Bovingdon, was inaugurated in 1833, after years of disagreement with the Mother Church of St Mary's. Prior to that time, from the thirteenth century, the vicar of Hemel Hempstead was ordered to serve the chapels of Bovingdon and Flaunden 'by means of two fit chaplains', for whose upkeep he received twenty shillings annually. A church terrier* of 1638 declared that the inhabitants of the hamlets provided this allowance and the chaplains shared a house, orchard and garden, at West Bovingdon.

A lookout was posted on the top of the tower at Bovingdon to warn the congregation by the ringing of a bell when the parson was spied approaching for his monthly sermon. There was no point in doing so in bad weather since the parson would not be expected to appear. The hamlet had to provide a bell rope for St Mary's and help repair its fabric and fences.

From such small matters bitter disputes can, and did, arise. The Church of St Lawrence, Bovingdon, dates back to medieval times and still contains one tomb of this period. It was thoroughly restored in the Gothic style in 1845 by Thomas Talbot Bury FSA to whom a stained-glass window is dedicated. The south porch has puddingstone as well as flint in its south gable and there are numerous monuments to the Ryder family of Westbrook Hay. The Hon. Granville Dudley Ryder, a Box Moor Trustee and local benefactor, who died in 1879, helped to renovate the old church. The stately avenue of yew trees is reminiscent of battles such as that at Crécy in 1346, when the English bowmen were at their most formidable and where the entombed knight may have fought. Yew was the material traditionally used for making bows and where better to keep a supply than in the village churchyard, away from stock. The Bovingdon churchyard was also used as pasturage for sheep until 1872 when the evergreens were planted.

The Surplus income from the Box Moor Trust is first mentioned as being applied directly to the church in 1853 when the sum of £30 may have offset some of the restoration expenses. The public path through the churchyard also deserved funding in 1891, when £8 10s was specifically granted and further minor grants were made over the next two decades. The church clock needed winding and cleaning from time to time and this was yet another object to benefit from the Surplus. The intervening years saw a decline in the income and extra funds were just not available. In the 1970s the Revd George Molyneux, the Vicar of Bovingdon, was told that his request for help could not be granted, not even for trimming the overgrown yew trees in the churchyard. In fact, the last meeting held in the Vestry of St Lawrence took place in 1964, when £25 was the total amount distributed. The village continues to grow and a new generation enjoys the rural atmosphere of the area, unaware that many of the features they take for granted now could not have existed without support from the Box Moor Trust and that the former manorial estate at Westbrook Hay is part of their heritage now.

Bovingdon has long had a strong non-conformist tradition: Lollards, Presbyterians, Wesleyans, Baptists and Anabaptists all held sway at some point in time. Joshua Lomax was indicted in the Archdeacon's Court for non-observation of his duties as a member of the Establishment. The Mayne family, previous Lords of the Manor of Westbrook Hay, probably founded Box Lane Chapel, the secluded site of which continued as a place of worship from before 1668 to the middle of the twentieth century. Thomas Lomax rebuilt it in 1690 and seven years later he and his wife Mary transferred it to trustees, some of whom were also named as Feoffes in the Box Moor recitals of 1711. Thomas Cromwell is believed to have once received the Lord's Supper at its old oak communion table. The historic building ended its days as a Congregational Chapel on 29 June 1969, after which it was converted into a private house.

The following rather bland statement appeared in the *Victoria County History*, first published in 1908, but no mention was made of the story behind these words:

'The first Church of St John the Evangelist at Boxmoor was opened in 1830, and the present structure was finished in 1874 and enlarged westward in 1893. It was a Chapel-of-Ease* to the Parish Church of Hemel Hempstead until 1844, when, by an order in council, its own ecclesiastical parish was formed. The living is a vicarage in the gift of the vicar for the time being of the collegiate and Parish Church of St Mary, Hemel Hempstead. The registers date from 1820.'

St John's Church, Boxmoor, in fact owes its pleasant location on the Moor to the Trustees of 1829. An application to erect a Chapel-of-Ease to St Mary's, Hemel Hempstead, was first discussed at the Trust meeting of 12 November 1828. The decision was made to call a Vestry Meeting on 3 December, the Trust intending to offer £200 towards the building costs.

Revd White was in the chair when, at the subsequent Trust meeting of 25 April 1829, the Trustees consented to the committee appointed to oversee the building of the new chapel to treat with the Parliamentary Commissioners. They submitted a plan, which needed amending, for a chapel and burial ground near the Heath, but the Trustees on the whole were 'willing and desirous of treating for the sale of the ground required for the above purpose'. This conveyance was then executed on 17 September 1829, 'Messrs Creed and Griffin having valued the site required for the new chapel at £71'. What the price at today's valuation would be is anyone's guess! According to *Kelly's Directory*, this extra place of worship for Anglicans was needed because of the growth of the town on the southern side, partly due to the establishment of the paper mills at Apsley and later due to the proximity of the railway. Boxmoor became a separate parish and welcomed its first vicar, Revd Henry Lister, at the inauguration of the church on 25 May 1830; Ann White, a co-founder of the church and Revd White's sister, laid the foundation stone. Separate registers were kept at the chapel from 1 January 1843.

The next reference to the chapel in the Trust minutes does not occur until 1866, a period of high activity concerning negotiations with the Hemel Hempstead and London and North Western Railway Company who wanted to construct a new railway line. Revd Richings had already contacted the Trust in December 1865 to enquire whether he could build on Roughdown Common. He followed this request with an application to purchase a part of the Moor for the site of a new church, the congregation having outgrown the original Chapel-of-Ease. The Trustees considered the idea and asked if a suitable application could be made through the Ecclesiastical Commissioners. Matters must have gone ahead successfully because the issue does not appear to have been raised again until permission was sought by the contractors in January 1873 to place their workshops on the Moor.

The Church of St John the Evangelist, rebuilt and consecrated in 1874, is an edifice of stone with dressings of Bath stone in the Early English style, erected at a cost of £4,800 from designs by R. Norman Shaw RA architect. The east window, erected in 1868, is a memorial to the late Revd Thomas White and Miss Ann White, formerly of The Lawn and Corner Hall, who were co-founders of this church. There are others to Thomas Woodman, 29 years churchwarden, who died on 28 February 1889, to the Revd A. C. Richings 1865–99 and to Mrs Richings who died on 27 June 1885.

The unusual, medieval-style brass memorial to Edward Mitchell-Innes KC CBG can also be found in this lovely church; his only son Gilbert was killed at Ypres in 1915.

Henry Balderson and Thomas Woodman were both churchwardens as well as Box Moor Trustees in 1865, but they were to be frustrated in their efforts to acquire an extra plot of land to extend the burial ground on the Moor. Several further attempts were made to enlarge the churchyard, but to

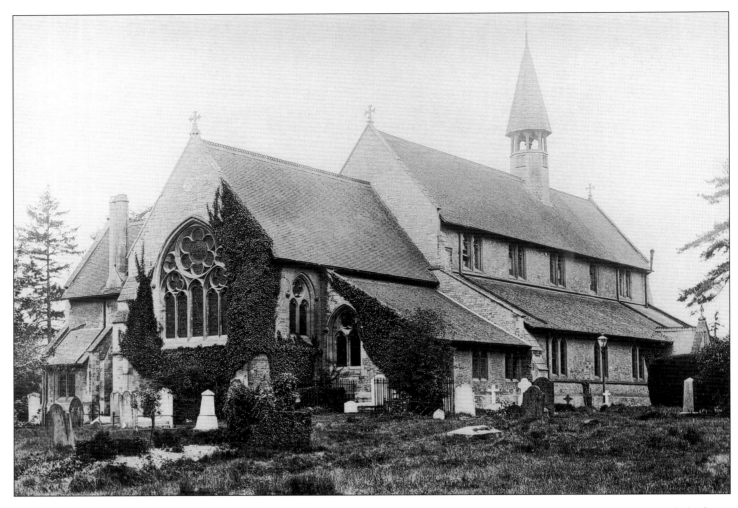

St John's, Boxmoor. The first Church of St John the Evangelist at Boxmoor began as a Chapel-of-Ease to St Mary's in May 1830. The land was sold by the Box Moor Trustees under the Church Buildings Act for £71 and this helped to pay off the Land Tax on Boxmoor Wharf. The chapel was originally served by curates appointed by the vicar of the Mother Church. It became an independent parish in April 1844 and the first vicar was Revd Henry Lister. The congregation rapidly increased and appeals were made for funds to rebuild the church, under the ministry of Revd A. C. Richings. The present structure, built to the designs of Norman Shaw, was consecrated in 1874 and further enlargements took place in 1895. Even more impressive alterations took place recently when the Vestry was demolished and a church hall complex was built on the south side; this was officially opened on 7 July 2002. This list of dates does not do justice to the aesthetic charm of the church, splendidly situated on the Moor at Heath Park.

begin with the land was leased rather than sold outright. Revd Richings's name appeared again in 1889 when he asked the Trust to either donate or to sell the piece of land in question, leased by then to the church at £1 per annum. He offered £50 but Mr Stallon thought it was worth £100; in the end, the churchwardens paid £75 and all costs. Meanwhile, Revd Richings had built a 'handsome vicarage' in the locality, at his own expense. The church was enlarged in 1893 to seat 850 people and this was much appreciated by the majority at the time. However, one resident complained that the older chapel was to be preferred to the newer 'ugly structure with its half-opened umbrella spire'. There are nineteenth- and twentieth-century stained and painted glass windows, three panels in the east window coming from the original Chapel-of-Ease. A painting of the Last Supper was installed in the Chancel in 1908 and in the following year a Vestry was added. Even more impressive alterations took place when a new church hall complex was added on the south side, which was officially opened on 7 July 2002. This has given St John's a new dimension of available meeting space, for both church and community events.

Box Lane Chapel. An early view with typical wooden marker boards in the graveyard. It is believed Oliver Cromwell once took Communion there. It was re-built in 1690, by Thomas Lomax. In 1857, Roman remains were discovered in the churchyard by the Sexton, Moses Puddephatt. It closed in June 1969, after 370 years of worship, and the historic chapel became a private house.

39. THE OLD TOWN HALL

'Hemel Hempstead has been fortunate in the possession of two revenue earning undertakings, the Bailiwick and the Box Moor Trust, both of which over the years have provided amenities which other places of similar size were denied.'
History of Hemel Hempstead – Hemel Hempstead Local History and Records Society.

The ancient Market House adjacent to St Mary's Church had seen better days; therefore, as long ago as 1806, the Trustees were being asked to help in the repair of the premises. A Trust meeting of January 1817 recorded that the Bailiff and Jury were empowered to apply the surplus rents and profits of Boxmoor Wharf, in addition to the Bailiwick funds, in order to defray the expense. The total cost of the repairs was not cleared until 1829, when the Trust again stepped into the breach and gave £100 to settle the arrears.

Local directories of the time give the background information to the later re-building in their own inimitable style:

'At the beginning of 1851 the inhabitants of Hemel Hempstead determined to rebuild the town hall and at the same time to combine with it a more commodious market which the increasing trade of the town urgently demanded.'

By this time the back part adjoining the churchyard required demolishing and the frontage was irregular with hanging projecting eaves; parts were so dark they could not be used properly, making it difficult for the corn dealers upon whom the town relied for its prosperity. There was traditionally a large corn and plait market held on Thursdays.

'Accordingly a new edifice was commenced in July, 1851 and has just been completed [May 1852]. It is entirely supported on piers and arches and has a frontage of 85 feet next the High Street. The lower portion of the building is appropriated to the Corn Market. The access to the principal floor is from a spacious stone staircase situated at the northern end of the building leading into an anteroom from which the hall is approached. The style of architecture adopted is that which was prevalent during the reign of James I.'

The Trust was able to give £50 in 1850 towards this scheme and in 1853, a further £45 'for liquidating debt on the Town Hall'. The architect was George Low and the overall cost was £1,278. The open colonnade was filled in during 1857 to make a more enclosed Corn Exchange, wheat still being a major commodity in Hemel Hempstead at that period. A Reading Room with a Vestry Hall below were added in 1861; a few other improvements also took place and the street was slightly widened.

The pride of one local, 'an old inhabitant', shines through in the following, written in 1880:

'A very handsome and commodious Corn Exchange and Town Hall has been recently erected in the principal street; the building is an excellent specimen of ornamental brick and stonework and has a Reading Room, as well as a large Assembly Room. The Magistrates for the district hold a Petty Sessions in the Hall every fortnight. The London and County Bank occupies a portion of the building, and the under-Bailiff resides here.'

Similarly, in 1890, the local directory states: 'The Town Hall, Corn Exchange, Market House and Vestry Hall, with a handsome new erection in the same style comprising three excellent shops and a market place with shambles, present together one of the finest piles of buildings in the County …' The building was also used for Bailiwick dinners, lectures, social events, religious services, Sunday School meetings and has even accommodated a School of Industry.

William Henry Cranstone, the iron founder, following in his father, Joseph's, footsteps, became Bailiff in 1871. To celebrate his year of office, he gave the splendid wrought iron gates which still bear his name. Continuous amounts of money were donated by the Trust to the 'Town Improvement Fund' and the 'debt on the municipal buildings' throughout the nineteenth century. When the Borough Charter was given to the town in 1898 and the ancient title of Bailiff was combined with that of Mayor, the Town Hall was witness to yet another historic event in the town.

The building of the New Town in the 1950s gave rise to a brand new Civic Centre in Marlowes and the fate of the Victorian building was in the balance. It was transformed into the Old Town Hall Arts Centre and has continued to play its part in the life of the town; hopefully it will do so for many years to come.

The Shambles, Market House and Butter Market, High Street, Hemel Hempstead. There was a disastrous fire at the Market House on 2 January 1749, a portion of which was pulled down in 1851.

PLAIT AND PLAITERS.

Straw plaiters. The straw in this district grew tall, straight and thin, ideal for plaiting to make into straw hats. The straw was split into splints, allowing up to as many as sixteen ends to be woven into intricate patterns. It proved to be an important addition to the income of many families in the area and children were taught to plait at an early age. Hemel Hempstead had a thriving market for the trade in finished plait, which was then sent to the hatters in Luton and Dunstable.

The Town Hall, High Street, Hemel Hempstead, erected in 1852 from designs by George Low. The open colonnade was filled in during 1857 to make a more enclosed Corn Exchange.

Town Hall, Hemel Hempstead. A Reading Room with a Vestry below were added in 1861 and the High Street was widened.

W. H. Cranstone's gates at the entrance of the Town Hall were given by him to celebrate his year of office as High Bailiff in 1871. The cast iron gates were supplied by the Coalbrookdale Company and were officially opened on 17 November 1872, on the day of the Corporation's annual dinner.

40. The Workhouse

'The practice of enlarging and engrossing of farms, and especially that of depriving the peasantry of all landed property, have contributed greatly to increase the number of dependent poor.'
Quoted by the Revd D. Davies in *The case of the labourers in husbandry*, 1795.

The above article continues: *'Thus an amazing number of people have been reduced from a comfortable state of partial independence to the precarious position of hirelings who, when out of work, must immediately come to their parish. And the great plenty of working hands always to be had when wanted, having kept down the price of labour below its proper level, the consequence is universally felt in the increased number of dependent poor'.*

The town and rural district of Hemel Hempstead probably had its fair share of the 'dependent poor', but at least some commoners could still graze their livestock on the lands belonging to them by virtue of their status as inhabitant householders in the Area of Benefit of the Box Moor Trust. The issues raised above were, however, causing many a sleepless night for those humanitarians who thought things ought to be better managed. None more so than Augustus Smith of Ashlyns, Berkhamsted, who was so convinced of his own forthright and radical ideas to make the lot of the common

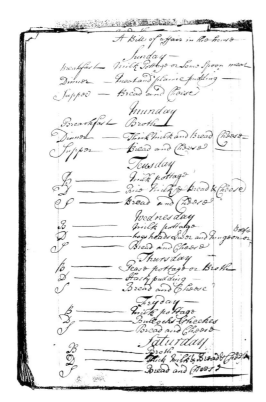

Bill of Fare for Hemel Hempstead Workhouse, 16 December 1741: 'The Workhouse should be a place of hardship, of coarse fare, of degradation and humility; it should be administered with strictness, with severity; it should be as repulsive as is consistent with humanity'. The Revd H. H. Milman, 1852.

man a far better one, that he spent his time and fortune on rescuing the Isles of Scilly from a spiral of destitution and despair. One of his innovations on the neglected islands was compulsory schooling, forty years before its introduction on the mainland. Parents had to pay a penny a day in attendance fees, or two pence a day for non-attendance!

Reminders of the Peasants' Revolt in the fourteenth century, when the monastery at Ashridge had been forced to grant a charter to allow more freedom to the people of Hemel Hempstead and Berkhamsted, together with the subsequent harsh putting down of the leaders of the rebellion, might still have survived in folk memory. The Elizabethan Poor Laws, commencing with the establishment of 'overseers of the poor' and the parish Poor Rate in 1572 and continuing with the Act for the Relief of the Poor in 1598, had not solved the national problem of the destitute peasantry.

The Acts of 1598 and 1601 authorised, without compulsion, the erection of 'poor houses' to deal with the parish paupers. A much later Act in 1722 encouraged the provision of 'workhouses' with the proviso that relief could only be given to those who agreed to the rules of these dire sounding establishments. The Accounts for inside and outside the workhouse show the assessments of the rates to be paid for the necessary relief of the poor. Henry Fourdrinier was charged £15 whilst George Howard was assessed for £1 and John Dickinson for only twelve shillings. The Speenhamland System*, by which parochial rates were used to supplement wages linked to the price of bread, became common from 1795. In 1800 the respective amounts raised for the relief of the poor in the Area of Benefit were Bovingdon: £634 12s 8d; Flaunden: £151 8s 7d and Hemel Hempstead: £1,142 5s 6d. The Accounts for 1814 included burial and marriage fees as well as midwives', surgeons', barbers' and grocers' bills.

In December 1817 the Box Moor Trustees unanimously agreed to lease to the Church Wardens of Hemel Hempstead a tract of land on the right-hand side of the road leading to Berkhamsted, over the new bridge extending up to Haybarns House, at a yearly rent of twenty shillings an acre, for the employment of the 'labouring poor'.

The new Poor Law Amendment Act of 1834 instituted Unions of parishes and so-called 'Guardians' instead of Vestries and overseers. Prior to the Act, 'the Vestry decided on the poor rate, and it was the duty of the overseer to make, collect and disburse the same, making him the sole guardian of the public purse and investing him with the power to relieve the poor at his own discretion'. The opportunities for abuse and neglect arising from this system are obvious. The Act tried to address the lack of uniformity across the country under the old system and was based on the principles of 'less eligibility' and the 'workhouse test', i.e. 'that subsistence in a workhouse must be made less desirable to the recipient than subsistence obtained by independent effort'. This sorting out of the sheep from the goats, born of the pervading work ethic and an increasing number of applicants for relief at the end of the Napoleonic Wars, gave rise to the erection of many foreboding workhouse premises across the land.

The first building to claim this title in Hemel Hempstead stood from 1723 in Saffron Lane, later called Queen Street, and then Queensway. The site comprised a cottage, malt house, kiln house, straw house and barn, occupying an area of 3 acres. There the inhabitants could work at activities such as straw plaiting, sack making, weaving, stone breaking for the roads, or maintaining the workhouse garden. Matthew Marriott of Olney, Buckinghamshire, an early entrepreneur, added to his control of his own local workhouse by taking over the management of those in Hemel Hempstead, Berkhamsted and Tring as well as others. It must have been a profitable business for some!

The building of Boxmoor Wharf gave a much needed injection into the expenses of the local workhouse, since the Trust Surplus could be directed to the relief of the poor, if so agreed at Vestry meetings.

By 1835 this district had its own Poor Law Union, comprising the parishes of Bovingdon, Flamstead, Flaunden, Great Gaddesden and Kings Langley, as well as Hemel Hempstead, which used the Select Vestry to raise the necessary rates. A Board of Guardians, elected from each parish in the Union, was supposed to both raise and allocate the spending of the poor rate, appoint staff and supervise the granting of relief to 'indoor' and 'outdoor' paupers. One of their first actions was to pull down the old workhouse. A larger building, which could accommodate 120 inmates, replaced it by 1837. One of the stipulations of the 1834 Poor Law Amendment Act was that workhouses should contain Infirmaries or sick wards. The building was further extended in 1869 and again in 1916 when a children's home with twenty-four beds was added, in Cattsdell.

In April 1839 it was reported that the Overseers had refused to pay any further rent for the eight cottages on Trust land near Haybarns, that the occupiers should have notice to quit and that, when empty, the houses were to be sold by auction, demolished and the spoil carried away at the expense of the purchaser. One can imagine the state the buildings must have been in, to be refused even by the Guardians of the Poor. They had been used for parish paupers at a ground rent to the Overseers of £1 9s 6d per annum; two sitting tenants, however, refused to leave. Their eviction necessitated legal

Workhouse Account of 1800 to be paid out of produce of Boxmoor Wharf.

An early photograph by F. Margrave of Catlin Street, Boxmoor of stone pickers, Ann Hobbs and Ann Burgin, of Bovingdon, in 1898. Clearing the fields of flints was an important part of the work on farms in the district.

Sketch by Dennis Edmonds, July 1990, of the former workhouse in its later guise as St Paul's Hospital. The site is now occupied by a housing estate. The Hemel Hempstead Institution, with frontages to Redbourn Road and Highfield Lane, was built in 1836 and could accommodate 120 inmates. In 1869 the infirmary was built and enlarged in 1935 to accommodate a further 76 beds. Work started on its demolition in 1968.

proceedings which eventually bore fruit in November 1839, but whatever became of the unfortunate tenants is not recorded.

The Trust continued to help out with finances over the years, as in 1840 when £225 was handed to the Overseers to liquefy the Bailiff's debt. The workhouse was inspected in 1899 and the recommendation made that the dangerous old oil lamps should be replaced by gas, but such an innovation would have been expensive and so the Guardians deferred their decision. The master and matron's request for an increase in their annual salary was met more sympathetically; the additional expense of topping up the £90 per annum already received by Mr and Mrs Burnett was anticipated to be met by an increase in the sales of firewood chopped by the inmates. The disposal of over ten tons of granite which had been broken up by the male inmates also added to the income, the council buying it to repair local roads. In May 1849 the able-bodied were ordered to pick half a ton of oakum*, a painstaking task.

The Board of Guardians was taken to task in 1883 because ninety occupants of the workhouse had consumed 38 pints of wine, 68 pints of gin, 162 pints of brandy and 1,167 gallons of malt liquor in only six months!

The 1929 Local Government Act transferred powers to the County Council from the Board of Guardians. The workhouse at Berkhamsted was closed and in 1935 one local committee of Dacorum Guardians was formed to serve both Hemel Hempstead and Berkhamsted. The old workhouse, sometimes known as Hempstead House, was re-named the Public Assistance Institution of Dacorum. During the Second World War, it served as a Base Hospital under the Emergency Medical Service and had closer links with the voluntary West Herts Hospital. At the end of the war and at the start of the National Health Service, it was re-named St Paul's Hospital, after the nearby church, which was demolished in the early 1960s. The remaining residents of what was by then the Hertfordshire County Council's old people's home were not sorry to move out in April 1966 to their new home at Queensway House in Highfield. March 1990 saw the transfer of 130 patients from the St Paul's Hospital Wing to either the new Windsor Wing or the refurbished Queen Elizabeth Wing at West Herts Hospital. Many local residents were born in the maternity wards which existed at St Paul's until its winding down and subsequent demolition. Now it is all a distant memory and an attractive housing development occupies the site.

Bovingdon, too, had its own poor house. In 1836 it was said to be by the side of Bovingdon Green, probably near the aptly named Workhouse Meadow, and could accommodate up to thirty persons who had no other means of sustenance. There was reputed to be a cage or lock-up for people who misbehaved. The parish often had to try to return paupers, who were a burden on the rates, back to their original parishes, but it was not an easy task. The poor house closed in August 1835, at the inauguration of the Poor Law Union, and the remaining six inhabitants were transferred to the workhouse in Hemel Hempstead.

41. FIRES AND LIGHTS

'Wednesday was a sad day for the villagers of Great Gaddesden and the townsfolk of Hemel Hempstead. Those wended their way to the scenes of the fire [Gaddesden Place] by hundreds ... what a powerful lesson did the lost glory of the noble mansion convey to the wondering crowd. The fearful and rapid destructiveness of fire; the possible outcome of just a spark; the swift and awful reduction of grandeur and beauty to ignominious ruin.'
Hemel Hempstead Gazette, 4 February 1905.

There may not appear to be any obvious links between the history of the fire brigade in the parish of Hemel Hempstead and the Box Moor Trust, but a closer look at the Trust's minute books reveals a different picture. The provision of early primitive fire engines (little more than a large tub of water on wheels) and the cost of maintaining fire-fighting equipment, vital in the days of timber-framed houses, thatched roofs and candle light, were undertaken by the Bailiwick. Many local names were underwritten in its accounts as contributors to the engine purchased in 1659 for £30 from Anthony Greene of Lothbury, London. A second engine was purchased in 1676. In 1787, William Ginger offered to remove the engine shed from the lower end of the town to a place between Bury Yard and the blacksmith's shop, wherever that might have been. He was permitted to do this with the proviso that even if it was on his own land and at his own cost, he should sign a contract to convey it all to the Bailiwick on demand.

The engine was used on occasion as the centrepiece of local festivities, the cost of 'playing the engine' for the amusement of the crowd being recorded along with the cost of the beer that helped the thirsty stalwarts after the event.

The Hemel Hempstead Fire Brigade officially started in 1845 and was reputed to have been one of the oldest in the country. In those early Victorian times there were twenty-four firemen; half were volunteers and the other half were paid for their services, in effect two brigades. The volunteers used the manual engine that belonged to the parish, whilst the men paid by the Phoenix Fire Insurance Company used their own manual engine. This engine, although kept in a praiseworthy condition, was only called to attend fires in properties insured by the company, identified by a firemark on the wall of the building. Joseph Cranstone was the company's local agent and he looked after the engine, appropriately called the Phoenix. He was appointed General Superintendent of both brigades and, as a Box Moor Trustee, may have inspired the decision to allocate £28 5s 7d for repairs to the engine house in 1847. The following year an allowance of £15 was provided for the Hemel Hempstead Fire Brigade. They were distinguished by their uniforms: the volunteers wore brown leather belts and the paid men wore webbing. Joseph Cranstone was replaced as Superintendent by his son, William, in 1872.

The situation altered in 1884, from which date the fire brigade became a solely voluntary affair. The annual grants of £25 to £50 out of the Box Moor Surplus from 1888 to 1906 must have been gratefully received. The brigade had to wait until April 1907 for their first steam engine, affectionately known as Mabel, and the Trust provided £10 10s towards the new fire station. The brigade had a variety of homes, including premises next to the present main entrance to Gadebridge Park at 1, The Broadway (1906), then in Alexandra Road (1938), and finally in the modern fire station in Queensway, nowadays the responsibility of Hertfordshire County Council.

The earliest known photograph of a British fire brigade, reputed to have been taken in Hemel Hempstead. The Hemel Hempstead Volunteers were formed in 1845 'to cope with the spate of incendiarism which has made its appearance in the area'. Hoses, helmets and buckets were all made of leather.

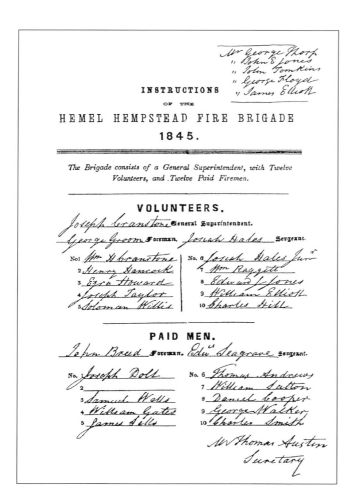

INSTRUCTIONS
OF THE
HEMEL HEMPSTEAD FIRE BRIGADE
1845.

The Brigade consists of a General Superintendent, with Twelve Volunteers, and Twelve Paid Firemen.

VOLUNTEERS.

Joseph Cranstone General Superintendent.

George Groom Foreman.   *Josiah Hales* Sergeant.

No. 1 *Wm Cranstone*	No. 6 *Josiah Hales Junr*
2 *Henry Hancock*	7 *Wm Raggett*
3 *Ezra Howard*	8 *Edward J. Jones*
4 *Joseph Taylor*	9 *William Elliott*
5 *Solomon Willis*	10 *Charles Hill*

PAID MEN.

John Breed Foreman.   *Edwd Seagrave* Sergeant.

No. 1 *Joseph Doll*	No. 6 *Thomas Andrews*
2	7 *William Sutton*
3 *Samuel Wells*	8 *Daniel Cooper*
4 *William Gates*	9 *George Walker*
5 *James Hills*	10 *Charles Smith*

Mr Thomas Austin
Secretary

The fire brigade at John Dickinson's paper mills is well documented and its official foundation has been traced as far back as August 1883, when Lewis Evans was the captain. It was one of the foremost private brigades in the county until its demise in 1990.

On the occasion of the serious fire in 1905 at Gaddesden Place, seat of the Halsey family, the Hemel Hempstead crew arrived quickly with their horse-drawn manual engine, but were relieved to see that Dickinson's Brigade had arrived with their steamer. The Frogmore and Berkhamsted Brigades joined in the frantic efforts to save the house and its valuable contents. In spite of the combined forces, the mansion burned relentlessly and two of the household staff lost their lives; after nearly two days' work the exhausted firemen returned to base. This incident prompted the purchase of the Hemel Hempstead Fire Brigade's own steam engine.

The British Paper Company at Frogmore Mill also maintained its own private fire brigade and engine, and they would be called upon to help out in major emergencies, such as that described above. There was a serious fire at the Mill in 1942, caused not by enemy action but by a driveshaft overheating. The brigade, consisting of employees (including the Managing Director, Cecil Sanguinetti), remained until the 1970s and many competitions were held between the local firemen in a spirit of friendly rivalry. Their fire station was demolished in 2003 to make way for a housing development, but the 1938 Dennis Ace fire engine, nicknamed the Flying Pig, is still intact and forms part of Apsley Paper Trail's collection.

Other public benefactions resulting from the Trust's Surplus included street lighting for the town and neighbourhood, for example, in October 1850, an expenditure of £40 was proposed by the Bailiff. However, the Trustees of the time were not in too much of a hurry to alter their quiet existence, since they refused point blank to have anything to do with the Electric Telegraph Company who had dared, in 1853, to dig trenches across the Moor. They were ordered to 'take up their wires and tubes now laid down on the Moor and restore the pasture in a sound and workmanlike manner'.

Another £45 was given for street lighting in that year and in 1856 the Street Lighting Act was adopted. The foundation of the Boxmoor, Two Waters and Crouchfield Gas Light and Coke Company in 1868 gave those districts their first glimmer of street lights. The Hemel Hempstead Gas Light and Coke Company had been established years before, in 1835, with premises in Popes Lane, Bury Mill End. It was owned by none other than Joseph Cranstone junior. In 1885, William Henry Cranstone, son of the enterprising Joseph, made the provision of a splendid lamp post and fountain.

Frequent references were made to the lamps in the parish of Bovingdon and regular amounts were paid from 1888 onwards. 'Public lighting, public clocks, public buildings were all supported or provided out of the annual Surplus of the Trust', although even by 1973 there was still no street lighting in the village.

Lamp post and fountain, High Street, Hemel Hempstead, provided by William H. Cranstone, local iron founder, in 1885. William took over from his father, Joseph, as Superintendent of the Hemel Hempstead Fire Brigade in 1872.

*Firemark for the Sun Assurance Company, dated 1710,
fixed to a wall in the High Street, Hemel Hempstead.*

*Hemel Hempstead Volunteer Fire Brigade (pre-1906), resplendent in their
uniforms, outside a very early engine house.*

*A proud line-up of firemen and horse-drawn appliances. The mock Tudor
buildings still stand in Queensway, but have a quieter existence as offices
and shops.*

*Hemel Hempstead Volunteer Fire Brigade (post-1906) with its 'Leyland
Cub' petrol-driven engine outside their former Fire Station at 1, Broadway
(now Queensway), opened in 1906 by Alderman Henry Balderson. A new
steamer engine was bought in 1907, christened 'Mabel' after Balderson's
daughter, who performed the christening at the market square by smashing
a bottle of champagne over it.*

*The Bovingdon Fire Brigade in the 1950s, with the village's first proper fire
engine. Bob Adams, Chris Parish, Fred Parish, Pat Parish, Eric Blundell
and 'Ponny' Jones formed the gallant crew in this line up.*

42. BOXMOOR HALL

The Box Moor Act of 1809 required that any Surplus of the Estate be distributed within the Area of Benefit. For many years, specified purposes that were always meant to be for the good of the whole community were decided at specially convened Vestry meetings. It was not always a straightforward task.

One project which seemed to fulfil this strict criterion was the building of a large public meeting place to satisfy many needs in Hemel Hempstead and the expanding Boxmoor. In 1878 a Special Vestry Meeting set the ball rolling by asking the Trustees to consider releasing some land on which to erect such a building. They objected to the first proposed site, on the east side of St John's Church, although they liked the accompanying plans of Messrs Coe and Robinson. A further Vestry Meeting was held in the National Schools, Boxmoor, on 16 May and a site near Boxmoor Baths was initially agreed. Then Revd Richings's idea of a plot between the Midland Railway arch and the river Gade, near the Heath Park Hotel, was accepted as being more suitable. The matter was then left to 'stand over' and subsequently everyone seems to have lost interest in the idea. A minute of 1885 refers to Mr Draper, representing the Boxmoor Reading Room Committee, who attended the Trust meeting and was asked to make fresh proposals. Other affairs, such as the purchase of Roughdown and Sheethanger Commons, then became more pressing.

The Reading Room Committee was not pleased to be told in 1886 that the sum voted by the Vestry for premises had 'fallen into the general funds of the Trust' and accordingly sent in a letter of protest. This situation eventually gave rise to a formal complaint to the Charity Commission in December 1886. There was still no agreement on a site for the building by 1887, in spite of a petition from the Boxmoor Improvement Fund Committee. However, by 1888 matters moved forward, and the first contribution was made from Trust funds towards the project.

Although not quite on a par with the Assembly Rooms in Bath, Boxmoor Hall was nevertheless a useful addition to the town. It was constructed by a local builder, James Payne; the architect had premises in Marlowes. The hall is mentioned in the directories of the time as follows:

'The Public Hall, St John's Road, Boxmoor, was erected in 1889–90 at a total cost, including fittings, of about £1,300, derived from funds produced by the annual Surplus of Box Moor for this purpose about twelve years since at the annual Vestry. The building is of grey and red brick and Bath stone in the Flemish style of the seventeenth century, from designs by William Albert Fisher. On the ground floor is a large room which is used for various purposes; the upper storey consists of a public assembly room with permanent stage and three retiring rooms.'

The hall has had many functions over the years; the Justices of the Peace used it for their petty sessions, formerly held in the Town Hall in the High Street. One of their early secretaries was Henry Balderson, a well known Box Moor Trustee. After much debate it was agreed that religious services could be held there. On Empire Days children were given refreshments in the hall, duly decorated to fit the occasion. Soldiers were billeted there at the outbreak of the First World War. The hall served for many years as the venue for the meetings of the Hemel Hempstead Teachers' Association.

The clock on the front of the building became a landmark feature, funds being allocated for it over several years. It kept time well into the twentieth century and even survived being hit by cricket balls from the Hemel Hempstead Cricket Club opposite. In 1978 an estimate for repair came in at nearly £1,000 and it was not until 1990 that the money could be spared for the work to be carried out. The clock's original dial was restored and a modern electric movement installed. This enabled the hands to be moved automatically by radio impulses emitted from a master controller in Rugby. It is now the most accurate clock in the district, justifying the £2,794 paid for its renovation after twenty-five years of neglect.

In the early 1950s the New Town was established, offering a greater provision of meeting places, including the Pavilion and a new Civic Centre. All this made the hall seem rather redundant, but in 1971 it was given a new lease of life as the Boxmoor Arts Centre. The centre continued to offer a lively programme of courses and events organised by Dacorum Borough Council until a cost-cutting exercise by the council brought about its closure in 2004. The Trustees of 1890 would have been pleased to see it serving a useful purpose for a wide section of the community's youth, but its future is now uncertain.

Children on stage at a workshop in the Boxmoor Arts Centre. Painting, pottery and drama were all part of the activities organised at Boxmoor Hall by Dacorum Borough Council since 1971. The Centre closed down in 2004. The future of the hall is uncertain since the adjacent Heath Park (Ye Olde Projectionist) has been demolished for housing. Efforts are currently being made by a group of local residents to achieve Listed status for this historic building.

Boxmoor Hall was erected in 1890. The funds were provided from the Box Moor Trust Surplus. The architect was W. A. Fisher and the builder was James Payne, both local men. It was often decorated for special occasions, such as on Peace Day 19 July 1919. Long before the New Town and the now non-existent Pavilion, local people had somewhere to hold functions, both formal and informal.

ADMINISTRATION OF THE TRUST

43. NOTABLE TRUSTEES OF BOX MOOR

Windmills Crompton, a man with an evocative name, was listed as a Feoffe in 1757. He was from London and a haberdasher by trade, not a local or a farmer or a miller, as might be assumed. He was associated with the beginnings of the Sparrow's Herne Turnpike Trust and was wealthy enough to live comfortably at Piccotts End in the house which his wife Elizabeth inherited from her family, the Partridges. One of their two daughters married the last Earl of Marchmont and the house became known by that name. Crompton died in 1771 when he was seventy years old; his wife died the previous year.

Thomas Elisha Deacon had a family history in the area stretching back to the sixteenth century. His predecessor, Thomas Deacon, owned property at Corner Hall and became an affluent tanner and farmer, rising to the office of Bailiff in 1637; the family at one time lived in The Gables. An Elisha Deacon was nominated a Feoffe in 1659 and others of the same name were listed in 1711 and 1757. By 1832 Thomas Elisha Deacon occupied the house, tanning yard and land at Corner Hall, where he found the Moor opposite to be very useful for dumping waste materials. His other interests included the trades of brewer and maltster, operating from Bury Mill End in the 1840s; Deacon's Anchor Brewery had its tap in Anchor Lane and the brewery itself was behind the old police station at the bottom of Bury Hill. He served as a Trustee from 1816 to 1857 and was the Treasurer until his bankruptcy in around 1846. Only two years previously he had been given a purse of ten sovereigns for 'having kept with the utmost accuracy and neatness the Trust's accounts for the last 11 years'. It was found later that there was a discrepancy with the books and in October 1846 it was decided that the Clerks should do the job instead. The tannery was later taken over by Henry Balderson, another notable Box Moor Trustee.

Hon. Granville Dudley Ryder was elected a Trustee in 1833, shortly after succeeding to the Westbrook Hay Estate on the death of his uncle in 1832. He was the son of Dudley, the first Earl of Harrowby and was, it seems, the only Trustee in four hundred years of the Trust with a title. He appears always to have been interested in the welfare of his employees and in that of the local villagers. He established schools in Berkhamsted and Bovingdon as well as building the school-cum-chapel in Bourne End. He resigned from the Trust in October 1846 and died in 1879, leaving affectionate memories amongst the people whose lives he had made a little easier by his thoughtful generosity. The well cover at the bottom of Bovingdon High Street was erected in 1881 in his memory.

Joseph Cranstone junior was probably one of the most locally influential men of all the Victorian worthies who came to be elected as Trustees. His father, also called Joseph, originated in Horsham and came to Hemel Hempstead in 1798 to take up an ironmongery business. The father died in 1811 and the younger son, Joseph, then developed the foundry side of the business. He became involved in the Gas Works at Bury Mill End and experimented with steam travel, producing the first steam 'road motor' to make the journey from his works in the High Street all the way to London. Unfortunately, it misbehaved at Stanmore on the return leg by running backwards downhill and was written off. Joseph married Maria Lefevre in 1819. Their second child was Lefevre James Cranstone, who became a well known artist.

Joseph formed the Volunteer Fire Brigade in 1845 and remained its Superintendent for 35 years. The brigade boasted an engine and twelve paid men as well as twelve volunteers; another engine belonged to the Phoenix Fire Office, for which company he was the insurance agent. Needless to say, Joseph's ironworks produced both appliances. His activities in the community were wide ranging, since he was also a Quaker and treasurer of the Mechanics' Institute*. He was the Bailiff from 1839 to 1840, signifying his standing in local affairs. He became a Trustee in 1833 and served for forty-five years, being unanimously voted the permanent Chairman from December 1846. The remaining Trustees sent a memorial to the family on his death in 1878, expressing their gratitude to their faithful and valued friend. They mourned his loss as a 'representative man and as a pattern to other men'.

Shadrach Godwin, or 'Squire Godwin' as he was popularly known, gave his name to a Halt on the Hemel Hempstead to Harpenden Railway. It was built in 1905, along with the Halts at Heath Park and Beaumont's Lane, to accommodate passengers using the new 'Railmotor' on the railway. Godwin's sidings, near his estate at Grove Hill, were already in existence. These were at the summit of the line, and from this point it was a hazardous descent on a gradient 1/39 down to the platform of the station in Midland Road. He was a generous man and sometimes held suppers for his employees in the King's Arms in Hemel Hempstead. He was a Box Moor Trustee from November 1846 to 1892, becoming the permanent Vice-Chairman from December 1846, a long period of service and one which witnessed many changes in local life. His ancestors, Shadrach Godwin the elder and the younger, had both been named as Feoffes in 1757 and one was Bailiff in 1733. Squire Godwin was himself Bailiff in 1842 – continuing a fine family tradition.

The Hon. Granville Dudley Ryder, elected 1833.

Joseph Cranstone, elected 1833.

Daniel How, elected 1871.

Henry Balderson, elected 1871.

Daniel How was born in Flaunden in 1826 and died in 1889; his grave is in the Parish Church, Leverstock Green. He lived at Little Colliers Farm, Pockets Dell in Bovingdon, moving to Corner Farm, Cupid Green in around 1855–6, and then to Wood Lane End Farm. He was elected a Box Moor Trustee on 28 October 1871. He became High Bailiff in 1882 and was also a member of the Board of Guardians, the Committee of the Burial Society, the Cottage Garden Society and the Oddfellows. He was described as 'possessing a good strong sense, a straightforward nature and a kindly and genial spirit' – high praise indeed. The How family served the Trust well over many generations, including William Henry How (elected 1890), Harry How (elected 1912) and Leonard Leno How (elected 1922). The family has a long history of involvement in the local community: a Daniel How was recorded as one of the original Feoffes of 1594.

Samuel Stallon also was elected in October 1871, following a series of letters to the Charity Commission regarding the legality and correctness of the proceedings of the poll for new Trustees taken at a Vestry meeting on 28 May 1870. He was the Chief Clerk in the employ of Charles Ehret Grover, a respected solicitor of Hemel Hempstead. Stallon was Clerk to many local government bodies and Chairman of some; his roles included the duties of superintendent registrar and he was often appointed as auditor to the Trust. Both the gas and water companies were amongst his directorships and he sanctioned the earlier plan to build a railway from Boxmoor to Harpenden, to link into the Great Northern network. His social and business interests in the town led to him becoming one of Hemel Hempstead's first Aldermen*; he also served as High Bailiff from 1866–69. In 1897 he instigated a library for the working-classes, to be paid for by a penny rate and from time to time he held the office of Honorary Secretary of the Literary and Mechanics' Institute. It appears that he was not universally liked, and he opposed the idea of a Charter for Hemel Hempstead in 1896, perhaps because he felt some of his influence would be eroded. He lived to be eighty-four and his obituary when he died in Bournemouth on 11 May 1906, said: 'And so Samuel Stallon has passed away at last'.

Henry Balderson was another Box Moor Trustee who served from 1871. His name was synonymous with Boxmoor Wharf, which he leased from the Trust for the latter half of the nineteenth century. Here he carried on a multiplicity of businesses, as is evident from the directories of the time, listing him as a tanner, coal, corn, stone, timber, wholesale wine and spirit merchant, as well as a dealer in artificial manures. Henry Balderson was heavily involved in the plans for a railway to link the town of Hemel Hempstead and Boxmoor Wharf to one of the main lines which had by-passed it, becoming one of the first Directors of the ambitiously titled 'Hemel Hempstead and London and North Western Railway Company'. He served as High Bailiff in 1859 and was elected mayor in 1900 (shortly after the Borough received its charter). Amusingly, the opulence of the event was commented on at the time: 'Like four geraniums lost in a bed of violets the red robes of

Aldermen Stallon, Dowling, Balderson and Gray are thrown out by more sombre tints around them'. Sir Astley Paston Cooper relinquished the role in 1899, leaving a contest that had its own drama. In the end, Balderson won the day, as his supporters claimed 'he is excellently fitted by ability, by associations and by position to fill this honourable post'. He died in October 1908 and his passing marked the end of an era, which started at the beginning of the century with the Box Moor Act of 1809.

Adam Joseph Chennells was an active Trustee from 1890 until his death in 1923. He owned a family grocery business in the High Street, having been apprenticed there to Mr Lewin in 1859. It became a limited company in 1915 and served an area of twelve miles around, delivering both wholesale and retail goods by motor and horse van. The family originated from Bellingdon Farm, near Chesham and his father farmed land at Bourne End. Adam Joseph gave his time to public duties, becoming High Bailiff of Hemel Hempstead in 1879. He also served again, as Town Mayor in 1901.

Edward Alfred Mitchell-Innes KC was Mayor in 1911 and elected a Trustee in 1912, just before the outbreak of the First World War in which his only son, Gilbert, was killed. He became Commandant of the Hemel Hempstead Volunteer Company on 9 January 1915, which it is claimed was the first in Hertfordshire to be fully armed. He had a great deal of military experience, gained as a member of the Inns of Court Rifle Volunteer Corps, before accepting a commission in the 2nd (Herts) Volunteer Battalion, Bedfordshire Regiment in 1903. He was born in 1866 and married a Yorkshire lass, Barbara Laycock, in 1893. The family lived in the gracious house named Churchill (once known as The Heath) opposite St John's Church, Boxmoor. He died in 1932, two years before the Borough Council bought his property to accommodate the new swimming baths. This site eventually became the present Hemel Hempstead Sports Centre. The unusual, medieval-style brass memorial to his family is in St John's Church, Boxmoor.

Churchill was the home of E. A. Mitchell-Innes KC. It was formerly known as The Heath, built by William Howard some time before 1850. Demolished in the 1960s, having been used as council offices and a health clinic. The Dacorum Sports Centre was sited there; it is now called the Hemel Hempstead Sports Centre.

Percy Christopherson joined the Trust in 1912 and was a Trustee for about ten years. He was a sporting Headmaster of Lockers Park School, from 1901 to 1919, and arranged cricket matches with leading personalities of the day to play Hemel Hempstead teams. He gained his Rugby Blue from Oxford and even played for England. His earlier education was at Marlborough and Bedford. He was described as 'decent, kindly and conventional; the boys liked him and he liked them'. Prince Maurice of Battenburg and his cousin Louis 'Dickie' Mountbatten (later Earl Mountbatten of Burma) were boarders at the school during his headship. He served as a JP and as President of the Hemel Hempstead Cricket and Swimming Clubs, also becoming involved in the West Herts Hospital, the Military Tribunal and the Working Men's Club. During the First World War, Christopherson allowed the Volunteer Corps to use the school's cricket ground for drill and rifle practice. By all accounts he was an active and caring man whose illness and early death in 1921, aged fifty-five, was mourned by many. His obituary stated that 'in his demise, Hemel Hempstead is left the poorer'.

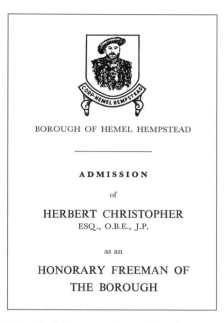

BOROUGH OF HEMEL HEMPSTEAD

_____

ADMISSION

of

HERBERT CHRISTOPHER
ESQ., O.B.E., J.P.

as an

HONORARY FREEMAN OF
THE BOROUGH

Herbert Christopher's Inauguration at Hemel Hempstead School on 7 December 1970; he was elected in 1964.

Herbert Christopher OBE, JP was elected a Box Moor Trustee in March 1964 and honoured as a Freeman of Hemel Hempstead at a ceremony in 1970. He was a Londoner by birth and was in the 12th London Rangers Regiment when he was wounded during the second battle at Ypres in 1915. After the war, he came to the area to take up a position with the newly formed Hemel Hempstead Engineering Company Ltd. His association with the local Council continued from 1930 for a further thirty-one years. He was Chairman of a number of committees, in particular the Emergency Committee throughout the Second World War. He also found time to be part of most, if not all, of the social and sporting societies of the town as well as continuing an active role in business. He rose to become Chairman and Managing Director of three Hemel-based engineering companies, besides being a Director of two other companies out of town. In 1952 he was appointed to the Commission of the Peace for Hertfordshire and was for some time a Deputy Chairman of the Dacorum Magistrates. He was also a Commissioner of Taxes and an Alderman, becoming Mayor in 1951. He received Queen Elizabeth II on her visit to lay the foundation stone of St Barnabas Church, the first New Town church, in June 1952. His services and talents were recognised in 1964 when he was awarded an OBE. He served the Trust well until his resignation in December 1977 on grounds of ill-health.

William George Seymour Crook is a name from within living memory, 'Billy' Crook having become a Trustee in 1964. He was not a native of the town, but of Buckingham, where he was born in 1893. He later attended St Mark's College, Chelsea. During the First World War he served as a naval schoolmaster and immediately after the war was appointed Headmaster of Piccotts End School. He then became Head of Boxmoor School (St John's) in 1929 and it is in this capacity that most people remember him. Incidentally, Billy Crook was the first teacher in the Borough to become the County President of the National Union of Teachers. A stalwart member of the Home Guard in the Second World War, he took his public duties seriously and was a member or chairman of so many local bodies that it was not surprising that he was eventually honoured as a Freeman of Hemel Hempstead in 1965. He retired from teaching in 1954, having been Mayor the year before. He must have enjoyed the office, since he acted as Mayor again in 1955. He was a JP from his retirement year and was even a Commissioner of Income Taxes from 1960. Throughout his life, Billy Crook had been interested in history and enjoyed his time as Chairman of the Hemel Hempstead Local History and Records Society. He wrote several popular children's books and booklets, as well as many articles on local history. He passed away in October 1977, having spent his life in service to the community of which he became a well-respected member.

To all the above Trustees and the many more Feoffes and Trustees whose names grace the centuries, we owe a debt of gratitude that such people existed; as can be seen, many were involved in more than one aspect of local civil life. Long may the tradition continue!

W. G. S. Crook, elected 1964.

44. Clerks to the Box Moor Trust

'The good of the people is the chief law.'
Cicero, *De Legibus III.*

The term 'Clerk' dates back over the centuries and, in modern times, refers to someone who keeps the records and accounts or generally acts as secretary of official bodies, such as the Town and Parish Councils. It could also refer to the Clerk to the Justices, a legally qualified person who sits in court to advise lay justices on points of law. It seems to have been an amalgamation of these roles that the Clerks to the Box Moor Trust undertook over the years and the title has been handed on, mostly within one local firm of attorneys, since its inception.

In Hemel Hempstead's case, the ancient term 'scrivener'* covered these legal and secretarial duties up until the 1600s, after which the title 'Clerk' appeared in the Bailiwick records. It may well be that some of these early Clerks were also involved in the paperwork of the Box Moor Trust, but this is only conjecture. The first definite mention in the Trust minutes appears on 22 June 1809, at a meeting at the Court Loft of the Market House 'for the purpose of electing some person to act as their Secretary or Clerk'. Adam Casebourn was duly chosen and served the Trust for nearly four years; he also acted as the Clerk to the Bailiff from 1806 until 1812. At that stage the Clerk to the Trust also dealt with the finances.

Casebourn resigned in 1813, for reasons unknown, and his place was taken by Mr Downing. He stayed the course for over twenty years, but informed the Trust on 15 February 1836 that his health incapacitated him from carrying out his duties any longer. The Clerk's salary at that time was in the order of £15 per annum.

Messrs Smith and Grover were next to take on the role. Harry Grover was the Clerk to the Bailiff from 1794 for twelve years and High Bailiff in 1798, as well as being a Trustee from 1809 up until his death in August 1835. He was the leading banker and solicitor in the town. He married Sibylla Ehret and together they had fifteen children, making The Bury into a true family home. His second daughter, Ann, married John Dickinson and lived at the nearby Abbot's Hill. His solicitor son, Charles Ehret Grover, continued in his father's footsteps, being elected as High Bailiff in 1835. Charles lived in the High Street and was listed in the census of 1861 as having six children, one of whom, Walter, at only nineteen years old was already an articled Clerk and solicitor.

After the Trust elections of 1846 it was proposed that Messrs Smith and Whithingstall should be Treasurers and that Smith and C. E. Grover should continue as Clerks to the Trust. William Smith was later declared a bankrupt. William Stocken, another solicitor, in partnership with Grover, was the next separate appointee, as Collector of the rents. That job

Mr Ginger's Villa at Hemel Hempsted, Herts. *(1 Feb. 1796). William Ginger the younger, a local attorney and a Feoffe of Box Moor, died in August 1795 during his year of office as Bailiff. He served as Town Clerk from 1757 and it is likely that the roles of Clerk to the Box Moor Trust and Clerk to the Bailiff were often combined. In or about 1790 the old Bury was demolished and a grander house was built nearby, now known as The Bury. Richard Ginger, thought to be William's brother, a dealer in the City of London, next acquired it. He had bought a lot of other property in the area, but he became bankrupt in c.1797. Harry Grover lived at The Bury in the early nineteenth century. The house and grounds were bought in 1853 and added to Sir Astley Paston Cooper's Gadebridge Estate. It is now the local Registry Office.*

lasted from 1847 until 1857, when the Clerks were made Collectors in his place. There seems to have been a close connection between the Bailiff's and the Trust's Clerks during this period.

Frederick and Henry Day were the preferred choice of the majority of Trustees in 1857 when the post of Clerk again became vacant: the two Clerk's posts became one sometime between April and May, 1861. However, by January 1858 they had not received all the documents from the previous Clerks, nor the draft of Mr Davison's agreement with regard to his encroachment on the Moor. Frustrations existed even in those less pressured times! Henry Day's continuing service was noted in July 1870, as Clerk and Collector to the Trust for the combined yearly salary of £30.

Lovel Smeathman JP in his Town Clerk's robes, post-1898. He was Clerk to the Box Moor Trust from 1884–1928. His obituary stated that Hemel Hempstead had lost a great leader in the official sense, but the Borough had lost a great and real friend.

At the meeting on 9 January 1884 the Trustees confirmed the appointment of Lovel Smeathman as the new Clerk, since Henry Day was deceased. The tenants were sent letters telling them of the change and reminding them of rent due. Smeathman had been admitted as a solicitor in 1875 and took over the offices of Henry Day in the High Street, opposite the Town Hall, in 1883. A few years later he went into partnership with Walter Grover of Grover and Son, and when the latter retired, Smeathman became the sole owner. Lovel Smeathman himself played many parts. As well as holding the office of Clerk to the Box Moor Trust, he was the first Town Clerk

after its incorporation, the Council's solicitor, Clerk to the Rural District Council, the Education Committee, the Assessment Committee, the Guardians of the Poor, the Joint Hospital Boards and the Magistrates. He also became High Bailiff in 1890 and 1891 and served as Steward of the manor, Justice of the Peace, Coroner, President of the Hertfordshire Law Society and as a St Mary's Churchwarden. He was instituted as the first Freeman of the Borough in 1929, in recognition of the many years of devoted public service he had given. Smeathman was living at South Hill at the time, now the name of a local Primary School.

He died on 2 June 1932, aged seventy-nine, and deservedly had a long and complimentary obituary in the *Hemel Hempstead Gazette*. The many bodies with which he was associated acknowledged the debt they owed to him and the fact that his offices were no sinecure. His very first public post had been with the Box Moor Trust until he had reached the stage of having more public appointments than any other practising solicitor in the county. Two of his sons lost their lives in the First World War and the third surviving son, Lovel Francis Smeathman, followed the family tradition of service in the community. His father retired from the Clerkship of the Trust in January 1928, on medical advice, and Lovel Francis was appointed to the post of Clerk and Collector in April of the same year.

Lt. Col. Lovel Francis Smeathman, DSO, MC, DL, still referred to locally as 'the Colonel', qualified as a solicitor in 1909, so he was well placed to continue the Trust's work in the firm where he had been a partner for some time. He was the last to head the family partnership, but the name survived as Picton Smeathman's until the 1990s, with premises in Hemel Hempstead and the Home Counties. It is now known simply as Pictons.

Lovel Francis was President of the Hemel Hempstead Rifle Club at the outbreak of the Second World War. He became Clerk to the Rural District Council and was firmly opposed to the idea of a New Town in the area. He was interested in the hospital and served on the Area Management Committee, representing Boxmoor. Lovel Francis stayed as Clerk to the Trust until 30 June 1956, throughout all the traumas of the Second World War and the major changes brought about by the eventual New Town. He presented the evidence for the Box Moor Trust to the Royal Commission on Common Land in March, 1957.

When Lt. Col. Smeathman retired, his many local public appointments were divided amongst his continuing partners, and so began Richard W. H. Raikes's formal association with the Trust. He had started life on distant shores, having been born in Karachi in 1919. He was educated in England, at Denstone College, Staffordshire and served as a Regimental Infantry Officer with the Hampshire Regiment during the Second World War. After the war, he studied to become a solicitor and was admitted in 1947, upon which he joined

The Firs, Green End, *by Peter Wagon (1971), the home of Lovel Francis Smeathman. (Dacorum Heritage Trust Collection).*

Lovel Smeathman and Son in January 1948 at their premises at 10 Queensway. He was offered a partnership in 1953, living in Kings Langley and then Frithsden Copse, both residences outside the Area of Benefit of the Box Moor Trust. Raikes was subsequently appointed Clerk on 30 June 1956 and was made a Coroner in 1966. He stayed with the firm until his retirement in 1984.

He wrote recently that one of the main activities he remembered was the felling of a number of horse chestnut trees along the former A41. He believed that the Trustees of his time were rugged individualists who would not tolerate 'interference' from outside agencies. The independence of the Trust from local authority control was jealously guarded in his time.

The last Clerk to the Trust had his origins closer to the area, having been a pupil of Berkhamsted School (1946–55). R. T. 'Tarn' Hodder was born in Southgate in 1938, but lived in Berkhamsted from the age of nine until 1967 when he moved to Piccotts End. He became articled in the City of London and joined Smeathman's in 1962, where he remained for forty years. The post of Clerk to the Box Moor Trust was offered to him in 1971 and he enjoyed the challenge of this extraordinary office. Tarn's many pastimes include golf: he is a Director of the Berkhamsted Golf Club Trust, as well as being a past Captain and President of the Club. He is also a keen non-competitive bridge player, a supporter of Arsenal

Football Club and a member of MCC. His interest in social and political history underpinned his involvement with the Trust and, more recently, his professional support of the Apsley Paper Trail. He represented the Trust in the A41 By-pass Inquiry in 1988 and combined legal and general advice on a day to day basis for the many aspects of the work. Tarn retired from his position on 13 February 2002, justly proud of the fact that he was one of only four Clerks throughout the twentieth century and that they all came from Smeathman's.

R. T. 'Tarn' Hodder, Clerk to the Box Moor Trust from 1971–2002. The Office of Clerk no longer exists.

45. TRUST ELECTIONS

'COLLIVER WILL CONCENTRATE COMMONSENSE ON THE CONDUCT OF THE COMMON.'
Headline from the *Hemel Hempstead Gazette*, 3 August 1912.

Since the Trust's inception in 1594 to the end of the twentieth century, Box Moor Trustees had always been elected for life, unless they moved away from the Area of Benefit or resigned, often not by choice. Indeed, a simple move to the main farmhouse on the other side of his family farm placed Paul Stanbridge's residence just a few metres outside the Area of Benefit, which then required him reluctantly to resign his Trusteeship in December 1984. In a few instances, Trustees have been deemed by their continued non-attendance to no longer desire to serve, such as Joseph Hight and Ephraim Ware in 1816, and new elections have taken place.

The original Indenture of 1594 stipulated that the Trustees should number twelve in all to manage the day-to-day business of the Trust, but sometimes the local inhabitants felt it necessary to ask for elections when the numbers fell due perhaps to death or removal from the parish, as in 1845.

From 1809, Trustees were appointed at open Vestry meetings. These elections generally relied on a simple show of hands. This system of polling had many critics, some of whom wished for proper balloting to take its place. The Mayor said in 1912 that the Ballot Act only applied in its original form to municipal and parliamentary elections and had since been extended by Statute to a few others, but could not be applied to just any election. Different feelings were expressed in the *Hemel Hempstead Gazette*, where it was boldly stated:

'We cannot see the Moor for the Act. And yet that Act must have been conveniently shelved on many occasions. Who is there in authority, or out of authority, who would have endeavoured to lift a finger in opposition if this election had been conducted by ballot? The intrinsic and palpable virtue of the ballot would have been ample protection to the Trustees if they had decided upon a ballot. But because the Act did not prescribe a ballot, and because the Ballot Act did not specifically apply to such an election, the people were subjected to the antiquated and repulsive mode of election which prevailed on Friday and Saturday If the Ballot Act could not apply, with all its penalties and regulations, most people feel that its principle could have been adopted.'

The 1970 election was the first in the Trust's history for which a completely secret ballot was held. There should not, in accordance with the 1809 Act, be less than seven Trustees for a majority vote on important concerns such as the making of Bye Laws but, as the minutes illustrate, on many occasions numbers at quarterly meetings fell to only three or four attendees. Sometimes the elections were not held until there were seven or eight vacancies to fill. From 1809 to the beginning of 2000 there have been 108 Trustees, most of whom have given long and generous service to the Trust.

Venues for the elections have varied. Nineteenth-century electors favoured the Vestry Room or the Town Hall, but in the twentieth century as numbers grew, the Corn Exchange, St John's Hall, St Mary's Hall, Bovingdon Village Hall and Baptist Church and even Hemel Hempstead Pavilion have been made into temporary polling stations. Notices were formerly posted two Sundays prior to the day of the elections on the doors of every church and chapel in the Area of Benefit. Nowadays, local newspapers and media carry the information. Often there have been many more candidates than vacant positions, proving the high regard in which the Trust and its activities are viewed.

There are several examples of family names reappearing as possible or elected Trustees since 1809: Chennells, Snoxall, Stanbridge and Williams, for instance. It is reassuring to note that having seen the workings of the Trust at close hand, it does not seem to have put off the next generation from applying on their own behalf. However, too patriarchal a membership may not serve the best interests of what is a democratic, charitable body.

In 1890 two gentlemen were elected with the same surname and similar sounding forenames (Frederic and Fredrick) Saunders. Fortunately, one was a farmer and the other was a saddler, and it was as such that they were known. Three vicars have so far (2004) been elected to the Trust, all early in the nineteenth century: Revd D. Hamilton in 1820; Revd T. White in 1827 and the Revd J. H. B. Mountain in 1833. Julia Lowe gained the distinction of becoming the first ever female Trustee in 1979.

Before this turns into something resembling the *Guinness Book of Records*, it may be as well to sample the flavour of the old time hustings which can be gained from the detailed accounts in the local press. At the 1890 event it was said: 'The poll was a heavy one. There was no actual rioting and perhaps little ill-feeling, but there was a great amount of excitement in the latter part of the afternoon and evening, which reached to commotion as the hour for the closing of the poll arrived. That the excitement was in a considerable degree physical and was something STRONGER THAN WATER there can be no denying.' The local publicans certainly benefited from the day's activity.

In the 1912 elections, although much literature was distributed, some of the candidates never left the vicinity of the Town Hall. Others were out and about scouring the locality, to the amusement of tourists who were visiting the town and who thought it was an antiquated mode of election. 'Many voters were brought to the poll at the Corn Exchange in motor cars and other vehicles and had to run the gauntlet of candidates crying "Give me one; give me one."' What some people would do for a ride in an automobile! Nevertheless, at the end of the day, over 1,906 inhabitants had registered their votes, compared with a total eligible population of about 3,000. In fact the voting was something between the old open system and a parliamentary ballot on that occasion, the first election for nearly a quarter of a century. It was reputedly carried out 'without any regrettable scenes'; the polling took place over two days and it took a longer time than usual to count all the votes.

Back copies of local newspapers, such as the *Hemel Hempstead Gazette,* make fascinating reading, recording the full details of all the candidates and their often fanciful opinions, including letters of thanks from the successful ones. More publicity was called for at that time, despite the presence of the press at quarterly meetings, to show doubters that the Trust was not behind the times and out of touch with the modern spirit of local government. There was a strong feeling, often repeated, that 'little of real importance as to the conduct of the Common has filtered into the public ear. The vast majority of the people are ignorant and they have never had an opportunity of learning of the powers which the Trust can exercise'. These sentiments have surfaced many times in the long history of the Trust.

BOXMOOR TRUST.

ELECTION OF
8 NEW TRUSTEES.

Notice is Hereby Given that a

POLL

HAVING BEEN DEMANDED IT WILL BE TAKEN ON

FRIDAY next the 2nd of August
AND
SATURDAY the 3rd of August,

Between the Hours of 10 a.m. and 8 p.m.
on each day at the

CORN EXCHANGE,
HEMEL HEMPSTEAD.

The following is a LIST of the CANDIDATES who have been duly nominated and in respect of whom the POLL will be taken :

ALLISON, William F.	**HIGGINS,** Herbert
ANDERSON, Henry	**HINSON,** Alfred
BADCOCK, Frederick St. J.	**HOW,** Harry
BADCOCK, Charles F.	**KERRIDGE,** Arthur J.
CHRISTOPHERSON, Percy	**McCARTHY,** Thomas H.
COLLIVER, Frederick P.	**MITCHELL-INNES,** Edward A.
CRAFT, John G.	**NEEDHAM,** Edgar
CHENNELLS, George L.	**OLIVER,** Charles R.
DAY, Alfred G.	**PEMSEL,** Arthur F.
DODGSON, Henley F.	**ROBERTS,** Joseph
FROGLEY, Frederic	**RUNHAM,** Walter
GLADSTONE, Samuel H.	**THOMPSON,** Maitland
GUTHRIE, James	**TODD,** William L.
HEBERT, Henry F.	**WILLIAMS,** William J.

LOVEL SMEATHMAN,
26th July, 1912.   Clerk to Boxmoor Trustees.

Printed by F. BREED & SON, Gordon Printing Works Alexandra Road, Hemel Hempstead.

To the Electors of the Trustees of Boxmoor.

LADIES AND GENTLEMEN,

Not having been asked by anybody, I think it my duty to come out as a Candidate for a Trustee, as some clever men may be wanted on the board.

I shall do as follows when Chairman–

I shall abolish all pigstyes on the Trustees' property, and turn out any tenant who keeps a pig. I shall vote for the entire omission of pork from the domestic sausage, and polonies (all hot) I shall altogether prohibit.

Italian barrel organs I shall encourage and give every itinerant Italian musician the right to graze his barrel organ on the Moor, and to wash himself in the Baths, this I consider necessary.

I shall order the Cricket Club to provide Champagne at Luncheon for the *scorer*, and all the members to have their full-length portraits in oils (gas tar not allowed) taken by some celebrated local A.R.S. (Associate Royal Society).

I shall not support the temperance movement, as I consider the movement of an inebriate requires more supporting.

On the subject of Compensation, I think if you take a glass of beer from a Landlord you should compensate him to the extent of twopence.

On the Irish question I shall say nothing, except remark an objection (hereditary) to the bacon trade.

With regard to abolishing the Coal Dues, I should like to abolish the dues on my coal.

On the Channel Tunnel Scheme I am silent.

Yours truly,

J. ALLFUN.

P.S.–I forgot to mention I am, among other things, The Poor Man's Friend, The Working Man's Friend, The Wontworking Man's Friend, The Independant Candidate, The Raiser of Wages.

In favour of a balance sheet (not having one) and in favour of dividing 400 shares among 1800 people, so that every one may have a little.

Boxmoor Trust Election, 1912.

To the Inhabitant Householders.

WE are being misrepresented, for purposes best known to THOSE WHO misrepresent us.

OUR PROPOSALS BRIEFLY ARE,
To have power by a New Act:—

1.—To dispose of LIFE Trusteeship.

2.—Bring Elections under the Ballot Act.

3.—Make it IMPOSSIBLE for a TRUSTEE to be a TENANT of a Trust Property.

4.—Make it impossible for ANYONE to be a Trustee who is a grazier on the property.

5.—To " Drain and Improve" the Moor for the best "use and advantage" of those to whom it belongs, as the Act provides.

6.—And DEMOLISH instead of to RE-BUILD unsanitary dwellings and to restore every inch to open space.

7.—To preserve the rural aspect of the Moor.

8.—To have proper machinery in the New Act so that Trustees have something to guide them in their duties.

These are some of the things we think desirable.

As public men we consider it a public duty to bring this election before you. We warn you that you may not have another opportunity of gaining proper control of your property.

Don't blame us if you lose what you have been asking for so long.

CRAFT, John G.
HEBERT, Henry F.
HIGGINS, Herbert
KERRIDGE, Arthur J.
McCARTHY, T. G. Hollands
PEMSEL, Arthur F.
RUNHAM, Walter

Printed and Published by Weston Bros., Printers, South Hill, Hemel Hempstead.

MUSTUR DUNEL HOW,
Trusthee on Boxmoore.

Sir,—

i bee a Wurkin Man, yew say yew bee my friend, lend mee a soveren to by a watch, Muster Peerman weel clene it for nothin; i bee prowd to bee the frend of sich men, i weel allis vote for Muster Peerman and yew. and i hope youl help us wurkin men to get our rites, and giv mee a bit on ground on Boxmore for a gardin; i shud like to have my bred on yew, and weel pay yew whin i sell the taters i mean to grow on mi ground at Boxmore. i shud like to hav my bit on ground at this eend on the more, becas it will bee andyest for mee; by doing this yew weel oblege yer frend

JIM SAWYER,

And i weel allis vote for yew sar.

On 18 October 2000 the first election of the third millennium was held, for three new Trustees. This was also the first election under the new Charity Commission's Scheme 2000 and the altered terms of office (elections every five years and abolition of life trusteeship) put into practice. The public in the extended Area of Benefit were sent polling cards, as in a Local Council or General Election, which carried information about the Trust on the reverse. With the help of Dacorum Borough Council, who organised the distribution, more residents were made aware of the election. Postal votes were encouraged and several hundred people took advantage of this innovation. The Hemel Hempstead Town Cricket Club's premises were used for the first time and in Bovingdon, the Memorial Hall. Details of all eight candidates were publicised in the local press and they could organise their own campaigns to drum up support.

In all 1,553 voting papers were counted, comprising 194 from Bovingdon, Bourne End, Felden and Flaunden and 996 from Hemel Hempstead, together with a further 363 postal votes. This compares with a total eligible population of 67,355 local inhabitants. The successful candidates were Will Hodgson, George Tite and Margaret Ward.

46. Appeals to the Charity Commission

Elections for Box Moor Trustees did not always run smoothly and there were four significant occasions when the Charity Commissioners were called upon to settle differences. The first dispute arose in 1870, following an election meeting on the 28 May which started in the Vestry Room and then had to be continued in the Town Hall, due to the large numbers of both candidates and inhabitants attending. Six Trustees had died and two more had left the Area of Benefit, so a new cohort of Trustees was urgently needed. Joseph Cranstone was appointed Chairman of the Vestry. Then Mr Day, Clerk to the Trust, read out the section of the 1809 Act pertaining to the election of Trustees. The two Bovingdon representatives, Hobbs and Austin, were elected unanimously, there being no other names from that district. There were a further twenty-six nominations to consider and it proved impossible to count a show of hands. The officials then tried calling out one name at a time and the people in favour went into an anteroom to be counted. In the end, six names were announced as new Trustees, whereupon the remaining disappointed candidates, including William Stocken, W. H. Cranstone and Samuel Stallon, demanded a poll. This took place two days later and when the votes were counted Henry Balderson, George Catling, Philip Evilthrift, Thomas Lendon, John George Smith and Thomas Woodman junior were found to have topped the poll. This result gave a slightly different line up to the previous vote. Joseph Cranstone then informed the Trustees of the decisions of the second election.

Not content with this state of affairs, Stocken duly wrote to the Trustees telling them of his disapproval of the proceedings and that he was going to contact the Court of Queen's Bench to have them made null and void. He required the Trustees not to convey anything to the 'new' members. This edict was discussed at a special Trust meeting on 7 July when the four 'older' members were present and, following advice, they declared the election of the two Bovingdon candidates to be a 'perfect' one. They believed the election of the other six 'probably to be good also', but, because of the controversy, they would wait for the Charity Commissioners to decide. In the meantime, the views of the prospective Trustees would be sought on current considerations and the leasing arrangements connected with Boxmoor Wharf, which involved Henry Balderson, were to be completed before he took up his office.

All of the new and old Trustees were present at the next quarterly meeting on 12 July. Under-Bailiffs Solomon Willis and Glenister were paid ten shillings each for their services at the election, but, more importantly, a letter in reply to Stocken was read stating that unless he took legal proceedings to restrain the old Trustees, they would act on their resolution and carry on regardless. To clarify their position, however, the Trustees wrote to the Charity Commission on 26 July giving full details of the preceding events. It transpired that there were not more than 200 inhabitant householders present for the first vote and only the 'ayes' in the anteroom were counted. The later poll of 30 May was closed at 5pm and at the time no one objected to this. A total of 938 householders took part and Henry Balderson was the only person who received more votes than half of this number. Following this, Stocken had threatened to file a Bill in Chancery.

The Trustees appealed to the Commissioners to give them guidance on the manner and place of future elections, as well as what to do about the controversial newly elected Trustees. Such advice was not forthcoming, although it took the Commissioners five months to decide they could not help. They did suggest, however, that in order to save future costs and inconvenience, the ownership of the Estate could be vested in the Official Trustee of Charity Lands. They thought that minor matters of management could be addressed 'with almost equal facility' by means of a Scheme – the first time this was mentioned.

This was not exactly the news the Trustees were waiting to hear and by May 1871 there were still many unresolved questions and so they consulted Trust solicitors Field Roscoe and Co. of Lincoln Inn Fields. Stocken, the originator of the complaint, was first approached to see what his views were, as he had not joined in the application to the Commissioners. The beginning of August saw the results of Counsel's deliberations, namely, that the election was 'good' for Hobbs and Austin but 'bad' for the rest and they were advised to hold yet another election. In proposing new Trustees, no distinction should be made between those for Bovingdon and those for Hemel Hempstead, since they served a united district. The Trustees then challenged Stocken to impeach the previous two elections.

The Trustees subsequently pre-empted this action by calling a third election themselves on Saturday 28 October. A show of hands gave six names but a poll was again demanded, from 1pm to 8pm on that same day and from 9am to 7pm on the following Monday. At length the High Bailiff gave out the names of H. Balderson, P. Evilthrift, Daniel How, G. A. Smith, S. Stallon and T. Woodman junior. The unfortunate W. Stocken was still not chosen, but there were some intriguing changes from the previous list. The long drawn-out matter was brought to a close with the letter dated 6 November 1871, from Frederick Mason, Chairman of the Vestry, to Joseph Cranstone, informing him that the above-named gentlemen were now officially the new Trustees. A fascinating story would emerge here, if only there were space for the full details of this 'bad' election.

The second occasion on which the Trust received a summons to action by the Charity Commissioners took place between 1886 and 1887. They reminded the Trust that no returns of the Accounts had been submitted for several years:

'I am also to state that representations have been made to the Commissioners that the number of Trustees is reduced to seven, that one of the Trustees is tenant of part of the Charity property, and that the

Population of Hemel Hempstead		
Year	Number	Increase
1801	2722	—
1811	3240	518
1821	3962	722
1831	4759	797
1841	5901	1142
1851	7073	1172
1861	7948	875
1871	8720	772
1881	9064	344
1891	9678	614
J. Harris CE. Borough of Hemel Hempstead: Notes on its Municipal History, 1898		

Trustees have failed to apply a sum of £50 in the manner directed by the inhabitants of Hemel Hempstead at a meeting held under the 8th clause of the Act 49, George III Cap. 169 whereby this Charity is regulated and governed.'

The Commissioners said that if they did not get a reply within fourteen days from 21 February they would take proceedings against the Trust, insisting that the Trust was obliged to submit information as and when requested. This meant that, as a Charity, the Trust would be under the jurisdiction of the Commission. Previously, the question had been raised but not solved and since the Trustees were now aware of the position, they would comply with all requests. They would, not unsurprisingly, also apply to the Inland Revenue for repayment of Income Tax if they were now exempt as a Charity. A search of the late Mr Day's papers revealed correspondence between himself and the Commission which appeared to indicate that the last three years' Accounts had been submitted. The Commissioners replied that the vacancies should be filled as soon as possible; they required a summary of all endowments and they accepted that in future the Trust would abide by a literal compliance to the provisions of the Charitable Trusts' Amendment Act of 1855.

The third time the Trustees were called to give account to the Charity Commission happened when they received a letter dated 13 March 1895, asking for observations on a formal request by four parish councillors of Hemel Hempstead.

The Commission mentioned that the Trust appeared to be within the provision of Section 14 (I) of the Local Government Act, 1894. They enclosed the councillors' submission, which asked for information as to whether the Parish Councils were empowered to take over the management of the Trust. Under Section 6 (III) the Parish Council could take over other property as well as ecclesiastical, including land such as village greens, and the correspondents thought that the Trust should come under such a class. The Trust was given ten days in which to reply. The Trustees' response was to write that 'as they were elected by the inhabitants of Hemel Hempstead and Bovingdon it was not their intention to transfer the Trust to the Parish Councils of those parishes or either of them'. This prompt decision was to have future implications.

The fourth occasion which entailed petitioning the Charity Commission occurred in 1896. An indignant local resident sent to the Commissioners some newspaper cuttings which disclosed that the Box Moor Trustees dined together at the expense of the Charity. These dinners traditionally took place on Pasture Ticket Days, when the Trustees were busy all day. In retrospect, it seems a little churlish to complain about this practice when all the time and effort by the Trustees was given voluntarily. The Charity Commission had no option but to follow up the complaints and the wheels were set in motion for a full inquiry later that year into the affairs of the Box Moor Trust: the Public Inquiry of 1896.

47. The Public Inquiry 1896

A large attendance was reported for the Public Inquiry held by the Charity Commissioners on 30 October 1896, at Hemel Hempstead Town Hall. As detailed previously, certain points in the administration of the Charity had been brought to the Commissioners notice, which was why an Inquiry was thought necessary. The Assistant Commissioner leading the proceedings was G. S. D. Murray; Lovel Smeathman, as Clerk, represented the Box Moor Trust; the High Bailiff represented the town's inhabitants and the Revd T. P. Stevens, Messrs C. Hinson and C. Sims were present on behalf of Bovingdon. Various Trustees and town officials also attended, as well as members of the public. The stage was set for a lengthy debate, but the Commissioner immediately decided that the evening would be a better time for suggestions and criticisms.

The Box Moor Trust had never been publicly scrutinised before and the Commissioner proposed that he would firstly discover the facts about the endowment and its administration. He wanted to know about the Trustees, their conduct of business, the history and present condition of the Trust and the administration of the income.

One of the first points made was that Henry Balderson was both a tenant and a Trustee. Smeathman responded that Balderson had been a tenant before he became a Trustee and that the tenancy was by then in the name of Balderson and Son. The Trustees in 1891 had been particularly keen that Balderson should renew his tenancy of Boxmoor Wharf, one of the Trust's main sources of income. Since the premises would have been most difficult to re-let, the Trust had even built new offices at the wharf as an inducement to the lessees. Secondly, the connection of Samuel Stallon with the Trust's firm of solicitors and Lovel Smeathman was queried, but again Smeathman answered that Stallon had been a Trustee long before he himself had joined the original firm of Grover's, where the gentleman in question was employed as Clerk to the Justices and to the Guardians of the Poor.

When questioned about meetings, the answer was that there were quarterly meetings, at one of which the Pasture Tickets were first distributed. They held special meetings from time to time and an Improvement Committee had been formed which met monthly. This Committee reported back at the quarterly sessions. A Trust bank account was held at the Bucks and Oxon Bank, and cheques had to be signed by three Trustees and countersigned by the Clerk. Two outside accountants were usually appointed to audit the end-of-year Accounts.

The Commissioner then moved on to the serious issues of the Trust dinners and the Accounts. Smeathman said that the practice of dinners on Pasture Ticket days went back at least to 1846. The Commissioner thought there was a difference between necessary refreshments and a banquet! The Bovingdon contingent was unhappy about their hamlet's lack of representation at that time and also stated that they never saw a copy of the Accounts. The Clerk assured them that they were displayed in the Vestry, at the Corn Exchange, in shop windows and, according to the Herdsman, in all the public houses. There were no statutory requirements to provide the Parish Council with copies, but the Commissioner thought this was possible to arrange.

Smeathman gave details of grazing rights, the two Herdsmen and their cottages, the Golf Club's rent of the common land for £7 10s a year and Mr Glover's use of the chalk pit on Roughdown Common for a further £5 a year. The gross income amounted to about £665. He explained the Surplus and some of the objects the money had been used for, including the Town Hall. The Revd Stevens gave a résumé of the uses of the Surplus for Bovingdon, but, having got the platform, he brought out all the past history of the purchase of the Commons and the aggravation that Bovingdon parishioners still felt about it. When asked what remedy he suggested, he was about to reply that: 'Bovingdon should have an opportunity …' when the Commissioner himself interjected: 'Of getting rid of the Common?' Smeathman tried to redress the balance by emphasising that the Trustees simply wanted to keep the Commons as open spaces for both parishes and that the chalk was for the use of them all. The sitting was adjourned shortly after that somewhat unusual exchange of views.

At the evening session the Town Hall was crowded. The impeachment of Trustees, in particular Balderson and Stallon, was raised at the outset, going back to the 1871 election. The Commissioner did not feel empowered to deal with questions arising under the Act of 1809, since he could not make any specific changes in Trustees.

Mr Rose, from the floor, suggested that the expensive Trust dinners should be abolished and that a fully qualified accountant should henceforth audit the Accounts. The Revd Stevens again put forward the Bovingdon grievances, saying especially that they would like to control their own Commons, notwithstanding that 'the administration of the present Trustees was very good indeed'. He felt that a flock of sheep and golf-playing did not go together, but the Commissioner rejoined 'They often do in practice!' The issue of taking chalk for agricultural purposes was explained by Smeathman and the regulations and charges that applied if it was used for manufacture into lime. Revd Stevens reiterated that the people of Bovingdon just wanted their rights preserved and respected.

A novel question was raised by Mr Pearman, who wished to know if there was an Act of Parliament that could deal with the giving away of beer and money at Trust elections. The Commissioner, not to be drawn, informed him that he should consult his solicitor. A further query about opening Trust meetings to the press was referred to the Clerk, but he could not indicate the feelings of the Trustees on that matter. A voice from the body of the Hall called out, 'Divided!', but all the same, Smeathman must have been aware of the meeting in 1890 when the vote went six to five against the press being

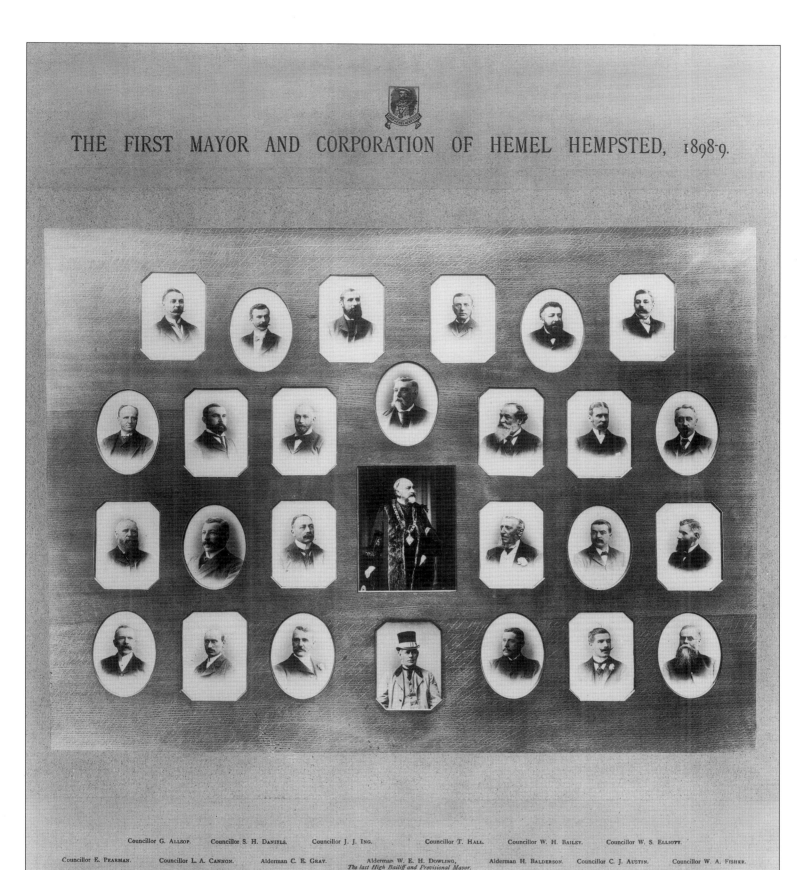

THE FIRST MAYOR AND CORPORATION OF HEMEL HEMPSTED, 1898-9.

Councillor G. ALLSOP.	Councillor S. H. DANIELS.	Councillor J. J. ING.	Councillor T. HALL.	Councillor W. H. BAILEY.	Councillor W. S. ELLIOTT.
Councillor E. PEARMAN.	Councillor L. A. CANNON.	Alderman C. E. GRAY.	Alderman W. E. H. DOWLING, *The last High Bailiff and Provisional Mayor.*	Alderman H. BALDERSON.	Councillor C. J. AUSTIN.	Councillor W. A. FISHER.
Councillor A. J. CHENNELLS.	Councillor Maitland THOMPSON.	Alderman C. A. COOPER, *Deputy Mayor.*	HIS WORSHIP THE MAYOR, Alderman Sir A. P. Paston-Cooper, Bart.	Alderman S. STALLON.	Councillor R. W. ROLFE.	Councillor H. PROCTER.
Councillor W. J. ORCHARD.	Councillor E. H. FLOWER.	Lovel SMEATHMAN, *Town Clerk.*	S. WILLIS, *Sergeant-at-Mace.*	W. SUMMERFIELD, *Treasurer.*	Councillor P. H. SANGUINETTI.	Councillor E. FULLER.

The first Mayor and Corporation of Hemel Hempstead 1898–9. Many Box Moor Feoffes, Trustees and Clerks played a prominent public role in local affairs. Henry Balderson, A.J. Chennells, W.S. Elliott and C.E. Gray were all Trustees in 1898. Lovel Smeathman was also Clerk to the Box Moor Trust.

admitted. The distribution of shares for grazing was also mentioned by Mr Pearman, but again the Commissioner referred to the Act of 1809. The issue of the handing over of Boxmoor Hall to the Town Council was next on the agenda, when Henry Balderson remarked (one imagines with a sardonic smile), that the committee would be pleased to hand it over immediately, including the debt of between £200 and £300 that was still outstanding.

Mr Hewitt then took Balderson to task over some alleged property, in particular the Heath Park Hotel and the two villas adjacent to Boxmoor Hall which he claimed did not have title deeds and were built on Box Moor. Henry Balderson, the owner of at least one of the houses, counter-claimed the land had formerly belonged to the Revd Brooke Mountain, Vicar of Hemel Hempstead, and had never been part of the Trust's Estate. Smeathman intervened on Balderson's behalf and the Commissioner dismissed the whole question.

The High Bailiff, Mr Dowling, summed up the meeting, stating there was not one of them present who did not think that he could manage the Box Moor Trust better than the Trustees. However, he could not help realising the great debt of gratitude they all owed to the Trustees and their predecessors. He had deprecated the arrival of the Commissioner since he felt things were getting on satisfactorily and, apart from the Trust dinners, which he would like to see dispensed with, he did not know of any other fault:

'What he did deprecate indeed was that by any want of unanimity they should lose what had been of great advantage to the town and would be in the future – the disposal of the Surplus from the fund. He wished to hold on to that like grim death. He was sure the agitation which had brought about the enquiry was not supported by the old inhabitants of the place … Perhaps the result of the enquiry would do good, but it probably might have done a great deal of harm. It had been the most unpopular thing in the town.'

The Assistant Commissioner's views were that the Trust had welcomed the Inquiry and 'would be glad to be shown any points in which they might have unwittingly transgressed or fallen short of their duties under the Charitable Trusts Act'. There were certain technical points in which the requirements of the law had not been strictly followed and these could be set right without detriment to the Charity. He thought the matter of the extravagant dinners was already under discussion and would be mitigated shortly, before the official communication was received from the Commissioners themselves. He thanked everyone for the interest they had taken in the proceedings and the order they had preserved, and also Mr Smeathman for the assistance he had rendered. The Inquiry was then closed and inhabitants and Trustees alike left to wonder what it had all been about.

The follow-up meeting of Trustees to discuss the Charity Commissioners' Report was held on 23 March 1897. The Report stated that the provisions of the Act of 1809 could not be varied by the Commissioners, including re-distribution of rights of pasturage or separate representation by Bovingdon. They felt that more frequent appointments of Trustees should be made rather than waiting until the numbers fell to four or below. They also advised the vesting of the legal estate in the Official Trustee of Charity Lands.

It was felt that insufficient authority had been obtained for exchanges of land on at least three occasions: with Revd Mountain in 1841; for the subsequent sales of 1869 and 1871, and then for the purchase of the Commons in 1886. However, the Commissioners could find no grounds for impeaching the validity of the position of Henry Balderson or Samuel Stallon as Trustees.

The new lease granted for the wharf to Henry Balderson in 1892 was inconsistent with the duty of the Trustees and they should have realised he could not properly become the lessee of a property vested in him as a Trustee. The money gained from past sales should be put into a Capital fund and paid to the Official Trustee of Charitable Funds for investment. The dividends from this sum would then go into the General fund. The net receipts from gravel quarried from the Moor ought also to be treated as Capital and invested accordingly. It was fully acknowledged that the Trust should be exempt from Income Tax and it was recommended they should renew their application on this matter.

Overall, the Commission wanted to place on record that, whilst some aspects of the Trustees' past actions were open to criticism, on the whole they had administered the Trust with prudence and to the general benefit of the inhabitants of the parishes involved.

No doubt many local residents felt disappointed by some of these findings, but at least they had had the chance to air their views. The Trustees tried to economise on the bill for the dinners, but the Commission would only allow them 3s 6d each for moderate refreshments, against their suggested 15s each, even after a special meeting on this delicate subject in the Commission's office in Whitehall. The threat of referring the matter to the Attorney General must have concentrated their minds and the excess was eventually refunded by the Trustees. Over such trifles empires are won or lost!

Hemel Hempstead's Changing Status	
1539	Bailiwick – Bailiff
1850s	Bailiwick – 'High Bailiff'
1898	Borough – Mayor and Bailiff
1974	Dacorum District Council – Chairperson
1984	Dacorum Borough Council – Mayor

48. Dreams of a Scheme 1922–9

'Such possessions as the Moor should be highly prized, but perhaps gently so and if, to show our diamond off well, we lose a little in the cutting, the loss is really gain.'
Hemel Hempstead Gazette, 1912.

The Public Inquiry of 1896 faded from memory and the Trust continued its business more or less unchanged.

Then in December 1921 the Trustees agreed to lease a triangular piece of land of about 3 acres. The purpose was to erect a bandstand, bowling-green or tennis courts, seats and a paddling pool. This area of Moor End later came to be known as Heath Park Recreation Ground or the George V Memorial Playground. The Moor was starting to be nibbled away.

The high-sounding Association of Borough Citizens was the next to make its voice heard in the on-going saga. In January 1922 they considered that the Act of 1809 was well and truly out of date and needed to be modernised. They recommended that Trustees should not be elected for life, but re-elected every three or five years. The elections should take place under the Ballot Act and nominations for vacancies should be made in accordance with the method of election to other local administrative bodies. By July matters had progressed in so far as the Clerk to Hemel Hempstead Town Council had visited the Charity Commissioners to talk about a completely new Act, but they felt that a Scheme would be less expensive and equally well able to effect the desired changes. On 11 October a reply arrived intimating that, because of the great pressure of work at the Commission, the subject should be allowed to stand over for a year or two. Consequently, the affair was shelved until April 1925, when the Council asked the Trust to pursue an alteration to the Act.

Nothing further seems to have been agreed and the next reference appeared in July 1929 with a letter from the Council suggesting it would be desirable if some of the Moors could be adapted for the fuller enjoyment of the public in general. 'This may need a revision of the Act to give more powers to the Trustees to deal with the Moors on more up to date lines.'

This innocuous sounding request was to have a chain reaction that far exceeded the wishes of those councillors. The Charity Commission was approached once again and on 30 July 1929 they responded by saying that the Trustees desired to transfer part of the Moors to the Town Council, to sell certain parts of the land which had good road frontages and to purchase other grasslands for the graziers. All of this would necessitate a Scheme approved by Parliament and it would all have to be discussed at a Public Inquiry, held by an Assistant Commissioner.

No time was wasted in producing the Draft Scheme and on 18 December 1929 it was agreed to forward it, together with the plan, to the Commission. Six months later a sealed Order from the Commission gave the Trustees the authority to grant a licence to Hemel Hempstead Council for twenty-one years at a nominal rent. Nothing more was mentioned about holding a Public Inquiry. Word must have leaked out, however, for behind the scenes rumours had already started circulating and people's emotions were aroused.

Publication of a series of letters and articles in the *Gazette* on the proposed sale of parts of the Moors for general building was the next outcome. Indeed, one irate resident went so far as to write a poem on this sensitive subject, after posing the rhetorical question as to whether the old church was the next to be pulled down to build a picture palace:

'Because it looked like an English town,
You pulled the famous shambles down,
Next the Samaritan window was smashed,
Because it taught you to love – and gave you cash,
Now you are going to destroy the Moor,
Because it belongs to the humble poor.'

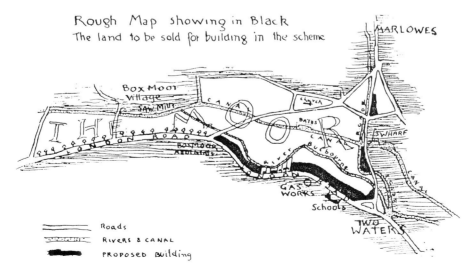

Map showing Trust land proposed for sale in 1929.

Two Waters Schools. A British School was started by non-conformists on 15 March 1869. The Baptist Minister, Revd H. C. Leonard, was the chief promoter. It was taken over by the School Board in 1875 and new buildings with a distinctive bell tower were added in 1878. In 1913 another school was built and by the late 1930s a Central School for older pupils was held in these premises. The modern Two Waters JMI School opened on the Manor Estate in June 1976.

What was all the fuss about? The Heath Park Recreation Ground, near the Heath Park Hotel, was apparently to be laid out as a formal park; the services of a Town Planning expert were being considered. Councillors Jarman and Moores were to visit other local authorities to obtain further information. The whole idea was heralded as a 'Big Improvement Scheme'. It had been devised in conjunction with the Charity Commissioners and major changes were envisaged, perhaps in reaction to the constant pressure for the Trust to 'modernise' itself and bring even more benefits, whether to the few or to the many being a part of the debate. A so-called 'gift of land to Hemel' was, in essence, a shift of land in the terms of the historic Box Moor Estate.

Under consideration was:

'The purchase of land on the Chaulden Estate to replace the land it is proposed to sell or to devote to other purposes. Through the generosity of the Playing Fields Association the Trustees, who had no funds, have been able to pay a deposit on the purchase of the land from Col. Mahoney. The Trustees propose to provide a recreation ground in the parish of Bovingdon. They also propose to sell, for building development, the frontage (to the depth of 150 feet), between the Bell Hotel to the Princes' Arms. They will leave sufficient ground at the back of these sites to allow for playing fields for the Central and Two Waters Schools.'

As if that were not enough, the statement continued:

'They will make a free gift to Hemel Hempstead Council of the Heath Park Recreation Ground, the land between that ground and the Canal, from Balderson's Wharf to Heath Park; the present Hemel Hempstead cricket ground and all that portion of ground down to the canal on the left going towards Boxmoor Station, including the present Boxmoor Baths; the piece of ground up to the wall of St John's Churchyard, on which the tank now stands and that piece of land on the right-hand side of the road running from the River Gade at Corner Hall to the railway bridge.

It is also proposed to offer for sale the frontage between the old Two Waters Mill and the Canal and on the opposite side of the road, the Trust property between Balderson's Wharf and the Triangle Garage; also the frontage of Moor on the left-hand side of the road running from St. John's Road (Three Blackbirds) to Horsecroft Road.'

What, we might ask, would have been left of the Moors today, for the benefit of the 'heirs and assigns' of the district? All the Trust had stood for during more than 300 years was to be swept away in the name of progress and improvement. Not only the Estate, but also the means of managing it, was to be demolished: 'The Scheme provides for the abolition of the old-time system of election of Trustees, and Hemel Hempstead Council and the Bovingdon Parish Council will be empowered to appoint members of the Trust'. In effect, the Council and the Trust were to become one, with all the hidden dangers that such a situation could provoke ignored or minimised by the powers that were then in control … or so they thought.

Eventually, the body of Trustees was to consist of ten 'competent persons', four of whom would be appointed by Hemel Hempstead Council and one by Bovingdon Parish Council. They would each serve for a term of four years. The other five would be co-opted by the Trustees themselves as vacancies occurred. To begin with, the nine Trustees in existence at the time would remain as 'Co-optative Trustees', until their number was reduced naturally to below five, when the new system would operate. Bovingdon was always to have two representatives, one co-opted and one appointed by the Parish Council.

All of these alarming proposals, it was claimed, could have been accomplished at very little expense by what was known as an 'omnibus Act of Parliament'. This would have been presented in January 1931, amongst other Schemes sanctioned by the Charity Commission. It was certainly the most far-reaching project presented to the inhabitants for many years, but not everybody wished to join in and congratulate the Clerk on his hard work to bring this about.

One of the main reasons given for these draconian measures was the general dissatisfaction with the method by which Trustees were elected, which in the past had given rise to the objections to the Charity Commission. Added to that, the Moors occupied a large proportion of the centre of the Borough, across which every municipal service, sewers, water pipes and so on, had to be laid and from which no rateable return was received. This, it was felt, caused local government services in Hemel Hempstead to be much more expensive than necessary. The Trust acknowledged its main considerations for the graziers and inhabitants of the two parishes but did not feel that its new Scheme would affect these in any deleterious way. The extra grazing land would become available at Chaulden Meadows: 26 acres between Chaulden House and the canal. The plots suggested for sale were 'of no particular importance from the grazing point of view, but were building frontages ripe for development'. They had jumped at the chance to make these changes by means of the omnibus Act, thereby cutting costs which would have been prohibitive for the Trust at that time. The perceived need of a public park and playing fields could also be incorporated into the Scheme. All parties concerned were obviously feeling very pleased with themselves.

However, they had reckoned without 'Joe Public': protests poured into the local paper from all sections of the community. Objections were raised on several counts, some disbelieving the Trust's expectations of being able to sell 'waste, boggy land' in a damp position as prime building land, preferring even more choice areas to be offered for redevelopment (but this may have been a deliberately sarcastic viewpoint, intended to irritate). Others were dismayed that the Trust should even contemplate selling open spaces, especially as the Salmon Meadow in Apsley had gone, since it was generally believed that the Trust was there to prevent that kind of thing from happening.

Councillor A. J. Chennells (also a Box Moor Trustee) had made the recommendation at the Council meeting of the previous 15 November, that the Council's agreement to the contentious Scheme put forward by the Box Moor Trustees should be referred back to the committee. His feelings were that there did not seem to be many in favour of it, that it would entail 'very big work to carry out' and that there should be an opportunity for all citizens of the Borough to have their say in such an important matter. He also thought that open spaces were better in their natural condition and should be left alone. The Town Clerk informed him that objections had to be handed in by the sixteenth of the month; the Mayor said that he thought it should be voted on there and then, but Col. Brereton asked if the recommendations of the public meeting had been forwarded to the Charity Commission. The Town Clerk (Lt. Col. Smeathman) replied that he had already done so. Councillor Neal stated that the people who were making the most noise about the Scheme were those who knew very little about it, but Chennell's recommendation was eventually carried.

The Water Tower, Chaulden, c.1915. Part of Chaulden Meadows, now the home of Hemel Hempstead (Camelot) Rugby Football Club, was eventually exchanged for land required by the New Town Commission at Moor End. The old water tower and wheel, which pumped water to Chaulden House, together with a similarly ornate boat house, have long since disappeared.

49. 'Hands Off the Moor!' 1930

'Our Common is Doomed!'
Hemel Hempstead Gazette, 15 November 1930.

Alderman A. H. Jarman, writing in the 1950s in his little book of memoirs about life in Hemel Hempstead, summed up the feelings of the time when the plans of the Trust and the Council were laid bare:

'The local inhabitants, certainly in recent years, have been very jealous to preserve the Moor as a public open space, and when a Scheme was propounded a few years ago to build on certain of its fringes, and in compensation to extend the Moor to include the Chaulden Meadows, there was quite a furore of opposition …'

One of the principal objectors was Nathaniel Micklem of Northridge. He wrote a long and scholarly letter to the *Gazette* on 3 November 1930, but ended by saying in plain English that the Scheme was a bad one:

'The desecration of the Moor must not be allowed. Our open spaces are too valuable to be handed over to the speculative builder. Undue encroachments have already been made; further encroachments should be strenuously resisted. I appeal to the promoters of this Scheme to burn and forget it.'

The implications today if this had all come into effect are obvious enough: there would, in all likelihood, be no Trust cattle or horses; landscaped acres would greet the eye instead of lush water meadows filled with buttercups and rarer wild flowers and, quite likely, much of the Moor could now be covered with housing. As it is, the land leased in good will to the Council for a recreation ground eventually became the site of Kodak's offices – the needs of business and the collection of rates seemingly more important than children's fun and games.

Councillor Jarman believed that one of the main difficulties lay in the election of new Trustees; under the provisions of the Act of 1809, only householders of Hemel Hempstead and Bovingdon had the right to vote and in those pre-computer days the compilation of such a list would have been 'a most difficult and expensive undertaking'. Owing to these organisational problems and the cost of such elections, the vacancies on the Trust were often left unfilled for a long time.

The largest and most interesting meeting to be held in the Borough for years subsequently took place in November 1930, appropriately in Boxmoor Hall. It lasted for three hours and the tone was definitely antagonistic. Lt. Col. F. S. Brereton presided and was assisted by the Mayor, Alderman F. Stratford; the Clerk to the Trust, Lt. Col. Lovel Smeathman; and the Chairman of the National Citizens' Association, Capt. H. E. Holme. The latter organisation had been approached by several members of the local branch and it was this group which had staged the meeting. The situation was initially explained by the Clerk, in particular stressing that there was no intention of building all over the Moor and also that in order for the Trust to 'get up to date' with a new Act, a large sum of money, in the region of £1,000, would have to be expended. The Trust simply did not have access to that kind of money and so the Scheme seemed to be a good idea. Further, it would answer the need for more recreational space and Smeathman reminded his audience that there had recently

Northridge, Boxmoor, residence of Nathaniel Micklem, KG, JP, who was also the Liberal MP for West Herts. Micklem opposed the sale of Trust lands and later strongly objected to the idea of the New Town; he died in 1954, at the age of one hundred. Northridge Park and Northridge Way in Warners End continue the name, but the house is no longer there.

been plans to purchase land in Marlowes for that very purpose. The Trustees were required by the Charity Commissioners to replace any grazing land disposed of, and the site in Chaulden, although more costly than they had originally thought, was a fair exchange.

He referred to Mr Micklem's letter as being 'not very kind' and said the Trust were not anxious to sell, but were anxious to raise the money to buy the other land, so that they could make a gift of the 17 acres to the Council. In the meantime, they had realised the error of their ways and were withdrawing from plans to sell the piece of land from the Three Blackbirds to Horsecroft Road. This raised loud applause. The total area for sale would be 7 acres of open Moor, made up to 13 acres because the County Council wanted land for road widening. One of the ultimate objectives was to finally get rid of the Star Cottages on Blackbirds' Moor and not many people disagreed with that. They could not sell a single portion without putting it into another Parliamentary Act or Scheme. He mentioned some old die-hard Tories who called themselves Liberals (amidst laughter) who detested change of any sort. He painted a vision of the future with 'a beautifully laid out public park, a magnificent swimming bath, filled with clean water and all heated, (more laughter), shady walks for the aged, paddling pools for the youngsters, a model yacht pond and other nice things'. He reminded his listeners that if there could possibly be any opposition to such an advantageous project then the whole thing would fall through (to more loud applause).

There were many no less persuasive arguments from the floor. Dr Macdonald believed the secretly concocted plan would deprive people of the use and advantage of the Moor, contrary to the 1809 Act and the original intent, and would deprive them of any voice in the election of Trustees. He called it a 'scandalous impertinence', amidst cheers. He was not at all happy about the choice of Chaulden Meadows or the asking price, which worked out at £200 an acre for mere grazing land, a price way above the usual sum. Finally, he was outraged at the notion that the Charity Commission would be allowed to establish further Schemes for the alteration of any of the provisions of the 1930s Scheme 'as if those provisions had been made by a founder in the case of a charity having a founder'. This last is an important point and one which had not been stressed up until that moment.

The dangers of having self-elected Trustees holding office for life were noted and the freedom of their curtailing the ancient rights of the local inhabitants, which must not be given up so lightly. Hugh Aronson, Chairman of Bovingdon Parish Council, felt that the Scheme had to be kept under wraps until the whole plan had been properly worked out. He welcomed the Scheme wholeheartedly, but living in Bovingdon, thought he was probably the least affected. R. T. Barnard, the Headmaster of Two Waters School, considered that, by rights, the Trustees themselves should have called that meeting in order to put the ideas to a ballot. He personally did not want

to lose the open nature of the Moor opposite the School. Jesse Hawkes, as a democrat, could not agree to the proposed system of election. Some thought the work of the Trustees was to keep their common land open. The irony of selling off the Moor in order to buy alternative grazing land was stressed by others. F. J. Mayo and Father Day were both opposed to the whole intention and the latter felt that a great injustice was being perpetrated against Apsley folk who would lose most of their open spaces.

Councillor Tozer mooted the undoubted advantages and Councillor Jarman said that no one had a monopoly of interests on behalf of the Borough – everyone was trying to do what they could in the interests of the town. He felt overall that the benefits would outweigh the disadvantages and that he wanted to get things moving. 'If they that night scotched the Scheme then scotched it would be, and then Box Moor would remain as it is.' At this point a heartfelt voice from the crowd called out, 'Thank God!'

Dr Macdonald subsequently put forward his resolution:

'That this meeting, having heard Col. Smeathman's statement of the proposed Scheme, and the objections to the proposed Scheme by other speakers, condemn the Scheme in its entirety and demand that it be abandoned for all time.'

This motion was seconded by Mr Boddington of Boxmoor, but it could not be taken forward by the Chairman. A further resolution by Jesse Hawkes, namely that the Charity Commissioners should be invited to hold a Public Inquiry into the matter, was accepted and carried by a large majority.

The letters swamped the local press over the next few weeks. People from as far away as Bournemouth wrote in, echoing the thoughts of many residents:

'If those who are seeking to destroy the amenities of the Moor are mentally incapable of valuing its aesthetic attraction and too stupid to see its future pecuniary value to the Box Moor of the next generation, then let them pause to think of the deep execrations that will follow those who first began to invade its quietness. For their example will inevitably lead to further desecration.'

Others were far more cynical, even to the extent of poking malicious fun at the whole concept. Mr Jolliffe suggested that since the Council had not yet installed its free crystal-gazing bothy in the market place he could only see one side of the question: 'How about commissioning Epstein for a few thousands to provide some figures for the bridges symbolical of councillors trying to "pinch" the Moor, and a few mermaids (with spots on) round the £50,000 public baths? Isn't there enough interesting work on the Council that you must needs look for Moor?' W. Christmas asked the *Gazette* to reprint the account of the 1896 Inquiry into the administration of the Box Moor Trust, which the paper duly did, and so the affair rattled on.

50. THE BOX MOOR DEFENCE LEAGUE

Cecil Sanguinetti in 1953; he devoted seventy years to the British Paper Company at Frogmore Mill. He was a member of the Moor Defence League in 1950.

Three Gables, Corner Hall, the former home of Cecil Sanguinetti. It is a late fifteenth- or sixteenth-century timber framed house, altered in the early seventeenth century.

Cecil H. Sanguinetti, Managing Director of the British Paper Company at Frogmore Mill, was the next to become involved in the great debate over the future of the Box Moor Estate. Another public meeting was quickly called for 4 December 1930, once again at Boxmoor Hall, with Sanguinetti in the Chair and Nathaniel Micklem KC as main speaker, together with Col. Blyth. The organisers termed themselves the 'Moor Defence League'. A capacity crowd of 250 people thronged the hall and even the Mayor could only find standing room in an ante-chamber. The resolution was put forward for a petition, which should be made available throughout the district for all interested parties to sign, namely:

'This meeting of inhabitants of the parishes of Hemel Hempstead and Bovingdon emphatically protests against the scheme of the Trustees of Box Moor, so far as it provides for the enclosure and sale of the Moor frontages along the London road and elsewhere, and so far as it provides for the purchase of 25.955 acres of the Chaulden Meadows for grazing purposes at the price of £5,000.'

Once again Micklem spoke movingly about the 'great tragedy' that would occur if the Scheme was adopted; one that was devised in the dark, behind people's backs and one that would have gone through without challenge. The Charity Commission had responded to his letter asking for a Public Inquiry with the conclusion that the Scheme had been so carefully considered that they did not think an Inquiry was necessary. The Society for Preserving Commons and Open Spaces, the Ministry of Agriculture and the National Playing Fields Association were said to have given their approval, but Micklem, in order to corroborate, had seen the Secretary of the latter organisation. He replied that he had not been shown the plans and did not realise they were taking away part of the existing Moor. The last vestige of control by the people would disappear and that was why there should be open elections and a public meeting held at least annually. This met with general approval and the meeting was concluded with enthusiastic applause.

The Charity Commission obviously relented and reacted to the depth of feeling shown in the public debates. On 11 December there was an Official Inquiry into the Scheme, held at the Town Hall. W. F. Fox, the Assistant Commissioner, conducted the affair which lasted from 2.30pm to 7.40pm. There was, once again, a healthy attendance by the general public and Micklem was in fighting form. He maintained that the Trustees were guilty of making the graziers' rights paramount compared with the rights of the inhabitants. Mr Capper, Secretary to the Hertfordshire branch of the Council for Preserving Rural England, spoke against the plans. H. D. Weston affirmed that he was prepared to contest any councillor shown to be in favour at the next local elections and this 'brought the house down'. The petition signed by more than 5,000 residents over the age of sixteen was then produced by A. J. Forshew, Chairman of the Defence League.

The defenders of the draft Scheme then had their say, noting that Hemel Hempstead was considered the 'most backward place in the county in respect of recreation grounds'. The Commissioner finally deduced that it was clear there could be no agreed Scheme whilst it was proposed to sell any of the frontages, following appeals for a compromise over the land for a recreation ground. In conclusion, it was decided that the Mayor would meet the Trustees and the main objectors to discuss the whole matter and to establish whether or not a Scheme of any kind could be the outcome. Mr Jolliffe handed in a written objection to the Charity Commission at the end of the long and sometimes heated meeting. There followed a full account in the local paper and then the news that the Charity Commissioners were not intending to proceed with the Scheme 'during the present year'. Since the year was almost at its close, that was not a difficult conclusion to reach.

Councillor Jarman felt moved to write to the paper that a similar impasse existed in Chippenham, where six 'Freemen cow-keepers' objected to the fencing of their ancient Borough lands for a recreation ground; the Council were the Trustees, but even they could not alter this situation. Therefore, they, too, could not proceed with a Scheme and he complained about the 'dead hand' which jealously guarded ancient grazing rights. Jolliffe accused the councillors of footling about with Boxmoor instead of doing more to make Hemel Hempstead town an attractive place. He tartly added, 'Keep the Council off the Moor', and that was finally what transpired.

However, the Defence League was still active in February 1931 and the Secretary, C. G. Jenkins, informed the press that any emergency that arose would be publicly announced. Alderman Fletcher was the most far sighted in the circumstances. He argued that the Trust should publish its Accounts, hold an Annual Public meeting and that Trustees should no longer be elected for life.

The Charity Commission produced their findings and a copy went into the *Gazette* in March 1931. They believed that the real benefit of the Scheme had been lost sight of, in objections to certain details, perhaps deliberately glossing over the main objection: the sale of any part of the inhabitants' inheritance. They emphasised the gain of 31 acres, even if it meant selling building frontages:

'The Commissioners have no wish to press on the inhabitants of Hemel Hempstead and Bovingdon a Scheme which is not generally acceptable, but they cannot help feeling that the opposition is partly based on misunderstanding, and that if this opportunity of adding 31 acres is lost the inhabitants a few years hence will regret the short-sighted opposition of today.'

The Commissioners did not intend to take any further steps themselves until the two parties had met to sort out their immediate differences, hopefully with a view to modifying the draft Scheme.

Micklem could not let any opportunity pass to underline the important issues and sent a reply to the *Gazette* on 11 March. He pointed out that the additional 31 acres (in fact about 25 acres) had been an afterthought to the idea of a Scheme and was for the benefit of a minority – the graziers – not the majority. The 'remote and unfrequented area' of Chaulden was a small recompense. The short-sightedness of the opposition was not a fact, merely the Commissioners' opinion.

The Trust minutes of 27 February record the formation of a joint committee, established in an attempt to resolve the issues. It consisted of three members of the Town Council, three Box Moor Trustees, one member appointed by Bovingdon Parish Council and four from the Moor Defence League. The points to be discussed were: a decrease in the area of the Moor to be sold; a decrease in the quantity of land proposed to be purchased and the question of grazing rights.

The Mayor, Councillors Jarman and Tozer subsequently had a 'very nice meeting with the Box Moor Trustees and representatives of the Moor Defence League' on 10 March and said they would be meeting again to discuss it further. Conversely, Micklem stated they had not had sufficient notice to properly appoint their members and he could not say the meeting was either particularly helpful or fruitful. The Council was still waiting for further suggestions from the Defence League in April, subsequent to a general meeting at Boxmoor Hall on 21 March. The prime objectives of the League were outlined: 'To retain the Moor for all time as an open space; the reconstruction of the Trust under which the Moor was held to bring it more up to date; to co-operate with the Box Moor Trustees in any scheme which, while retaining the Moor as an open space, would improve it for the benefit of the inhabitants of the parish of Hemel Hempstead and the hamlet of Bovingdon'. No-one voted against these objectives.

51. THE SCHEMING CONTINUES

The excitement of the 1930s 'Hands Off the Moor!' campaign rumbled on well into the following year. Walter Elwes, resident of Yew Tree Cottage, Boxmoor (now Yew Tree Court), complained to the press that Dr Macdonald's suggestion whereby the Box Moor Trustees should acquire the fishing pool known as Bourne End Mere would be very unpopular with the Boxmoor and District Angling Society who leased the fishing rights from the Westbrook Hay Estate. He hoped that: 'the Trustees will keep their hands off the one place in the neighbourhood where local anglers can enjoy their sport without interference by the general public'.

The Council's Development Committee turned itself into the Town Planning Committee and the Draft Scheme of the Box Moor Trust was left on hold, pending the receipt of suggestions from the Box Moor Defence League. There was a struggle between two opposing views, that of the graziers and the public at large, which was believed by some to be at the heart of the dispute, and the proposed new Scheme was thought to be a chance to bring these things into conformity with the new times.

'They give insufficient weight to the fact that what has been done by an Act of Parliament is not eternal. It is frequently an act of new wisdom, avowedly wiping out the old and effete.'

The compliance of the then Trustees was being questioned, also the Council's tame acceptance of the status quo, all of which just added to the impression that the public protest was viewed as a temporary wave of feeling. A strong argument was made for not maintaining the old grazing acreage, in the name of justice and common sense. A postponement of a final decision by the Charity Commission until after the election of 1 November was requested.

The Box Moor Defence League went ahead with their open meeting at Boxmoor Hall on the evening of 21 March. Nathaniel Micklem KC was Chairman and attendance was good. The opposition to the sale of any frontages of the Moor and to the consequent purchase of Chaulden Meadows in lieu of land lost was as vehement as ever. One resident commented that he foresaw that the trend of development in the Borough was to make the Moor as much in the middle of Hemel Hempstead as Hyde Park was in the centre of London. Another thought that if they gave up one inch of the Moor they would regret it. Micklem himself stressed that the point of public meetings was to decide on the Trust's Surplus which had fallen into abeyance for some years, mainly because there had been no Surplus to distribute, but that should not negate the beneficiaries' involvement in the Trust's affairs. If the policy of the Trust had been openly declared, he felt there would not have been any Scheme to debate in the first place. He called for the removal of the iron railings around certain enclosed stretches of the Moors and asked that the Trust itself should consider holding all the grazing rights to let as needed. The final vote was unanimously in favour of the resolution and the action points that had been sent to the Clerk to the Trustees.

At the April meetings of the Box Moor Trust there was no further mention of the Scheme or of the Box Moor Defence League. However, in May, a further meeting with all parties was contemplated. This took place on the 9 July 1931 at the Town Hall. The grant of the lease to the Town Council of two pieces of land at Moor End, for recreational purposes only, was under discussion. This idea progressed in October, with the added request of £150 in cash for the Trust and yet more meetings were envisaged. The Heath Park Recreation Ground was formally opened to the public on 29 June 1932. Another six years were to pass before the word 'Scheme' surfaced again and it was brought forward that a revival of the idea should be discussed with the Council. Recreational land and Trust Elections were then seen as key issues.

The Trust minutes of 5 July reflected the change of attitude since the previous attempt to introduce a Scheme: 'It was further agreed that the Public should be fully informed from time to time of the discussions which were proceeding and the various suggestions made on both sides'. Nevertheless, a year later the Council were again suggesting that the Trustees should have powers to sell part of the Moor.

The new proposals were agreed in principle, apart from the suggestion that the Council wanted to appoint six Trustees out of twelve. The Trustees carefully considered this option but decided that three from Hemel Hempstead and one from Bovingdon would be a sufficient number of appointed representatives.

This contentious Scheme never came to fruition, due this time to Britain's formal declaration of entry into the Second World War on 3 September 1939. This paramount event overshadowed the need for a resolution. Five days later the Charity Commission postponed any further proposals. The whole question was shelved until after the war.

The George V Memorial Playground, a favourite spot for children until the early 1960s. It was moved to the Water Gardens to accommodate Kodak House, and then to Gadebridge Park. There were swings, a see-saw, a rocking cradle, a paddling pool and later, a roundabout.

52. THE WAR YEARS

'Dulce et decorum est pro patria mori.' (It is sweet and fitting to die for one's country).
Horace II *Odes* ii, 13

There is a trench in the Newfoundland War Graves Cemetery on the Somme simply called St John's Road. It is as far distant from the leafy Moors and sparkling streams of St John's Road, Boxmoor, as anywhere on earth could be, yet it sums up the feeling of the ever present reality of life and death on this planet as men have made it. No war has inflicted such a scourge on our own landscape, and gruesome relics of former battles are not commonplace here, but this district has sent many men and women away to war and not always seen their safe return.

The Loyal Hemel Hempstead Volunteer Infantry Corps was formed in Hemel Hempstead in the nineteenth century, shortly after the 1798 Defence of the Realm Act of George III which authorised associations for local defence. There were one hundred men in one company and the uniform was red, with yellow facings and silver lace. The company was disbanded in 1808, when it was partially absorbed into the Western Regiment of Hertfordshire Local Militia.

The Government of 1812 had earmarked Box Moor as suitable land on which to erect powder magazines. The Trust asked for £150 per acre, which the Board of Ordinance thought was far too much and therefore it appears unlikely that this affair was ever concluded.

The Hertfordshire Yeomanry, like their later counterparts, were involved in drill practice on the Moor opposite the Swan in 1891. The end of the Boer War was marked by celebrations paid for out of the Hemel Hempstead share of the Surplus from the Box Moor Estate.

Troops and the blacksmith outside the forge, Fishery Road, during the First World War. The 7th Brigade of the Royal Field Artillery occupied Box Moor with their horse lines. Hemel Hempstead was a garrison town and many London army units came to the area's open land for training.

As a sign of the changing times at the outset of the First World War, Robert Balderson asked if Boxmoor Wharf could be insured against aircraft and bombs. Mr Prudance, the vet, was on military duties and, owing to the exigencies of war, grazing was extended until 12 December in 1917.

During that period, troops had encamped on the Moors without the consent of the Trustees and caused damage. The 7th Brigade Royal Field Artillery needed to use Blackbirds' Moor to picket 540 horses, guns and ammunition. They were given permission to swim in Boxmoor Baths, but were told to keep off the Boxmoor cricket pitch! It must have been a constant reminder of the battles being fought on foreign soil to see all those signs of weaponry. Mr Edney and Mr Luck of Hollybush Row helped to look after the horses that returned from the Front and gave them a chance to recuperate on the Moor.

Postcard by Edward Sammes. Money was raised locally to sponsor battleships, such as HMS New Zealand. Her Captain was Sir Lionel Halsey during the First World War. This appealing photograph of the model battle cruiser, made for the Oxford Club Brotherhood Parade, was taken on Blackbirds' Moor near to Star Cottages.

The official Declaration of Peace at the end of the First World War took place on the Moor on 19 July 1919. Lt Col. Lovel Francis Smeathman received the DSO and MC.

The National War Savings Tank at Heath Park, Boxmoor. It was given to the town in 1920 in recognition of record savings. There was some controversy later when E. A. Mitchell-Innes KC CBG of Churchill wanted the 'rusting old heap' removed, which eventually happened in 1931.

Celebrations on Peace Day, 19 July 1919. Church bells were rung, a grand parade with decorated floats and a children's tea party were held. The day culminated in a torchlight procession and bonfire on Roughdown Common.

Memorial Hall, Bovingdon. A memorial to those who lost their lives in the First World War; the land was given by the Ryder family and during the Second World War it was used as a classroom for London evacuees and as a recreation centre for locally based troops. The front extension, added in the 1960s, covered the original inscription: 'To the Glory of God in thankfulness for Services Sacrifices and Victory 1914–1918'.

War Memorial, unveiled in 1921, on its earlier site near the Plough Inn. Both were removed when the Plough Roundabout was constructed c.1954.

The War Memorial in its present position, near St John's Church. Services are held there on Remembrance Sunday.

From the outbreak of the Second World War in 1939, the military utilised the Moor for infantry drills and the cattle were allowed to stay on the pastures to eat off the surplus grass. Guns were placed on the Moor early in 1940, but the Herdsman was more concerned about the troops stationed at Boxmoor Hall who were continually playing football on the Hemel Hempstead Club's cricket pitch. The troops were allowed to play on the pitch opposite Boxmoor Wharf, however. The railway arch was designated an air raid shelter, as well as others which were purpose built on the recreation ground at Moor End. Coal was stored on the Moor at Cotterells and suitable sites were discussed for growing potatoes. Eventually 6 acres of the Moor opposite Westbrook Hay Lodge were planted with potatoes and in these small ways the Trust helped with the war effort.

The Trust also opened a Post Office Savings Account for Warship Week in March 1942, and for War Weapons Week in the previous year permission was given to the Auxiliary Fire Service to give a display on the Moor opposite the Three Blackbirds. The Moor was used for drill practice and there are still concrete gun mountings near the former Herdsman's Cottage. The Army (Eastern Command 7th Devonshire Regiment) was renting the car park opposite Dunbar's Nursery in Park Road for their trucks. This continued up to Christmas Day, 1944. The Commons were requisitioned for military training until mid-summer 1946.

Work on widening Box Lane commenced in 1942, partly due to the extra traffic necessitated by the airfield at Bovingdon. The American 8th Army Air Force took over the base from No. 7 Group RAF Bomber Command during August 1942. The 'Memphis Belle' was often to be seen there and the airmen's presence was certainly felt in the local shops and pubs. Celebrities of the day, including Glenn Miller, Clark Gable, James Stewart, William Holden and Bob Hope all visited the base, either as entertainers or as servicemen in transit. The airfield reverted to the control of the RAF in 1946 and it was eventually closed in 1972. Part of the site is now HM Prison, The Mount, (Bovingdon) and an open-air market is held where once bombers took off for daring missions in enemy territory.

The Home Guard, or Local Defence Volunteers as they were first styled, was active in the Hemel Hempstead area. Ernest Maurer, a teacher at Corner Hall Senior School, wrote down his experiences of that traumatic period. He thought that he would like living in Boxmoor, with 'its open land like a big village green, if Hitler will leave us alone'. In August 1940 he wrote to his fiancée in Sheffield:

'There has been plenty of aerial activity over here lately, bombers and fighters going to and fro, … it does seem a shame that such lovely days and nights should be spoiled by shadows of fear and destruction … I learnt this morning that a bomb fell in the next road and flattened four houses. Two people have died from the effects and there are about ten injured, which I think is amazing as the houses are just heaps of rubble.'

On Wednesdays the Home Guard met at the Heath Park Hotel for talks and lectures on important matters such as map-reading skills. The uniforms were patchy and ill-fitting, the equipment often non-existent, but they played a vital part in the defence of the realm in those depressing days, their presence helping to boost morale. At the end of the War they were asked by the Trust to fill in the three gun pits they had constructed.

Hemel Hempstead Home Guard, spigot mortar training beside the railway embankment on Fishery Moor, during the Second World War.

'Wings for Victory' baseball game, 30 May 1943, organised on the Moor by American airmen stationed at Bovingdon airfield. Boxmoor Cricket Club played return matches of cricket with the airmen.

September 1945, Victory in Japan Day Party for local children at Heath Park. Street parties were held throughout the district to celebrate the end of the Second World War. The Stars and Stripes as well as the Union Jack were proudly displayed possibly in recognition of the American airmen stationed at Bovingdon Airfield.

Remembrance Day Parade, November 2000.

Howes Retreat was transformed into a prisoner-of-war camp just after the Second World War. The inmates lived in ten huts with eight men to a hut. The old kitchen and dining room of Howe's occupancy, when it was a pleasure ground, were utilised and attached to the outside was the 'glasshouse' that was used for detentions. The POWs worked in the area as farm labourers and they also laid drains, built houses and, for relaxation, made slippers out of sacking, which were very popular with the local residents. They sometimes worked at clearance on Roughdown Common and it was recorded in 1946 that 'the work had been done very satisfactorily'. The prisoners were paid a token shilling a day in wages and supplemented this revenue from the slippers which were sold in a shop in Gossoms End.

At the end of the war they became civilians and some went back to Germany, but many stayed on to live in England and make a new life for themselves with their former enemies. The Government paid their return fare, but if they failed to return, they had to pay the money back. The camp was finally

de-requisitioned in 1950. The site was purchased by the Trust in 1979 and transformed yet again from a run-down pig farm into a winter shelter for stock. The large old brick building still remained for some years as a relic of its time as a POW centre.

The War Memorial at Heath Park, near St John's Church, is situated on land belonging to the Box Moor Trust but leased to Dacorum Borough Council. It had not been erected there originally, but was moved to that site after the construction of the Plough or Moor End Roundabout in about 1954. The Council were discussing with the Trust re-location of the Memorial in 1938 to take account of road improvements then under consideration. They did not envisage at the time all the extra names that would shortly be added to those from the First World War. The nearby Memorial Garden was later laid out for those who lost their lives in the Second World War. The names of the fallen in the Falklands War were also added to the War Memorial and Remembrance Day services are still held to honour those local people who have made the ultimate sacrifice.

53. SCHEME STALEMATE

The idea of major changes to the Box Moor Trust was taken up again in 1946 and the Trustees were asked to bring copies of the draft Scheme of 1930 and the suggestions of 1939 to the Town Hall meeting that was scheduled for 8 February. Tabled plans for a Scheme which had been presented confidentially to the Council at that meeting followed in the main those devised in October 1939, pending the end of international hostilities.

The Scheme made the following recommendations: that the twelve Trustees were to be made up from three appointed by Hemel Hempstead Council, one from Bovingdon Parish Council, six co-optative Trustees representing Hemel Hempstead and two representing Bovingdon. They would now only serve for three years at a time, not for life, but could be re-appointed. The control of the Box Moor Estate would thus have become intertwined with the local authority in a formal and defined way. The Trustees would have the power to decide on the application of the Surplus fund, providing it was for the benefit of the inhabitants, in the historic portions. The new Trustees would also have the power to buy, sell and exchange land, apart from the main Moors and Commons. They would be able to borrow money and let land for a longer period than the existing twenty-one-year leases. All the assets of the Trust were to be vested in the Official Trustee (Charity Commission), but the Trustees would still have the power to make Bye Laws enforceable before a Magistrate's Court.

The Trust was to address the long-standing debate over recreational land by giving the Council various lands that were at the time leased. These comprised land at Heath Park, together with the grounds of the Hemel Hempstead Cricket Club. It included land to the south of Heath Park, land between Two Waters Road and Old Corner Hall as well as the triangle opposite Park Road used as a car park. It also incorporated the triangle of land at the junction of Lawn Lane and Two Waters Road, which at the time accommodated public conveniences and a bus shelter.

The decision was taken not to proceed with the Trust's purchase of grazing rights by agreement, nor the idea of using the land at the junction of Two Waters Road and London Road, opposite the Transport garage, as a fairground in lieu of the usual site at Handpost Farm. The general feeling was that these two proposals would 'kill the Scheme'. The document finished with the words:

'The Trustees are particularly anxious that there shall be no public misunderstanding about the Scheme or the motives of the Trustees or the Council in propounding it and they say special consideration should be given at the appropriate time as to the best means of informing the public of the proposals.'

It was decided on 8 April 1946, that the Clerk to the Trust should interview the Charity Commission on the whole subject. Nothing materialised for another two years until 29 July 1948 when it was reported that the Clerk had corresponded with the Charity Commission; by 4 April 1949 it was noted that the matter of the appointment of new Trustees had become urgent and the Commission's views were imperative. They finally met on 22 April, but the Commissioners intimated that they still could not yet consider any general Scheme.

An important meeting was held between all the interested parties at the Town Hall on 28 June 1949, with the Mayor, Councillor P. White, in the Chair. The number of active Trustees had fallen drastically to only three. The Charity Commission had felt unable to consider a Scheme to modernise the Trust at that date, but would be prepared to appoint Trustees to fill the vacancies. They stated that any names submitted should be generally acceptable and two at least of the twelve should be resident in the parish of Bovingdon. It appeared doubtful that the Commission, in fact, had any powers to make appointments of this nature, but a shortlist of names was drawn up on the proviso that these Trustees would only serve for a limited period of ten years.

The local reaction to this plan was evident in a petition dated 27 July 1949 in which fifty-six residents asked the Council (not the Trust) to postpone their decision on the matter of new Trustees for Box Moor. They felt that consideration should be given to other nominations representing wider public interests. A public meeting was called for, to be arranged by the Trustees; failing that, the Council was asked to call such a meeting. The expense of holding a proper election was to be put on the agenda. A stalemate situation was averted by a more provident project.

Dacorum Borough Council erected and still maintain this playground on Blackbirds' Moor, by agreement with the Trustees. More play equipment has been added and it has been fenced since this photograph was taken.

54. THE NEW TOWN

'It may be that the village of Hemel Hempstead must die in order for Greater London to live.'
Attorney General Sir Hartley Shawcross, July 1947.

One of the aftermaths of the Second World War was the concept of the 'New Town'. The streets of London had been devastated by the Blitz; there were increasing numbers of people who wanted to work there and space was at a premium. Professor Abercrombie's Greater London Plan of 1944 proposed the novel idea of satellite towns around the capital, which would require wholesale movement of industry as well as a major population shift. Hemel Hempstead was first considered, then rejected, and finally chosen as one of the sites. The New Towns' Bill of 1946 had an immediate effect on the district. Not since the 'Hands Off The Moor!' campaign of the 1930s had there been such a flurry of public dissent. All the protests proved to be in vain, however, and the newly appointed Development Corporation had the unenviable task of transforming a quiet market town of 22,700 into a mini-metropolis of 60,000 inhabitants.

G. A. Jellicoe was the fortunate choice as general planning consultant. His vision for the metamorphosis of this large, virtually green-field site, was intended 'to include all human diversifications and should be the modern counterpart of the cathedral city'. His overall plan of 'neighbourhoods', rather like little villages, surrounded by open land, remains relatively intact today. The area was already well known for all its 'Ends', or nearby hamlets, such as Bourne End, Piccotts End and Potten End, and to these hamlets brand new neighbourhoods were to be added, with all the facilities of established villages. The existing outlying areas of Apsley and Boxmoor became a trifle overlooked in the process, however. Many of Jellicoe's grander ideas were never put into practice, such as the closing of Apsley and Boxmoor stations to build one central passenger station at Two Waters, or the diversion of the A41 south of the railway line. The West Herts Hospital was to be moved, possibly out of the town itself, and its position used as a market place. The industrial area that centred on Cupid Green was to boast a sports stadium and arena. The plans for the leisure facilities were amazing – art galleries, golf courses, museums, theatres, artificial lakes and no less than three Country Clubs:

'The valleys become water meadows, parks and gardens – beyond the encircling road lies the unchanged countryside of cultivated fields and farms, hamlets and woodlands which in Spring are carpeted with bluebells and primroses.'

The Moor was to be cleared ultimately of all obstructions, short lengths of road across it being suppressed so that it could become a 'leisurely summer resort with boating and bathing, the pace being set by barges on the canal and swans on the river'. In one sense, these things have come to pass and the Grand Union Canal has seen the end of its former use as a commercial waterway. In 1968 it was officially designated as a cruising waterway. Another element of the planner's vision, the public ownership of the 'fine parklands at Westbrook Hay', was also to come to pass, albeit nearly fifty years later!

Naturally, the Trustees were represented at the Public Inquiry about the proposed New Town on 2 December 1946 at St John's Hall. The Trust had just learned that the Charity Commission could not go ahead with a Scheme on their behalf, but that they were prepared to entertain an application for an Order to appoint new Trustees, so there was plenty to debate at the time. An objection to the New Town's Draft Order was sent in by the Clerk after he had interviewed four of the Trustees. By April 1947, the Clerk had received a copy of the Notice from the Ministry of Town and Country Planning designating the area of the proposed New Town. Mundane matters then took over the Trust meetings until September 1948 when the Trust gave permission to the Hemel Hempstead Development Corporation to sink exploratory boreholes for building suitability near the Plough Inn and at Cotterells. A stronger feeling was expressed in August 1949 when it was reported that the New Town Scheme would affect Trust property by encroachment of roads on the Moor, for instance, as well as the inevitable demolition of properties that would result; for those reasons it would be opposed. The next Public Inquiry was scheduled for 15 November 1949 in order to comment on amendments to the original 1947 Master Plan.

The Trust was by then down to only five members and the Chairman, Col. Middleton, wanted to resign owing to ill health. St John's Hall was becoming a busy place for public meetings and another was held on 4 May 1950 to consider the method of appointing further Trustees. The Mayor, Councillor P. White, took the Chair and approximately 100 people attended. It was finally agreed on 9 June that nine new nominees should be appointed to bring the number once more to twelve active Trustees. A show of hands then gave the vote to Aronson and Jolliffe from Bovingdon; of the eighteen nominations from Hemel Hempstead, MacDonald, Procter, Oliver, Osborne, Snoxall, Day and Webb were elected according to a ballot of inhabitant householders.

Later that year it was resolved to allow the Charity Commission to incorporate a clause vesting the legal Estate of the Trust properties to the Official Trustee of Charity Lands. This Order was eventually sealed on the 21 March 1951, but when the process was finally completed on 18 June, the above clause was not, after all, included.

Compensation was requested from the Development Corporation for damage done to the Moor by the installation of sewers and surface-water drains from the pumping station at Apsley to Moor End in August 1951. Once again, vigilance was needed to protect the Estate from developers. The area opposite Boxmoor Wharf was to be re-instated suitably for a playing field after the work. Holes were dug all over the Moor at that time.

An aerial view of Moor End, 17 September 1954. Part of the Box Moor Trust Estate is shown, including Boxmoor Wharf, the allotments, the bandstand on the Moor and the sidings in Cotterells for the Hemel Hempstead to Harpenden Railway, prior to the development of the New Town. Today, the Box Moor Trust manages an estate of approximately 480 acres on behalf of the inhabitants of Hemel Hempstead and Bovingdon who live within the Trust's Area of Benefit.

Aerial view of Hemel Hempstead Town Centre. Work started on the new town centre in the early 1950s. The railway sidings alongside Cotterells were once on the left; the George V Memorial Playground and the railway embankment were where Kodak House now stands. The open ground on the left was formerly part of the original Trust lands.

Work started on the first new factory for the Central Tool and Equipment Co. Ltd from Richmond, in what was to become the Maylands Avenue Industrial Estate. New Town tenants began to move into the Adeyfield neighbourhood from February 1950 and sometimes had to climb the steep hill to Westbrook Hay to contact their landlord, the Development Corporation, on housing matters; the Estate Office was based at the former manor house.

Chaulden Meadows featured yet again and at last it seemed likely that the Development Corporation would allow the Trust to have 12 acres for grazing, subject to them agreeing to some part of the land being used for football and cricket if required. The Trust did not think they could accept the exchange on any terms tied to existing tenancies. This is now the ground leased to the Hemel Hempstead (Camelot) Rugby Club and the cattle peacefully graze elsewhere. The land was eventually exchanged for part of Cotterells and the triangular piece of land at Two Waters Road near Moor End Roundabout.

The old Harpenden line railway viaduct had been demolished in 1959 and offices for BP erected in 1963 to straddle Marlowes were an echo of the former railway bridge.

One controversial new development was the building of an eighteen-storey skyscraper for Kodak at Moor End in the early 1970s on the site leased to the Council since 1930. The Trust land previously occupied by the Heath Park Recreation Ground, or the George V Memorial Playground as it was then known, suddenly became transformed, dominated by an office block that can be seen from miles around. A Deed of Covenant for the exchange of the land was signed on 30 January 1968 by the Commission for the New Towns and nine Trustees. In return, the Trust re-possessed a similar sized plot of land previously bought by the Hemel Hempstead to Harpenden Railway Company, as well as the large sum (at the time) of £7,974 12s 'by way of equality of exchange'. It is quite possible that the Trustees of later years would have preferred to retain the Trust's part of the site and receive a share of the rental income from Kodak.

It took until 1971 before an Arts Centre was opened in Boxmoor Hall, but the promised art gallery and museum never did materialise. The Sports Centre was a little later in coming to fruition and the new indoor swimming pool, a welcome successor to the Boxmoor Baths, was officially opened in 1974. It was sited at Heath Park, where once had stood the house known as Churchill and where the large outdoor pool still existed. This was finally altered again in 1998–9 to become a complex of indoor and outdoor pools, but each one smaller in length and depth than the original 50-metre outdoor pool. The indoor diving pool was retained in the alterations.

Lower Marlowes, taken from the railway viaduct, prior to the coming of the New Town. The Waggon and Horses public house can be seen on the left. A pedestrianisation scheme began in March 1994 and further new developments are currently taking place to transform this area, once a neglected part of the town, into its modern centre.

Land Girls, working at Marchmont Farm, Piccotts End. The Second World War saw a huge increase in women's employment, especially in war work. By June 1944 the Women's Land Army had 80,000 members.

Harvest time at St Agnells Farm, Cupid Green in 1939. Several generations of the Stanbridge family farmed in Cupid Green and these photographs record familiar scenes of the past.

Prior to the arrival of the New Town, Cupid Green was a very small hamlet with its own shop, post office and hostelry; the latter was called The Cupid Inn, managed by Mr Minister.

Squire Godwin adapted his railway sidings in order that horse droppings cleaned from the streets of London could be brought to Hemel Hempstead and supplied to local farmers to spread on their fields.

Several farms were affected by the New Town development, changing the centuries-old landscape.

Rows of houses replaced fields and hedgerows as the building work advanced.

The brave new buildings of the satellite neighbourhoods and Marlowes, transformed into the main shopping precinct of the town, continued to appear throughout the 1950s and 60s. The first tenants mostly came from Acton and Willesden and were glad to have more space and cleaner air to breathe. The sight of so much open common land on their doorsteps must have come as a surprise to many and bus tours were organised to give the prospective residents some idea of the district. Industrial premises and schools followed and soon the Area of Benefit had expanded so much in terms of its beneficiaries that it would have been totally unrecognisable to the Trustees of 1809.

The new town centre, no longer in the High Street, but in Marlowes. The Odeon and Pavilion, major buildings of that time, have either changed their function or disappeared from the scene. This section is now pedestrianised.

Hemel Hempstead Engineering Company. The company was the first tenant of the newly constructed industrial estate near Cupid Green in 1950. The photo shows their new premises; Herbert Christopher was Chairman and Managing Director. Other relocated companies at that time included Alford and Alder, Rolls Razor Ltd and Addressograph Multigraph. Rotax Ltd (later Lucas Aerospace) followed in 1952.

The Water Gardens were designed by Geoffrey Jellicoe and completed in 1961. They remain an important feature, but all the buildings in the foreground have been demolished. This photograph was taken just before the office block (owned by BP) was razed in the 1980s, leaving a vacant site at the entrance to the town for many years. The proposals for the re-development include an enhanced setting for the river Gade. The covered shopping mall named 'The Marlowes Centre' now lies to the east.

The curved building echoed the former railway viaduct over Lower Marlowes. A complex called Riverside is now under construction. It will provide a major retail-led, mixed use development, comprising shops, a hotel, a health and fitness centre, car parks and a bus link. It is planned to create a pedestrian-friendly environment, similar to the existing pedestrianised area of Marlowes, and re-establish a fitting gateway to the town centre.

ENVIRONMENTAL ASPECTS

55. THE A41 BY-PASS

One of the greatest impacts on the Box Moor Estate in the twentieth century was the construction of the A41 By-pass, or, to give it its full title, the Kings Langley, Apsley and Berkhamsted By-passes. The ideas, debates, planning and public consultations instigated by such a major alteration to an existing road took up much time and effort from the middle to almost the end of the century. The Trust land was at the heart of this involvement.

It was said in olden days that whoever bought a home in Hertfordshire paid two years' purchase for the air. Certainly there seems to be no lack of people who want to come and live or work in Hertfordshire, but they all generate traffic. The Chiltern Gap formerly served the need for a communication route and so it was inevitable that this passage from London to the Midlands or the West should eventually be considered for general improvement. The volume and speed of modern traffic had made the older roads, cutting through towns and settlements, extremely uneconomical as well as environmentally damaging. Long before Professor Abercrombie reported on the Greater London Plan of 1944, which proposed a new highway network of ring and radial roads for the capital, schemes had been suggested to relieve the A41 in Hertfordshire and Buckinghamshire.

Protesters at the 1971 Public Inquiry, outside the Pavilion in Hemel Hempstead. The slogan of the 1930s appeared again!

Chelsea Speleological Society members surveyed the chalk mine on Roughdown Common in 1971, prior to the Public Inquiry that year.

The A41 Motorway was one solution offered up to alleviate the problem. By 1949 both County Councils had agreed that a completely new route was unnecessary. The preferred idea, of local by-passes together with general improvements along the existing route, was promoted. Such a route was included in the Hertfordshire Development Plan for 1953, confirmed again in 1958 and re-confirmed in 1963.

Pressure mounted on the Ministry of Transport in the 1960s to rectify the situation and a Public Inquiry was held in 1971. At the preliminary meeting at the Hemel Hempstead Pavilion in February, recordings of birdsong on Roughdown at dawn were played to the Inspector and contrasted with the harsh, incessant noise from traffic on the M1. The view of the Ministry was that their by-pass schemes would bring environmental benefit to Berkhamsted, Two Waters, Apsley and Kings Langley. The proposed new roads, however, would regrettably dissect Roughdown Common and parts of Box Moor.

In February 1974 Jack Bandle, the Property Agent for the Box Moor Trust, was instructed to prepare a map showing all the land that was affected and the land being offered in exchange.

The allotments at Two Waters were severely affected by the Link road to the A41 By-pass and were discontinued as a result. The allotment holders were informed of the Trust's intention to phase out their use by the end of January 1996. The first allotments on this site were started in 1903, when the land which was used by the GJCC for mud-tipping was let. The request to build pig sties on the site was refused in 1906 and no further areas of the Moor that were suitable for grazing were ever enclosed for allotments. During the Second World War, however, food was grown temporarily on other parts of the Estate.

Nothing further materialised from the Ministry and in 1980 it was noted that the Trustees' consensus of opinion was that they accepted that Dacorum had a traffic problem, but they should lodge a formal objection and also request a full traffic survey of the A41 in the area. They rejected the Trunk Road Action Committee's proposal of a route closer to Bovingdon, feeling that it was 'too far out' and appointed transport consultant Stefan Tietz to investigate alternative routes in November 1982.

The Motorway never came (paradoxically, for economic reasons), but the idea of an altered A41 did not disappear. Another Public Inquiry was set up in 1983 to look into the same vexed question. One active campaigner attended dressed all in black, in supposed mourning for the Moor. The local press called it 'a road to destruction'.

Peter Carter, for the Department of Transport, acknowledged 'in seeking to achieve these objectives regard has to be paid to obtaining value for money, to the inevitable loss of land, property and amenity that will result and the way people feel about the proposals'. The latter part of his statement certainly rang true. A special meeting was called by the Trustees together with representatives from the Eastern Road Construction Unit to consider the effect this would have on Trust lands and the possibility of Exchange land. Since up to 40 acres of land were affected, the Trustees' approach was to object to the scheme but not to suggest any alternative route.

There was no lack of local objectors to the proposals. The Boxmoor Residents, the A41 Trunk Road Action Committee (TRAC), the original Dacorum Environmental Forum and the Save Our Moors Committee joined forces to reject the idea of a major road taking away grazing and common land as well as people's homes. Twenty or so alternatives were put forward, either for minor variations, large sectional changes or for totally different routes. The Department of Transport, according to the Trust's Counsel, had had a long time to prepare its route compared with the objectors, but to many the outcome was a foregone conclusion anyway. The Department of Transport's need to weigh economics against environmental impact resulted in their preferred route being chosen. The land offered as Exchange land at that time was considered to be quite unsuitable and the Trustees decided to expend their energies and limited resources in fighting for a better deal in this regard.

A public meeting was called by the newly formed Save Our Moors Committee on 20 April 1983 at St John's Hall and the Trust's Chairman was its spokesperson. He indicated that the Trust would try for a route that would leave as much common land as possible intact.

By April 1985, following the Inspector's recommendation that no alternative routes were acceptable, the official announcement confirmed the preferred route: a mixed dual-carriageway and single lane road, not a motorway. A re-alignment of the road was allowed at Bourne End so that the new roundabout would take less of the Moor. In September 1987 a public statement was made regarding the Trust's objection to the route the road was to take and to the Compulsory Purchase Orders necessary to build it.

Still nothing happened on the ground and in April 1988 a further Inquiry was ordered. This was to investigate the revised route proposed by STAG (Save Trust Lands Action Group, an offshoot of TRAC). The Trust was now looking into supporting this route, which seemed to take as little common land as possible, subject to an analysis of costs

View from the top of the Kodak building, Moor End, summer 1985. The link road to the By-pass now crosses the allotments seen here on the left.

The famous 'Magic Roundabout' at Moor End in 1985. A flyover was proposed at one stage of the debate. The two-way system at this roundabout is unique and is now a landmark of Hemel Hempstead.

The beginnings of the Two Waters Link Road with the Engineers' compound on the left, looking towards Hemel Hempstead Town Centre, 24 November 1991.

against benefits. The Inquiry at its completion had covered forty-eight days, in over half of which the Trust had been involved. 'The Exchange land submission had been dealt with in a crisp, concise and logical manner in two days.' The Trust's case was ably presented by its Clerk, Tarn Hodder, assisted by Verity Calderan.

The STAG revision was to no avail and early in 1990 the Secretary of State confirmed the Department of Transport's preferred route. The proposal for a single lane across Trust lands was, however, replaced with a dual carriageway, a feature both Dacorum and Hertfordshire County Council had originally requested. One outcome which aroused some public interest was the demolition of the Herdsman's cottage, sited beside the Stevenson's skew railway bridge on the London Road, which happened to be directly in line with the new road bridge. A replacement house, with all modern amenities, was duly built on Exchange Land at Gee's Meadow (Box Hill) for the proposed new Estate Manager and his family before formal transfer of ownership was completed. This attractive accommodation was appropriately named Snook's End, the result of a different kind of 'highway robbery'.

From its initial conception in the 1950s to its final realisation in 1993, the cost of the By-pass had risen steeply, but one factor which had kept a high profile throughout was the environmental cost. This issue had always been at the heart of the Trustees' objections and, if they could not influence the route of the new By-pass exactly, at least they could ensure that a high standard of preservation and conservation of the local flora and fauna was part of the agreement.

The self-generating junipers on Roughdown Common, which were anyway part of the debate on saving the area from excavation, were scheduled for a programme of cultivation off-site by staff and students at the Writtle College of Agriculture

in Essex. This was undertaken on behalf of the Trust, the Department of Transport and English Nature. If successful, these young plants would then be re-planted on the Exchange Land and the embankment, which did indeed happen in 1996. The chalk downland features of the Common, a decreasing habitat in Hertfordshire as well as nationally, were to be replicated on the newly acquired Further Roughdown. The original nutrient-rich, arable topsoil was removed and the land was top dressed with a one-inch layer of the carefully retained topsoil from the Common which held the existing seed bank. The field was then sown with a selected wild-flower seed mixture. The presence of thousands of cowslips in the spring now bears witness to the success of the project. The exposed chalk of the steep embankments was mostly left to regenerate naturally, but in some areas more cowslips and other wild flowers were sown.

When the Trustees took over the management of Box Hill, known for many years as Gee's Meadow, it had been neglected for some time. They had quickly to establish grassland for immediate grazing needs to replace that taken by the By-pass on Snook's, Herdsman's and Snoxall's Moors. It has been a valuable addition to the Estate for grazing ever since. The cattle are nowadays joined by a flock of Norfolk Horn sheep, which would cause some amazement to those early Trustees who once banned sheep, stating 'they were an improper description of cattle to de-pasture on the Moor'.

The local badger community was also protected during the excavations for the By-pass and particular care was taken by the engineers, Brian Colquhon and Partners, to the extent of slightly re-aligning the embankment to save existing setts. Unfortunately, the necessary badger crossings were not put in place until some time after the opening of the Berkhamsted section, resulting in many badger fatalities along that stretch of the new road.

Desolation on the lower slopes of Roughdown Common as clearance gets underway, 28 July 1991.

Featherbed Lane crossing facing north, 31 May 1992.

The new bridge at Roughdown, over the A41 By-pass, during its construction in November 1993. At the Public Inquiry in 1983 the decision had been made not to site a new roundabout on Mugford's Moor at Bourne End, but on the hillside adjacent to Westbrook Hay.

This new bridge was necessary to carry the By-pass over the former A41 (now the A4251). The original Herdsman's cottage was pulled down as a consequence; the railway bridge is in the distance.

The A41 By-pass in 2000, cutting through Roughdown Common. The dissection of the Common was one of the major features in the debate. It was a fine line between seeking to achieve the best benefits to the Box Moor Estate against those to the community at large, by meeting local transport needs. The glimpse of cows peacefully chewing the cud whilst drivers wait impatiently at the link road traffic lights might help to alleviate some of the tensions of everyday life.

Junipers and chalk downland flora are slowly being regenerated on Roughdown Common and Further Roughdown. The buttercups, such a cheerful sight on the Moors in early summer, still thrive and give pleasure now to ever more travellers. The newly acquired land at Westbrook Hay and the Bovingdon Brickworks' quarry, although not Exchange Land, are a welcome extension to the Estate. Whether they will ever compensate for the loss of the quiet glades on Roughdown is a matter for personal reflection.

56. EXCHANGE LAND

The Box Moor Trust has for centuries been morally bound by its constitution never to sell land. It has, in the past, leased land for a variety of reasons and also leased properties built on its land. The exceptions have been very few, notably the sale of part of its holdings in the area of Two Waters Mill to the Fourdrinier brothers in the early days of machine paper-making and prior to the 1809 Act of Parliament.

The compulsory purchase of land for the building of the Grand Junction Canal, the London and Birmingham Railway and the Hemel Hempstead to Harpenden Railway has been dealt with in detail in other sections of this book.

Land has, on occasions, been exchanged instead. On 10 February 1875 the proposal by the Hon. G. D. Ryder of Westbrook Hay to exchange part of his estate, comprising the field opposite the gates to his drive that was once known as Mugford's Moor, for the house and garden at Old Pastures in London Road, was accepted. There was a proviso that he should level the field, make a fence throughout and keep it in good repair.

The major exchange of land in recent times has been part and parcel of the negotiations over the construction of the A41 By-pass. Further Roughdown and Gee's Meadow (Box Hill) were obtained through this deal. The former has been carefully reinstated with wildflowers and junipers, using the original top soil from Roughdown Common.

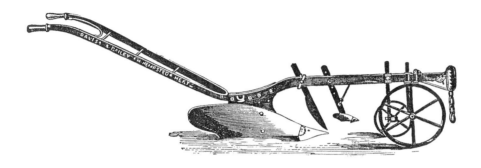

Plough manufactured by Davis and Bailey of Boxmoor Ironworks, Marlowes, Hemel Hempstead, c.1930

White Hill, (now called Further Roughdown), c.1900. Long before it became part of the Box Moor Estate, the land was used for arable farming up until the time of the exchange for the construction of the A41 By-pass. Landmarks such as the Gas Works, the Hemel Hempstead to Harpenden Railway embankment, Two Waters Mill chimney, the Lock House, Boxmoor Hall and Heath Park Hotel can also been seen in the distance.

Gee's Meadow (re-named Box Hill in 1993 by the Trustees, as previously shown on the Tithe Map of 1841). Children enjoyed fresh air and exercise on a railway excursion from London. Its acquisition as part of the Exchange Land proved to be an important link, leading to the Trust's expansion into the Westbrook Hay Estate.

Cowslips proliferate now on Further Roughdown, as part of the re-instatement of the land. It was sown with a wild-flower seed mixture. Junipers have also been planted here, with cuttings taken from Roughdown Common.

Common Juniper (Juniperus communis)

Old Pastures. *Sketch by Miss Ethel Salisbury, c.1930. The house is still in existence; it belonged to the Box Moor Estate until it was exchanged in 1875 with G. D. Ryder for land at the end of Snook's Moor, opposite the entrance to Westbrook Hay.*

Box Hill in 1999, important as a lambing station for the Norfolk Horn flock. The Estate Manager's home, Snook's End, is adjacent to the barn.

57. Environmental Management

The importance of the entire Box Moor Estate, which includes a designated Site of Special Scientific Interest (SSSI) as well as two Countryside Heritage Sites, necessitates the on-going involvement of many local and national bodies in the planning of its management policies. In 1977 the Nature Conservancy Council prepared some recommendations at the request of the Trustees. They emphasised that the interesting plant communities and rare species that still existed had been shaped and conserved by centuries of grazing, a beneficial regime that should, therefore, continue.

'The landscape of Box Moor is one of the few fragments remaining in Hertfordshire of ancient grassland on alluvial soils, unmodified by agricultural improvement and rich in wild plants and the insects they support. This type of vegetation, as well as being a valuable biological resource, is clearly more attractive to the general public than grassland which is managed by either modern agricultural methods or conventional municipal park treatment.

The area of greatest botanical interest is that part which lies north of the railway line and between the A41 (now the A4251) and the Grand Union Canal. The grassland here has suffered fewer changes than elsewhere and most of the rare plants occur in this part ... the maintenance of a high water table is essential for their conservation. The plant community would also be adversely affected by the application of fertilisers or herbicides.'

In the 1970s, the Trust, along with the majority of landowners, was unaware of the damaging effects of fertilisers and herbicides that were used in all innocence to improve the grazing on some parts of the Moor. Times have changed since then and the move towards broadly organic methods is impacting on planning.

This report of 1977 also stressed the value of Roughdown Common, particularly since the exposure of the chalk rock, a stratum of the chalk which is rarely seen in Hertfordshire. The Common, with its chalk grassland flora, boasts the only colony of regenerating juniper in the county and many species

Belted Galloways on Snoxall's Moor, 2000; grazing is used as an environmentally friendly management tool.

Norfolk Horn sheep graze on Westbrook Hay Estate, another example of environmentally friendly management, since they minimise the thatch smothering finer grasses and wild flowers. Soay sheep were initially introduced as part of the management approach, replaced by Norfolk Horns.

characteristic of former grazing land on chalk soils, such as orchids, and also gentians which rely on grazing to flourish. Rare breeds of sheep and cattle were recommended as the best choice to utilise agriculturally poor, but botanically rich, grassland. The fencing of Roughdown Common was seen as essential to this programme, together with the removal of ever encroaching scrub, whilst avoiding chemical treatment of the area. The report also recommended contact with the Hertfordshire and Middlesex Trust for Nature Conservation and firm links were established with that organisation.

The Box Moor Trust's current initiatives and management methods are important to continued conservation in the area, which is supported by initiatives such as: the Dacorum Nature Conservation Strategy; the Dacorum Agenda for Sustainability and the Environment Agency's Action Plan for the Colne Valley (which includes the rivers Bulbourne and Gade). These have all arisen in recent years to address the wider issues, as well as Dacorum's own Environmental Forum. English Nature advises nationally and, on 9 August 2000, the Trust received an award from them for the sensitive management of Lower Roughdown Common after the construction of the A41 By-pass.

The river Bulbourne and its associated wetlands, as well as the disused watercress beds in the Area of Benefit, have been identified as priority areas by the Box Moor Trust. Monitoring is crucial and a great deal more up-to-date scientific data is being compiled. Voluntary bodies such as the Hertfordshire Natural History Society, Hertfordshire and Middlesex Wildlife Trust as well as Hertfordshire Biological Records Centre can all help in this regard. The existence

of staff knowledgeable in these matters, along with their further training, are also seen as key factors for the future development of a sustainable Box Moor environment.

Re-introduction of species 'at risk' is one positive way in which the Trust can, and does, play a part. Duke of Burgundy Fritillary butterflies have already been released on the Estate since they were virtually extinct in Hertfordshire. Cowslips and orchids are now seen in profusion on Exchange land that was once extensively agriculturally cultivated. Water voles and white-clawed crayfish, two species causing concern nationally, are also under consideration for this programme, which is sometimes, but not always, achieved solely by providing suitable environments. However, the Trust's determination to manage its wide range of habitats in a way conducive to biodiversity will encourage many other species to re-colonise the area naturally. One of the key issues is to demonstrate, develop and encourage the links between people, wildlife and their environment. All the relevant associations, such as the Hertfordshire and Middlesex Wildlife Trust, are consulted and the Trust considers itself at the forefront in estate management techniques.

The former Bovingdon Brickworks quarry, acquired in 2000 has its own well-prepared management plan and this will become more obvious over the next ten years, offering all kinds of exciting possibilities for sensitive environmental enhancement. The Estate Manager and his team are all well aware of the huge scope and responsibility they have in putting these plans into practice, so that in the next 400 years the ecological treasury that we have inherited can develop naturally and have an assured future.

The water courses throughout the Estate have been receiving serious consideration for many years. This photograph shows the result of some of the initial work on the old watercress beds above Fishery Moor in May 1993. Surveys by John Leonhardt have shown that the water courses are in very poor condition overall, but have recently begun to show some minor improvement.

Lady's Smock on Fishery Moor, April 1987. This ancient water meadow has always been traditionally managed by grazing and is designated a Heritage Site. It is one of the most important and botanically rich water meadows on the Estate, and perhaps even in Hertfordshire, as the surveys by Rachel Hemming, Gerald Salisbury and Jill Saunders have shown.

Bluebells in Ramacre Wood, 2000. These familiar plants are believed to be vulnerable to the effects of global warming. Woodland management is aimed at preserving the trees and the under-storey of flora, as well as the wide variety of wildlife they support.

This wonderful display is the result of sympathetic re-instatement after the construction of the A41 By-pass. Roughdown Common SSSI was reduced in size prior to the planning of the new road. Is the time now ripe to consider expanding the SSSI, to include this area of orchids, gentians and other chalk grassland flora?

Cowslips on Further Roughdown, 2004. Childhood memories of fields full of wild flowers will hopefully continue to be part of life's experiences for future generations in the Area of Benefit.

The river Bulbourne and other watercourses on the Estate are receiving a great deal of consideration in an effort to increase their quality. Some improvement to the water meadows will be the next step.

58. FLORA AND FAUNA

'In the bottom of the river Bulbourne on each side be very faire meadows …'
John Leland, 1546.

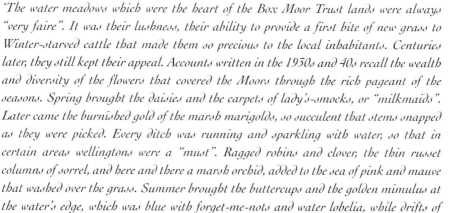

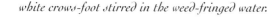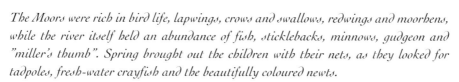

'The water meadows which were the heart of the Box Moor Trust lands were always "very faire". It was their lushness, their ability to provide a first bite of new grass to Winter-starved cattle that made them so precious to the local inhabitants. Centuries later, they still kept their appeal. Accounts written in the 1930s and 40s recall the wealth and diversity of the flowers that covered the Moors through the rich pageant of the seasons. Spring brought the daisies and the carpets of lady's-smocks, or "milkmaids". Later came the burnished gold of the marsh marigolds, so succulent that stems snapped as they were picked. Every ditch was running and sparkling with water, so that in certain areas wellingtons were a "must". Ragged robins and clover, the thin russet columns of sorrel, and here and there a marsh orchid, added to the sea of pink and mauve that washed over the grass. Summer brought the buttercups and the golden mimulus at the water's edge, which was blue with forget-me-nots and water lobelia, while drifts of white crows-foot stirred in the weed-fringed water.

The Moors were rich in bird life, lapwings, crows and swallows, redwings and moorhens, while the river itself held an abundance of fish, sticklebacks, minnows, gudgeon and "miller's thumb". Spring brought out the children with their nets, as they looked for tadpoles, fresh-water crayfish and the beautifully coloured newts.

There were also the annual rituals of waiting for the first horse-chestnut sticky buds to appear, to open out into the green fans of leaves which could be made into fish-bone patterns. There was the beauty of the white candle-like flowers and then the excitement of the first conkers. No local child could forget the thrill of seeing the white-silk lined prickly cases split open to reveal the polished brown chestnuts inside.

With some alteration in river flow, the canal and the new drainage systems necessary to cope with the increasing size of Hemel Hempstead, the Moors became drier and lost most of the flowers that depended on the watery habitat. Today, the Moors which most nearly resemble the original water meadows are Harrison's Moor and Fishery Moor, opposite the Fishery Inn in Boxmoor. They have been designated as a Heritage Site as part of Hertfordshire County Council's Heritage Project and are being managed in such a way that as many as possible of the water-loving plants and grasses may survive. People can thus have a reminder of the habitat which made the meadows so "very faire" in years gone by. In such a small compass it was a naturalist's paradise.'

In 1994 the Box Moor Trust celebrated its Four Hundred Years Anniversary and on that notable occasion Jean Stevens wrote the above in the *Hemel Hempstead Gazette's* special supplement. Jean produced regular monthly articles on behalf of the Trust, under the pseudonym 'Wayfarer' from 1987–92, and for *Bovingdon News* from 1991–8.

Various botanical surveys over the years show the veracity of this article. The restoration of the water meadows is a long-term aim of the Trust. Both controlling the flow and minimalising pollution of the rivers are important factors in this effort. To achieve this aim the Trust is currently trying to improve the overall environment of the rivers Bulbourne and Gade before improving the adjacent Moors.

Ornithologists find there is much of interest still to be seen on the Moors and Commons and, with over seventy different species represented, there are not many groups of British birds that are not seen in the local area. The open nature of Box Moor is attractive to space-loving birds and the avenues of chestnut trees are likely places to spot pied wagtails and thrushes. Redwing and fieldfare are regular winter visitors, also coal, marsh and long-tailed tits join the blue and great tits at this time, or even the elusive lesser-spotted woodpecker. More noteworthy is that siskins have been recorded breeding adjacent to the Moor and recently, hobbies, meadow pipits, warblers and woodcocks have all been sighted.

The former Bovingdon Brickworks now has one of the largest populations of nesting whitethroats in Hertfordshire and rare wasps found there mark only the tip of an iceberg in species conservation, once this unique habitat has been fully investigated. Bovingdon Reach has brought many nesting skylarks back to the district.

Roughdown Common is particularly rewarding for birdwatchers, with sightings of the green or the great-spotted woodpecker as well as fair numbers of blackbirds, dunnock, finches, robins, thrushes, tits, woodpigeon and wrens. One may occasionally catch a glimpse of sparrowhawks intent on their prey. Nuthatches and treecreepers are also residents of the Common; the rarer hawfinches and tree sparrows have been recorded in the past. Nightingales, unfortunately, no longer sing on the night air.

Sheethanger Common, especially Bury Wood, is an equally excellent and varied habitat attracting yellowhammers and linnets, besides all the above-named species. Kestrels join sparrowhawks to hunt the more open areas. Nocturnal birds of prey, such as tawny owls, are relatively widespread, while the new owl loft at Westbrook Hay Barn will hopefully become a permanent, safe residence for barn owls. These birds have been introduced from St Tiggywinkle's Animal Hospital, having recovered from accidental damage elsewhere, and care will be taken that they retain their wild instincts and are not dependent upon human support. The Trust has undertaken surveys for small mammals in the vicinity, to ensure that there is a natural food source available. Glis-glis, an escape from the Rothschild's estate in Tring in 1902, have also been sighted, and heard, since they make such a patter on the ceiling if they take up residence.

The presence of the Grand Union Canal, together with the rivers, brings the added bonus of water birds, such as heron, mallards, moorhen and coot. The tranquil and majestic swans contrast with the vividly flashing blue of a passing kingfisher. The muddied area alongside the river Bulbourne where it emerges from under the canal (known locally as 'The Chunks') is a place not to be missed early on a summer's morning. House martins congregate there to collect mud with which to build their nests on the sides of nearby houses. Swallows swoop down to drink and to hawk the low-flying insects.

The river in the Old Fishery Lane area, which formerly thrived with watercress beds fed by several artesian wells, was at one time full of fish, crayfish and invertebrates. Gudgeon, miller's thumb, minnow, stickleback and stoneloach could all still be found and even caught bare-handed by eager youngsters. Common snipe were regular visitors and occasionally water rail or the scarce Jack snipe might be seen. It is now an increasingly rare habitat and will need careful and informed management in the future to realise its undoubted potential. Fortunately, the newly instigated reed-bed for water cleansing has been a success, attracting water rails back to the area for the first time in twenty years. Reed bunting and sedge warbler now nest there too.

David Lees, a local contributor to the nest-recording scheme of the British Trust for Ornithology, spent many hours on Trust lands in the 1980s to record his observations in a booklet for the Trust:

'It is not unknown for redshank, snipe, water-rail, sandpipers and plovers to call into the cress beds on their way to Tring Reservoirs. It has become quite normal over the last few years to regularly see species such as goosander, goldeneye and widgeon, although the chance of them staying very long in this area is extremely remote. Among the regulars on the former cress beds is the grey heron which arrives first thing in the morning to catch what it can before being disturbed by the increase in human activity along the towpath.'

David also set up nesting boxes on the Estate, since Box Moor is an important part of the migration corridor as many species of birds fly up the waterways to the Tring Reservoirs; even ospreys have been recorded passing through.

In more recent years, the bat population has been ideally catered for with the establishment of a *hibernaculum* for winter hibernation in the recesses of the old chalk mines on Roughdown. These were sealed to human access in 1994 and the Hertfordshire and Middlesex Bat Group have carried out annual surveys since then. In 1995 some droppings were found, then nothing until 1998 when three brown long-eared bats were discovered. Two bats of the same species (*Plecotus auritus*) were reported in both 1999 and 2000 and the hope is that this number will gradually increase.

Larger mammals are not forgotten by the Trust and badgers can be seen on various parts of the Estate if one exercises caution. Particular locations cannot be identified because of problems in the past with badger baiters actually digging out the setts for their own despicable objectives. To the credit of the Department of Transport, they took a great deal of trouble with two long-established setts, particularly on the route for the new road, by ensuring that no badgers were present before excavations began.

Butterflies have always been a major feature of the Trust's Estate, especially in recent years with the further acreage at Bovingdon Brickworks and Westbrook Hay. The areas of woodland and surrounding meadows, with wide rides covered in clover on the latter site, have attracted large skippers, marbled whites, meadow browns, peacocks, red admirals,

ringlets and small skippers as well as numerous burnet moths. A keen eye on the shorter grassland may spot a small copper or a small heath. The beautiful holly and common blue are always a thrill to behold and the hope is that these will multiply if conditions are right. The tranquility of this area is exceptional, as one walks along the broad swathes of grassy paths with scores of marbled whites fluttering up to the overhead song of skylarks. Fifty years ago, brimstones, cabbage whites, red admirals, orange tips, peacocks and tortoiseshells were commonplace as well as damselflies and dragonflies. Recent years have seen regular sightings of clouded yellow and painted lady from the continent, as they are particularly attracted to the flowers of knapweed and thistle.

The huge success of the recent work on Further Roughdown, besides the springtime carpet of cowslips, has seen the return of an appreciable number of green hairstreak, a species rare in Hertfordshire. In June, the common blue butterflies are a delight to see. Watch out for unusual day-flying moths as well, such as the strange Mother Shipton.

The Box Moor Estate has already benefited from the philosophy of past generations of Box Moor Trustees. In ensuring the future of grazing by establishing its own herd and flock, a most important management tool has remained available for much of the land. Monitoring will be a crucial part of the process in the future and the assistance of volunteers in their own areas of expertise will be welcomed.

Sketches by Dennis Furnell, from The Country Book of the Year. *Stickleback, Sparrowhawk, Common Shrew, Skylark, Dragonfly, Water Vole.*

Common Blue Butterfly (Polyommatus icarus).

Duke of Burgundy Fritillary (Hamearis lucina).

Stoat (Mustela erminea) *painting by Dennis Furnell, 2004. The stoat is a fearless hunter but a caring mother. In the south of England it rarely changes its coat to the white ermine of winter.*

59. EDUCATION MATTERS

'Education is a major contributor to quality of life.'
Hertfordshire Environmental Forum 2002.

The Countryside Management Service collaborated with the Box Moor Trust for an environmental education event on Roughdown Common in June 1998. Local children were taken on an enjoyable and informative field trip. A programme of involvement with the environment for local inhabitants is seen as an intrinsic part of the Trust's future role.

The Box Moor Trust has been steadily increasing its provision and budget for educational purposes over the last few years, due to an increase in funds which has allowed the Trustees to be more pro-active generally. Initial consultation with professionals has led to ideas for future projects, which include changes to the environmental areas and the old barn (for health and safety reasons), the building of an outside teaching area, the employment of qualified education staff and the building up of a volunteer base to support the Trust's work.

The Trust aims to increase the number of visits made to local schools and encourage schools to make use of on-site educational activities. Recently the Trust produced an education pack aimed at National Curriculum Key Stages 1 and 2. The existing Wildlife Watch Group's activities could be furthered and perhaps a group for older children introduced.

A series of free leaflets showing various walks around the Moors and Commons is available and this area of the Trust's interpretation work could be further enhanced. The annual production of a calendar with photographs of the area taken by local people adds to the general interest. The publication of this book and earlier booklets all lie within the Trust's proposals for a more comprehensive education programme.

The Heritage Lottery Fund has been approached with these objectives in mind, paving the way for greater local awareness and understanding of the Box Moor Trust Estate's unique position and history.

'Education is simply the soul of a society as it
passes from one generation to another.'
(G. K. Chesterton)

'Tis education forms the common mind, just as
the twig is bent, the tree's inclined.'
(Alexander Pope)

'When he has learnt that bottiney [botany] means
a knowledge of plants, he goes and knows them.'
(Charles Dickens, from Nicholas Nickleby)

'To me education is a leading out of what is already there in a pupil's soul.'
(Muriel Spark)

'Discovery consists of seeing what everybody has seen and thinking what nobody has thought.'
(Albert Szent-Gyorgyi)

'We teachers can only help the work going on, as servants wait upon a master'
(Maria Montessori)

A re-enactment in costume by Prince Rupert's men of the Sealed Knot in October 1999, managing to bring history to life and appealing to all ages.

Countryside craft skills being demonstrated at the annual Conker Festival. The Trust tries to ensure that these traditional pursuits continue to be appreciated.

'Hands on' activity with badger skulls, obviously a captivating subject! School groups are encouraged to use the resources provided by the diverse environments of the Trust's Estate.

Pond dipping in Hay Wood at the Education launch in 2004. It is just one of the many activities organised by the Trust's newly appointed Education Officer, Beth Brierley.

'Getting their eye in': members of the Wildlife Watch group taking part in an activity day at Westbrook Hay Barn.

An enthusiastic group of Junior Wildlife Watch youngsters with Dacorum's Mayor, Derek Townsend, and some Trustees at the renovated Westbrook Hay Barn in April 2002.

60. TREES IN TRUST

The Box Moor Estate is on the fringe of the Chilterns, the second largest wooded area in England, which has remained an historical unity since the Norman Conquest in 1066, when Hertfordshire itself was among the most densely wooded of the English counties. 'In the time of Elizabeth I a squirrel could have jumped from the border country of Wales to the outskirts of London without having to come down to the ground.'

Up until the acquisition of Westbrook Hay Farm in 1995, the Trust managed relatively little woodland and that was mainly secondary in nature; the ecologically more valuable part of Bury Wood was owned by Dacorum Borough Council until the Trust purchased it in 2003. All this, however, is not to negate the benefits that can accrue from the gradual establishment of other vegetation and wildlife that enjoys woodland protection or low density tree cover, such as on Roughdown and Sheethanger Commons. Most of the western part of the latter is broad-leaved. The eastern (SSSI) section is a mosaic of calcareous grassland and scrub on an old chalk quarry. Apart from the 'cricket bat' willows, there has not been a commercial spin off from Trust trees for some time.

On the occasion of the Trust's Four Hundred Years Anniversary in 1994 four trees were planted at Heath Park, one tree for each century. The species were carefully chosen as notable examples of those introduced into this country during each of the centuries: thus holly for the sixteenth; medlar for the seventeenth; quince for the eighteenth and a Wellingtonia for the nineteenth century. There are not many specimens that are over 100 years old on the Estate, but there are some worthy of mention. A fine pollarded* black poplar stands proudly on Hardings Moor, whilst in Ramacre Wood there is a remnant of a pollarded hornbeam dating to the 1700s, as well as an important area of very old yew trees. A magnificent ancient oak tree covers a large plot of the aptly named Oak Tree Field at Howe's Retreat. The remains of an orchard can still be found on Harding's Moor and the Ryder family's avenue of mistletoe-bedecked limes still ascends the hill at Westbrook Hay. All these treasures are there to be discovered and, together with the indigenous beech, ash and wild cherry, add to the delight of the rambler or naturalist as well as providing habitats for wildlife.

Single or small groups of trees are occasionally planted as memorials at the request of relatives or friends of deceased local people. Storm damage, as in 1987 and 1990, is another reason for re-planting in specific areas. A major programme of scrub clearance was begun in 1977 with the help of volunteers in the vicinity of the SSSI on Roughdown, in order to give the existing colony of junipers some breathing space. Woodchips from clearance projects were used effectively to surface the paths and bridleways the Trust has made in the last few years. The woodland on Roughdown has been improved recently, necessitating the removal of some established trees such as sycamore, ash and oak which were either poor specimens or too densely placed. Some hollies, hawthorn and hazel were coppiced* at the same time. These efforts sometimes meet with mixed reactions from the public, to whom the destruction of any tree is a sacrilege, but it is all done on good advice and not wantonly.

The intrusion of the A41 By-pass brought many of these matters into focus, since tree cover was an important aspect of the proposed route. The re-generation of ancient indigenous junipers, a planting scheme made necessary by the By-pass cutting through Roughdown, has been a great success. These have now become established, guaranteeing a continuity of species which is environmentally satisfying to all concerned.

On the run-up to the Trust election of 1870–1, Henry Balderson, lessee of Boxmoor Wharf, requested permission to plant a row of chestnut trees by the side of the high road leading from the Wharf to Albion Place; this was granted, perhaps marking the beginning of the association of the Trust with the horse chestnut tree. The avenues of red and white varieties still bring pleasure year after year to passers by.

The new logo of the Box Moor Trust, a chestnut leaf, reflects this aspect of the Trust's green heritage. However, the periodic replacement of the long-established avenues of chestnuts, which criss-cross the Moors is another area of concern and monitoring of these stately specimens is an on-going task. The loss of mature trees due to road schemes imposed on the Trust by outside agencies has also occasioned thoughts of asking for semi-mature trees as replacements rather than saplings. The chestnut avenue bordering Blackbirds' Moor on St John's Road, Boxmoor, is now the responsibility of Dacorum Borough Council. A number of these trees were deemed to be diseased and were removed in recent times, but the replacement trees are now catching up on their older cousins in terms of stature. In the autumn, a Conker Festival has been held annually since 1996 and the fallen chestnuts provide ammunition for the knock-out competitions.

The various woodlands at Westbrook Hay are now managed in conjunction with the Forestry Authority within the Woodland Grants Scheme and are subject to a general Tree Preservation Order. A ten-year management plan covers the period 1995 to 2005. Historic records show the existence of woodland and walks on this land dating back to 1760. Formerly, coppicing took place regularly and specimen trees were planted, such as the giant Wellingtonia. Yearly Trust meetings with Dacorum Borough Council and other organisations will help to keep track of this plan and, overall, the trees and hedges will be treated in a sympathetic manner.

The Trust's long-term plans for the woodland in its care will include some areas of coppicing and pollarding (age-old practices), some removal of mature and diseased trees, as well as thinning of overcrowded sections. Re-planting of local species such as ash, cherry, hornbeam and oak, together with crab apple and hazel to soften the edges, is envisaged over the

Aesculus hippocastanum by John Miller. The stages of the horse chestnut are all worth observing in detail, as this lovely watercolour illustrates. (Reproduced by kind permission of the Royal Horticultural Society, Lindley Library).

The magnificent horse chestnuts that grace the Moors have become a symbol of today's Box Moor Trust. The avenues were mostly planted to mark Royal occasions. The latest row of red and white varieties borders Snoxall's Moor, London Road, and commemorates the late Queen Mother's eightieth birthday.

Copper Beech (Fagus sylvatica cuprea). *Trees, such as this on Blackbirds' Moor, are sometimes planted on Trust land as a memorial to local residents.*

next few years. Left to themselves and the ravages of pests like the grey squirrel, the woods would gradually degenerate and the wide diversity of wildlife they sustain would suffer with them, so the Trust's staff plays a very important role in the strategy to keep the trees in Trust.

Occasionally in the past the Trustees sold dead trees for timber. The presence of yew trees sometimes caused a problem, since cattle could, and did, die from eating this poisonous plant.

The Trust's interest in trees seems to have escalated during the nineteenth century and, in October 1876, 50 horse chestnut trees were ordered, with 'standard guards' to protect them when planted on the Moor. Willows were to be planted from the Boxmoor Baths to the bridge in 1883, to form a fence. Further willows were planted in 1890 along the canal bank opposite the Star beerhouse. Seats were placed on the Moors and Commons at this time, costing thirty-three shillings each. More expenditure was allowed in 1891, when the avenue of trees from St John's Church to the Three Blackbirds was sanctioned. The land for a path along this route was agreed and a strip six feet wide was offered to the Highways Board. In the end, 30 chestnuts and 16 limes were bought as well as 24 iron plates to fix to the seats. The bug seems to have bitten, for in October another 25 trees were ordered. Planting continued into 1892, when 20 chestnut and 14 sycamore trees were recorded; all the tree guards and iron hurdles were re-tarred and the widening of St John's Road was then a topical point of discussion. Mr Dunbar's Nursery in Park Road supplied trees in 1893. In 1902 the avenue of horse chestnuts from the canal bridge to Boxmoor Station was commissioned as well as 27 trees from Two Waters Mill to the Bell Inn. The Trust sometimes gave a reward for evidence in a prosecution for tree damage, emphasising the high esteem in which they

held this aspect of their custodianship. One novel event in the Trust's calendar until recently was Tree Dressing, organised in the winter in conjunction with the Countryside Management Service, when schoolchildren hung their prepared 'dressings' to celebrate the life of the tree. This may well have its roots in pagan times, but it does focus attention on these often overlooked but vital parts of our lives.

Common Oak (Quercus robur) *is one of the best-known deciduous trees; this towering specimen at Howe's Retreat gives shelter to a myriad of wildlife. Oaks can live to a great age, up to 1,000 years, and they are one of our most valuable native hardwoods.*

61. WATERCRESS AND OSIER BEDS

'Down the valley where the waters of the spring run, as indeed down nearly every other dene where a chalk stream bursts out, are watercress beds.'
Henry Taunt.

The healthy spring waters and chalk streams of this area of Hertfordshire have long been renowned for commercial watercress growing. The turnpike road and then the railway, followed by the modern road transport systems, ensured that fresh crops reached the markets in London. In the 1920s watercress was transported to the station by horse-drawn trolleys and at one time it was a common sight to see large wicker baskets full of watercress bunches waiting to be loaded onto the trains at Boxmoor and Hemel Hempstead Station.

The rivers Gade and Bulbourne, which meander across the Moors, contributed to the flourishing watercress business and the Trust leased ditches and grounds to the trade for the best part of 200 years. Watercress is a native plant of the chalk or limestone regions of southern England, where alkaline water coming up from deep springs is at a constant temperature of about 10°C, enabling the cress to grow even in severe winter weather. The Romans believed in the medicinal properties of the plant and it was extolled by herbalists of the sixteenth and seventeenth centuries. It is a good source of vitamins, iron and calcium and at one time it was a popular breakfast food of the labourers, often sold by children on the streets of London, their cries documented by Henry Mayhew:

'The first coster-cry heard of a morning in the London streets is that of "Fresh wo-orter-creases." Those that sell them have to be on their rounds in time for the mechanics' break-fast, or the day's gains are lost. As the stock-money for this calling need only consist of a few.'

The main cutting season was from February to June. It was an important industry in the Chilterns until recently and there were many growers in the Hemel Hempstead area. At the time of the New Town Public Inquiry in 1946, it was stated that the area produced one-sixteenth of the country's valuable watercress supply and the growers strongly objected to their land being taken. The Williams family had watercress beds in Marlowes and W. J. Williams, W. F. Williams and W. T. (Tom) Williams were all successive Box Moor Trustees.

The name William Durrant first appeared in the Trust minutes in 1826 when he wanted to lease a cottage and garden at Box Moor. He attended a Trust meeting in April 1848 and expressed a wish to rent the ditch at the side of the Bulbourne to grow watercress 'from the stone bridge to Mr Steven's Mill [Two Waters Mill] and also the pond on part of the Moor'. A fourteen-year lease was subsequently settled at a cost of £10 per annum. The meeting of 27 June 1862 considered his request for an extension of the lease but the new terms were not acceptable to him and he was summarily told to quit, not even being given time to remove his seed plants. An invitation to watercress growers to tender for the next fourteen-year lease was printed in both the local and national press. Durrant re-applied but the highest bidder was Joseph Harrison. He had entered the Trust's records in 1848 when he offered £10 per year for the piece of ground opposite Cangles for watercress growing, possibly on the site of old fishponds which dated back to the medieval period or earlier. He was named as a fishmonger at that date and the Trust had no objection to his offer.

Harrison must have made a success of the venture, since two years later he asked for the lease of two more ditches, nearly opposite the Swan Inn on the London Road. He wanted to make the Trust a special offer for the continuation of his lease in 1870 and, again being the highest bidder, he contracted to build a house of not less than £12 annual value within twelve months on the Trust's usual terms. This had not happened by the following April, but the time limit was extended and the lease was mentioned as a forty-year one – a big increase. Still no sign of a house in early 1872; by July of that year, however, two small cottages had been erected next to the watercress beds in Old Fishery Lane. His expansion continued, as in 1873 he took out yet another lease on land near the Boxmoor Baths and the canal.

Harrison was out-bid, however, on 10 May 1876, when William Durrant secured the four pieces of land that Harrison had been leasing near Two Waters Mill. Durrant transferred the lease on his watercress beds to Charles Sansum of King's Langley later that year. Sansum was in trouble for putting up a fence in October 1882 and for blocking back the water in 1884. The Trustees tightened up their grip on illicit use of watercress ditches on the Moor without proper leases from that year.

Watercress beds at Old Fishery Lane. Harrison's cottages can be seen on the right-hand side of the canal. In the early days, a pipe was added to the canal to feed the watercress beds near Lock 62. The scene is reminiscent of an industry which has all but died out in Hertfordshire. The two derelict cottages were demolished in 2003. The Trust is planning to replace them with two new houses and an Environmental Education Centre.

The Williams family's watercress beds in Hemel Hempstead, before the New Town. In the mid-1900s the town produced one-sixteenth of the country's watercress.

Another name enters the picture in 1887, when John Ing applied for two watercress ditches to be cut, one behind the Lock and the other behind Boxmoor Baths. Three ditches were later mentioned and the price of £10 per annum agreed. Sansum's lease was due to expire in midsummer 1890 and this was finalised for twenty-one years at a rent of £40 a year. He saw fit to complain in 1895 that 'the River Bulbourne on Box Moor from Foster's Ltd. to Two Waters Mill is in a very bad state from overgrowth of weeds in the bed ...' This was a continual problem. The executors of William Sansum's estate in November 1896 asked for the transfer of the lease to Charles Sansum and Mr Williams, for which application was granted. When the County Council suggested the construction of a new bridge at Two Waters, concern was raised as to how it might affect the watercourse of the cress beds situated there, evidence that the industry, albeit small in scale, was seen to be a noteworthy one in the area.

Harrison asked the Trustees for an abatement of his rent in 1880, due to adverse seasons, and again in 1890 when the lease still had twenty years to run, but the reply was in the negative. Instead, the Trust agreed to convert another part of the property into a watercress bed and so create work for a number of unemployed local men, the lease to run for the same period as the others. In April he was requested to put a fence around the new watercress bed at once, before the cattle were turned out.

By 1893 Harrison had found that the new bed was 'useless' and he wrote in the hope of a return of rent already paid. Not surprisingly, the Trust could not accede to this. Harrison was also in dispute with the LNWR for encroaching on their land; the Trust gave the Company a nominal 2s 6d and then marked the boundary with posts. Joseph Harrison died but his widow continued the business. In 1905, Mrs Harrison was left in a poor financial state and was unable to pay the rent. The firm of Harrison Bros. watercress growers was still listed in the local directory of 1937 and the Ordnance Survey map of 1940 shows a large outbuilding adjacent to the railway line. This area was later used by the Box Moor Trust as an Estate workshop.

At some stage, Grimwoods took over the business until 1971, when it was leased to R. E. Gabell for ten years. He did not finish this term, surrendering the lease back to the Trust on 24 June 1976. The last residential occupant of the site was Charlie Walker who passed away on 14 February 2001 aged ninety-five; he was a familiar figure for over forty years in the Boxmoor area and loved the Moors.

The industry generally declined in the 1950s and Hertfordshire watercress eventually ceased to be viable commercially, so Harrison's old watercress beds that ran between the railway embankment and the canal were given a facelift in the mid-1980s. The stream was cleared, the verge grassed over and an open area allowed to develop for the enjoyment of school children and ramblers. Whatever the day-to-day working relationship was, Harrison's name lived on, being the recent title of the Moor between Old Fishery Lane and Fishery Road. It is now known as Fishery Moor.

In 2001 the Trust applied for planning permission to replace the two former Harrison's cottages with something more modern, in keeping with the canal-side location. The Trustees hope that an Environmental Education Centre, based on the wildlife of the former watercress beds, will be built alongside the replacement homes.

The baskets for transporting watercress may well have been made from the flexible branches of osier, a small willow of which there are several varieties. Common Osier (*salix viminalis*) was often used to make baskets before the advent of man-made materials. The first reference to osier beds in the Trust minutes is on 2 January 1817, when the Trust met to look at whether part of the Moor could be used for their cultivation. George Alexander Smith's Map of 1842 shows osier beds and in 1829 George Weedon, a basket-maker, was the lessee of two pieces of osier ground. Nine years later he proposed to give up part of his holding, as long as he could remove his osier stubs. The Trust agreed to take back part of the leased lands for £60 in 1839. By 1861, the Trust was taking proceedings against Alfred Weedon for the recovery of the house and premises at Moor End. This was finalised early in 1862 and the Trustees were considering re-letting the property. The building was to be demolished and new cottages erected with very precise specifications, but no mention was made of any osier beds then. Today, Dacorum Borough Council maintains the colourful gardens on the old osier site at the entrance to the town.

Common Watercress (Radicula nasturtium-aquaticum).

Watercress packed and ready for delivery to the railway station from John Sharp's watercress farm at Bourne End.

The cottages by the river Gade at Moor End, where once there were osier beds. Riverside, the house on the right, was the home of Mary Carey, Hannah and Ann Hobson (nee Carey). They were all involved in the foundation of the Boxmoor Baptist Church. William Carey was well-known as a Baptist missionary.

BOX MOOR TRUST PROPERTY

62. TRUST PROPERTY

At the time of the 1809 Box Moor Trust Act, there were already twenty-six cottages or tenements erected on various parts of the Moor; the tenants were all listed including William Howard at Boxmoor Wharf. The Lock House erected by the Grand Junction Canal Company (GJCC) was occupied by William Berry. The shop at Moor End, Gade Villas, Cox's, Bolton's, Lawrence's, Green's and Picton's Cottages are all now faded memories. Rose Cottage, sold on a long-term ground lease in 1986, and those opposite the former Bell at Two Waters, still survive. The cottages at numbers 1, and 2, Station Road were demolished by order of the Chief Public Health Inspector some time after the autumn of 1965.

It was not until relatively recently that the Box Moor Trust owned any property; instead it leased parts of the land under its control, which was a major source of income. There were always difficulties with collecting the rents and in January 1836 the Trustees resolved that, 'considering the inconvenience and loss arising from the irregularity of the payments made by [their] tenants, the rents due at Christmas

shall be paid by Lady Day and those due at mid-summer shall be paid at Michaelmas'. Two important decisions were made at the following meeting in February, when it was agreed that the sum of £100 out of the profits of the Moor was to be spent on a warehouse and cottage at Boxmoor Wharf, for which it was suggested to George Howard, lessee of the Wharf, that an annual rent of £5 would be payable. Howard subsequently asked for £130 to be expended, but the final bill came to £162 3s 3d and included a warehouse and lean-to, as well as the cottage. It was fully understood that these were the property of the Trust. The Herdsman, too, was to be housed in a cottage with a kitchen, a back kitchen, two bedrooms and a shed for barrows and tools.

Some tenants who were erecting some expensive buildings on Trust land had misunderstood, perhaps deliberately, that their cottages still belonged to the Trust at the end of their forty-year lease. The Clerk wrote to them reminding them of the terms of their holdings:

'In the year 1849 the cottages and every building which during the term may be erected upon the ground will belong absolutely to the Trustees who will then be at liberty to take possession of it, and sell it for the best price it will produce, and that in the meantime you are bound to keep the buildings in repair.'

This letter must have provoked some acrid remarks about the workings of the Trust, but it was within its rights to stipulate this action.

The feeling of disappointment may have caused Thomas Barnett, Thomas Vyse, James Fenn and James Homans to refuse to pay their rent arrears in October, but, undaunted, the Trustees threatened them with summons to the County Court if they did not pay up by Christmas. The bills were still unsettled by all of them except James Homans in March 1837. Whether they ever did pay is not stated, but the gardens 'late in the occupation of James Fenn, James Homans and Daniel Collins' were let to Dr Davis of Boxmoor House, Box Lane, in 1837, along with about 67 poles of land opposite his property, 'considering such slip to be incapable of drainage or improvement for the purposes of the Moor'. The boundary of the Moor property was not to be obliterated, but landmarks were to be put down and maintained by Dr Davis. The subject of boundaries became an important one at the beginning of this century, when the question of proper compensation to the Charity for way-leaves* was under debate.

The Estate was considerably enlarged in October 1837 when roughly 7 acres of Haybarns Meadows, near Cotterells, were purchased at the asking price of £550, which came from the money received from the London and Birmingham Railway

Account of rents due, 25 December 1835.

Company (L&BRC) for the compulsory purchase of Trust land. The owner who had put the land up for auction was Mr Tower of Gadebridge. This family also owned Frogmore (Covent) Mill and leased it out to the Fourdrinier brothers for paper-making in 1803, thus contributing to a sequence of events of historic importance for the area.

Previous offers of land for sale included Cangles Meadow, also 50 acres near Corner Hall belonging to the Deacon family, at £50 per acre, but both of these had been rejected by the Trustees, for reasons unknown. It may be conjectured that, financial implications apart, the land was simply not suitable, being too segmented. They did, however, want to own the slip of land by the side of the canal called Tree Farm, from which the GJCC had dug clay; this land was to become the site of Boxmoor Baths. But the Trustees declined to bid for the 'Workhouse Meadows'; these decisions may again have been because the land in question was not considered good enough for grazing, the main objective of the Trust at that time. The Trustees were not necessarily thinking in terms of future investment, although in hindsight it seems a pity these opportunities were passed by.

Occasionally, the Trust allowed cottages to be erected for specific purposes, such as in the case of Mrs Smith in 1839. Samuel Smith was named as a tenant in the 1809 Act of Parliament and after his death his widow could not simply be turned out of her home, which was one of the eight cottages near Haybarns. The Overseers of the Poor had acquired them more than twenty years previously, but they were to be demolished. The Trust spent the magnanimous sum of £15 to build a small cottage on the Heath opposite Heath Farm for her. Unfortunately, Mrs Smith died on the same morning of the meeting in which the costs were sanctioned to be paid and, without more ado, the order was given to remove the house!

Sometimes the Trust leased further land themselves, such as George Holloway's Half Moon Meadow, or exchanged land, for example Revd J. B. Mountain's Little Cotterell's field, next to the Moor. These deals were not without their own difficulties however, for the tenant of the Half Moon Meadow did not want to relinquish possession. The arrangements with Revd Mountain, resident of The Heath, were protracted also, for he later asked for an exchange of the whole of Little Cotterells for the 'narrow slip of ground opposite Box Moor Chapel-of-Ease on which my laundry Cottage, Childs Beer Shop and Bates' two Cottages stand, so as to make me a straight frontage on the road'. At last, in May 1841, the exchange was agreed; the value of Revd Mountain's land being put at £80, the total amounting to £114. A plan of Box Moor was ordered at the same meeting to be made by George Alexander Smith and a small sub-committee was given the task of organising the matter. This fascinating map now hangs in the Trust's new office at Westbrook Hay Farm.

Interestingly, the familiar name of Fourdrinier appears once more in a dispute of 1842 over land on the western side of

Minutes of a Box Moor Trust property meeting, 13 July 1847.

Two Waters Mill. The GJCC let this site to a Mr Stevens who then sub-let it to Richard W. Cooper; he subsequently moved his cart shed onto the Moor. The two tenants argued that the land belonged to the GJCC and to the Fourdriniers before that. To no avail, because the Trust made further enquiries and satisfied themselves that the land in question was part of the Moor and therefore part of the Trust Estate. The debate did not rest there, however, and the GJCC Chairman, Sir Francis Head, became involved in January 1843, when a meeting was held. Nothing transpired from this, however, and so the Trustees ordered the shed be pulled down. In the end, Cooper moved it back to the original boundary. These constant efforts to enlarge properties at the expense of the Trust seemed to take up an inordinate amount of time.

The Trustees had always been without a proper base in which to hold their meetings and, to rectify this, it was suggested in July 1841 that a room should be added to the Herdsman's cottage for this purpose. They could not see fit to allow another Herdsman's cottage to be built next to Boxmoor Baths, as requested by the Bath Committee, and the project was never concluded.

More land was added to the Estate in November 1842 on the purchase of 'two fields of arable land with three cottages erected on Lot 2 belonging to Norris and Pedley'. The land

Trust houses, numbers 114–120, London Road, Two Waters, alongside the river Gade. These properties have recently been modernised and a single-storey extension added.

Rose Cottage, 353, London Road, is let on a long-term lease.

was purchased by the Trust for £500, covered by the fees from the compulsory sale of land to L&BRC. The Box Moor Trustees then arranged to pull down the dilapidated houses and to sell any re-usable building materials. They also needed to fell some of the timber, to plough and sow the ground. Once known locally as St John's Moor, or simply the Moor, today it is called Blackbirds' Moor and is the home of Boxmoor Cricket Club.

Joseph Cranstone felt the need to protest in writing to his fellow Trustees in 1845 about their idea of purchasing back the six mud cottages near Tomlin's Corner for the sum of thirty guineas in order to pull them down and fill up the adjoining pond. He thought it was impolitic to set such a precedent, since the cottages would eventually revert back to the Trust, it would cost more money to fill in the pond and it would reduce the Trust's income in the short term. He also stated it was not consistent with the Act of Parliament. However, an earlier Vestry meeting had approved an amendment to the Act that the surplus profits should be invested, either in the purchase of the unexpired terms of such leases as could be obtained, or in the purchase of land as contiguous to the Moor as possible. This money was to be held in an Accumulation fund and was to be spent as soon as the occasion arose.

The meeting of 20 October 1847 gave a résumé of the rents and values of the cottages; the weekly rents were in the range of 1s 6d to 4s 6d and, on the basis of improved rental fees, further leases were arranged. The Trustees also decided to allow certain pieces of land, including that opposite the former Bell Inn at Two Waters, to be auctioned for a term of forty years as building ground. The houses were to have not less than two rooms on the ground floor and the same above; not less than six feet from the floor to the plate* was to be built of flint or brick and the walls were not to be less than nine inches

thick, the roofs being covered with slate or tiles. These cottages are still standing.

T. E. Deacon was alarmed by all the land being leased and registered his disapproval in a signed letter. In spite of this, four lots were auctioned on 19 November and only the piece of ground opposite Cangles was not spoken for. Joseph Harrison, a fishmonger, came forward the following January, to request a lease for this land as a watercress bed, on the terms of a fourteen-year lease at £10 per annum. This was agreed; he extended the lease and in 1872 constructed two small cottages on the site. Harrison's watercress business survived well into the twentieth century. The cottages existed until 2003, but were declared unfit for human habitation for some years before that.

The acquisition of Trust land in the 1860s by the Hemel Hempstead and London and North Western Railway Company gave rise to an offer by George Alexander Smith, the Trust's Surveyor, of about 4 acres of his own freehold land to the Trust, together with four houses; he valued it at £200 an acre. This was probably in the area of Duckhall and the Gas Works, opposite what is now known as Harding's Moor.

A forty-year lease on premises at Moor End was offered to Joseph Benskin of the Cannon Brewery, Watford, on 8 April 1874 at £5 per annum. Leases for other properties at Moor End came up for renewal at the same time and a Mr Rolf offered to re-build 'that portion of the old cottage left standing where the Grocer's Shop and Bakehouse was built by Liddall and the shed or stable at the back'.

The possibility of a Reading Room for Boxmoor's inhabitants was debated in 1878 and a suitable site was declared to be between Mr Stringer's garden and the new railway near the

Midland Railway arch and the Heath Park Hotel. There the matter seems to have rested until 1885 when Mr Draper, representing the Boxmoor Reading Room Committee, attended a Trust meeting. He was asked to re-submit his committee's proposals. Suitable premises were procured by 1886 and the committee demanded the £50 that had been agreed at a Vestry meeting for this purpose. The Trustees replied that this money had gone into the General fund and, as it was a new financial year, a fresh application should be made. This did not please the committee who sent a letter of protest to the Clerk. The Trust then became entangled with the Charity Commission, since it was decided not to send in the Accounts until the matter had been cleared up. At last, in 1887, the sum of £50 was agreed to be paid over to the parish of Hemel Hempstead. The next mention of a Reading Room is in a minute dated 13 April 1887 when J. Glenister, Secretary of the Boxmoor Institute and Reading Room, asked for a piece of ground for cricket opposite the National Schools (St John's). This request was refused. Half of the money had still not been claimed by November 1888 and this was then spent on two lamp posts and a fountain on the verge of the new Market Place.

A Special meeting was called on 15 November 1888 at the Vestry Room to consider reports on Trust properties such as Gade Villas, the Boatman, the Artichoke and the Star, all of which were due for repairs. Locke and Smith, the brewers, tendered for the latter plus two cottages and the rest were re-let. In 1889 many of the Trust's leases expired and an overview of all the properties was carried out. Some of these properties

were actually sub-let, which made it even more difficult for the Trust to manage. At the request of H. D. Woodman, those tenants of certain cottages who paid their rent punctually were given a Christmas box of one shilling.

Another minor asset of the Trust was the mineral wealth of its land, aspects of which were a concern for some. For instance, anguish was caused by the 'enormous and continuous removal of the chalk and the damage consequently done to the downs, especially Roughdown, not merely for the accommodation of the commoners but really for the purpose of carrying on the trade of a lime burner'. By 1890 the Trustees were unanimously of the opinion that the time had arrived when decisive steps should be taken to resolve their problems. As well as taking Counsel's advice, it was voted to fill in and level the pits.

The severe winter of 1893 caused unemployment to rise in the area and forty local men applied for work. To alleviate the situation, a gravel pit was opened near Hollybush Row, which made a profit of £96 in the sale of gravel. In 1893 the Telephone Company was charged three shillings per post for 38 posts placed across the Moor, but 50 posts were, in fact, erected. Time and again, people seemed to want to get away with a little more than their due.

The story of all the Trust's former properties as recorded in the minute books reveals a wealth of detail about the everyday concerns of ordinary folk in the Area of Benefit, particularly in the Victorian period.

Old Fishery Cottages, 1 and 2, Old Fishery Lane, Boxmoor. These were built by Joseph Harrison a local watercress grower, in the nineteenth century. They were condemned as structurally dangerous. The last tenant, Charlie Walker, wished to remain on the site and was therefore re-housed in a mobile home. It is now planned to re-develop part of this area with two houses and an Environmental Centre.

Charlie Walker, aged 95, enjoyed the peace and quiet of the old watercress beds and his colourful garden. He called his secluded canal-side home his 'little piece of heaven'. His recipe for a healthy life was hard work and plain cooking! Charlie was one of the Trust's oldest tenants, living for over forty years in Old Fishery Lane, until his death on 14 February 2001.

Trust Offices: the Trust's first designated office was set up in 1979 in the small room at the front of St John's Hall, which is now part of Hemel Hempstead Operatic and Dramatic Society's very own Boxmoor Playhouse. Jack Marshall was appointed as the part-time Administrator. All legal matters were still dealt with by the Clerk's offices at Smeathman's, in Queensway, Hemel Hempstead. These offices were occupied by Smeathman's until the move to Waterhouse Street in the late 1900s. The firm is now known as Pictons and still assists the Trust in legal matters. The Trust moved to the first floor of 69, High Street in 1993. Jean Sniders had taken over as Office Manager from Shirley Selwyn and Jack Marshall had already retired. The role of Office Manager had grown to a full-time responsibility, in conjunction with the Estate Manager; an assistant, Caralyn Duignan, was also appointed. The office was rented and the Trust was in need of a more permanent home.

The barn at Westbrook Hay Farm, before it was destroyed by fire in 2000. The story came full circle in that year, when the Trust's own offices were at last established at Westbrook Hay Farm, in what is now termed the Box Moor Trust Centre. Fate played a harsh trick when fire damaged the newly furnished offices on Christmas Day. The year finished with portacabins acting as a temporary home. The New Year brought the tribulations of foot and mouth disease and so the offices were closed to all but the regular Staff. Since then, the Centre has re-opened and a busy schedule is followed by all the former and new Staff.

63. TRUST HOUSES AND THE ARTICHOKE PROJECT

Up until 1908 there is no record of the Trust building its own houses, apart from the Herdsman's cottage. Land was leased out for building and at the end of the lease the dwellings became Trust property. However, in March 1908, one of the Trustees, Mr Saunders, asked if the money held by the Paymaster General could be used for new buildings. The Charity Commission felt that the Trustees had no power to invest capital in building projects and they very much doubted if the High Court could give them this power. The only course of action was to obtain additional Parliamentary authority. Nevertheless, in the following month the Trustees approved a plan for two semi-detached cottages. They may have decided on this course of action because a number of their properties whose leases had expired were unfit for habitation and were, economically speaking, beyond repair. The work was duly carried out in July by the builder Sydney Smith, at an agreed tendered price of £590. Cooper and Harrison were the first tenants and the rent was fixed at £19 10s per annum with the tenants paying the rates.

The proposal to erect these houses was to form part of the Scheme to be laid before the Charity Commission. By 1910 the Commissioners had agreed a loan from the Lands Improvement Company of up to £4,000. The Artichoke site and the new houses were put up as security and the Board of Agriculture gave its approval. Mr Gold won the contract and four houses as well as eight cottages were completed in 1912. This loan was eventually settled in September 1941.

Jack Bandle, the Manager of the local branch of estate agents Brown and Merry, was retained by the Trust as a surveyor and rent collector for the residential properties. He attended most Trust meetings between 1965 and 1984, but sadly died on 23 June 1998.

The Artichoke public house and its neighbouring cottages on the London Road had long been part of the Box Moor Estate. These premises, although on Trust land, were not built by the Trust; they were leased over many years, mainly to the tenants themselves or Trust staff. In 1985 the two Hope Cottages were closed down, as was number 142 London Road in 1993.

Numbers 339–353, London Road, adjacent to the former Gas Works; the redundant works are now being considered for redevelopment. The first pair of semi-detached cottages were built in 1908, followed by a further eight cottages and four houses in 1912. These were the first houses to be built by the Trust itself, apart from the Herdsman's cottage.

The Artichoke site, including Hope Cottages, in 1999. Another long-vanished public house called The Three Crowns was at 359, London Road. The Trust owned the way-leave rights but not the building. Its Pasture Plaque was removed to the Trust's keeping when it was demolished.

Later that year a deputation from Bovingdon asked for 'the power to raise money on mortgage for the purpose of erecting buildings'. The Clerk to the Trust replied it would need a Parliamentary Scheme to alter the 1809 Act to meet their requirements. In the meantime, work went ahead for plans for more houses along the London Road. The Commissioners asked for the average annual cost of keeping the houses in good repair and the Trustees responded at a tangent, saying that they never thought it probable that the rents would cover the whole of the principle and interest on the money borrowed. They also answered that these new homes would replace those they had pulled down.

The Artichoke subsequently became a grocery shop and then a pet food store and this was finally vacated on 24 July 1996. The last property became vacant on 28 February 1997, leaving the way open for the Trust to comprehensively re-develop the whole site.

This successful project which started during 1999 was completed on target in February 2000. There are four semi-detached and three terraced houses, forming an attractive complex called Artichoke Court and constructed in keeping with the surrounding properties. The total capital cost was £453,700 against an estimated budget of £460,000 and they were all let within a month of completion.

No record of an inn sign exists, so necessity being the mother of invention, we invented one!

The Artichoke was the name of the public house that once occupied this site. It has long been a part of the Box Moor Estate, although the premises were not originally built by the Trust. It later became the Artichoke Pet Shop, pictured here in May 1998, several years after closure.

The last inhabited property became vacant on 28 February 1997, leaving the way open for the Trust to comprehensively re-develop the area. The knapped flint facings of the old cottages were replicated in the modern design. Flint is a common feature on buildings in the Area of Benefit.

Artichoke Court in 2000: one of the houses has been designed to accommodate physically disabled tenants.

Artichoke Court in 2000: showing two pairs of three-bedroom houses.

Trust Staff, 2004. Left to right: Alison Shipley (Assistant Estate Manager), Ray Timberlake (part-time Estate Worker), Paul Redding (Estate Worker), Beth Brierley (Education and Community Manager), Phil Pennington (Estate Manager), Elaine Rushton (Administrative Assistant), Jean Sniders (Administration Manager), Christopher Bartlett (Estate Worker), Toby Proctor (part-time Estate Worker).

Beth Brierley joined the Trust in January 2004 as Education and Community Manager to implement the Trust's policy to offer a more formal educational provision, a job that was previously undertaken by Estate staff. Beth already has a good deal of experience in the field: the first few years of her career were spent as a classroom teacher, both in mainstream and special needs schools, and more recently she was Education Officer at Banham Zoo in Norfolk. She has also worked as a researcher and was head of an education programme in East Africa. Beth enjoys hands-on conservation and getting out into the countryside. In her spare time, she enjoys painting and singing.

John 'Jack' Thomas Marshall (1914–2001) was born locally, the son of a baker, and educated at Berkhamsted School. He worked for John Dickinson's and was part of the second rising of Camelot Rugby Union Football Club, playing as a winger, and he soon became its Treasurer. During the Second World War he rose to the rank of Captain in the 8th Army in North Africa. On demobilisation, he re-joined John Dickinson's and was instrumental in reviving Camelot for its third existence. He worked indefatigably for rugby and was President of the County from 1966–9. He was appointed as the first Administrator to the Box Moor Trust in 1979 and his local knowledge was of considerable benefit. He was married with two daughters and sadly passed away in 2001, before this book was published. He was researching the history of the Hemel Hempstead (Camelot) Rugby Club right up until the end and the authors are grateful for the assistance he gave them in writing that particular article.

'Jack' Marshall (1914–2001).

Phil Pennington was Farm Manager and Head of Rural Studies at a Community school near Blackpool before he joined the Trust as Estate Manager in 1993. Previously he had been a shepherd, farm manager and lecturer in livestock management. Phil holds City and Guilds qualifications and a National Certificate in Agriculture as well as a Diploma in Environmental Management; he also has a BA Honours Degree in Art History and Social Studies. Phil is the Secretary of the National Breed Society for Norfolk Horn sheep and puts conservation at the top of his list of interests. He is Chairman of Dacorum Environmental Forum and a Governor of a local secondary school. Married with two children, Phil himself is something of a rare breed within the community: a man of forethought and commitment.

Toby Proctor's part-time post complements that of Ray Timberlake; both men have similar duties, road verge strimming and litter picking, amongst other things. Toby is at the beginning of his career and hopes to go to college, using his time with the Trust to gain experience.

Paul Redding is the longest serving member, joining the Trust staff in 1982 as Estate Worker. Over the years he has worked on both the Moors and Commons and has come to know the land very well, witnessing the Trust's acquisition of both Westbrook Hay and Bovingdon Brickworks. He is a skilled carpenter and takes an interest in the general maintenance of the Trust's residential properties. Paul now heads the Estate team and also assists in the welfare of the livestock. In his spare time Paul enjoys using his craft skills for the benefit of family and friends.

Elaine Rushton has been a resident of Boxmoor since 1984 and may often be seen out on the Moors walking her dogs. She has a deep appreciation of the local countryside and became a member of Friends of the Box Moor Trust when it was established in 1996. She joined the staff as part-time Administrative Assistant in September 2002; it is likely to be her voice you will hear if you ring the Trust office on a weekday morning. Elaine is married and has two children. In her spare time, Elaine edits a charity newsletter, attends dog shows with her two salukis and enjoys practising archery with a local club, the Berkhamsted Bowmen.

Shirley Selwyn can be seen planting a tree on Sheethanger Common, shortly after her retirement as Secretary to the Trust in 1988. Martin Hicks, of the Hertfordshire Environmental Record Centre and Jean Sniders watch the proceedings, which marked the designation of Sheethanger Common as a Heritage Site. Shirley worked for MIND before joining the Box Moor Trust.

Alison Shipley joined the Trust as Assistant Estate Manager in 1999 and is responsible for the day-to-day running of the Estate as well as the Staff and work programmes. Alison's duties also include working with the livestock and she played a key role in setting up the Junior Wildlife Watch Group at Westbrook Hay. Alison has a Degree in Environmental Science and previously worked as a Countryside Warden at Hainault Forest Country Park, where she was responsible for estate maintenance, the rare breeds' farm and environmental education. Previously, Alison was a full-time volunteer for Sandwich Bay Bird Observatory and Mid-Suffolk District Council. In her spare time Alison can be found working out at the gym and dancing until dawn at Old Skool and Drum 'n' Bass all night events.

Jean Sniders started work as Secretary to the Box Moor Trust in 1988 and has since moved office three times to her present location at the Box Moor Trust Centre on London Road as Administration Manager. Jean received her BA Honours Degree in Social Administration at Nottingham; she also has a teaching qualification. The fact that she was born in Yorkshire gives Jean the gritty tenacity to run the Trust Office. Jean loves walking and now that her children have grown up she dabbles in many other activities, including reading, music and arts and crafts.

Ray Timberlake initially started work with the Trust as its litter picker but since his retirement as a caretaker for a local school he has increased his hours, helping to maintain Trust properties as well as taking on other odd jobs around the Office and Estate. Ray started his working life as a printer and he has varied outside interests, such as bowls and independent travel. You will often see Ray on the Moors, with his litter picker, always cheerful in any weather.

Shirley Selwyn (foreground), Martin Hicks and Jean Sniders, in 1988.

André Couzens and Paul Redding manufacturing hurdles, kissing gates, tree guards and other items for the upkeep of the Estate as required, in one of the workshops at Howe's Retreat.

André was a familiar figure on the Estate for over twenty years, until he retired in 2002. As well as assisting with the increasing number of livestock, his particuluar skills were in the maintenance of the Trust's tractors and machinery.

Trust Staff in front of the Box Moor Trust Centre in autumn 2000, back row: Paul Redding (Estate Worker); Alison Shipley (Assistant Estate Manager); Caralyn Duignan and Jaine Irish (former Assistant Administration Managers) and André Couzens (Estate Worker); front row: Jean Sniders (Administration Manager); Phil Pennington (Estate Manager).

65. HOWE'S RETREAT

The parcel of land known as Howe's Retreat has had a chequered history during the last hundred years. A favourite venue as a pleasure ground, a prisoner-of-war camp during the Second World War, a pig farm and, finally, part of the Box Moor Trust Estate. It serves today as an area of workshops, cattle barns and a bull pen as well as grazing land for the Trust's herd of Belted Galloways. The sale by auction in 1978 of Felden Farmhouse and adjoining land, including Howe's Retreat, led to a bid by Robert Pooley to secure the whole property. Subsequently, Howe's Retreat was purchased by the Trust for £25,378.50 on 13 December 1978. The adjacent 2 acres were purchased from All Souls College, Oxford, for £6,000 in August 1981.

HOWE'S PLEASURE GROUND

View of Howe's Pleasure Ground, c.1900. The Pleasure Ground was a popular feature in the early twentieth century on the land now called Howe's Retreat. C. H. Howe, a contractor of refreshments from Rickmansworth, originated the idea in c.1896.

A railway excursion from London to Boxmoor Station in 1906, probably destined for Howe's Retreat. 'Charles Howe was desirous of bringing London Sunday School children to Boxmoor for their summer picnic.'

The dining hall at Howe's Retreat. Bovingdon farmers would help to convey local children to enjoy the merry-go-rounds, followed by tea and buns.

View of the elegant tea gardens and tea rooms, which were part of the provision in 1906 for visitors to the Pleasure Ground.

Helmut Maros, a German prisoner-of-war, resident of Howe's Retreat POW Camp, 1948. According to Helmut's wife, Heather: 'When the prisoners arrived at Boxmoor in 1947 it was deep in snow. They were marched up Felden Lane from the station to Howe's Retreat. It was a bitterly cold winter and they only had their battledresses, but no underclothes. Forays into the woods helped to keep the big, black iron stoves giving out a little heat. They had to work hard, but worst of all was the mental anguish, worrying about their families in Germany.'

After the Trust purchased Howe's Retreat in 1978, the land was restored from a pig farm to winter quarters for the Trust's own herd, since the lower Moors became too waterlogged in winter. The small herd of Shetland cattle was sold as a unit and returned to Scotland.

The Shetland cattle were replaced with Belted Galloways and a substantial herd of about fifty animals has now been built up. On the right in the background is the new cattle barn, erected in 2000, and on the left is the equipment barn and workshop, originally a brick building.

66. WESTBROOK HAY

It is appropriate that to mark the Four Hundred Years Anniversary of the Box Moor Trust a large parcel of land was acquired, formerly part of the Ryder family's estate, which then brought the area managed by the Trust up to 400 acres. This new land was by that time in the possession of the Enid Linder Foundation.

The following press statement is worth quoting in full, for the acquisition of Westbrook Hay was an important addition to the Box Moor Estate:

'Subject to contract and approval by the full Council when it next meets on 12 October [1994] Dacorum Borough Council intends to purchase land at Westbrook Hay Farm, off Box Lane. It is also intended, subject to negotiation, to lease the land into the care of the Box Moor Trust for public use and enjoyment.

The land, which measures approximately 168 acres of mixed woodland and pasture, joins existing Box Moor Trust land, creating a green corridor from Two Waters all the way to Little Hay Golf Course. In addition, it adjoins land which has been provided by the Department of Transport to replace lands taken for the new A41 By-pass.

The buy-and-lease deal will be similar to the arrangement made very recently for Tring Park, when Dacorum Borough Council bought 254 acres of open parkland and immediately leased it to the Woodland Trust for management.'

The news was received enthusiastically by local residents and signified the tip of a proverbial iceberg, since it was the result of months of careful negotiations between the Trust, the Council and the Enid Linder Foundation. The full meeting of Dacorum Borough Council on 12 October ratified the agreement to purchase the land, a momentous decision that was followed by a meeting of the Trustees on 26 October. This meeting focused on the lease, the terms of which provided the opportunity for the Trust to consider buying the land at some future date, when its finances allowed. The Trustees had been advised that it would be difficult for them to satisfy the Charity Commissioners that Trust resources would be properly employed in setting up Westbrook Hay Estate and maintaining it as a public open space if they could never be sure of eventually owning the freehold reversion, no matter how long the lease or nominal the rent. However, the Trust was fortunately able to purchase the freehold in March 2003 for £330,000 and thereby fully safeguard the land for all to enjoy as part of the growing Box Moor Estate.

There was a strong emotional element to the leasing and eventual acquisition of this land. The Trust Chairman wrote to the Council reminding them that during the four hundred years of its history, the Moors and Commons had been severed, first by the canal, then the railway and now by the A41 By-pass. Although the Trust had been compensated in accordance with the law for these invasions, they had left it

with a seriously fractured estate. The area under scrutiny linked sensibly to other Trust lands and redressed the balance, particularly for the inhabitants of Bovingdon.

The Trust needed to draw up a management plan and present it to the Council. Five or six years of neglect meant that there were some urgent matters to attend to, such as fencing, which needed addressing before the full plan could be put into action. There were 36 acres of woodland, 22 acres reinstated from use as a chalk pit for the construction of the By-pass and some 'set aside'* areas, as well as grassland. Ramacre Wood had been used for war games by the California Commandos for several years. The Plan was to include the provision of new footpaths and hedges serving as wildlife corridors in the long term. It was to become open amenity land, with the emphasis on species-rich grasslands. Grazing would be used as a management tool. As there were no natural water sources on Westbrook Hay, it was decided to establish a large pond on Preston Hill. A further woodland pond has since been installed, an important feature in these days of diminishing natural watering places for all kinds of wild creatures and plants.

Education and information is incorporated into the overall future planning, with the whole area accessible to everyone, except for unauthorised vehicles and motorcycles. Wheelchair users are accommodated with extra wide kissing gates that offer easier access; in fact, the needs of disabled visitors are at the forefront of future planning.

To continue the educational theme, the Trust has enabled the old barn on the crest of the hill opposite Westbrook Hay School to be rebuilt in a sympathetic style based on the original design. This came into use during 2000 as a shelter, visitors' information point and a classroom for environmental studies. The Chiltern Society honoured the project with a Highly Commended Award in its annual architectural competition in that same year.

A small car park has been built for those who wish to drive and then to walk the Estate's extensive footpaths. For equestrians, there are many attractive bridle paths now open, linking into other paths in the vicinity. Tom Horn of Dacorum Borough Council was especially active in this respect and worked closely with the Trust to ensure a good circular network of routes. The more ambitious project of the Box Moor Trust Centre, based in the former farm buildings close to the road, will take further thought and meticulous planning.

Marbled White (Melanargia galathea).

The old barn at the summit of Westbrook Hay, believed to date to c.1820, was derelict for many years. When the Trust took over the Estate lease in 1995 it was in a sorry state.

The restoration of the old barn was completed in November 2000, aided by a grant from the Countryside Stewardship Scheme. It comprises a classroom, a ramblers' shelter, toilets and an owl loft.

Sketch by Peter Mitchell of the excavation at Westbrook Hay undertaken by the Berkhamsted and District Archaeological Society from September 1998 to June 1999. Finds included two glass bottles c.1850 and broken Victorian pottery. Peter Mitchell, the Society's Excavations Officer, was joined by a team of volunteers which included D. Burgess, M. Cherry, J. Hunn, R. McFadden, Ann Nath and B. Sparks.

Barn Owl (Tyto alba) a sketch by Dennis Furnell, 2004. Once a common feature of the Hertfordshire countryside, it is now down to a population of below ten pairs county-wide. Barn owl nest boxes have been placed in quiet parts of the Box Moor Estate.

This pond was recently established on Preston Hill at Westbrook Hay, in order to provide a habitat for aquatic as well as other species dependent on the availability of fresh water. It will be a key feature of the educational programme in the future, with activities such as pond dipping.

Westbrook Hay Farm was originally mainly an arable holding. These two barns and a grain-drying unit are situated behind the new Box Moor Trust Centre, but there are plans to modify or replace them in the near future by buildings more appropriate for Trust activities.

Westbrook Hay's gamekeeper, John Wilkins. He was a servant of the Hon. Granville Dudley Ryder.

The Westbrook Hay Estate dates back to the thirteenth century, when it was first mentioned in grants of land to Queen Eleanor. 'Robert de Hagh, Clerk at Hayha' is referred to in 1238, when he was allowed to have a small private chapel on his lands. John de la Hay, later the Sheriff for Hertfordshire, received a grant for life of all lands at La Hay and in 1312 he obtained a licence to have an oratory. By 1334 the estate comprised about 100 acres.

The last de la Hay recorded locally was the wealthy Edward, who was a close friend of Cecily, Duchess of York the devout mother of King Edward IV. She resided at the nearby Berkhamsted Castle and left clothing and money to her friend in her will of 1495. Edward's daughters inherited the estate and so it passed into the Parre and Butter families. Incidentally, the Bounds of the Manor of 1650 are described in a document which lists the customs of the manor of Hemel Hempstead, in which both 'Hay Hill' and the 'manor of Westbrooke Hayne' are mentioned. The latter was then held by Mr Richard Woode and Mrs Sarah Mayne.

The Mayne family of Ascot became lessees and then owners of the estate from the late 1580s; they were sympathetic to the Puritans and it is probably during their occupancy that the chapel in Box Lane came into being. There existed brasses in the chancel of Bovingdon Church to the Maynes, the last one being to James Mayne dated 1642.

They in turn were replaced by the Lomax family, when Joshua Lomax of Bolton gave Westbrook Hay to his youngest son, Thomas, who rebuilt the house. It was described by Chauncey as 'a very fair Mansion house of Brick'. It was by marriage that his daughter, Ann Lomax, brought the manor into the ownership of Richard Ryder MP whose brother was Sir Dudley Ryder, the first Earl of Harrowby, and MP for Tiverton. Dudley later became Attorney General (1737–57) and Chief Justice of the King's Bench. The house was then left to Richard's nephew, the Hon. Granville Dudley Ryder, MP for the County of Hertfordshire. He became a Box Moor Trustee in 1833 and served for thirteen years.

Granville took an active interest in the surrounding communities and was a kind benefactor to local schools and churches. He died in 1879 and was succeeded by his son, Dudley Henry Ryder who continued his father's good works until his own death in 1911. Many memorials to the Ryder family, as well as to the Mayne's, exist in St Lawrence Church, Bovingdon. The last member of the family to own the estate was Frederick Granville Ryder and in 1920 it was rented by the Parry's. From 1947 to 1962 it was the Head Office of the Hemel Hempstead Development Corporation (later taken over by the Commission for New Towns). The memory of a long walk up the steeply rising and twisting lane still lingers for some early New Town residents.

The Commission for New Towns, in effect, swapped Westbrook Hay for Gadebridge House, Hemel Hempstead, which was at the time an independent boys' boarding school. The move took place in the severe winter of 1963, leaving the Gadebridge site to become both a public open space and the Kodak Training Centre. An Educational Trust was formed in 1985 at Westbrook Hay School, as it is now known, and the co-educational day and boarding school continues to the present.

Westbrook Hay, the former Manor House. It is now a preparatory school for boys and girls, who still use the mansion and grounds.

Gadebridge House, Hemel Hempstead, once the home of Sir Astley Paston Cooper, surgeon to George IV. The preparatory school vacated the premises and moved to Westbrook Hay in 1963.

Memories of Westbrook Hay by Alice Wear

Alice Wear, who now lives in the United States, wrote the following about her memories of Westbrook Hay in spring 1999. It is a sad piece, as she laments the changes that have been brought about over the last thirty years, but she ends on a note of positive trust in the protectors of her beloved Westbrook Hay.

'It was strange, after thirty years, to be going back to Westbrook Hay; after all, it had been my home for nearly two decades. My home was Moor End Farm and the Westbrook Hay Estate was incorporated into it. The estate added considerably to the acreage, although most of it was parkland.

My husband was the Farm Manager there from the mid-1940s to around 1963. I used to help him with the dairy herd and tractor work. I also exercised the hunters and looked after the poultry.

It was a busy life. Our day started at 5.30am with the milking. We milked about 30 cows and there were calves to raise as well. However, it wasn't always hard graft. I always had the compensation of the Westbrook Hay woods and I looked forward to the light evenings when I would take my Jack Russell terrier up to the woods.

How he delighted in the scent of fox, badger, hedgehog and squirrel while I found my joy in the scent of the bluebells and primroses. For me, in those days, the woods were my one source of entertainment, always something new, always something to wonder at. In the main wood there were six rides, three running parallel with the Box Lane houses and three running down towards the lower one. The furthermost one was close to the field now known as Preston Hill; we knew it as Bun-Baum fields (there were two at one time, divided by an old hedge).

The centre ride we always referred to as the Cathedral Nave; here there were some wonderful mature beeches and the canopy they formed resembled a cathedral roof. We always kept a dignified respect when we walked this ride and the children were always taught to behave as though in church.

The other ride, near the old barn – or the 'granary' as we used to call it – was the Heronry Ride. This was a wonderful heronry, built high in the beech tops. The herons used the same nests each year and started in very early spring to mate and rear their young. Often one would find a

The Norfolk Horn sheep are used to manage the grassland at Westbrook Hay. The tree on the left is a specimen Wellingtonia, a legacy from the former Ryder family's Estate.

Visitors to Westbrook Hay being shown Bovingdon Reach. Grassy paths are mown to provide easy access through undisturbed grassland where several pairs of skylarks are already established and butterflies abound.

discarded egg shell at the foot of the trees and the smell of fish was very strong. We used to press our ears to the trunks to hear the young herons 'grunting' in the nests.

Spring in the Westbrook Hay woods was really something. There were great drifts of primroses and acres of bluebells, often white ones and on rare occasions there were orchids and cowslips too. It all seemed so permanent, so peaceful.

Now here I was after thirty odd years once more at the lodge gates of Westbrook Hay, looking across at the lime avenue and across to the Shanty Field – or where it used to be because the new By-pass had gouged such a hole in it that there was hardly any Shanty Field left. Most of the mature trees had gone too. We walked on up to the drive, to find that Green Croft, on our right, was about four feet higher than it used to be. Infill from the By-pass had made it into a field, nice and green; the sheep seemed to be enjoying it.

Over on our left was the old redwood tree: he used to be the marker on the corner of the wood. Now he stood, stark and lonely, for the woodland had been cut away, just leaving him on his own. Likewise the old barn, that used to be well into the wood but now it stood isolated and abandoned. I felt I was in a strange place; where had the woodland gone? Had some dreadful Old Father Time of immense proportions come along with a huge scythe and swathed it all away? Where were the Heronry and the Cathedral Nave? There certainly was a muddy ride ahead of us but it was all so dark and seemingly bereft.

We pressed on and eventually came back to the Preston Hill field. I remembered how the herons used to take their rest periods in that field; they would just stand there for hours on end while the yellowhammers would sing blithely on the tops of the hazels. The woodland on our left had been coppiced well; it seemed that somebody cared. In due course it would probably be a fine bit of woodland again and perhaps the green woodpeckers would return.

"Now, where does one go from here?" I ask. Then I tell myself that the whole thing could not be in better hands. Neither the Box Moor Trust nor Dacorum Borough Council would exploit the once-beloved woodland. Surely in years to come – not in my lifetime but fifty or sixty years hence – it will without a doubt return to its former glory.'

The Mayor of Dacorum, Councillor Catherine Appleby, presented the Trust's Chairman, David Furnell, with the Deeds of Westbrook Hay, Bury Woods and Ramacre. The freehold was purchased by the Trust in 2003. The aim is to create and preserve for future generations this area of rural delight by careful husbandry of the woodlands, grassland and scrubland, using the skills in estate management that the Trust has developed over many years.

The boardwalk, Hay Wood. The Trust has recently provided facilities for disabled people to better enjoy the Estate. A small pond has been established nearby to assist ecological studies. A motorised wheelchair, specially designed to travel over rough ground, is available on request from the Box Moor Trust Centre.

The quality of the local lakes and rivers is crucial for all forms of wildlife.

Westbrook Hay Barn is proving to be a useful base for indoor events.

PAST, PRESENT AND FUTURE

67. CELEBRATIONS!

The year 1994 marked four hundred years in the history of the Box Moor Trust. A multitude of events were planned to ensure that the quartercentenary should be remembered by the local inhabitants, old townees and newcomers alike. On 4 September a grand day was arranged on Snook's Moor entitled 'Moor Time'. This included a Wild West Show, a band, parachute jumps, helicopter rides, the re-telling of Snook's story by an actor in role, and the laying of Snook's Foot-stone at the memorial grave. There were sports, rural crafts, a treasure hunt … and much more. The occasion was also in aid of the West Herts Hospital Scanner Appeal, harking back to the times earlier in the century when many Hospital fund raising events were staged on the Moors.

A special supplement in the *Hemel Hempstead Gazette* featured many stories and details about the Four Hundred Years Anniversary. Concerts in the parish churches, celebration cricket matches and barbecues, a library display, a travelling display for schools and a guided walk were a few of the other activities arranged during that year. Time capsules were placed on the Moor on 26 April by local schoolchildren and the age-old tradition of Beating the Bounds with willow wands so that the boundaries would not be forgotten was resurrected by Lois Gurney and the Open Spaces Society.

Another popular attraction that year, bringing back memories of Victorian and Edwardian times, was Carter's Steam Fair. This red and gold cornucopia of delights from another era of popular entertainment gave enjoyment to all ages on the Moor opposite St John's Hall. Most of the beautifully crafted traditional rides have been rescued by John Carter from scrap heaps or at auction. The 1895 carousel, driven by a period steam engine and accompanied by a genuine Gavioli organ, made a particularly splendid sight. The thrills of the dodgems, with some of the last British cars ever built, were contrasted with the nostalgic penny slot machines that still worked, using old copper pennies.

Fairs are not new to the Moors and Commons, but form part of a tradition spanning the last four hundred years. The town of Hemel Hempstead was granted a fair by Henry VIII and the September Statute or 'Statty' Fair for hiring servants had long been held at Handpost Farm, near the present-day Queensway. There are early photographs showing horse-drawn caravans, swing boats and rides on Roughdown Common. In 1896 C. H. Howe, a refreshment's contractor from Rickmansworth, was 'desirous of bringing London Sunday School children to Boxmoor for their summer picnic'. He assured everyone that the children he brought would not be a nuisance and would do no damage. He bought a plot of land in Felden which later became known as Howe's Retreat and was eventually purchased by the Box Moor Trust. The erection of a building which could seat 400 people for refreshments gives an idea of the scale of the venture that made Boxmoor a focal point for day trippers who came from London by train and by bus to enjoy the fresh country air and pleasure grounds.

Fireworks have also been a time-honoured way to celebrate in the area since they were first introduced into England. They were mentioned as long ago as the Coronation of Anne Boleyn on Whit Sunday 1533. Indeed, Brocks Crystal Palace Fireworks, one of the largest British manufacturers, had their premises in Hemel Hempstead at Cupid Green from 1933 until closure in the 1970s. Major national events were once illuminated by fires and fireworks on vantage points such as Roughdown Common and there was always a large community bonfire for Guy Fawkes' night on Blackbirds' Moor. Nowadays, the safer approach of an organised display, such as those held on the Saturday evening of Carter's Steam Fair, seems to be more acceptable.

A local resident, Jean Stevens, wrote in her diary for 1946:

'… 8 June was the official Victory day, with great parades in London, banners, tassels and a general air of celebration. At home the day itself was uneventful, rather drizzling and chilly, but at night we made our way to Roughdown Common, to the head of the chalkpit, where a huge bonfire waited to be lit. Turning up our coat collars we stood in the damp grass waiting for the torchlight procession to appear. At last, on the skyline, appeared a dull moving glow. We followed it with our eyes, straining into the windy darkness, until the glow became distinguishable as 500 bobbing lights. The lights drew nearer, becoming flaring torches held by shadowy figures, a winding caterpillar of light that moved to the foot of the chalkpit and climbed towards us. The flames flickered in the wind; while we dimly appreciated that this particular evening was a landmark in history, a history we were uneasily making …'

In the past, Royal occasions often necessitated a bonfire celebration and in 1911 permission was granted to Mr Flint to build a bonfire on Roughdown Common for the Coronation of George V. The King's Jubilee of 1935 was another occasion for celebration, this time on Blackbirds' Moor, with a blazing bonfire as before. This was allowed on condition that 'no damage was done and that the site was completely tidied up when the bonfire was over'. The abdication of Edward VIII in December 1936 led to the Coronation of his brother George VI in 1937, which year again saw many activities on the Moor as well as the traditional bonfire. Forty chestnut trees were planted to mark the occasion, in the so-called 'Coronation Avenue', from Picton's Bridge to the Three Blackbirds.

Charter Day procession crossing the Moor near St John's Church. Queen Victoria's Charter conferred Borough status on Hemel Hempstead. The Charter of Incorporation was granted on 8 June 1898 and came into operation on 9 November of that year. The official deputation arrived in a decorated train at Boxmoor Station.

Empire Day, 8 June 1910, at Hemel Hempstead Town cricket ground at Heath Park. The children marched to the Moor, saluted the flag and sang special Empire Day songs. Refreshments at Boxmoor Hall were followed by races on the Moor.

Hospital Parades to raise funds for West Herts Hospital were popular local events. This group, possibly from the Oxford Club Brotherhood that was associated with the Baptist Church opposite, were pleased when their horse and harness won first prize. The annual procession was in two sections; one started at Salmon Meadow, Apsley, the other from St John's Hall, Boxmoor.

This tree planting idea was followed up in the reign of Elizabeth II, when a copse with mixed varieties was dedicated, adjoining Station Road, in recognition of the Queen's Silver Jubilee. In 1983 bluebells and daffodils were added to the plantation. The late Queen Mother was similarly honoured in 1980, when a row of eighty red and white chestnuts was placed alongside the former A41 leading to Bourne End, to commemorate her eightieth birthday.

The Coronation of our present Queen in 1953 was well supported by a week of locally organised activities, such as an open-air service with combined church choirs, country dancing, a military parade and a cricket match between Hemel Hempstead and Gidea Park.

Queen Elizabeth's Silver Jubilee in 1977 was similarly celebrated with many 'family fun' events, such as an ox roast at Chaulden Meadows, the Boxmoor Silver Band, a steam organ, five-a-side football and a yard of ale competition. The money raised from this event went to the Prince of Wales Jubilee Fund. Many community-minded people gathered together for street parties, such as that held in Sebright Road, Boxmoor, in an attempt to keep alive some of the spirit of the past.

Fairs have always been a feature of the locality since the time of Henry VIII. A sheep and cattle fair was held on Holy Thursday in the Rose and Crown Yard, a wool fair on the last Friday in June and a pleasure fair on the third Monday in September.

May Day ceremonies were an important part of the year's activities. The local schools made full use of their open space – the Moor.

Pageants and processions were a part of local life, as in this twentieth-century version of Henry VIII and his Court on the Moor. The young Elizabeth II visited the new developments at Adeyfield and Bennetts End on 20 July 1952. In 1953, her Coronation was joyfully celebrated, with fireworks, fairs and bonfires as well as many other special events.

Beating the Bounds, 1990. An old custom was revived on Box Moor in 1985 by the Open Spaces Society. In the modern version, children took willow wands supplied by the Trust and had fun beating the bounds of the Estate.

Carter's Steam Fair helped to add colour to the scene of the Trust's Four Hundred Years Anniversary in 1994.

In 1993, a copy of This is your heritage, the Trust's booklet, was personally presented to the town of Hempstead on Long Island, New York, on the occasion of its three hundred and fifty years' celebrations. This picture shows the first real-estate transaction in Hempstead on 13 December 1643. Tackapousha and the 'One Eyed Sachem' with other native Americans conveyed to the Revd Robert Fordham and John Carman [both possibly from Hemel Hempstead] all the land that comprised the Township of Hempstead. Local Councillor Derek Townsend represented the Dacorum Borough Council at the celebrations in 1993 and was given a copy of this print, which now hangs in the Mayor's Parlour, Hemel Hempstead.

68. FRIENDS OF THE BOX MOOR TRUST

The annual Conker Festival, inaugurated in October 1996, has grown into a popular family event. The venue on Blackbirds' Moor is appropriately adjacent to an avenue of mature chestnut trees, planted to celebrate Queen Victoria's Diamond Jubilee in 1897.

Charities have proliferated in the last few hundred years, and there does not seem to be any area of the common good which does not receive some kind of support from voluntary contributors. The Box Moor Trust is unusual in this respect; it enjoys charitable status but does not rely on regular contributions from individuals in monetary terms. It was, nevertheless, seen as a useful development to involve a wider cross section of the community it serves in its operations. Therefore, in recent years, in keeping with its aims and with modern trends for disseminating more information, for 'mission statements' and partnerships, the Trust has undergone some radical changes.

In 1976 a small, inexpensive booklet called *This is your heritage* was published in order to publicise the aims and history of the Trust. This was followed in 1986 by a second edition, which included many superb colour photographs by Keith Huggett.

In order to appeal to a wider audience and to record the history and current work of the Trust, David Stevens, a former Trustee, undertook the ambitious project of a cine film. He has shown this fascinating portrait, entitled *A Green Oasis*, on more than one hundred different occasions to date, to many interested organisations around the district. In 2003, David produced an up-dated slide show, appropriately called *A Trust for all Seasons*, which is also being shown to local groups.

On 1 May 1996, Friends of the Box Moor Trust was launched to better inform interested people about all aspects of the Trust's work. For a small annual fee, members receive a regular newsletter detailing special Trust events during the year and a handsome folder in which to keep back copies. Membership has risen to over 400 and the idea has been well received locally. A web site is now part of the forward-thinking approach of the modern Box Moor Trust.

In the autumn of the same year the first Conker Festival was held; an appropriate event for an area planted with mature chestnut trees. This has become an annual event, with a variety of ancillary craft stalls, environmental exhibits and even visits by the Sealed Knot, a company which re-enacts life at the time of the English Civil War.

The Trust's display stands have become sought after at many other local events, especially the Council's 'Lark in the Park' in Gadebridge Park, the Hertfordshire Environmental Forum and a successful exhibition called *Looking through the Lens* at Westbrook Hay School, besides school fetes and other similar occasions.

There are from time to time guided walks, covering different aspects of the Trust's environmental work and a series of free leaflets have been produced giving directions for short walks all over the Estate. A commemorative walk to 'Beat the Bounds' has been a regular part of the Open Spaces Society's programme and enjoyed every year since it was instigated by the late Lois Gurney in 1985.

Litter is a constant problem and the Trustees ask all Friends to help in this respect, as well as officially appointing Ray Timberlake as a part-time litter collector. He had kindly undertaken this task enthusiastically for some years. Unruly dogs worrying the sheep have also been a cause for concern and, in fact, it is a great reassurance to know that there are residents who are interested enough in their local environment to report misuse of the amenities.

The Estate Manager's role has naturally encompassed an educational strand. Junior Wildlife Watch is one of several schemes which aim to involve youngsters in country pursuits, besides allowing the Trust to be associated with the Royal Society for the Protection of Birds. Young Friends can participate in a variety of informal, fun investigations and the support of volunteers in this context is much appreciated.

An innovative and ambitious event was planned for summer 2001, when a free concert entitled *Music on the Moor* took place. This was the first time that a major event such as this had been staged by the Trust, although there is a long tradition of bands playing on or near the Moor for special occasions. Owing to its success, it was repeated over two days on 5 and 6 July 2003, to wide public acclaim. It seems set to become a regular feature of the Trust's benefit to the community in the future.

A library of natural history books and the proper maintenance of the archives are all progressing to further expand the educational and informational aspects of the Trust. Photographic and painting competitions, puzzles and articles, help to keep the Trust and its activities alive for the voters of the future, who will one day decide on the next Trustees and their responsibilities.

Visits to the Trust's extensive Estate are organised by the Staff on a regular basis, or the Friends of the Box Moor Trust and the public at large can ramble at their leisure.

Fund-raising events for local charities and schools rely on voluntary effort.

The Trustees and Staff encourage people of all ages to take part in exploring the Estate's environmental diversity.

Imaginative exhibits, such as this make-believe badger sett, provide fun for youngsters attending Trust events.

One of the many groups of volunteers who assist the Trust in tasks such as hedge-laying and scrub clearance. Their support is an important part of the overall upkeep of the Estate.

The Box Moor Trust continues to branch out!

We are very pleased to welcome our new Community and Education Manager, Beth Brierley, to the Trust. She joined us in January this year. Beth feels that encouraging a passion for discovery is something often reserved for educators working with children. Her belief is that this can be life-long, and exciting opportunities for people to gain knowledge and skills and access inspiring environments should be available for everyone.

The Trust is already known for its links with many schools and community groups, and has been successfully delivering both formal and informal education for over a decade. Beth has come along to build on these foundations, with a view to making our heritage accessible to all. Her diverse role within the Trust will encompass the development and management of the community and education programme, facilities and resources.

Coming from a varied background, Beth already has a good deal of experience in this line of work. The first few years of her career were spent as a classroom teacher, both in mainstream and special schools. More recently she was an education officer at Banham Zoo in Norfolk. She has also worked as a researcher and was head of an education programme in East Africa.

New developments: Improvements to our outdoor amenities for all visitors are currently taking place in and around Hay Wood. These improvements include a larger pond with shallows to encourage water-loving species, a new bird hide (constructed of natural materials) and a pond dipping area for use by visiting groups. Access routes are being modified in order to create a safe and exciting base, usable by all visitors including those with disabilities.

Courses available for schools and community

groups: All programmes have been designed with health and safety as a priority as well as being carefully linked to curricula requirements for schools. There has already been much interest from schools this year; some popular areas of study include pond-dipping, study of local flora and fauna, farming, lambing, hedge laying, living sculpture, and rocks and soils. You may wish to come and undertake one of these subjects (depending on the season) or suggest your own area for study.

Volunteers: Local volunteer groups have been responsible for some fantastic work over the years on the Box Moor Trust land. We are keen to maintain these links, but also wish to start up our own volunteer base for people of all ages. Work could include conservation, giving guided walks, talks, filling bird feeders, helping out or running events, archiving, setting up databases, research, wildlife monitoring, you name it! Whether you have an hour a week to spare or a couple of days we would love to see you. So, if there is something you would like to get involved with, come along!

For any community groups and schools that are still wondering where to go for a thought-provoking AND fun outing, the answer could be on you back doorstep! If you would like to know more or if you live locally and are interested in volunteering please feel free to give us a ring, or email: **bethbrierley@boxmoortrust.org.uk**

The Box Moor Trust

NEWSLETTER

The Box Moor
Trust Centre
London Road
Hemel Hempstead
Herts HP1 2RE
Tel: 01442 253300
Fax: 01442 253800
Registered Charity
No 206142

Friends of the Box Moor Trust Newsletter, Spring 2004.

69. TRUSTEES TODAY

The job description of a present-day Box Moor Trustee might read as follows:

'Applicants must have commitment, motivation and keen interest in keeping the Moors and Commons safe for future generations. He/she must live locally. No formal qualifications required but diverse experience welcomed. A part-time post, mainly evenings. This is a rewarding and important job, sometimes frustrating but increasingly necessary in a fast-changing world. Remuneration nil.'

David Furnell (photograph courtesy of Hemel Hempstead Gazette)

David Furnell moved to Hemel Hempstead when he was fourteen years old. He has two daughters, Emma and Claire, and now lives in Piccotts End village on the northern outskirts of the town. David founded Furnell Transport in 1967 and his company continues to thrive. Strong support of interaction between business and the community have prompted him to become a committee member of the local Industrial Association, Enterprise Agency and Business Network Link and a Trustee of the local Dacorum Community Trust. He was a member of the Association of Round Tables in Great Britain and Northern Ireland and is now a 41 Clubber. Through the Round Table, David was involved with the Anthony Nolan Bone Marrow Trust for twenty years and is a staunch supporter of the Woodfield School for children with severe learning difficulties in Leverstock Green. An enthusiastic member of the Veteran Sports Car Club, David owns a 1930 Austin Seven 'The Toy' and a 1926 Austin Burghley. Elected a Trustee in 1995, David became Chairman in 2001 and served until 2004.

Dennis Furnell has lived in Hemel Hempstead since 1962. Elected to the Box Moor Trust in 1986 as a lifetime Trustee, his work as a natural history author, broadcaster and acknowledged expert on the problems and solutions of access to the countryside for the disabled, has enabled him to focus on the various environmental aspects of Trust land. During the course of his Trusteeship he has welcomed a more holistic regime that, among other things, has seen the instigation of a traditional wild flower hay meadow and memorial orchard, a bat *hibernaculum*, a common tern raft on the lake at Pixies

Mere, a wildlife pond on Preston Hill, improvements to the Fishery wetland site and a plan to return Hay Wood from a conifer plantation to a broadleaved wood with coppice management and natural under-storey of wild plants.

Dennis Furnell

Roger Hands was born in Edmonton in 1937 and attended Enfield Grammar School. He moved to Boxmoor with his wife, Joan, in 1964. They have two grown-up sons, David and Stephen. His reason for seeking election as a Box Moor Trustee in 1979 stemmed from a determination that future generations might enjoy similar pleasures in the local environment during their formative years. He is a founder member of a nursery and landscape gardening business that has won numerous medals, including Gold at the Royal

Roger Hands

Chelsea Flower Show, and which recently celebrated forty years of consistent partnership. Roger assists in managing the Boxmoor Trout Fishery, and although he does not get much spare time to fish nowadays, he remembers with pleasure a trip to the Alaskan wilderness. There he caught a 40lb King salmon on a barbless fly on the Togiak River, which was in full flood at the time. Roger enjoys holidays in the UK and abroad, especially if they include visits to his grandchildren in Holland and the United States. Roger appreciated the challenge of serving as Chairman of the Trust from 1988–96 and is still very committed to the principles of the Trust's historic foundations.

Claire Hughes

Claire Hughes has lived in Boxmoor all her life. She has two young children at local schools and works as a Resource Centre Manager at Bovingdon Primary School. Her main objective is to raise the Trust's profile within the local community generally and, with the introduction of recent events like *Music on the Moor* and the annual Conker Festival, feels that the Trust can now offer something for everyone. Recognising the wonderful educational resources that the Trust has to offer and the difficulty schools have in providing interesting, relevant, local and cost-effective environmental trips, she will also assist the Trust in improving and expanding its facilities to offer educational visits to local schools and other interested groups.

William Hodgson

William Hodgson, Chairman of the Trust in 2004, considers himself fortunate, not only because he was nurtured in Bovingdon, but that he now lives in the family house in which he was born. In his youth, Will roamed over land owned by the Trust; a privilege that, as a Trustee, he concedes should be the right of future beneficiaries. Around 1980 he met his wife Caroline and they have two children, Natalie and Olivia. In 1982 he joined the Police Service and has served people ever since; at the Trust, through his work and through the Round Table. In 2000 Will was elected to the Trust promising greater access and use for education, although on election, he discovered that plans towards these, his personal aims, were in place, albeit in their infancy. As Chairman, Will believes it is paramount that he is at all times approachable and, like all Trustees, feels a responsibility to safeguard the Trust by constantly monitoring and ensuring its relevance to today's beneficiaries.

David Kirk

David Kirk, an accountant, grew up enjoying the sanctuary of the woods, fields and streams of the Trust Estate at a time when wildlife was plentiful and children could roam for miles in safety. David feels that many young people are deprived of this opportunity today; hence, along with other Trustees, he is keen to promote education and the environment with the aim of encouraging the return of lost wildlife species. The Trust's weekend children's wildlife group – The Boxmoor Birds – run together with the Royal Society for the Protection of Birds, is particularly relevant to David's belief in the benefits of environmental education for children. David, along with the other Trustees, supports fully the *Music on the Moor* initiative that gives hundreds of young musicians a chance to play to a wide audience. If you see a lone figure on the estate with binoculars in hand and camera at the ready, surveying birds, insects and plants, it may well be David; do have a chat with him.

Reg Sear (1913–2003)

Reg Sear was born on 17 June 1913 and was elected as a Box Moor Trustee in 1975. He actively and conscientiously served on all the various sub-committees over the last twenty-eight years. He was always dedicated to promoting local heritage, as well as giving a number of talks on the Trust. He spent a considerable amount of time putting together a dossier of past decisions and events in the Trust's history. As well as his many church activities, Reg was associated with the Scouting movement. He served on many committees for local clubs, often in a financial role, and had been Club Captain and Vice-President of the Chesham and Ley Hill Golf Club. After a short illness, Reg died on 1 December 2003 at the age of ninety. He leaves a widow, Nancy, and two sons. He was a remarkable character and an invaluable asset to the Trust. His enthusiasm and detailed knowledge will be sorely missed.

John Poole

John Poole was elected as a Trustee in 1975 to help improve the condition of the Moors with his expertise and knowledge of agriculture and cattle. He is the last yeoman farmer to be elected for life. John is a member of the Estates Committee and was its Chairman for six years. Along with other colleagues, John has witnessed the introduction of the Trust's stock, starting with the Shetland cattle in conjunction with the Rare Breeds Survival Trust, which were then replaced by the Belted Galloways. He also saw the purchase of Howe's Retreat in Felden, a derelict POW camp which has been demolished and replaced with the Trust's machinery store and winter quarters for cattle. John was Chairman of the Trust for two years.

John Steele

John Steele, born into a family of builders and owner farmers, can trace his yeoman ancestry back to 1620 in North Oxfordshire. On finishing his education, John joined the Royal Navy until 1947 and then pursued a career in road haulage and distribution. With his wife and two sons he moved to Berkhamsted in 1966 and Hemel Hempstead in 1970. In 1972 John joined Whitbread (London) as Distribution Director. In 1982 he became Facilities Director of Stowells of Chelsea and in 1986 was appointed Operations Planning Director of European Cellars, finally retiring in 1990. After his retirement he felt keenly that he should put something back into the community using the skills and experience gained in business. He joined the Box Moor Trust in 1995 and was appointed Chairman in 1996, a position he held until 2002. He is a Board Member of the Hanover Housing Association and Chairman of Hanover Property Management. He retains membership of the Chartered Institute of Transport and Chartered Management Institute.

Margaret Ward

Margaret Ward was elected as a Trustee in October 2000, under the new Charity Commission Scheme of that year. The commonsense and versatility acquired to bring up a family combined with a twenty-year career in a variety of roles with Kodak seemed to be a useful preparation for work as a Trustee. Margaret's aim in standing for election was to ensure that the public had a greater awareness of why the Trust exists and its purpose in the local community. She also believes that women are under-represented in so many areas of life and that it was timely to address this imbalance within the Trust. She is keen to promote future community activities, such as *Music on the Moor*, and to expand in general the recreational, educational and social uses of the Moor within the community.

George Tite

George Tite was born and brought up in Apsley and went to a school at Two Waters, now the site of the Pilling Volvo garage; he then went to Berkhamsted School. As a child he spent a lot of time on Two Waters Moor and Roughdown Common, experiences that inspired his keen interest in wildlife. On leaving school he began his career in agriculture. He later joined John Dickinson in Apsley as a fireman, rising to the rank of Station Officer. George has had a smallholding for many years, during which time he has kept a variety of livestock; now he has ponies and a few sheep. His main hobby is carriage-driving and he is often to be seen driving his piebald mare round Felden and Bovingdon. Townspeople, George believes, should be given a taste of the countryside in an urban setting and not just another park. He believes that the Trust must ensure the maintenance of grazing land and use the Moors for as many different outdoor, educational and recreational pursuits as possible.

The boardroom in the Box Moor Trust Centre, 2004.

70. THE BOX MOOR TRUST ORCHARD

'Go, bind thou up yon dangling apricocks, which, like unruly children, make their sire stoop with oppression of their prodigal weight.'
Richard II, by William Shakespeare, Scene IV, Act III in Langley [Kings Langley], the Duke of York's garden.

Hertfordshire contained up to 6,000 orchards 100 years ago, of which only about 2,500 survive, mostly in poor condition. The district of Hemel Hempstead and Bovingdon was once covered in cherry blossom and wild cherry trees in the hedgerows are a reminder of those days. The Prunus varieties are well suited to the chalky soil of this region and once grew in abundance; similarly, the 'Coroon', 'Croon' or 'Keroon' was a popular variety of Hertfordshire black cherry also grown locally. 'Merries', a word derived from the French *merises*, were another variety, the fruit nowadays only recalled in names like Cherry Bounce* in Hemel Hempstead's old town. The villagers of Potten End were known as 'cherry pickers' and children were kept busy scaring birds away from the ripening crops. Pears were cultivated in England from about the time of the Norman Conquest, and in the early sixteenth century several new varieties were introduced. In his *Weather Diary* of 1684–9, Sir John Wittewronge of Rothamsted recorded 'Bergomot, Spannish, Bon Chritien and Bury du Roy'.

Yet the fruit for which this part of the world was best known was the apple. The famous Lane's Prince Albert and the lesser known Oakland Seedling were two varieties developed at John Lane's Potten End Nurseries. In 1880 nearly 80 acres of his holdings lay in or around the village and all kinds of nursery stock was grown. Chiefly admired for its azaleas and rhododendrons, the firm employed over 100 men by 1892, together with another 100 during the fruit-picking season.

Gradually, over the next fifty years the trade declined and the Broadway Nurseries near Bourne End were sold. The business, founded in 1777, never did reach its second centennial and closed in the 1950s. There are still, however, a few remaining Prince Albert trees left in the district.

It seems right and fitting, therefore, that one of the varieties chosen for the Trust's own memorial orchard should be the Prince Albert apple, and also that the piece of land chosen for the plantation should be very close to the original Lane's Nurseries at Broadway. The orchard, sited at the northern end of the footbridge over the A41 By-pass at Bourne End, will serve three main purposes. As a supporter of the Hertfordshire Orchard Project, the Trust will enable local people to plant fruit trees in memory of their loved ones; the plants will be mainly old species, some of them endangered local varieties, and will include ancient fruits such as greengage, medlar, quince and prune. (The words of Shakespeare come to mind even as one says the names.) Most importantly, the Trust's concerns for conservation will be met, with Trust Staff given training in how to care for these wonderful, but rarely seen, plants.

One day the Trust hopes to be able to provide a gene bank of local trees and helping the Trust work towards this enterprising objective are the keepers of the National Apple Collection at The Brogdale Horticultural Trust in Kent and the Tewin Orchard Nature Reserve. The fallen fruits will also aid wildlife, especially bullfinches and wrynecks. So one day, in the not too distant future, local inhabitants may once again be fortunate enough to see rows of apple, pear and cherry trees in all their blossoming beauty in the spring. Perhaps some of the local traditions associated with fruit growing, long vanished from the Area of Benefit, will be revived.

Fruit pickers at Lane's Nurseries, c.1900. The firm was founded in 1777 by Henry Lane. He was succeeded by his son John who introduced the apples known as Lane's Prince Albert and Oakland Seedling. Lane's had holdings at Broadway, Bourne End, not far from the Box Moor Trust Orchard.

Cherries: Early Rivers (black); Emperor Francis (red); Bigarreau (white).

Illustrations from The Gardener's Assistant, *by Robert Thompson. First edition published in 1859; this edition 1925, William Watson (Ed.).*

Webb's Prize Cob

Spanish Prize Filbert

Mulberry

Medlar

71. Bovingdon Brickworks

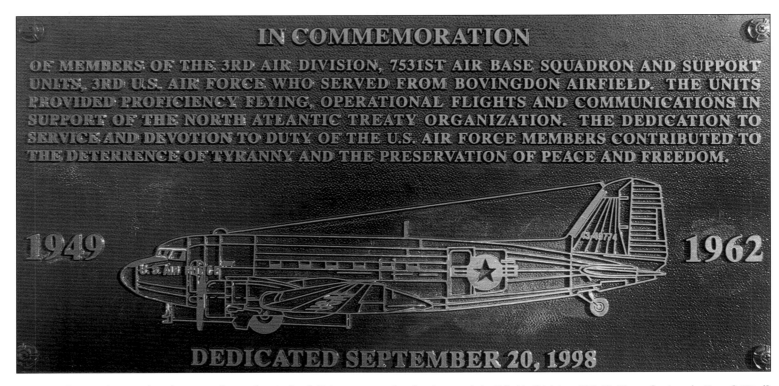

IN COMMEMORATION

OF MEMBERS OF THE 3RD AIR DIVISION, 7531ST AIR BASE SQUADRON AND SUPPORT UNITS, 3RD U.S. AIR FORCE WHO SERVED FROM BOVINGDON AIRFIELD. THE UNITS PROVIDED PROFICIENCY FLYING, OPERATIONAL FLIGHTS AND COMMUNICATIONS IN SUPPORT OF THE NORTH ATLANTIC TREATY ORGANIZATION. THE DEDICATION TO SERVICE AND DEVOTION TO DUTY OF THE U.S. AIR FORCE MEMBERS CONTRIBUTED TO THE DETERRENCE OF TYRANNY AND THE PRESERVATION OF PEACE AND FREEDOM.

1949   1962

DEDICATED SEPTEMBER 20, 1998

The site of Bovingdon Brickworks was used as a hospital and living quarters for the airmen of the 3rd Air Division, US Air Force, during the Second World War. The airfield was built in 1941–2 as a bomber base for the Royal Air Force, which reclaimed control of it in April 1946 until the late 1960s.

The addition of Westbrook Hay to the lands managed by the Box Moor Trust was a very welcome one, yet to receive another opportunity to substantially increase the acreage of the Estate within a few years seemed too good to be true. The old clay quarries at Pudds Cross were no longer viable for the production of quality bricks and so Bovingdon Brickworks' managers were looking for another site in the locality. Dacorum Borough Council and Hertfordshire County Council felt that to start another extraction site in the vicinity, when the previous one was not reclaimed, was unsound and environmentally unfriendly.

The solution to the problem lay in finding an organisation capable of taking on the long-term environmental reclamation, for which the Trust seemed admirably suited. Thus, after several months of negotiations, in January 2000 the new Box Moor Trust Bovingdon Brickworks Conservation Area was born, adding another 36 acres to the Estate at a relatively minimal initial cost.

The land is unlike any other part of the Moors or Commons: a green-fringed lunar landscape with deep clay-lined holes and a myriad of tracks amongst mature blackberries and scrub. The comprehensive ten-year management plan is monitored by Hertfordshire Council. The old clay pits have an established colony of flora and fauna, attracting bird life, but the aim is to increase this in an ecological manner and diversify where possible. The hope for the future is that even some currently endangered species may be encouraged to thrive there.

Before the Trust took over the site, a decontamination survey was carried out. A botanical survey is being carried out by local residents Gerald Salisbury and Jill Saunders, working as volunteer recording officers for the Hertfordshire Environmental Records Centre, which will prove an invaluable baseline for future activities. (See Appendix 9)

The area will be fenced, using sheep as an organic management tool. There will be footpaths, hides and seats so that eventually the public can have unlimited access, although the Trust asks that the existing footpaths are used as little as possible whilst reinstatement with heavy machinery is taking place. Bovingdon Brickworks themselves will be assisting with some of the hard landscaping and contouring of the site. Care will be taken to retain small ponds and to protect many parts that have been regenerating naturally.

The educational potential of the site is an exciting dimension of the project and the outcome of chemical-free management can be demonstrated to future generations. All in all, it will be a great amenity for the local communities of Bovingdon and Hemel Hempstead alike and a real challenge for the Trust in the twenty-first century.

Inside the brickworks. Originally part of Green Farm, the land was bought by Alfred Matthews, a brickmaker from Bellingdon. Over one million bricks were made annually before the Second World War.

Bricks ready for the kiln. There is still a strong demand for good quality hand-made bricks. In 1960 E. H. Smith Ltd took over the enterprise.

Digging out the clay in the new quarry. There were Nissen huts, a tennis court and a service bay for vehicle repairs in the vicinity of the brickworks. The clay in the old quarry was worked out and a new source of reliable clay was needed for brickmaking at the end of the twentieth century.

Gerald Salisbury and Jill Saunders are seen here recording the flora of the quarry in 2003. Reclamation of the old quarry by the Box Moor Trust has already started in accordance with a ten-year management plan to achieve the maximum environmental benefit.

72. THE BOX MOOR SCHEME 2000

It has been a surprising feature over many years that the Trust minutes, as well as various articles in the local press, have recorded the concerns of the beneficiaries regarding the conduct of the Trustees in interpreting and administering the 1809 Act of Parliament. Conversely, the Trustees themselves have felt constraints upon some of their plans, such as in the purchases of suitable adjoining land. In the past, this could only be obtained as replacement for existing permanent endowment land which had been taken under Compulsory Purchase Orders, such as in the cases of the canal and railways, or by application to the Charity Commission and public meetings, as in the case of Roughdown and Sheethanger Commons. Investment property, consisting of the assets of the Trust that have been acquired since 1594, was not subject to the strict interpretation relating to the original land.

Reference has already been made to the first serious attempts to devise a Scheme for the better management and re-organisation of the Box Moor Trust in the 1930s. It was clear from the original Act and the 1594 Conveyance that the Trust was not a 'free-standing charity with relief objects', but that it was primarily to hold land for the benefit of the residents and in so far as there were profits or a surplus, these had to be applied for the benefit of residents, facts that any new Scheme would have to reflect.

The Charities (Boxmoor Estate, Hemel Hempstead) Order 2000, which finally came into effect on 12 April 2000, had taken fourteen years of careful thought and planning to achieve. This new constitution was prepared by the Charity Commission in close consultation with the Trustees. It took the form of a Scheme, after receiving Parliamentary approval, rather than a completely new Act of Parliament, which in effect replaced the majority of the 1809 Act.

Towards the end of the twentieth century, the Act was felt to be neither flexible nor wide ranging enough to reflect present-day needs, modern legislation, or the foreseeable needs of future generations. If left unaltered it might well have resulted in expensive litigation for the Trust as it became increasingly unworkable. It was also considered that the Trust's income, expected to increase from the late 1980s, could have an impact on the financial organisation of the Box Moor Estate. In order to keep matters simple, yet fair to all concerned, it seemed in the best interests of all beneficiaries of the Estate to proceed with the Commission's suggested Charity Scheme and this has now been accomplished.

The move towards this momentous event formally began within the Trust on 12 May 1986, involving many lengthy discussions at all levels at Trust meetings, as well as on-site meetings with the Commissioners. To record all these details would take another book written solely about the Scheme.

It was not until 12 July 1990 that George Lawrence QC was instructed to advise the Trust on the Act. He recommended that the personal advice of Francis Bennion, an ex-Parliamentary Draughtsman, should be sought; this was followed up. On 12 December 1990, the Charity Commission decided that the proposed amendment to the Act could go forward as a Scheme rather than as a private Act of Parliament and informed the Trustees that they should take reasonable steps to ensure that 'any proposals for the Scheme were neither contentious nor controversial'. It is perhaps a contradiction to this sweeping statement that the Commissioners themselves then insisted that the established principle of life Trusteeship should be abandoned. Further, they raised the question of including representatives of the Local Authority to serve on the Trust, an idea that had never come to fruition in previous attempts to alter the workings of the Trust and that was now perceived as an unnecessary restriction to the Trustee's services to the community, by whom they are directly elected.

The Trustees were satisfied that the Scheme would equip them to serve the public efficiently and to meet the conditions arising in the years ahead. It will also preserve the traditions and good reputation of the Trust and make it fully accountable to the public it serves. The Scheme includes the retention of the original Area of Benefit, namely the boundaries of the parishes of Hemel Hempstead, Boxmoor and Bovingdon, with certain changes in accordance with modern urban developments. The original Area of Benefit in 1995 consisted of 54,506 inhabitants on the electoral roll. By extending this to include the New Town areas, an additional 6,419 residents became beneficiaries in Hemel Hempstead; in Bovingdon there were 4,225 on the electoral roll. After considering these figures, the Trustees decided upon new proportions: nine-tenths to Hemel Hempstead and one-tenth to Bovingdon.

There is to be an Annual Public meeting, open to all residents, in order to present the Annual Report and Accounts and outline future plans. This continues the tradition of the Vestry meetings of the past. All electors within the Area of Benefit have the right to vote in Trust elections. There are still twelve elected Trustees, but the current life Trusteeship is being replaced gradually by periodic elections under which Trustees stand for re-election from time to time. The Trustees elected in accordance with the 1809 Act still serve for life – not a prison sentence exactly – but nonetheless a major commitment! The hours, days, weeks of debate which, over time, eventually gave birth to the new Scheme have not been wasted if it can take the Box Moor Trust forward, democratically and responsibly, to meet the challenges of the future.

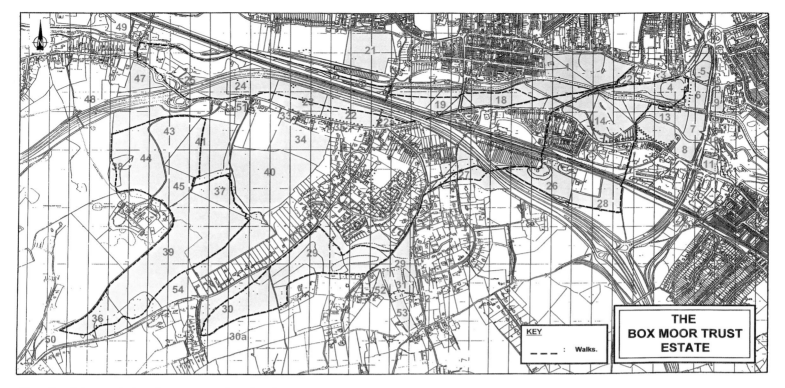

Field Names of the Box Moor Trust Estate

Name	No.	Hectares	Acres	Name	No.	Hectares	Acres
All Souls	52	0.86	2.12	London Road Verges	35	0.19	0.46
Amen Corner	25	0.36	0.88	Lower Roughdown	26	4.82	11.91
Apsley Triangle	12	0.41	1.01	Oak Tree Field	53	0.78	1.93
Balderson's Moor	6	1.55	3.83	Old Fishery	20	1.55	3.83
Barn Field	45	2.01	4.96	Orchard	48	0.78	1.92
Blackbirds' Moor	1	5.58	13.79	Overbourne	44	9.09	22.46
Bourne End Field	47	1.87	4.62	Pixies Mere	49	6.45	15.93
Bovingdon Reach	39	16.07	39.70	Plough Gardens	5	1.64	4.05
Box Hill	34	4.10	10.13	Preston Hill	40	8.10	20.00
Boxmoor Wharf	9	0.83	2.05	Ramacre Wood	36	5.77	14.25
Bulbourne Meadow	13	4.01	9.92	Ryder's	43	3.23	7.98
Bulbourne Moor	7	1.27	3.13	St John's Gardens	2	0.39	0.96
Bury Wood	30 & 30a	9.21	22.75	Sheethanger Common	29	16.48	40.72
Chaulden Meadow	21	4.26	10.52	(including Dew Green)			
Dellfield	41	7.15	17.66	Snook's End	33	0.50	1.23
Felden Verges	32	0.59	1.45	Snook's Moor	24	3.13	7.73
Fishery Moor	19	3.53	8.72	(including Mugford's)			
Further Roughdown	28	2.77	6.84	Snoxall's Moor	23	3.26	8.06
Gorsefield Wood	50	2.25	5.55	Station Moor	18	6.25	15.44
Green Croft	38	1.21	2.98	Three Crofts	54	0.72	1.77
Harding's Moor	14	6.38	15.76	Two Waters Moor East	11	0.61	1.50
Hay Wood	37	8.12	20.06	Two Waters Moor West	8	1.03	2.54
Heath Park	4	3.16	7.80	Two Waters Halt	10	0.10	0.25
Herdsman's Cottage	22a	0.63	1.55	Upper Roughdown	27	4.14	10.23
Herdsman's Moor	22	2.97	7.33	War Memorial Gardens	3	0.32	0.79
Howe's Retreat	31	1.97	4.86	Westbrook Hay Paddock	51	0.64	1.58

Bovingdon Brickworks	–	14.57	36.00

Bovingdon Brickworks and 30a, 45, 49, 50 purchased since map was produced.

Very small plots 15, 16, 17, 42 and 46 have been omitted.

73. THE TRUST IN THE TWENTY-FIRST CENTURY

The land owned by the Box Moor Trust is the source of a multitude of enjoyable activities, used as it is by groups as varied as the land itself. Spontaneous pleasures are mixed with more structured ones and a variety of club events also feature, mainly during the summer months, such as those organised by the Pony Club, Local Residents' Associations, the Rathbone Society, Guide Dogs for the Blind, the Open Spaces Society and many more. All this is a far cry from those original Feoffes and inhabitants whose lives were more restricted to the everyday burdens of living and whose leisure time was far less defined.

The canal has been the scene of boat rallies and the Great Inflatable Boat Race, with its finishing line adjacent to Station Moor. Only at these times can the Moor be seen to be covered in cars as well as buttercups. The Hertfordshire County Council's Library Service has also regularly brought its lively 'Story Boat' to Blackbirds' Moor and pirates have been known to invade Box Moor! The education of the young, as well as the young-at-heart, is an important aspect of the Trust's work. The Countryside Management Service have also organised rural events on the Commons. Local environmental volunteers have been involved in clearance of the scrub despoiling the Commons over the years. An unusual project carried out by pupils at Boxmoor House School in 1994 was the building of a dew pond on the aptly named Dew Green at Felden to celebrate four hundred years of the Trust. The frog population must have been grateful for that addition to their diminishing breeding grounds.

Sheethanger Common sets the scene for a day's outing in 2000, organised by the Chiltern Harness Driving Club, which was formed about twenty years ago and is still going strong.

The general policies of the Trust remain as close to the original intent as possible, incorporating the management and enhancement of the land, for grazing and amenity purposes, with public access. The raising of public awareness, especially in the fields of environment and education, is also an important maxim and one of the reasons for the publication of this book. The distribution of any available funds, after the needs of the Estate and suitable further purchases of land have been answered, is an on-going commitment, although in the immediate past this was not always possible. Therefore, the need is ever present to obtain sufficient income to further the Trust's policies.

The prosperity brought about in recent years by judicious use of the Trust's assets will have as yet unseen implications for the future, but the foundations have been slowly but consistently built upon to serve the 'heirs and assigns' forever. It is evident that as society changes, so too must the Trust and it is appreciated that this century's Scheme may not suit successive generations. Whatever else happens, however, the Trust will continue, and perhaps one day there will be another book about the first *thousand* years of the Box Moor Trust – your green heritage.

An exciting finish to the Inflatable Boat Race at the Fishery Inn, Boxmoor, in June 1989. This annual event has now ceased, but others will take its place.

The Hertfordshire Library Service's Story Boat in July 1982 drew crowds of youngsters onto Blackbirds' Moor. It is hoped that similar special events will continue to be a part of the appeal of the Trust's Estate.

Music on the Moor, 2003. The Berkhamsted Choral Society enjoyed the challenge of the open-air venue. The music was non-stop, with a jazz group filling in the intervals between items. Crowds of up to 5,000 people really appreciated the amenity of the Moor: their very own four hundred year-old heritage.

Music on the Moor was first held in the summer of 2001 and proved to be so popular that it was repeated on 5 and 6 July 2003. Celebrating the One World Community Arts Festival, in conjunction with Hemel Hempstead School and Dacorum Arts Education, a wide range of music was performed – from popular music to classics and jazz, from choral works to brass ensembles, as well as cameos of drama and dance staged at the School. A 'Green Village', organised by Dacorum Borough Council, with many stands making an environmental appeal, was part of the event. Family picnics on the grass were the order of the day and, fortunately, the weather was kind.

The newest calf on Snook's Moor, May 2004; a good sign for the future of the Trust's herd and grazing rights.

'Trust in the future...'

An Environmental Centre, based on the ecology of the river and surrounding water meadows, is planned for the former watercress beds at Old Fishery Lane.

This paddock, adjacent to the proposed Box Moor Trust's Visitors' Centre, is scheduled to become a microcosm of all the types of flora and habitats which are found on the Estate.

Pixies Mere, Bourne End, 2003. The lake was bought by the Box Moor Trust in the spring of 2003. The coarse fishery still operates and the aims are to provide good fishing, educational links for young people, bird watching facilities and protection for the existing wildlife.

A Letter to Future Generations

To Our Unknown Friends of the Future

The following letter was written by Jean Stevens, a long-time Boxmoor resident, and was placed in a special Time Capsule which was buried on Station Moor on 26 April 1994 to commemorate the first four hundred years of the Box Moor Trust.

'This letter is being written in the forty-second year of the reign of Her Majesty Queen Elizabeth II, but our thoughts are turning to the April day in 1594, in the reign of Queen Elizabeth I when the institution which we know as the Box Moor Trust came officially into being.

The local folk of that first Elizabethan era would scarcely recognise the valleys and water meadows of their day, even as you will look in amazement at the maps and papers which tell the story of this present time. The past centuries have brought a canal, a railway and a road system beyond the imagining of our forebears. New implements, machinery, new systems of husbandry, new breeds of cattle, horses and sheep have all played their part in creating the landscape that we know and love today and which, in trust, we have bequeathed to you.

In recent times we have had to give much time and thought to the effect of the By-pass running between Kings Langley and Berkhamsted. It has made inroads into the land, changed the shape of the Estate and posed problems which we are still in the process of trying to solve. How successful we are, we shall have to leave you to judge.

More important than anything else, however, is the land which has been entrusted to our care, on behalf of the local inhabitants. It is land which is still used for pasture and our own herd of Belted Galloway cattle take full advantage of this. It is land where people can walk, can watch the birdlife and wildlife of the district. Its Moors and Commons are still beautiful with trees, shrubs and flowers which delight the eye. There are areas where sports of many kinds can be played. People can still walk by the rivers Bulbourne and Gade, which were the source of the water meadows long ago.

In this special anniversary year we shall be celebrating the four hundred years which have elapsed since 26 April 1594. There will be many different events which we hope will bring pleasure and interest to many people. Tonight we shall drink a toast to the Box Moor Trust and our thoughts will turn to the past, to the present which we are helping to shape, and to the future, which will belong to you. We have been privileged to serve as Trustees; we pass this privilege to you and we wish you well.'

Grasses by Ann Johnson, 2002.

APPENDICES

APPENDIX 1

CONVEYANCE OF BOX MOOR DATED 26TH APRIL 1594

This parchment writing was produced by Joshua Pembroke at the time of his examination for the complainant in this cause before us
Will House   J Geo Bingham   P Bennett   John Mariott

1. JOHN ROLFE AND RICHARD POPE

to

2. FRANCIS COMBES, SETH GLADMAN & OTHERS

THIS INDENTURE made the six and twentieth day of April in the six and thirtieth year of the reign of our most gracious sovereign Lady Elizabeth by the grace of God Queen of England France and Ireland Defender of the Faith BETWEEN JOHN ROLFE of Boxted in the Parish of Hemel Hempstead in the County of Herts Yeoman and RICHARD POPE of Hemel Hempstead aforesaid Inn holder of the one party and FRANCIS COMBES the younger Gentleman (and others) of the other party

WITNESSETH that whereas all the Meadowe in Hemel Hempstead aforesaid commonly called or known by the names of Castle Mead Haywardes Mead Baylie Mead Haybourne Mead the Common Mead alias Two Waters Moor together with the liberty of fishing in the Water that runneth in and through the said Meadowe and all profits commodities and advantages thereunto in any wise belonging (amongst divers other things) by good and sufficient conveyance and assurance in the same as lawfully conveyed and assured to the said JOHN ROLFE and RICHARD POPE and one WILLIAM GLADMAN their heirs and assigns for ever the intent and purpose of which conveyance and assurance so to them made was by a secret trust to them committed to and for the benefit and only use whereby the inhabitants of Hemel Hempstead aforesaid and of Bovingdon their heirs and assigns might and should for ever hereafter have hold and enjoy the said Meadowe and all the commodities and profits that may or shall arise therefrom in as full ample and beneficial manner to all intents and purposes and by reason of any grant or conveyance made thereof by the Queens most Excellent Majesty to the late Right Honourable Robert Earl of Leicester deceased and his heirs the said Right Honourable Earl should or might have take and enjoy the same since the which assurance and conveyance made to the said JOHN ROLFE RICHARD POPE and WILLIAM GLADMAN as is aforesaid the said WILLIAM GLADMAN by force whereof the said JOHN ROLFE and RICHARD POPE are seised of the said Meadowe and premises in their demesne as of Fee by the right of survivor in manner and form aforesaid

NOW the said JOHN ROLFE and RICHARD POPE for and in consideration that the money wherewith they bought and purchased the said Meadowe and premises was disbursed by and paid at the costs and charges of divers and of most of the inhabitants of Hemel Hempstead and Bovingdon aforesaid in performance of the said intent and purpose videlicet that the said inhabitants of Hemel Hempstead and Bovingdon aforesaid in performance of the said intent and purpose videlicet that the said inhabitants of Hemel Hempstead and Bovingdon might for ever hereafter have hold and freely enjoy all the profits commodities and benefits of the said Meadowe and fishings as is aforesaid

HAVE GRANTED for feoffee and confirmed by these Presents do grant in feoffee and confirm unto the said FRANCIS COMBES and OTHERS all the said Meadowe or Moor and the liberty of fishing of the River and Water therein and all the rents profits privileges commodities and advantages thereof or thereunto belonging arising or in any wise appertaining Together with all the Deeds Evidences Charters muniments and writings concerning the premises only or only any part or parcel thereof which are in their or in any of their possession or in the possession of any other person or persons by their or either of their delivery or consent which they may lawfully come by without suit in the law which said Charters and Evidences the said JOHN ROLFE and RICHARD POPE for them their heirs and assigns do covenant and grant to and with the said FRANCIS COMBES THOMAS HOWE ZACHARY ROLFE ROBERT POPE and to and with all and every the other feoffees before named their heirs and assigns by these Presents to deliver to them or some of them safe whole undefaced and uncancelled before the feast of St Michael of Archangel next ensuing the date hereof

TO HAVE and to hold the said Meadow and all other the aforesaid premises with the appurtenances to the said FRANCIS COMBES and OTHERS and their heirs

TO THE USE AND behoofe as well of the said JOHN ROLFE and RICHARD POPE and their heirs as of the said FRANCIS COMBES THOMAS HOWE ZACHARY ROLFE ROBERT POPE and all other the feofees aforenamed and of all other person or persons whatsoever by what name or names so ever they be called or known which now dwell or inhabit within Hemel Hempstead and Bovingdon aforesaid and of all and every their heirs by equal portions thereof in common so long as they or every each of them or their heirs shall dwell and inhabit within Hemel Hempstead or Bovingdon aforesaid and if they or any of them or the heirs of them or any of them shall depart remove and not dwell there then to the use of such other person or persons and their heirs for such portion or portions of him or them so departing removing and not dwelling there in common with the rest of the inhabitants there as successively shall in their places and steads so departing and removing than dwell and inhabit within the said town or hamlet so long as such person or persons and their heirs shall so dwell and inhabit in their place and stead aforesaid and so from time to time and after every departing and removing so dwell within the said town or hamlet then to the use of such other person or persons and their heirs in common with the rest then inhabiting there as successively from time to time shall in their places and steads so departing and removing and all and every time hereafter dwell and inhabit within the town or hamlet aforesaid and to none other uses intents or purposes nor in any other manner or form than is before expressed mentioned and declared

To Be Holden of our Sovereign Lady the Queen as of her Manor of Eastgreene which within the county of Kent by fealty only in free socage for all manner of services exactions demands whatsoever and not in capise or knights service as by Her said Majesty's Letters Patent made unto the said Right Honourable Robert Earl of Leicester bearing date at Gorhambury in the nineteenth day of July and in the sixteenth year of her Majesty's reign to be unto Her said Majesty preserve doth and may appear

And The said John Rolfe and Richard Pope for them their heirs and assigns do covenant and grant to and with the said Francis Combes Thomas Howe Zachary Rolfe Robert Pope and to and with all the rest of the other before named feofees and inhabitants of Hemel Hempstead or Bovingdon aforesaid their heirs and assigns by these presents that they the said John Rolfe and Richard Pope their heirs and assigns and all and every other person and persons having claiming or pretending to have any estate right title use or interest of or in or to the premises or any part or parcel thereof by from or under the said John Rolfe and Richard Pope shall at all times within one year and a day next ensuing the date hereof upon reasonable request to them in that behalf to be made by the said Francis Combes Zachary Rolfe Thomas Howe Robert Pope and the rest of the said feoffees and inhabitants or any of them or by their heirs or assigns shall do knowledge execute and suffer to be done knowledged and executed all and every such further act or acts thing or things devise or devises in the law whatsoever be it by fine feoffment deed or deeds enrolled enrolment of these Presents reconvey or reconveys with single or double voucher release with warranty or warranties only against the said John Rolfe and Richard Pope and their heirs for ever for better and more sure making and assurance of the said Meadowe and other the premises to the uses and purposes before mentioned as by the counsel learned in the laws of the said Francis Combes Thomas Howe Zachary Rolfe Robert Pope and the rest of and other feoffees and inhabitants shall reasonably devised and required at the cost and charges of the said inhabitants

And Also that it shall and may be lawful to and for the said Francis Combes Thomas Howe Zachary Rolfe Robert Pope and all other the said feoffees and inhabitants their heirs and assigns peacefully and quietly to have hold occupy possess and enjoy the said premises with the appurtenances before mentioned to be granted by these presents according to the true intent and meaning in these presents expressed together with all and singular the said deeds evidences charters muniments and writing whatsoever

And That the said John Rolfe and Richard Pope have not made suffered or procured any act or acts thing or things encumbrance or encumbrances whatsoever whereby the said meadowe and premises should not or may not be lawfully conveyed and quietly enjoyed in manner and form and to such use and intent as in and by these Presents is before specified and declared

And Also covenanted granted and agreed upon by and between the said parties for these presents for them and every of them their heirs and assigns and every of them that as well the said Francis Combes Thomas Howe Zachary Rolfe Robert Pope and all others the aforenamed feoffees and inhabitants of Hemel Hempstead and Bovingdon aforesaid

As Also their heirs and assigns which at any time thereafter forever successively shall and ought to have and enjoy the said Meadowe and premises in manner and form aforesaid shall and will so long as they and every each of them shall be inhabitants and dwellers there maintain keep observe perform and fulfil all such and so many orders and bylaws as now are or hereafter shall be made at any time forever by twelve of the best of the inhabitants of Hemel Hempstead and Bovingdon aforesaid concerning the using enjoying and possession of the said Meadowe and fishing to the best commodity and benefit of all and every of the said inhabitants their heirs and assigns being inhabitants there

As Also for the felling cutting down and converting of the woods underwoods bushes fursines and trees now growing and being or which shall grow and be in and upon the said premises to be employed converted and used to the best commodity and benefit of the said feoffees and inhabitants their heirs and assigns inhabitants there for the time being

Provided always and it is nevertheless concluded and fully agreed upon between all the said parties the these Presents and their true intent and meaning is that whensoever twenty thirty or forty of the said feoffees shall depart out of this natural life and die then at all times after (or if it be thought needful) upon reasonable request on that behalf to be made by the then surviving feoffees they shall make or cause to be made a new feoffment to as many and the like number of the then inhabitants of Hemel Hempstead and Bovingdon aforesaid to be elected feoffees by the then Baylie of the said town of Hemel Hempstead for the time being and the greater part of inhabitants of Hemel Hempstead and Bovingdon aforesaid and to the like use and behoof as in these presents is declared with the like covenants grantees articles and agreements therein to be contained as in these presents are mentioned and not other wise

In Witness whereof the parties aforesaid either to other interchangeably to these present Indentures have set their hands and seals the day and year first above written 1594

Sealed and delivered in the presence of Richard Bosse and others

APPENDIX 2

FEOFFES APPOINTED BY INDENTURE 26.4.1594

[This list shows the names on each Indenture of the Act of 1809 together with as much information about family relationships, residence, occupation, civic duty and death as can be confirmed. It has been difficult at times to precisely ascertain to which family with the same name the information applied. Names have been spelt as listed in the original Indenture. Spellings of family names varied over time and even within the same document. It appears that young sons were sometimes included to ensure the continuity of the feoffement; this also avoided the expense of too frequent Indentures.]

Of the First Part	[i.e. surviving Feoffes from the original purchase]
Rolfe, John	Yeoman, of The Wood; Bailiff of Hemel Hempstead in 1631
Pope, Richard	Shoemaker of Hemel Hempstead

Of the Second Part	[i.e. newly confirmed Feoffes]
Axtell, Nathaniell	
Axtell, Philip	
Axtell, Thomas	Of Two Waters in 1632; Bailiff in 1618 and 1632
Baker, John	The younger
Besowth, Christopher	
Besowth, John	Of Aignells
Besowth, Zephaniah	
Birchemore, Richard	Bailiff in 1646
Blisse, John	
Colman, Robert	
Colman, William	
Combes, Francis	The younger, Gentleman. [He was not more than eleven years of age.]
Coxe, Simon	The younger
Doult, Richard	The younger
Feild, Nathaniell	
Feild, Thomas	Of the Hill
Gladman, Abiell	
Gladman, Seath	
Glenister, Mathew	
Gould, Francis	
Gould, John	Of the Street
Gould, Thomas	Of Newhall
Gould, Thomas	Of the Lane
Hall, John	
Hawkins, William	
Hay, Abieza	
Hearne, William	The younger
Howe, Daniell[1]	Bailiff in 1623
Howe, Edmund	The younger
Howe, John	
Howe, Michael	
Howe, Richard	Of Bury Mill End
Howe, Thomas	Of High Street; Bailiff in 1572
Howe, William	
Howe, William	
Humphry, Micah	
Knevat, John	
Knight, Jeromye	
Longe, William	
Maine, Francis	
Maine, James	Gentleman
Marstone, Thomas	

Newman, William	
Partridge, Edmund	
Partridge, Roger	Of Tile Kiln; Bailiff in 1628
Pope, John	Of the Wood; Bailiff in 1631
Pope, John	Of Hillend
Pope, Ralfe	
Pope, Robert	[This name appears in the indenture but not in the 1809 Act.]
Priest, John	
Puddevat, James	
Puddevat, Ralph	
Rogers, John	
Rolfe, Jeromy[2]	
Rolfe, Richard	
Rolfe, William	Of Pigotts End; Bailiff in 1619
Rolfe, William	Of the Towne
Rolfe, Zachary	
Rose, Henry	Of Green End; Bailiff in 1647
Shadde, John	
Shakmaple, William	
Southen, John	Of Bod's End; Bailiff in 1638
Sowthen, Richard	
Turner, John, (Captain)	Of High Street Side; Bailiff in 1655
Turner, John	
Turner, Roger	
Younge, William	Of Field's End; Bailiff in 1620

[1] *A Daniel Howe was christened on 6 December 1578 in Hemel Hempstead, son of a William Howe. Therefore he may have been only sixteen years old when becoming a Feoffe.*

[2] *A Jeremie Rolfe was christened on 5 April 1580 in Hemel Hempstead, son of a William Rolfe. Therefore he may have been only fourteen years old when becoming a Feoffe.*

The Arms of the Combes family of Hemel Hempstead.

In 1594 Queen Elizabeth I was in the thirty-sixth year of her reign and was considered by many to be the head of the Reformation movement. The Spanish Armada had been defeated in 1588. The year was a plague year in London and even the small town of Hemel Hempstead was affected by the terrible disease.

Indenture Of Feoffement 26.4.1659

Of the First Part — [i.e. surviving Feoffes of the previous Indenture of 26.4.1594]

Dolt, Richard	
Field, Nathaniel	
Gladman, Seth	
Gould, Thomas	The elder, of the Lane
Haye, Abieza	
Hearne, William	
Howe, Daniel	Of Felden; Bailiff in 1665
Newman, William	
Priest, John	The elder
Rolfe, Jeremy	
Rose, Henry	

Of the Second Part — [i.e. newly confirmed Feoffes]

Aberry, Thomas	Of Southfield
Belton, Joseph	
Clark, John	The younger, of Bury Mill End; Bailiff in 1653 and 1674
Combe, Richard	Gentleman
Combes, Sir Richard	Knight
Crawley, John	The younger, Maltster of Two Waters
Deacon, Elisha	
Field, Isaac	The younger; Bailiff in 1672
Field, John	The younger, of Fields End; Bailiff in 1662
Field, John	The younger, son of Nathaniel Field, of Lovetts End
Fryor, Thomas	
Garrett, William	Bailiff in 1671
Gate, John	The younger, of Boxted; Bailiff in 1641
Goodwin, Francis	Bailiff in 1669
Gould, Jeremiah	
Gould, Jeremy	The younger
Gould, John	
Gould, Thomas	The younger, of Bovingdon
Hallsey, Thomas	
Hayes, Thomas	The younger
Hitchcock, William	The younger
Howe, John	The son of Francis Howe of Pixe
Howe, John	The younger
Howe, Josias	Gentleman
Howe, Michael	
Howe, Samuel	
Knight, Jeremy	The younger
King, Francis	Gentleman of Lockers; Bailiff in 1677
King, Nicholas	The younger [This name appears in the Indenture but not in the 1809 Act.]
King, Zachary	The younger
Knight, Jeremy	[This name appears in the Indenture but not in the 1809 Act.]
Knight, John	
Longe, William	Of Cox Pond; Bailiff in 1658
Long, William	The younger, of Cox Pond; Bailiff in 1679 and 1706
Marston, Joseph	Gentleman
Marston, William	The son of Joseph Marston
Martyn, Josias	Gentleman [This name appears in the Indenture but not in the 1809 Act.]
Martyn, Josias	The younger
Munn, William	[This name appears as Bunn in the Indenture but not in the 1809 Act.]
Nash, Nathaniel	The younger

Newman, George	
King, Nicolas	The younger
Owen, John	
Partridge, Seth	The younger, of the Town; Bailiff in 1663
Pratt, Jonathan	Victualler [The Black Lion, Hemel Hempstead]; Bailiff in 1693; died 1709
Preist, John	
Priest, Thomas	
Puddephatt, John	Of New End; Bailiff in 1676
Reeve, John	
Rolfe, John	The younger; Bailiff in 1675
Ruckett, John	
Salter, Richard	The elder, of High Street; Bailiff in 1652, 1673 and 1689
Salter, Richard	The younger, of High Street; Bailiff in 1703
Sawcer, Robert	Gentleman
Settle, Elkanah	Bailiff in 1654
Shakemaple, Richard	The younger
Sowthen, John	The son of Samuel Sowthen of Warners End; Bailiff in 1638
Stratford, William	
Turner, John, (Captain)	Of High Street side; Bailiff in 1655
Turner, John	The younger, of Wards End
Turner, John	Of Waterside
Turner, Joseph	The younger
Turner, Richard	The younger; Bailiff in 1657 and 1681
Turner, Samuel	The younger, of High Street
Turner, Samuel	The son of Captain John Turner
Turney, Thomas	
Walker, Henry	Bailiff in 1678
Wright, William	Bailiff in 1683
Young, William	The younger; Bailiff in 1668 and 1686

The Arms of the Halsey family of Gaddesden.

1659 was one year after the death of Oliver Cromwell and one year before the restoration of the monarch Charles II, who was proclaimed King on 8 May 1660. Following that event, Daniel Axtell of Berkhamsted Place was executed for the regicide of Charles I.

Indenture Of Feoffement 7.8.1711

Of the First Part   [i.e. surviving Feoffes of the previous Indenture 26.4.1659]

Crawley, John	Gentleman of Hemel Hempstead
Deacon, Elisha	Tanner of Hemel Hempstead
King, Zachariah	The elder, Yeoman of Bovingdon
Marston, William	Gentleman of Hemel Hempstead
Nash, Nathaniel	The elder, Maltster of Hemel Hempstead
Shakemaple, Richard	Yeoman of Bovingdon
Sowthen, John	Yeoman of Warners End
Turner, Joseph	Yeoman of Hemel Hempstead
Turner, Samuel	Yeoman of Hemel Hempstead
Young, William	Yeoman of Hemel Hempstead

Of the Second Part   [i.e. newly confirmed Feoffes]

Beldon, Joseph	The elder, Yeoman of Hemel Hempstead
Beldon, Joseph	The younger, son of Joseph Beldon, the elder
Brandley, Nathaniel	Innholder/Yeoman of Hemel Hempstead
Budd, John	Yeoman of Bovingdon
Bunn, John	The younger, son of John Bunn, the elder, Yeoman of Bovingdon
Bunn, Thomas	Yeoman of Bovingdon
Bunn, William	Yeoman of Bovingdon
Burch, Thomas	The elder, Draper of Hemel Hempstead
Burch, Thomas	The younger, son of Thomas Burch, the elder
Crawley, Edmund	Yeoman of Hemel Hempstead
Crawley, John	The younger, son of John Crawley dec'd, (late of Two Waters, Maltster)
Crawley, Thomas	The younger, son of Thomas Crawley, the elder
Crawley, Thomas	The elder, Grocer; Bailiff in 1691
Field, John	Yeoman of Field's End; Bailiff in 1662 and 1716
Field, Ralph	The younger, Yeoman of Green End; Bailiff in 1728
Fuller, William	Grocer of Hemel Hempstead
Gladman, John	Tailor of Hemel Hempstead,
Gould, Joseph	Yeoman of Bovingdon
Gregory, Robert	Gentleman of Hemel Hempstead; Bailiff in 1690
Halsey, Robert	Yeoman of Hemel Hempstead; Bailiff in 1685
How, Ephraim	Draper of Hemel Hempstead; Bailiff in 1711
How, Francis	Yeoman of Pix
How, John	Son of Ephraim How
Francis King	The elder, Yeoman of Bovingdon
King, John	The elder, Yeoman of Bovingdon
King, John	The younger, son of John King, the elder
King, Jonathan	The younger, Yeoman of Bovingdon
King, Zachariah	The younger, Yeoman of Bovingdon, son of Zachariah King, the elder
Knight, Jeremiah	Yeoman of Felden
Knight, John	Brother of Jeremiah Knight, the younger
Lewis, George	Gentleman of Hemel Hempstead; Bailiff in 1710
Lewis, Luke	The younger, son of Luke Lewis, the elder
Lewis, Luke	The elder, Gentleman of Corner Hall; Bailiff in 1736
Lewis, Samuel	Gentleman of Hemel Hempstead
Long, William	Yeoman of Hemel Hempstead; Bailiff in 1679 and 1706
Meadowes, Peter	Miller of Hemel Hempstead
Nash, Nathaniel	The younger, son of Nathaniel Nash, the elder
Neale, Edmund	Yeoman of Bovingdon
Oliver, James	The elder, Yeoman of Hemel Hempstead; Bailiff in 1707
Oliver, James	The younger, son of Jonah Oliver dec'd
Pryor, John	Innholder of Hemel Hempstead
Puddephatt, Bennett	Tallow Chandler of Hemel Hempstead
Puddephatt, Jeremiah	Yeoman of Hemel Hempstead
Puddephatt, John	The son of Jeremiah Puddephatt; Bailiff in 1756
Puddephatt, John	The elder, Yeoman of Bennetts End; Bailiff in 1676 and 1709
Puddephatt, John	The younger, son of John Puddephatt, the elder
Puddephatt, Joseph	The son of Bennett Puddephat
Puttnam, John	The younger, Yeoman of Bovingdon
Rittman, John	The younger, Yeoman of Bovingdon [This name appears in the Indenture but not in the 1809 Act.]
Sage, Samuel	Maltster of Hemel Hempstead
Salter, John	Son of Richard Salter, the elder
Salter, Richard	The elder, Yeoman of High Street; Bailiff in 1673 and 1689
Salter, Richard	Son of Richard Salter the elder; Bailiff in 1703 and 1727
Salter, Thomas	Son, of Richard Salter the elder
Seare, Thomas	Innholder of Hemel Hempstead
Sheppard, Shem	Yeoman of Hemel Hempstead; Bailiff in 1725
Shipton, Daniel	The elder, Tanner of Corner Hall; Bailiff in 1694
Shipton, Daniel	The younger, son of Daniel Shipton, the elder
Smith, William	The elder, Yeoman of Bovingdon; Bailiff in 1723
Sparling, Moses	The elder, Haberdasher of Hemel Hempstead; Bailiff in 1708
Sparling, Moses	The younger, son of Moses Sparling, the elder
Turner, William	Yeoman of Hemel Hempstead
Turney, Edward	The younger, Maltster of Hemel Hempstead; Bailiff in 1684
Walker, Richard	Joiner of Hemel Hempstead; Bailiff in 1714
West, Moses	The elder, Gentleman
West, Moses	The younger, son of Moses West, the elder
Wheeler, John	Yeoman of Boxted; Bailiff in 1704

In 1711 Queen Anne, younger daughter of James II, was on the throne. Defoe, Swift, Congreve, Addison and Pope were amongst the notable writers of the day. Christopher Wren had just rebuilt St Paul's in London and Thomas Newcomen developed the steam pump. The population of England and Wales was in the region of six million and turnpike roads were spreading over the country.

Indenture Of Feoffement 26.11.1757

Of the First Part — [i.e. surviving Feoffes of the previous Indenture 7.8.1711]

Crawley, John	The elder, Yeoman of Roberts Lane, Hemel Hempstead
Puddephatt, John	The elder, Yeoman of Bennetts End; Bailiff in 1756
Puttnam, John	Yeoman, of Bovingdon

Of the Second Part — [i.e. newly confirmed Feoffes]

Arnott, William	Turner of Hemel Hempstead
Austen, John	Blacksmith of Bovingdon
Avis, Daniel	Maltster of Piccotts End
Batcheldor, John	Husbandman of Bovingdon
Bedford, John	Maltster of Bury Mill End
Bedford, William	Maltster of Bury Mill End
Birch, Richard	Gentleman of the Town; Bailiff in 1745
Brickland, Matthew	Leather Breeches Maker of Hemel Hempstead
Brooks, John	The younger, Husbandman of Bovingdon
Bryant, John	Yeoman of Green End
Bunn, George	Yeoman of Bovingdon
Camfield, Joseph	Yeoman of Hemel Hempstead
Cater, William	Yeoman of Boxmore
Clark, Richard	Yeoman of Longcroft, Bovingdon
Cole, Nicholas	Gardener of Green End
Collett, Joseph	Draper of Hemel Hempstead
Cosier, Thomas	Leather Breeches Maker of Hemel Hempstead
Crawley, John	The younger, Maltster of Piccotts End
Crompton, Windmills	Gentleman of Piccotts End, born 1701, died 13.3.1771
Deacon, Elisha	Gentleman of Hemel Hempstead
Dell, Joseph	Yeoman of Bovingdon
Field, Isaac	Maltster of Bury Mill End; Bailiff in 1672
Field, Isaac	Gardener of Hemel Hempstead
Field, John	The elder, Yeoman of Green End
Field, John	The younger, Yeoman of Field's End; Bailiff in 1716
Ginger, William	Gentleman of Hemel Hempstead; Bailiff in 1792
Glenister, William	The younger, Husbandman of Bovingdon
Glover, Jacob	Draper of Hemel Hempstead
Glover, Thomas	Innholder of the Town; Bailiff in 1748 and 1793
Godwin, Shadrach	The elder, Farrier of Hemel Hempstead
Godwin, Shadrach	The younger, Farrier of Agnells; Bailiff in 1733
Harding, John	Glazier of Hemel Hempstead
Hawkins, John	Surgeon of Hemel Hempstead; Bailiff in 1761
Hughes, Edward	Miller of Two Waters
Ivory, Edward	Husbandman of Bovingdon
Kellam, Thomas	Innholder of Hemel Hempstead; Bailiff in 1776
King, Francis	The elder, Yeoman of Few Onions, Bovingdon
King, Francis	The younger, Husbandman of Few Onions, Bovingdon
Knowlton, Thomas	The elder, Gentleman of Crouchfield
Knowlton, Thomas	The younger, Gentleman of Crouchfield
Lawrance, Samuel	Husbandman of Corner Hall
Lea, Michael	Maltster of Piccotts End; Bailiff in 1768
Love, Ephraim	Gentleman of Crouchfield
Lovell, John	Victualler of Two Waters
Moore, Henry	Butcher of Hemel Hempstead
Newman, John	Grocer of the Town; Bailiff in 1732 and 1750
Newman, Joseph	Draper of Hemel Hempstead; Bailiff in 1762 and 1777
Orchard, John	Mealman of Hemel Hempstead
Perry, Robert	Mealman of Two Waters; Bailiff in 1766
Puddefoote, William	Tanner of Waterside; Bailiff in 1757
Puddephatt, Bennett	Innholder of Hemel Hempstead
Puddephatt, Jeremiah	The elder, Yeoman of the Wood; Bailiff in 1763
Puddephatt, Jeremiah	The younger, Husbandman of the Wood
Puddephatt, John	The younger, Husbandman of Bennetts End; Bailiff in 1756
Smith, Hugh	Doctor of Physick of Hemel Hempstead
Smith, John	Yeoman of Shantock, Bovingdon
Smith, Thomas	Youngest son of John Smith, Husbandman of Shantock, Bovingdon
Smith, William	Grocer of Hemel Hempstead; Bailiff in 1723
Squire, Thomas	Schoolmaster of Hemel Hempstead
Tiverton, William	Miller of Piccotts End; Bailiff in 1759
Trott, William	Yeoman of Boxmore
Turfrey, John	Draper of Hemel Hempstead; Bailiff in 1755
Turner, John	Yeoman of Two Beeches; Bailiff in 1722
Walker, Richard	Ironmonger of Hemel Hempstead; Bailiff in 1714
Wardall, John	Shoemaker of Boxmore
Warren, Francis	Baker of Hemel Hempstead
Warren, Richard	Baker of Hemel Hempstead
Weedon, William	Carpenter of the Lodge; Bailiff in 1774
Whiteley, Thomas	Husbandman of Heath Farm, Boxmore; Bailiff in 1740
Willshaw, Clerke	Doctor of Physick of Marlowes

Longcroft Cottages in 1902.

In 1757 George II was King and Robert Clive's victory at Plassey assured English rule in India for the best part of the next 200 years. Nearer home, Britain and France had declared war in May 1756 and the Seven Years War had begun. Francis, third Duke of Bridgewater, succeeded to the Ashridge Estate in Hertfordshire and devoted himself to canal building, somewhat neglecting the property he had inherited.

Indenture Of Feoffement 20.4.1787

Of the First Part — [i.e. surviving Feoffes of the previous Indenture 26.11.1757]

Brickland, Matthew	Breeches Maker of Hemel Hempstead
Deacon, Elisha	The elder, Tanner of Bury Mill End
Field, John	Carpenter of Hemel Hempstead
Godwin, Shadrach	The elder, Farrier of Agnells; Bailiff in 1733, died 13.5.1789
Kellam, Thomas	Innholder of the Town; Bailiff in 1776
Knowlton, Thomas	Draper of Bury Mill End
Moore, Henry	Butcher of Hemel Hempstead
Newman, Joseph	Draper of the Town; Bailiff in 1762 and 1777
Puddephatt, Jeremiah	Husbandman of the Wood, Piccotts End; Bailiff in 1763
Tiverton, William	Gentleman of Piccotts End; Bailiff in 1759

Of the Second Part — [i.e. newly confirmed Feoffes]

Batcheldor, John	Husbandman of Bovingdon
Bedford, William	Maltster of Bury Mill End
Birdsey, John	Grocer of Hemel Hempstead; Bailiff in 1773
Blacknell, Daniel	Senior, Husbandman of Boxmoor in hamlet of Bovingdon
Blacknell, John	Husbandman of Box Lane, Bovingdon
Bolton, Francis	Miller of Hemel Hempstead
Bolton, William	Miller of Hemel Hempstead
Brashier, William	Baker of Hemel Hempstead; Bailiff in 1737 and 1782
Camfield, John	Yeoman of Cox Pond
Camfield, Joseph	Husbandman of Wood Lane End
Collett, Samuel	Farmer of Two Waters
Collett, Thomas	Draper of Hemel Hempstead
Collett, William	Grocer of Hemel Hempstead
Cotton, John	Esquire of Felden
Crawley, John	The younger, Mealman of Piccotts End
Darley, William	Esquire of Bovingdon
Deacon, Elisha	The younger, Tanner of Corner Hall
Field, Isaac	Maltster of Bury Mill End
Field, James	Of Hemel Hempstead
Furnival, Thomas	The elder, Linen Draper of the Town; Bailiff in 1779 and 1800
Furnival, Thomas	The younger, Draper of Hemel Hempstead
Gilham, John	Brazier of Hemel Hempstead; Bailiff in 1797
Ginger, William	Gentleman of the Town, died 8.8.1793; Bailiff in 1792
Glover, John	Grocer of the Town; Bailiff in 1789
Godwin, Shadrach	The younger, Farrier of Agnells
Hagger, Joseph	Miller of Piccotts End
Harding, Edward	Husbandman of Woodhall
Hight, John	Husbandman of the Hay, Bovingdon
Hight, Joseph	Son of John Hight, Husbandman of Bovingdon
Hodgson, Robert John	Gentleman of Hemel Hempstead
Holloway, George	Brewer of Hemel Hempstead
Holloway, James	Draper of Hemel Hempstead
Holmes, Edward	Papermaker of Hemel Hempstead
Hudson, George	Draper of the Town; Bailiff in 1790
Hudson, Thomas	Silk Throwster of the Town; Bailiff in 1775 and 1785
Hudson, Thomas	Gentleman of Bovingdon
Jennings, John	Husbandman of Corner Hall
Jennings, William	Yeoman of the Wood; Bailiff in 1819
Johnson, William	Husbandman of Boxted
Lines, Thomas	Gentleman of Hemel Hempstead
Mills, William	Husbandman of Lockers
Newman, John	Draper of Hemel Hempstead
Nicholls, David	Husbandman of Warners End
Preedy, Benjamin	Farmer of Piccotts End
Redding, Samuel	Yeoman of Wards End
Roberts, William	Blacksmith of the Town; Bailiff in 1784 and 1787
Squire, Samuel	Ironmonger of Hemel Hempstead
Squire, Thomas	Mealman of Hemel Hempstead
Suffolk, Edward	Husbandman of Bourn End
Suffolk, Joseph	The son of Edward Suffolk, of Bourn End
Tompson, George	Barber of the Town; Bailiff in 1781 and 1788
Tompson, John	Innholder of Hemel Hempstead
Trott, Thomas	Esquire of Gadebridge
Warren, Francis	Baker of Hemel Hempstead
Warren, Thomas	Baker of Hemel Hempstead
Weedon, William	Carpenter of the Lodge; Bailiff in 1774

Great Coxpond Farm, Hemel Hempstead c.1925

> *In 1787 George III, grandson of George II, was on the throne. He was sometimes known as 'Farmer George' to his people. He suffered from porphyria, a hereditary metabolic illness which produces abdominal pain and mental confusion. The American War of Independence was fought during his long reign and some compassionate Quakers formed a Society for the Abolition of the Slave Trade. Hemel Hempstead was described as the greatest market for wheat in the county.*

INDENTURE OF 1.6.1797

[This is not an Indenture of Feoffement.]

'Yes' indicates that the name is recorded on the Indentures of Feoffement 1757 and 1787.

		1757	1787
Batcheldor, John	Husbandman of Bovingdon	Yes	Yes
Bedford, William	Maltster of Bury Mill End	Yes	Yes
Birdsey, John	Grocer of Hemel Hempstead	No	Yes
Bolton, Francis	Miller of Hemel Hempstead	No	Yes
Bolton, William	Miller of Hemel Hempstead	No	Yes
Brashier, William	Baker of Hemel Hempstead; Bailiff in 1782	No	Yes
Brickland, Matthew	Breeches maker of Hemel Hempstead	Yes	Yes
Camfield, Joseph	Farmer of Wood Lane End	No	Yes
Collett, Samuel	Farmer of Two Waters	No	Yes
Collett, Thomas	Draper of Hemel Hempstead	No	Yes
Collett, William	Grocer of Hemel Hempstead	No	Yes
Cotton, John	Esquire of Felden	No	Yes
Crawley, John	Mealman of Piccotts End	No	Yes
Deacon, Elisha	The elder, Tanner of Hemel Hempstead	Yes	Yes
Deacon, Elisha	The younger, Tanner of Corner Hall	No	Yes
Field, Isaac	Maltster of Bury Mill End, died in or before 1837	Yes	Yes
Field, John	Gentleman of Hemel Hempstead	No	No
Field, John	Carpenter of Hemel Hempstead [This name appears in the Indenture but not in the 1809 Act.]	?	Yes
Furnival, Thomas	Draper of Hemel Hempstead	No	Yes
Gilham, John	Brazier of Hemel Hempstead; Bailiff in 1797	No	Yes
Glover, John	Grocer of Hemel Hempstead; Bailiff in 1789	No	Yes
Harding, Edward	Farmer of Woodhall	No	Yes
Hight, John	Husbandman of the Hay, Bovingdon	No	Yes
Hight, Joseph	Son of John Hight of Bovingdon	No	Yes
Holloway, George	Brewer of Hemel Hempstead	No	Yes
Holloway, James	Yeoman, late of Hemel Hempstead, now of Chesham Parish	No	Yes
Hudson, Thomas	Gentleman, late of Bovingdon, now of Newington Green	No	Yes
Jennings, John	Husbandman of Corner Hall	No	Yes
Jennings, William	Yeoman of the Wood; Bailiff in 1819	No	Yes
Johnson, William	Husbandman of Boxted	No	Yes
Kellam, Thomas	Innholder of Hemel Hempstead; Bailiff in 1776	Yes	Yes
Lines, Thomas	Gentleman of Hemel Hempstead	No	Yes
Mills, William	Farmer, late of Hemel Hempstead, now of St. Michael's Parish	No	Yes
Newman, John	Esquire of Hemel Hempstead	Yes	Yes
Nicholls, David	Mealman of Piccotts End, late of Warners End	No	?
Puddephatt, Jeremiah	Husbandman of Hemel Hempstead, late of Piccotts End; Bailiff in 1763	Yes	Yes
Redding, Samuel	Yeoman of Wards End	No	Yes
Roberts, William	Blacksmith of Hemel Hempstead; Bailiff in 1784 and 1787	No	Yes
Squire, Samuel	Ironmonger of Hemel Hempstead	No	Yes
Squire, Thomas	Hardwareman of Hemel Hempstead	No	Yes
Suffolk, Edward	Husbandman of Bourn End	No	Yes
Suffolk, Joseph	Son of Edward Suffolk of Bourn End	No	Yes
Thompson, George	Gentleman of Hemel Hempstead	No	No
Thompson, John	Sheriff's Officer of Hemel Hempstead	No	No
Warren, Francis	Baker of Bury Mill End	Yes	Yes
Warren, Thomas	Gentleman of Hemel Hempstead	No	Yes
Weedon, William	Carpenter of the Lodge; Bailiff in 1774	Yes	Yes

who are all the surviving Feoffes and joint tenants of the land and hereditaments hereafter mentioned, of the one part and John Impey, Gentleman of the Inner Temple, London, of the other part. [John Impey was the lawyer who drew up the Indenture but he was not a Feoffe.]

The Lockers, Hemel Hempstead, associated with the Collett family.

In 1797 George III still reigned but the Bank of England was in crisis. John Jervis, helped by the tactics of Horatio Nelson, defeated the Spanish Navy at the Battle of Cape St Vincent. The concept of vaccination was successfully tested by Edward Jenner. Jane Austen's 'Sense and Sensibility' was published. The Loyal Hemel Hempstead Volunteers were formed.

Indenture Of Feoffement 14.9.1799

Meeting of Feoffes and appointment of committee for negotiation with the Company of Proprietors of the Grand Junction Canal.

Deed Poll or Instrument in Writing 14 September, 1799 under the hands and seals of:

John Batcheldor	Husbandman of Bovingdon
Samuel Collett	Farmer of Two Waters
Thomas Collett	Draper of Hemel Hempstead
William Collett	Grocer/Farmer of Hemel Hempstead (Replaced David Nicholls)
Godwin, Thomas	Farmer
Grover, Harry	Attorney; Bailiff in 1798
Hight, Joseph	Husbandman of Bovingdon
Howe, Charles	[An inhabitant but not an elected Feoffe]
Jennings, William	Farmer of The Wood; Bailiff in 1819
Roberts, William	Blacksmith/Farmer of Hemel Hempstead; Bailiff in 1784 and 1787
Squire, Thomas	Ironmonger of Hemel Hempstead; died in1805
Warren, Francis	Baker of Bury Mill End

Reciting that the inhabitants at large of Hemelhempsted and Bovingdon were exclusive owners of Box Moor.

At a meeting of Feoffes, Trustees and Inhabitants ... it was resolved that seven of these people should negotiate with the Grand Junction Canal proprietors for land and damages regarding the passage of the canal through Box Moor.

The seven were:

Batcheldor, John	Husbandman of Bovingdon
Collett, Samuel	Farmer of Two Waters
Grover, Harry	Of the Town, Attorney; Bailiff in 1798
Howe, Charles	[An inhabitant but not an elected Feoffe]
Jennings, William	Farmer of The Wood; Bailiff in 1819
Nicholls, David	Mealman, of Piccotts End
Squire, Thomas	Ironmonger of Hemel Hempstead; died in1805

any three of whom should be competent to act in any of the Matters to which the Committee was appointed.

Mr David Nicholls was then reported to have moved away from the relevant parish and was replaced by William Collett, thus reconstituting the Committee.

High Street, Hemel Hempstead. Many of the early Feoffes were traders in the town.

APPENDIX 3

BOX MOOR TRUSTEES 1809–2003

[The table shows their date of election, occupation, residence and the reason and date for ceasing to be a Trustee where known.]

Tower, Christopher Thomas	22.06.1809	Gentleman of Gadebridge and Weald Hall, Essex; resigned
Jennings, John	22.06.1809	Farmer/Schoolmaster of Corner Hall; died 11.06.1831
Grover, Harry	22.06.1809	Attorney of The Bury; 19.08.1835, Bailiff in 1798
Hight, Joseph	22.06.1809	Farmer, son of John Hight of Two Waters; resigned 03.1816
Ware, Ephraim	22.06.1809	resigned 03.1816
Godwin, Thomas	22.06.1809	Yeoman of Two Beeches; died 13.09.1820, Bailiff in 1816
Roberts, William	22.06.1809	Farmer/Blacksmith of Hemel Hempstead; died 04.1816, Bailiff in 1787
Holloway, George	22.06.1809	Brewer of Hemel Hempstead; died 12.1827
Collett, William	22.06.1809	Yeoman of Lockers; died 10.1811
Collett, Thomas	22.06.1809	Gentleman of Lockers; resigned 10.1811
Johnson, William	22.06.1809	Yeoman of New Lodge; resigned 05.1833
Warren, Francis	22.06.1809	Baker/Miller of Bury Mill; died 03.12.1813
Cato, James	24.01.1811	Yeoman of Hemel Hempstead; resigned 05.1833
Jennings, William	07.11.1811	Yeoman of Bennetts End Farm and Felden; died 05.1820, Bailiff in 1819
Field, John	07.11.1811	Yeoman of Pix Farm, Green End; died by 05.1833
Partridge, Thomas	11.04.1814	Yeoman/Butcher of Hemel Hempstead; resigned 05.1820
Bovingdon, John	29.04.1816	Farmer; resigned 06.1822
Brown, John	29.04.1816	Gentleman; resigned 05.1820
Deacon, Thomas Elisha	29.04.1816	Tanner of Corner Hall; Bailiff in 1823
Hamilton, Revd W. J. MA	02.06.1820	Clergyman of Marlowes
Blake, Ezekiel	02.06.1820	Shoemaker/Liquor Merchant of Hemel Hempstead; died by 05.1833
Suffolk, Edward	02.06.1820	Yeoman of Moor End Farm, Bourne End; died 07.1845
Tompson, William	01.08.1822	Draper/Tailor of Hemel Hempstead; resigned 05.1833, Bailiff in 1804
Austin, Thomas	01.08.1822	Farmer of Bovingdon; died by 1845
White, Rev Thomas	24.12.1827	Clergyman of The Lawn, Corner Hall; resigned 05.1833
Smith, William	24.12.1827	Solicitor of Hemel Hempstead; resigned 05.1833, Bailiff in 1812
Ryder, Granville Dudley	29.05 1833	Gentleman of Westbrook Hay; resigned 10.1846
Mountain, Revd Jacob H. B.	29.05.1833	Clergyman of The Heath; resigned before 1845
Stephens, John	29.05.1833	Gentleman of Rowdown; ? before 1846
White, Henry Campbell	29.05.1833	Gentleman of Corner Hall; resigned 1845, Bailiff in 1820
Field, William	29.05.1833	Yeoman of Green End; ? before 1846
Howard, William	29.05.1833	Corn Dealer/Merchant of Two Waters Wharf and Piccotts End Mill and Boxmoor Wharf; ? before 1870
Smith, Hugh	29.05.1833	Gentleman of Bury Mill End; ? before 1870
Cranstone, Joseph	29.05.1833	Ironmonger of High Street; died 1878, Bailiff in 1839
Austin, Giles M.	13.11.1846	Farmer of Bury Farm, Bovingdon; ? before 1870
Hobbs, William	13.11.1846	Farmer of New House Farm, Flaunden; ? before 1870
Beale, William	13.11.1846	Chemist of Hemel Hempstead; ? before 1870
Chennells, John	13.11.1846	Farmer of Bourne End; died 04.1886
Cross, James	13.11.1846	Grocer/Butcher of High Street; ? before 1870, Bailiff in 1847
Collins, Francis	13.11.1846	Butcher of High Street; ? before 1870
Godwin, Shadrach	13.11.1846	Farmer of Grove Hill; died 25.11.1892, Bailiff in 1842
Thorp, George	13.11.1846	Grocer of High Street; died 10.1880, Bailiff in 1845
Austin, John	28.05.1870	Farmer of Bury Farm, Bovingdon; ? before 1890
Hobbs, John	28.05.1870	Farmer of Moonshine Farm, Flaunden; ? before 1890
Evilthrift, Philip	28.10.1871	Baker/Innkeeper of Crouchfield, Boxmoor; died 04.1886, Bailiff in 1876
Stallon, Samuel	28.10.1871	Magistrate's Clerk of Hemel Hempstead; died before 1912, Bailiff in 1866 and 1869

How, Daniel	28.10.1871	Farmer (born in Flaunden) of Corner & Wood Lane End Farms; died 22.12.1889, Bailiff in 1882
Balderson, Henry	28.10.1871	Wine Merchant/Tanner of Boxmoor Wharf; died 10.1908, Bailiff in 1859; Mayor and Bailiff in 1900
Woodman, Thomas junior	28.10.1871	Corn Merchant/Auctioneer of Corner Hall; died 03.1889, Bailiff in 1860
Smith, George Alexander	28.10.1871	Surveyor of Marlowes House; died 01.1888, Bailiff in 1846
Woodman, Harry Daniel	20.06.1890	Estate Agent/Auctioneer of Corner Hall; died before 1912, Bailiff in 1894
Elliott, William Spicer	20.06.1890	Brewer & Maltster of Star Brewery, Bury Mill End; died 06.1913, Bailiff in 1889
Chennells, Adam Joseph	20.06.1890	Grocer of High Street; died 07.1923, Bailiff in 1879; Mayor and Bailiff in 1901
How, William Henry	20.06.1890	Dairyman, son of Daniel How, of Adeyfield Farm and Hand Post Farm; died 1911
Hall, Percy JP	20.06.1890	of Hammerfield; resigned 1919
Field, George	20.06.1890	Corn Dealer of Boxmoor; resigned 1912
Saunders, Fredrick	20.06.1890	Farmer of Belswains Farm; resigned 1912
Saunders, Frederic	20.06.1890	Master Saddler/Registrar of Hemel Hempstead; died 07.1929
Gray, Charles Edgar	20.06.1890	Draper of Marlowes; died 05.1909, Bailiff in 1892
Mitchell Innes, Edward Alfred KC	03.08.1912	Lawyer of Churchill, Boxmoor; died 06.03.1932; Mayor and Bailiff in 1911 and 1912
How, Harry	03.08.1912	Farmer/Baker, son of Daniel How of Corner Farm, Cupid Green; died 10.1918
Williams, William John	03.08.1912	Watercress grower of Hemel Hempstead; died 05.10.1919
Frogley, Frederick	03.08.1912	Superintendent of Police of Bury Mill End; died 01.1922
Oliver, Charles Robert	03.08.1912	Farmer of Wards End Farm; ? before 1950
Christopherson, Percy MA, JP	03.08.1912	Headmaster of Lockers Park School; died before 1922
Colliver, Frederick Pemberthy	03.08.1912	Stockbroker of Chaulden House; resigned 06.1916
Day, Alfred George	03.08.1912	Stationer of High Street; died 03.1946
McCarthy, Thomas George H.	26.07.1922	of Boxmoor; died 01.1928
Bradshaw, Reuben	26.07.1922	Merchant/Wheelwright etc. of Ebberns Wharf, Apsley; resigned 08.1963
Williams, William Frederick	26.07.1922	Watercress Grower of High Street; died 01.1969
Middleton, George James Lt. Col.	26.07.1922	Retired; resigned 06.1950
How, Leonard Leno	26.07.1922	Farmer of Piccotts End Farm (born at Corner Farm), son of Harry How of Gadebridge; died 12.1944
Brice, Charles William	26.07.1922	Coal Merchant of Boxmoor; resigned 01.1953
Hinson, William Collingwood	26.07.1922	Draper of Bovingdon; resigned 06.1950
Aronson, Hugh Douglas	09.06.1950	Barrister of Bovingdon; died 01.1969
Jolliffe, George William	09.06.1950	Farmer of Oakcroft Farm, Felden; died before 1970
MacDonald, William G.	09.06.1950	Doctor of Green End House, Boxmoor; died 30.06.1952
Proctor, Hugh Vernon	09.06.1950	Farmer of Boxmoor; died 08.1974
Day, William Henry	09.06.1950	Insurance Agent of Hemel Hempstead; died 15.01.1958
Oliver, Ernest William	09.06.1950	Farmer of Felden Farm; died 09.03.1964
Osborne, Warren James	09.06.1950	Wholesale Tobacconist (Retired) of Boxmoor; died 01.1969
Snoxall, Frederick David	09.06.1950	Garage Proprietor; resigned 23.07.1954
Webb, Reginald Basil	09.06.1950	Local Government Officer of Boxmoor; resigned before 1964
Crook, William George	20.03.1964	Schoolmaster of Hemel Hempstead; died 10.1977; Mayor and Bailiff in 1953 and 1955
Snoxall, Frederick Roy	20.03.1964	Company Director of Bourne End; resigned 10.1976
Williams, William Thomas	20.03.1964	Watercress Grower of Hemel Hempstead; died 12.1985
Choake, Charles Henry Eric	20.03.1964	Farmer of Wood Farm, Piccotts End; resigned 09.1971
Dunbar, William John	20.03.1964	Company Director of Boxmoor; died 02.1988
Christopher, Herbert	20.03.1964	Company Director of Hemel Hempstead; resigned 12.1977; Mayor and Bailiff in 1951
Martin, Leslie William	15.05.1970	Company Director of Bovingdon; died 01.1984

Parish, Frederick George 'Pat'	15.05.1970	Director of Bovingdon; died 18.8.2001
Archer, Peter George	15.05.1970	Bank Manager of Boxmoor; resigned 09.1971
Snoxall, Stanley John	15.05.1970	Company Director of Chaulden; died 07.1995
Wilshire, Arthur Sydney	15.05.1970	Surveyor of Felden; resigned 02.1979
Poole, John Arthur	30.04.1975	Farmer of Marchmont Farm, Piccotts End
Sear, Reginald Walter	30.04.1975	Office Manager of Boxmoor; died 1.11.2003
Stanbridge, Paul John	30.04.1975	Farmer of Lovetts Farm; resigned 12.1984
Hands, Roger James	16.03.1979	Gardener/Nurseryman of Boxmoor
Hopcroft, Timothy James	16.03.1979	Company Director of Rucklers Lane; resigned 03.1990
Pooley, Robert John	16.03.1979	Publisher of Felden; resigned 04.1992
Lowe, Julia (Mrs)	16.03.1979	Housewife of Felden; resigned 02.1993
Furnell, Dennis Leslie	22.04.1987	Writer/Broadcaster of Hemel Hempstead
Snoxall, Michael David	22.04.1987	Solicitor of Pudds Cross; resigned 04.1996
Stevens, David Richard	22.04.1987	Chartered Surveyor of Boxmoor; resigned 1999
Furnell, David James	27.04.1995	Managing Director of Piccotts End
Kirk, David Henry William	27.04.1995	Local Government Officer of Hemel Hempstead
Steele, Oliver Albert John	27.04.1995	Retired of Boxmoor
Hughes, Claire (Mrs)	27.04.1995	Housewife of Chaulden
Hodgson, William Adam	18.10.2000	Police Officer of Bovingdon
Tite, George Michael	18.10.2000	Smallholder of Two Waters
Ward, Margaret (Mrs)	18.10.2000	Product Manager of Felden

Corner Hall House.

APPENDIX 4

THE PUBLIC INQUIRY 1896 – RESPONSE BY THE CHARITY COMMISSION

'The Charity Commissioners have had under consideration the Report made to them by their Assistant Commissioner in the result of the Inquiry held on 30th October last, and I am now directed to address to you the following observations with the request that you will bring them to the notice of the Trustees –

1. At the Inquiry it was suggested among other things (1) that separate representation on the Trust ought to be secured to the parishioners of Bovingdon and (2) that a redistribution of the rights of pasturage on the Moor is desirable.

These matters are regulated by the Act of 1809 the provisions of which cannot be varied by the Commissioners.

2. The appointment of new Trustees is, it is understood, usually postponed until the number of continuing Trustees is reduced to, or below, four – more frequent appointments are clearly desirable on general grounds and particularly in view of the fact that at least seven Trustees are required for making regulations under Section 7 of the Act.

So long ago as 1871 the Commissioners pointed out to the Trustees that the main objection to frequent appointments, namely the expense of fresh Conveyances, would be obviated by vesting the property in the Official Trustee of Charity Lands, and it is gathered that the Trustees' Solicitors were at that time disposed to consider this course desirable.

I am directed to forward the enclosed Memorandum upon the subject and to suggest that the Trustees should make an application upon the accompanying form for vesting the legal estate in the Official Trustee. A Draft Schedule for the suggested application is also enclosed herewith.

3. With regard to the dealings with the property since the passing of the 1809 Act it appears that no sufficient authority was obtained by the Trustees for the Exchange with Mr. Mountain, for the sales in 1869 and 1871, or for the purchase of the Commons in 1886.

In this connection I am to remind the Trustees that this Trust is subject in all respects to the general law affecting Charities.

4. Upon consideration of the evidence obtained as to the Elections of 1870 and 1871 the Commissioners find no ground for impeaching the validity of the position of either Mr. H. Balderson or Mr. S. Stallon as a Trustee.

5. The expenditure incurred in respect of dinners for the Trustees is viewed by the Commissioners with disapprobation. No objection would be raised by them to moderate expense for refreshments in the course of the long Meetings which have hitherto been followed by a dinner – Indeed, such reasonable refreshment appears to be warranted by Section 16 of the Act of 1809 – but the dinners provided at the cost of the Trust funds are neither authorised by, nor necessary for the due performance of the Trust, and, moreover, the vouchers which have been produced to the Commissioners show that the expenditure has been upon a scale which cannot be regarded as otherwise than extravagant.

Before deciding what, if any, steps ought to be taken with reference to the past action of the Trustees in this matter, the Commissioners will be glad to learn how they propose to regulate the expenditure for the future.

6. The granting in 1892 of a fresh Lease of the Wharf to Mr. Balderson, a Trustee of the Charity, was obviously inconsistent with the duty of the Trustees. Such a Lease is voidable, and could only be granted at the risk of all parties concerned and the Commissioners regret to observe that the Trustees had ample opportunities of knowing beforehand that Mr. Balderson could not properly become the lessee of property vested in him as a Trustee.

7. It is observed that sums of cash derived from sales of land and amounting to £650.15s.9d in all have from time to time been carried to a fund on deposit, which fund has been augmented by accumulations of interest, and otherwise, and that out of this fund £121.0s.6d was paid for the purchase of the Commons and the attendant expenses, and further sums amounting to £492.3s.6d have been paid for improvements on the Charity property, with the result that the amount of the fund stood at £392.18s.6d on the 15th October last.

The Commissioners are in the circumstances, willing to consider the £121.0s.6d as properly invested in land and not liable to replacement. The remainder of the sum of £650.15s.9d ought, however, to be made up and retained in the form of capital, and it is suggested that the Trustees shall invest or pay to the Official Trustees of Charitable Funds for investment the amount now on deposit together with such sums out of general income as will bring the total up to £429.15s.3d. The dividends on such investment would properly be carried to the general account.

8. The net receipts from the sale of gravel dug from the Moor ought also to be treated as capital and invested and I am to request that this course may be adopted in future.

9. It will be convenient that the separate accounts of the Gravel and the Baths respectively should be rendered to the commissioners with the General Account, the balances on these subsidiary accounts being brought into the General Account.

I am to call the attention of the Trustees to the requirements of Section 44 of the Charitable Trusts Act 1855 and Section 14 of the Local Government Act 1894 as to the accounts of parochial Charities.

10. The Commissioners understand that no application for return of property or income tax has been made on behalf of the Trustees since the year 1888. In view of the decision of the house of Lords in 1891 in the case "Commissioners for special purposes of Income Tax v Pemsel (1891) A. C. 531" there appears to be no doubt that this Charity is entitled to exemption and I am to suggest that a renewed application should be made in the matter.

In making the foregoing comments and suggestions the Commissioners desire to place on record their opinion that, while the past action of the Trustees under the Act of 1809 is in some respects open to criticism, they have upon the whole administered the Trust with prudence and to the general benefit of the inhabitants of the parishes interested in the Charity.

I am to add that the Commissioners propose in due course to communicate to the local press for the general information of the inhabitants of the parishes the contents of this letter together with the reply to be received from the Trustees.'

> I am, Sir,
> Your obedient servant,
> G. Holford

Sheep grazing on Shothanger (Sheethanger) Common.

APPENDIX 5

PROPOSED SCHEME OF THE CHARITY COMMISSIONERS RELATING TO THE BOX MOOR TRUST 11TH OCTOBER 1930

'The Corporation would first submit the following observations on the Trust as at present existing:

1. They feel that the present administration is not in accordance with modern ideas, that the time has arisen when the administration of the Trust should be overhauled.

2. They feel that the present method of electing Trustees is antiquated.

3. The Moor is not being used to the best advantage of the inhabitants. There is a great need of the provision of recreational facilities within the Borough and the Corporation feel that the Moor is the best place on which these should be given.

4. From an administrative point of view the Moor creates certain difficulties. It is of course non-productive from a rating point of view, and the cost of such services as sewage disposal, road maintenance, water supply etc. is increased by the fact that long stretches of mains and roads are laid through the Moor, but as new houses are connected thereto the income from rates is very small. A more serious factor is that the Moor being situated between the three parts of the borough (Hemel Hempstead, Boxmoor and Apsley) it tends to accentuate the division. An ideal town is one which forms a comprehensive whole, with the different parts welded together, but it is not realised in the Borough.

5. Normally, a town grows around a centre, and the open spaces are provided away from the centre, but here the open spaces – which are very large – are in the centre. This must lead to the town being scattered over a wide area, and this point will be emphasised as the town grows.

As to the proposed Scheme –

1. The Development Committee of the corporation, in June 1929, met the Box Moor Trustees at the request of the Committee, to consider what steps could be taken to better develop the Moor, when the Trustees explained the Scheme they had in mind. The Development Committee and the Town Council have been in touch with the Trustees during the time the draft Scheme has been prepared, and at a meeting held………………………… they passed the following Resolution.

2. The Corporation appreciate the suggested alteration as to the appointment of Trustees.

3. They observe with pleasure the intention to transfer to them some 17 acres for use as a Park or Recreation Ground, and if the transfer is made are prepared to develop it. They have already decided to seek the advice of an expert in the laying-out of the ground should it be transferred to them.

4. They note the provision as to the acquisition of additional land for £5,000, but they would prefer that the 17 acres should be transferred to them, and that no additional land should be purchased. If it is essential that the additional land should be acquired, they are prepared to accept this, and generally approve the Scheme, being of opinion that the considerable advantages which accrue to the Inhabitants of the Borough outweigh the possible disadvantages of the Scheme.

5. In this connection it might be pointed out that considerable development has taken place within the Borough in recent years. According to the Census of 1921 there were 3,123 dwellings in the Borough, and it is estimated that since then some 850 houses have been erected, an increase of over 25%, the greater part of which has been built during the last three or four years. The population has grown as follows:

Census 1901	11,264
Census 1911	12,888
Census 1921	13,826
Registrar-General's Estimate 1929	15,070 (the Corporation feel this is a low one.)

6. As has already been said, there is a need for the provision of adequate recreational facilities. In 1922 part of the Moor was leased to a Committee to provide a recreation ground, on a voluntary basis, but this failed through lack of funds. The land has now been leased to the Corporation who are prepared to develop it, but are awaiting the carrying through of the present Scheme. They are also considering the question of the provision of facilities in the growing district of Bennetts End.

7. The Corporation are doubtful whether what are known as the "Graziers' Rights" are of very much value in these days, and they would suggest that enquiry should be made as to whether the time has not arrived when these should be restricted or abolished. They feel that the whole benefits of the Moor should inure to the Inhabitants generally and not partly to certain individuals only.'

Appendix 6

Charity Commission Scheme 2000

Statutory Instruments
2000 No. 844
Charities
The Charities (Boxmoor Estate, Hemel Hempstead) Order
2000

Made - - - -   *22nd March 2000*
Coming into force   *5th April 2000*

Whereas the Charity Commissioners for England and Wales, have in pursuance of section 17(1) of the Charities Act 1993, settled the Scheme set out in the Appendix to this order with a view to its being given effect under that section:

And whereas the Scheme does not alter any statutory provision contained in or having effect under any public general Act of Parliament:

And whereas a draft of this Order has been laid before Parliament the period of forty days mentioned in section 6(1) of the Statutory Instruments Act 1946 has expired, and neither House of Parliament has within that period resolved that the Order not be made:

Now, therefore, in pursuance of section 17(2) of the Charities Act 1993, The Secretary of State hereby makes the following Order:–

1. This Order may be cited as the Charities (Boxmoor Estate, Hemel Hempstead) Order 2000 and shall come into force on the fourteenth day after the day on which it is made.

2. The Scheme set out in the Appendix to this Order shall have effect.

Home Office   *Jack Straw*
22nd March 2000   One of Her Majesty's Principal Secretaries of State

APPENDIX

Scheme For The Administration Of The Charity Presently Called The Boxmoor Estate Situated At Hemel Hempstead

Whereas the Charity known as the Boxmoor Estate situated at Hemel Hempstead and Bovingdon in the County of Hertfordshire ("the Charity") is now regulated by the Boxmoor Act 1809 ("the Act") and by Schemes of the Charity Commissioners of 16th December 1921, 18th July 1930, 10th September 1935, 21st May 1951, 12th August 1952, 29th May 1956, 11th September 1956, 6th November 1962, 11th December 1967, 5th October 1970, 21st February 1979 and 1st May 1985:

And whereas the Trustees of the Charity have made application to the Charity Commissioners for England and Wales ("the Commissioners") for a Scheme for the administration of the Charity ("the Scheme"):

And whereas it appears to the Commissioners that a Scheme should be established for the administration of the Charity, but that it is necessary for the Scheme to make provision which goes beyond the powers exercisable by them apart from section 17 of the Charities Act 1993 ("the 1993 Act"):

And whereas in pursuance of section 20 of the 1993 Act public notice of the Commissioners' proposals for this Scheme has been given and the Commissioners have considered all the representations made to them:

Now, therefore, the Commissioners in pursuance of section 17(1) of the 1993 Act hereby settle the following Scheme:

SCHEME

Administration of Charity

1. (a) The provisions of the Act shall cease to have effect with the exception of sections 11, 12 and 13.

   (b) With effect from the date that this Scheme is given effect by an Order of the Secretary of State under section 17(2) of the 1993 Act, the Charity and the property thereof shall be administered and managed in accordance with the provisions of this Scheme by the body of Trustees hereinafter constituted.

   (c) The name of the Charity shall be the Box Moor Trust or such other name as the Trustees shall from time to time, with the consent of the Commissioners, decide.

Vesting

2. As from the date on which this Scheme is given effect by an Order of the Secretary of State under section 17(2) of the 1993 Act the property described in the Schedule to this Scheme and all other property of the Charity shall vest in the Trustees for all the estate and interest therein belonging to or held in trust for the Charity.

Investment of cash

3. All sums of cash now or at any time belonging to the Charity, other than sums of cash needed for immediate working purposes, shall be invested in trust for the Charity.

Investment in land

4. (a) The Trustees may retain and manage any land held as an investment at the date of this Scheme.

(b) The Trustees may sell or otherwise dispose of such land in accordance with the powers of sale of land contained in this Scheme.

(c) Subject to clause 31 of this Scheme and to sub-clause (e) below the Trustees may reinvest the proceeds of sale or other disposal of such land in land to be held as an investment.

(d) Subject to clause 31 of this Scheme and to sub-clause (e) below the Trustees may invest surplus cash in accordance with clause 3 above in land to be held as an investment.

(e) No re-investment or investment in land to be held as an investment shall be made by the Trustees except in accordance with professional advice taken from a person or persons having professional experience of investing in land to be held by way of investment.

Interpretation

5. In this Scheme the following expression shall have the following meanings:–

(a) "the deposited map" shall mean the map deposited in the office of the Commissioners and identified by the official seal of the Commissioners and the number 46047;

(b) "the Bovingdon area" shall mean the area coloured grey-green on the deposited map;

(c) "the Hemel Hempstead area" shall mean the area coloured buff on the deposited map;

(d) "the area of benefit" shall mean the area outlined in black on the deposited map, comprising both the Bovingdon area and the Hemel Hempstead area;

(e) "electors" shall mean persons resident in the area of benefit whose names are for the time being entered in the electoral register maintained for parliamentary and local government elections which covers the area of benefit; and

(f) "residence" means a dwelling house within the area of benefit in which a person normally lives and the expression "resident" shall be construed accordingly.

TRUSTEES

Trustees

6. (a) Subject to clause 7 of this Scheme the body of Trustees when complete shall consist of twelve competent persons who shall be elected in accordance with the provisions of this Scheme.

(b) The Trustees must be electors as defined in this Scheme.

Transitional Provisions and First Trustees

7. (a) The first Trustees for the purposes of this Scheme shall be those Trustees of the Charity holding office on the date that this Scheme is given effect by an Order of the Secretary of State under section 17(2) of the 1993 Act and who shall (subject to clause 9(c)(i) to (v) of this Scheme) hold office for life.

(b) All vacancies in the trusteeship of the Charity occurring after the date of this Scheme shall be filled by election as hereinafter provided.

Declaration by Trustees

8. No person shall be entitled to act as a Trustee whether on first or any subsequent entry into office until after signing in the minute book of the Trustees a declaration of acceptance and willingness to act in the trusts of this Scheme.

Termination of Trusteeship

9. (a) At every election held under the provisions of clause 11 of this Scheme, one quarter of the elected Trustees, or if their number is not a multiple of four, the number nearest to one quarter, shall retire from office. The elected Trustees to retire shall be those who have been longest in office since their last appointment or reappointment; but as between persons who were last appointed or re-appointed on the same day those to retire shall (unless they otherwise agree among themselves) be determined by lot. Subject to clause 11 (d) of this Scheme any competent Trustee shall be eligible for re-election.

(b) For the avoidance of doubt, in calculating the fraction of one quarter in sub-clause (a) above:

(i)   those Trustees serving for life shall not be required to retire and shall not be included in the total number of Trustees;

(ii) those Trustees who have ceased to be Trustees by virtue of sub-clause (c) below shall not be included in the total number of Trustees; and

(iii) if the number of Trustees is five or less, one Trustee shall retire; if the number of Trustees is between six and nine inclusive, two Trustees shall retire; and if the number of Trustees is between ten and twelve inclusive, three Trustees shall retire.

(c) A Trustee shall cease to be a Trustee if he or she:–

(i)   is disqualified from acting as a Trustee of a charity by virtue of section 72 of the 1993 Act;

(ii) becomes incapable (in the opinion of the Trustees) by reason of illness injury or mental disorder of managing his or her own affairs;

(iii) is absent without permission of the Trustees from all their ordinary meetings held within a period of six months and the Trustees resolve that his or her office be vacated;

(iv) gives not less than one month's notice in writing of his or her intention to resign (but only if at least the required quorum of Trustees will remain in office when the notice of resignation takes effect);

(v) ceases to be an elector; or

(vi) reaches the age of 75 and is not a Trustee serving for life.

Vacancies

10. Upon the occurrence of a vacancy the Trustees shall cause a note thereof to be entered in their minute book at their next meeting.

ELECTIONS

Elections

11. (a) For the purposes of appointing new elected Trustees of the Charity the Trustees shall call an election:
    (i) within three months of the number of Trustees falling to fewer than nine; and
    (ii) no later than five years after the date of the previous election or (in the case of the first election) the date on which this Scheme is given effect by an Order of the Secretary of State under section 17(2) of the 1993 Act.

    (b) All electors shall be entitled to vote in an election. Each elector shall be entitled to one vote in respect of each vacancy in the Trustee body but so that:
    (i) no person standing for office shall be entitled to vote; and
    (ii) no person shall cast more than one vote in favour of any one candidate.

    (c) Every election shall be conducted by the Trustees, who shall give at least 28 days public notice of the election in the area of benefit.

    (d) Every person standing for election shall be proposed and seconded by ten electors. No person shall be eligible for election if his or her term of office has been terminated under paragraphs (i), (ii), (iii) or (vi) of clause 9(c) above.

    (e) Voting at an election shall be by personal voting in a secret ballot.

    (f) Within the limits prescribed by this Scheme the Trustees shall have full power from time to time to make regulations for the conduct of elections, including the proposal and seconding. of candidates, the number and location of polling stations, the wording of voting papers, the date and time of voting and the counting and recording of votes.

    (g) Without prejudice to the generality of the power conferred by the preceding sub-clause, the Trustees may in particular divide the area of benefit into two or more electoral divisions for the purpose of holding elections, and require any candidate for election to be resident in a particular division. Any exercise of this power shall not derogate from the duty of every Trustee to act in the best interests of the Charity and its beneficiaries as a whole.

TRUST MEETINGS

Annual Trust Meeting

12. (a) There shall be an annual meeting of the electors, to be known as the Annual Trust Meeting, which shall be held in the month of April in each year or as soon as practicable thereafter.

    (b) The Trustees shall present to each Annual Trust Meeting the Report and Accounts of the Charity for the preceding year.

Special Trust Meetings

13. (a) The Trustees may at any time and shall if so requested in writing by at least 100 electors, call a special meeting of electors (to be known as a Special Trust Meeting) to discuss any question relating to the Charity.

    (b) Written requests for a Special Trust meeting shall be written individually by each elector and addressed to the Charity at its office for the time being.

Notice of Trust Meetings

14. Every Trust Meeting shall be called by the Trustees, who must give at least 21 days public notice in the area of benefit, specifying in the case of a Special Trust Meeting the matter or matters to be discussed.

Procedure at Trust Meetings

15. (a) All electors shall be entitled to attend and vote at any meeting.

    (b) If present, the presiding Trustee for the time being shall be the chairman of any Trust meeting. If he or she is not present, before any other business is transacted the persons present at the meeting shall appoint another of the Trustees to be chairman of the meeting.

    (c) The Trustees may place any matter they think fit before any Trust Meeting for consideration by those attending. The Trustees shall not, however, be required to submit any matter to the decision of those attending a Trust Meeting or be bound by any views expressed, whether by resolution or otherwise, by those attending any Trust Meeting, after the expiration of any agreed period of consultation or consideration in respect of those views.

MEETINGS AND PROCEEDINGS OF TRUSTEES

Ordinary Meetings

16. The Trustees shall hold at least two ordinary meetings in each year.

First meeting

17. The first meeting of the Trustees shall be summoned by the Clerk to the Trustees for the time being and if he or she fails to summon a meeting for three calendar months after the date on which this Scheme is given effect by an Order of the Secretary of State under section 17(2) of the 1933 Act, or if there is no Clerk, then a meeting may be summoned by any two of the Trustees.

Presiding Trustee

18. The Trustees at their first ordinary meeting after the date on which this Scheme is given effect by an Order of the Secretary of State under section 17(2) of the 1993 Act shall elect one of their number to preside over their meetings. Such person shall hold office until the third anniversary of his or her appointment or until he or she ceases to be a Trustee. In the event of a vacancy in the office for whatever reason the Trustees shall elect a replacement at their next ordinary meeting of the Trustees. The person so appointed (who may be known by the title of Chairman or such other name as the Trustees may from time to time agree) shall be eligible for re-election unless he or she ceases to be a Trustee. If at any meeting the presiding Trustee is not present within 10 minutes after the time appointed for holding the same or there is no presiding Trustee, the Trustees present shall choose one of their number to preside at that meeting.

Special Meetings

19. A special meeting may be summoned at any time by the presiding Trustee or any two Trustees upon not less than four day's notice being given to the other Trustees of the matters to be discussed. A special meeting may be summoned to take place immediately after an ordinary meeting.

Quorum

20. (a) Except as provided in sub-clause (b) below no business shall be transacted at any meeting unless there are present not less than the number of Trustees determined in accordance with the following table.

Number of Trustees	Quorum required
4–8	4 Trustees
9–12	5 Trustees

Voting

21. Every matter shall be determined by the majority of votes of the Trustees present and voting on the question. In case of equality of votes the Chairman of the meeting shall have a casting vote whether he or she has not voted previously on the same question but no Trustee in any other circumstance shall have more than one vote.

Minutes

22. The Trustees shall keep, in books maintained for the purpose, minutes of the proceedings of their meetings.

General power to make regulations

23. Within the limits prescribed by this Scheme the Trustees shall have full power from time to time to make regulations for the management of the Charity and for the conduct of their business including the summoning of meetings, the deposit of money at a bank and the custody of documents.

Chief Executive and other staff

24. The Trustees may appoint and dismiss, within the limits permitted by law, a Chief Executive, a Clerk, and such other employees (if any) as they consider necessary for the efficient operation of the Charity, and may pay such persons (who shall not be the Trustees) such reasonable remuneration as they think fit.

Committees

25. The Trustees may from time to time appoint any two or more of their number to be a committee for the purpose of discharging any duty which in their opinion would be more effectively undertaken by way of committee, provided that all acts and proceedings of the committee shall be fully and promptly reported to the Trustees.

USE OF LAND

Use of land

26. The land specified in the Schedule hereto shall continue to be appropriated and used for the provision, in the interests of social welfare, of facilities for the recreation and other leisure time occupation of the residents of the area of benefit; subject to this use, the land shall be available for access for recreation by the public at large.

MANAGEMENT OF PROPERTY

Management and letting of lands

27. The Trustees shall let or otherwise manage all the land belonging to the Charity not required to be appropriated and used for charitable purposes.

Leases

28. The Trustees shall provide that on the grant by them of any lease the lessee shall execute a counterpart thereof. Every lease shall contain covenants on the part of the lessee for the payment of rent, and all other usual and proper covenants applicable to the property comprised therein and a proviso for re-entry on non-payment of the rent or non-performance of the covenants.

Repair and Insurance

29. The Trustees shall keep in repair and insure to the full value thereof against fire and other usual risks all the buildings of the Charity not required to be kept in repair and insured by the lessees or tenants thereof and shall suitably insure in respect of public liability and employer's liability.

Sale or other disposal

30. The Trustees may sell or otherwise dispose of the whole or any part of the said land not required to be appropriated and used for charitable purposes. and may do and execute all proper acts and assurances for carrying any such sale into effect.

Proceeds of sale or other disposal

31. Unless the Commissioners otherwise direct the clear proceeds of any such sale or disposal as aforesaid shall be invested in trust for the Charity.

APPLICATION OF INCOME

Expenses of Management

32. (a) The Trustees shall first defray out of the income of the Charity the cost of maintaining the property of the Charity (including the repair and insurance of any buildings thereon) and all other charges and expenses of and incidental to the administration and management of the Charity.

(b) The Trustees may provide indemnity insurance for themselves out of the funds of the Charity provided that any such insurance shall not extend to any claim arising from any act or omission which the Trustees knew to be a breach of trust or breach of duty or which was committed by the Trustees in reckless disregard of whether it was a breach of trust or breach of duty or not.

Reserve Fund

33. (a) In the interests of prudent management the Trustees may establish and maintain a reserve fund, to be called the Reserve Fund ("he Fund"), for the purpose of providing:

  (i) for the management expenses of the Charity in the event of a deficiency of income;

  (ii) for the extraordinary repair, improvement and rebuilding of the buildings of the Charity; and

  (iii) for the maintenance and improvement of the assets of the Charity.

(b) Unless the Commissioners otherwise direct, the Fund shall be established and maintained out of the income of the Charity by the transfer to the Fund of such annual sum as is sufficient for the purpose.

(c) Income of the Charity which is attributable to the Fund shall form part of the Fund.

(d) The Trustees may at any time apply the Fund, or any part of it, for its purposes, but in so far as the Fund is not so applied it shall be invested in trust for the Charity.

Purchase of additional land

34. The Trustees may apply the income of the Charity in acquiring additional land to be appropriated and used for charitable purposes for the benefit of the residents of the area of benefit.

Application of income

35. (a) Subject to the payments aforesaid, the Trustees shall apply the income of the Charity as follows:

  (i) as to 90% thereof for the benefit of the residents of the Hemel Hempstead area in the manner hereinafter specified; and

  (ii) as to the remaining 10% thereof for the benefit of the residents of the Bovingdon area in the manner hereinafter specified.

(b) the income applicable under the preceding sub-clause for the benefit of the residents of either the Hemel Hempstead area or the Bovingdon area shall be applied by the Trustees in one or more of the following ways for:

  (i) the relief of the aged, sick, disabled or poor residents of that area;

  (ii) the provision, or assistance in the provision, for the benefit of the residents of that area and its neighbourhood or any section of those residents, of facilities for recreation or other leisure time occupation where that provision is charitable by virtue of section 1 of the Recreational Charities Act 1958 (facilities provided in the interests of social welfare);

  (iii) the advancement of education for the benefit of residents of that area; and

  (iv) the promotion of any other charitable purpose (whether or not of a nature similar to any purpose specified in paragraphs (i), (ii) and (iii) above) for the benefit of the residents of that area.

GENERAL PROVISIONS

Co-operation with local authorities

36. Where it appears to the Trustees that it is likely to advance or make more effective the work of the Charity (but not otherwise) they may co-operate with any local authority within or adjoining the area of benefit for purposes including (but without prejudice to the generality of the foregoing) the co-ordination of activities or participation in joint projects and the Trustees may defray the cost of such co-operation out of any income (or money applicable as income) of the Charity.

Temporary restriction of access to land

37. (a) Where the Trustees after taking appropriate technical or professional advice consider that it is necessary to restrict public access to a particular site or sites on the Charity's land which have hitherto been on open access to the public, such restriction being for the purposes of environmental protection or improvement of the site or sites, they may restrict public access to that site or sites on such terms and conditions as they think fit, but only for such period as is necessary to effect such protection or improvement.

(b) Where the Trustees have made a decision to restrict access under sub-clause (a) above they shall keep that decision under regular review and shall in any case review such decision annually.

Gifts

38. The Trustees may accept gifts for the general purposes of the Charity and may also accept gifts for any special objects connected with the Charity which are not inconsistent with this Scheme.

Appropriation of benefits

39. Subject to Clause 25 of this Scheme the appropriation of the benefits of the Charity shall be made by the Trustees at meetings of their body and not separately by any individual Trustee or Trustees.

Trustees not to be personally interested

40. No Trustee shall take or hold any interest in property belonging to the Charity otherwise than as a Trustee for the purposes thereof and no Trustee shall receive remuneration or be interested in the supply of work or goods at the cost of the Charity.

Charity not to relieve public funds

41. The Trustees shall not apply the income of the Charity directly in relief of rates taxes or other public funds but may apply the income in supplementing relief or assistance provided out of public funds.

Questions under the Scheme

42. Any question as to the construction of this Scheme or as to the regularity or the validity of any acts done or about to be done under this Scheme may be determined by the Commissioners upon such application made to them for the purpose as they think fit.

SCHEDULE

The following land situate at Hemel Hempstead in the County of Hertfordshire.

Freehold land

Description	Field No.	Size in hectares	Description	Field No.	Size in hectares
Snook's Moor	1513	3.13	Heath Park Car Park	3616	0.14
Snoxall's Moor	4606	3.26	War Memorial Gardens	2419	0.32
Herdsman's Moor	8995	0.63	St. John's Garden	0817	0.39
	6999	2.97	Plough Gardens	4423	1.64
Fishery Moor	1007	3.53	Sheethanger Common	7424	16.48
Old Fishery (part)	5918	1.55	Bury Wood	1500	6.96
Station Moor	5708	6.25	Felden Verges	0333	0.18
Harding's Moor	9898	6.38		0414	0.13
Bulbourne Meadow	2496	4.01		0604	0.28
Lock Cottage	2702	0.23	London Road Verges	7292	0.15
Railway Embankment	2984	0.23		4398	0.04
Chaulden Meadow	8031	4.26	Balderson's Moor	4108	1.55
Lower Roughdown	6864	4.82	Bulbourne Moor	4094	1.27
Upper Roughdown	2770	4.14	Two Waters Moor West	3581	1.03
Further Roughdown	9554	2.77	Two Waters Moor East	4774	0.61
Blackbirds' Moor	8822	5.58	Apsley Triangle (part)	5568	0.36
Heath Park	1411	3.16	Two Waters Halt	4886	0.10

A total of 88.53 hectares at Boxmoor in the Borough of Dacorum, Hertfordshire.

Sealed by Order of the Commissioners this 10th day of November 1999.

EXPLANATORY NOTE

(This note is not part of the Order)

This Order gives effect to a Scheme of the Charity Commissioners for the Charity presently known as the Boxmoor Estate. The Charity is of ancient origin being founded in 1594 and is now regulated by the Boxmoor Act 1809 ("the Act") and various Schemes of the Charity Commissioners ("the old Schemes").

The present Scheme replaces most of the provisions [of] the Act, and all of the old Schemes. The name of the Charity is changed to the Box Moor Trust which reflects the proper designation of the area as Box Moor. A new body of Trustees is created, which (subject to transitional arrangements) will in future be democratically elected. The area of benefit of the Charity is now clearly identified by means of a deposited map prepared by the Ordinance Survey. The constitution and powers of the Trustees are modernised.

Provision is made for the Charity's land (other than land held as an investment) to be held for the purposes of public recreation and such recreational land is identified in the Schedule to the Scheme. There is power to purchase additional land for recreational purposes.

There is power to apply the Charity's surplus income for various purposes within the Charity's area of benefit. Those purposes include the relief of the aged, sick, disabled and poor people, the promotion of recreational facilities and the advancement of education.

The deposited plan referred to in the Scheme may be examined by any member of the public, by appointment, during normal office hours, at the London office of the Charity Commissioners for England and Wales.

Appendix 7

Box Moor Pingos

The earliest evidence of the landscape of the Box Moor Trust Estate dates from the end of the last Ice Age. The discovery of exceedingly rare periglacial features on one of the Moors, during preliminary work for the A41 By-pass in 1992, aroused much archaeological interest. On melting, the ice can leave behind hollows filled with water and surrounded by a ring of soil and/or rock. These pond-like, circular depressions in which peat has accumulated on the borders of a former glacier are known as 'pingos', a word derived from an Eskimo term. The Trust followed up this discovery by permitting Hertfordshire Archaeological Trust (HAT) to organise a dig to take samples from various layers of these deposits. Examination of the peat could eventually result in the reconstruction of the vegetational history from c.12000BC through the Mesolithic (8300–4500BC) and Neolithic (4500–2500BC) periods. The Trust itself has had positive links with HAT for some years and a number of excavations have been carried out on Trust lands.

Specialists from English Heritage, the University of East Anglia and King's College, London, participated in this research. Very little is known of early post-glacial woodland development in southern England and these are the only known pingos immediately north of London. At least three pingos were identified, but one had been partly destroyed by the work on the A41 By-pass. The peat deposits were up to 2 metres deep; two samples were taken away in February 1992 to assess the peat for its pollen content and preservation.

The archaeologists then used a mechanical digger to cut through Pingo 2 on 12 June 1992 and took numerous samples of the peat. The crucial fact that this part of the Box Moor Estate had never been ploughed helped this initial assessment. From their later analysis, information came to light on the remains of plants, insects, snails and soil. Most importantly, samples were also taken for radio-carbon dating. The pollen analysis revealed characteristics of the late glacial (Devensian) to the post-glacial (Flandrian) periods; it indicated an open habitat dominated by dwarf shrubs and arctic- or alpine-type plants, rather than woodland. The climate appeared to have changed rapidly, becoming suitable for birch trees, pine and willow, although much of the landscape still remained open. Herbaceous plants included Mugwort (*Artemisia*), Rock rose (*Helianthemum*), Ranunculus and Potentilla-type species, all growing at the margin of the pool.

The immediate vicinity of the pingo later became colonised by a dense thicket of birch, the canopy of which, over time, opened out as hazel and pine became more established. Hazel then diminished as alder, elm, lime and oak emerged, producing a rich, mixed woodland. (Incidentally, it appeared that oak had a lower representation than either elm or lime in the prehistoric woodlands of this district.) The elm subsequently declined c.3000BC and the picture of the Neolithic woodland seems to be of a diverse habitat with evidence of soil disturbance and a much more open tree canopy than in the later Mesolithic era.

The discovery of the pollen from trees and shrubs such as dwarf birch, pine, juniper, sea buckthorn and willow therefore enables one to visualise this ancient scene. The find of a small, but vivid green leaf from a birch tree, possibly 4000 years old, gave rise to great excitement and it was carefully photographed before it lost its natural colouring, preserved expediently by the authors in a glass of vodka!

Some interesting finds of delicate flint barbs suitable for fishing spears, together with fragments of charcoal large enough to be visible to the naked eye, and heat-shattered flint, suggest that Mesolithic people had exploited this site long before the name 'Box Moor' was devised. Charred cereal remains might indicate the small-scale growing of cereal crops in the glades during Neolithic times and would tie in with other finds of this period along the route of the A41 By-Pass. These finds alone make the site of special importance to the researcher of prehistory.

The prospect of a co-ordinated analysis of these early sediments was viewed as an unusual opportunity, since it was likely that firmer evidence of the retreat of the glaciers could be obtained. It would be possible to follow the woodland succession of the Flandrian age in eastern England and even monitor the impact of early peoples on the changing landscape. It is hoped that this follow-up work will take place in the future and the results will be eagerly awaited. It is an expensive business to carry out a full environmental analysis, but the site is of national significance and may one day reveal previously unknown information.

APPENDIX 8

EARLY SETTLEMENT OF BOX MOOR

The archaeology of the Trust's Estate ties in closely with that of Dacorum as a whole and in particular with that of the Bulbourne and Gade valleys. The entire lengths of the Kings Langley and Berkhamsted By-passes were evaluated by the Hertfordshire Archaeological Trust (HAT) in 1991–2, but there has never been a systematic study of the locality.

In an exhibition about the archaeology of Dacorum, presented by the Dacorum Heritage Trust in 1996, the handbook stated: 'Our knowledge of the extent and significance of Neolithic and Bronze age occupation has increased because of this work. The rarity of the evidence is such that the excavations are of national importance.' Evidence was found that the clay and chalk uplands, as well as the river valleys, had been exploited since at least the Neolithic period (4500–2500BC). Eight previously unknown sites, dating mainly to the Neolithic and late Bronze/Iron Age periods (4500–400BC), were unearthed. All the evidence pointed to the suitability of this area for human settlement.

Two important sites at Apsley and Rucklers Lane were investigated, on the high ground overlooking the river Gade, which in those days would have been a more prominent feature. The most surprising finds were parallel ditches and post holes, similar to cursus monuments which are usually associated with funerary and religious rites. They intimated that large numbers of people must have visited this area for some far-off ceremonial purpose. The ditches were about 80 metres long and 75 metres apart. Archaeologists have found that the alignments of cursus ditches correspond with the midsummer sunset and moon's rising; monuments of this type typically date to 3000BC. Further prehistoric remains comparable to those found in this particular region were uncovered along the chosen route.

Pottery and worked flint, principally scrapers and some delicate leaf-shaped arrowheads, were recorded. The early Neolithic farmers herded wild cattle, goats, sheep and pigs as well as growing wheat *(emmet)* and barley. The sheep would have resembled the small Soay sheep which the Box Moor Trust introduced to Roughdown Common in the 1970s. The farmers were not just reliant on what they grew or reared, but gathered the fruits and nuts from the surrounding woodland.

During the late Bronze Age, enclosed as well as un-enclosed farmsteads sprang up in these warm, equable districts, evolving into sizeable settlements. Clay loom weights and spindle whorls proved that wool was spun and woven on upright looms. Querns, similar to the one found at the Boxmoor Trout Fishery, were used to grind cereal grains and bread was baked in clay ovens.

Neolithic and Bronze Age hand-made pottery was discovered. The potters of long ago used the coil method and fired their wares at a low heat, therefore making them more fragile. The later Romano-British pottery included flagons *(amphora)*, beakers, bowls, dishes, lids and heavy duty mixing bowls *(mortaria)*. There was also some finer Samian ware, a reddish coloured pottery imported from France.

The only known site to be truncated by the construction of the road was Grim's Ditch, a substantial linear earthwork consisting of a bank and ditch many kilometres long. The excavations defined the age of this feature for the first time, when early- to middle-Iron Age pottery was recovered from the basal fill of the ditch.

During the Iron Age (700BC–AD43), people continued to settle here. Dacorum then formed part of the territory of the Catevellauni tribe. Celtic invaders first introduced iron into Bronze Age Britain and both tools and weapons were made from this valuable metal. The excavations at Cow Roast, near Tring, indicated the presence of iron workings, probably utilising local coppiced woods, although the source of the iron ore has not yet been identified. A number of furnaces and very large quantities of slag were found. The ore may have originated in the marshy areas of the Bulbourne valley itself, since the archaeologists believed that iron smelting was a major activity in this area. Coins were unearthed which showed that the site was occupied at least until the end of the fourth century AD. Some fine Roman-style brooches and a bronze figurine have been preserved, to show future generations that our earlier ancestors were not all barbarians.

The Roman road known as Akeman Street, linking Bath to Colchester via St Albans *(Verulamium)*, once ran through the present day Box Moor Estate. The former route of the A41 traversed a whole chain of Roman villas and associated buildings. Boxmoor House Villa, adjoining the present Box Lane and close to Sheethanger Common, was discovered in the mid-nineteenth century when a tree was removed in the lawn of the then newly built Boxmoor House. It disclosed part of a mosaic floor and the area was subsequently excavated by Sir John Evans in 1852. A series of buildings had occupied this site, from the late first century to the fourth century. Traces of mosaic floors, painted plaster walls and a hypocaust system demonstrated the one-time importance of this estate. Dr David S. Neal and the Hemel Hempstead Excavation Society investigated the Villa from 1966–70; it is now a Scheduled Monument and lies securely under the grounds of Boxmoor House School.

A Roman cist, or chest-type grave, had already been discovered in 1837 in the churchyard of Box Lane Chapel and possibly the two young people, whose cremated remains were exposed in glass jars, were members of the family who once occupied the nearby Villa. Further discoveries were made in the vicinity of Boxmoor Station in 1851 and that area was also excavated by Sir John Evans. A statuette of Mercury was found opposite the station. When the stationmaster's house was demolished, Dr Neal again carried out archaeological work on the site, dated at no later than the middle of the second century AD.

Apart from the remains of these Roman villas along the Bulbourne valley, an impressive Roman bath and associated buildings were initially excavated at Gadebridge by Dr Neal, in 1963–8, and re-excavated in the summer of 2000, as part of the town's millennium celebrations. Dr Neal also uncovered five Romano-Celtic religious buildings at Wood Lane End, Hemel Hempstead. The existence of this mausoleum-temple complex again underlines the popularity of the area for human activity and settlement.

Excavations at nearby Bourne End produced pottery, tile and animal bones by the bucketful. Fine tableware and tiles indicated a substantial Roman building in the vicinity. Human burials and cremation remains were also found at various points along the route of the A41 By-pass, some of Bronze Age origin. The crystal clear streams rising in the Chilterns and flowing down gentle, tree-clad valleys must have attracted those Roman colonisers as much as they did later settlers.

The gap through the Chiltern hills was used over and over again as a main transport artery, not least in Roman times, and perhaps Akeman Street saw the legions of Imperial Rome march along its length. *Verulamium* was not very far away and some of the soldiers might have availed themselves of the facilities at the surprisingly large bath complex near the river Gade. When the Grand Junction Canal was being dug, a soldier's helmet dating from the first century AD was brought to light.

There is little archaeological evidence covering the Dark Ages after the fall of Rome and the abandonment of Britain to the booty-hungry Norsemen. The western part of Hertfordshire was incorporated into the kingdom of Mercia after the Anglo-Saxon invasions *c.*AD450. Offa, King of Mercia, gave generously to the foundation of the Monastery at St Albans in the eighth century.

An Anglo-Saxon disc brooch was found between St Mary's Church and the river Gade. Anglo-Saxon reminders still survive in the name of Hemel Hempstead, possibly signifying 'the hamlet on the hill', as well as in the term 'Hundred'. The latter was an area of one hundred hides, each of which could supply one warrior in times of hostility, a system which dated back to the time of Alfred the Great. Danish raiders later sailed up the Colne and the Lea and the name Dacorum derives from *'Daneis'*, meaning 'of the Danes'. There were frequent incursions of Danish raiding parties into Hertfordshire, including one in AD930 in which the shrine at St Albans was desecrated. There may well have been some form of Danish control at the end of the ninth and beginning of the tenth centuries in this district.

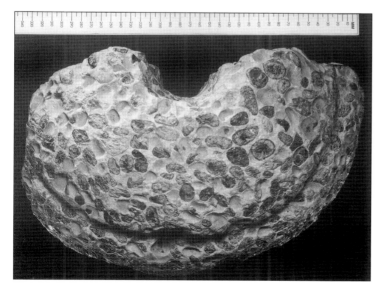

The puddingstone quern, or corn handmill, unearthed during excavations at Boxmoor Trout Fishery.

The figurine of Mercury was found on Box Moor, on the north bank of the river Bulbourne.

APPENDIX 9

BOTANICAL RECORD

It is a fortunate coincidence that some of Hertfordshire's best wild flower habitats are on land managed by the Box Moor Trust. Roughdown and Sheethanger Commons, Hay Wood and parts of the Moors themselves, all hold rarities and a wealth of plants that are becoming increasingly uncommon.

The Moors, most importantly Fishery Moor, as well as the river Bulbourne, have fifteen species not often found in Hertfordshire, including the only, recently recorded, site for Flat Sedge (*Blysmus compressus*). Other rarities include the Sedges (*Carex panicea, C. nigra* and *C. disticha*); Smooth Brome (*Bromus racemosus*); Ivy-leaved Water Crowfoot (*Ranunculus hederaceus*) which is only found in two or three other sites in this county and, occasionally, Marsh Orchids (*Dactylorhiza praetermissa*).

Roughdown Common, an old chalk quarry, is notable for the abundance of Juniper and a fine calcareous flora including Autumn Gentian (*Gentianella amerella*), Eyebright (*Euphrasia pseudokerneri*) and the Orchids (*Dactylorhiza fuchsii* and *D. praetermissa*), as well as the Pyramidal Orchid (*Anacamptis pyramidalis*). The Exchange land to the east has been seeded with a wild flower mixture including Cowslip (*Primula veris*), which has exploded, turning the hillside yellow in Spring with some half a million blooms. It is to be hoped that some of the special plants of the quarry may eventually spread to this site.

Sheethanger Common also has an abundance of chalk-loving plants, notably around the old chalk quarry opposite the Golf Club house. Here may be found Wild Thyme (*Thymus pulegioides*), Small Scabious (*Scabiosa columbaria*), Clustered Bell-flower (*Campanula glomerata*) and, most importantly, Frog Orchid (*Coeloglossum viride*). This has failed to appear in the last two years, due perhaps, to an over-zealous cutting of the banks of the Green where they once grew. Juniper also grows here but it is being crowded out by the invasion of scrub and trees.

Hay Wood, Bury Wood and Ramacre Wood all have interesting woodland plants, especially Hay Wood which has three members of the Orchid family, namely Fly Orchid (*Ophrys insectifera*), Greater Butterfly Orchid (*Platanthera chlorantha*) and the White Helleborine (*Cephalanthera damasonium*).

In all some 340 plant species have been recorded on the Trust lands in recent years. This is in part due to the diversity of natural habitats but also to the sensitive management of them by the Box Moor Trust, for which we should be grateful.

Gerald Salisbury and Jill Saunders, July 2003

Gerald Salisbury and Jill Saunders monitoring the flora on Further Roughdown in 2004.

APPENDIX 9A

PLANTS OF FISHERY MOOR, 1999–2000

Recorded by Gerald Salisbury and Jill Saunders.

This land has been designated by Hertfordshire County Council as a Heritage Site.

Common name	Botanical name
Field Horsetail	*Equisetum arvense*
Marsh Horsetail	*Equisetum palustre*
Adder's-tongue	*Ophioglossum vulgatum*[1]
Marsh Marigold	*Caltha palustris*
Meadow Buttercup	*Ranunculus acris*
Creeping Buttercup	*Ranunculus repens*
Bulbous Buttercup	*Ranunculus bulbosus*
Lesser Celandine	*Ranunculus ficaria*
Celery-leaved Buttercup	*Ranunculus sceleratus*
Ivy-leaved Crowfoot	*Ranunculus hederaceus*[1]
Water Crowfoot	*Ranunculus penicillatus*
	Ssp. Pseudofluitans
Shepherd's-purse	*Capsella bursa-pastoris*
Lady's Smock	*Cardamine pratensis*
Hairy Bitter-cress	*Cardamine hirsuta*
Wintercress	*Barbarea vulgaris*
Watercress	*Rorippa nasturtium-aquaticum*
Common Mouse-ear	*Cerastium fontanum*
Sticky Mouse-ear	*Cerastium glomeratum*
Chickweed	*Stellaria media*
Lesser Stitchwort	*Stellaria graminea*
Bog Stitchwort	*Stellaria uliginosa*
Pearlwort	*Sagina procumbens*
Common Orache	*Atriplex patula*
Common Mallow	*Malva sylvestris*
Cut-leaved Cranesbill	*Geranium dissectum*
Dove's-foot Cranesbill	*Geranium molle*
Orange Balsam	*Impatiens capensis*
Red Clover	*Trifolium pratense*
White Clover	*Trifolium repens*
Lesser Trefoil	*Trifolium dubium*
Bird's-foot Trefoil	*Lotus corniculatus*
Bush Vetch	*Vicia sepium*
Common Vetch	*Vicia sativa*
Meadow Vetchling	*Lathyrus pratensis*
Meadow Sweet	*Filipendula ulmaria*
Bramble	*Rubus fruticosus*
Silverweed	*Potentilla anserina*
Tormentil	*Potentilla erecta*
Creeping Cinquefoil	*Potentilla reptans*
Lady's Mantle	*Alchemilla vestita*
Great Hairy Willow-herb	*Epilobium hirsutum*
Hoary Willow-herb	*Epilobium parviflorum*
Broad-leaved Willow-herb	*Epilobium montanum*
American Willow-herb	*Epilobium ciliatum*
Rosebay Willow-herb	*Chamerion angustifolium*
Water Starwort	*Callitriche aggregate*
Cow Parsley	*Anthriscus sylvestris*
Fools Watercress	*Apium nodiflorum*
Pignut	*Conopodium majus*
Lesser Water-parsnip	*Berula erecta*[1]
Hogweed	*Heracleum sphondylium*
Knotgrass	*Polygonum aviculare*
Amphibious Bistort	*Polygonum amphibia*
Persicaria	*Polygonum maculosa*
Sorrel	*Rumex acetosa*
Sheep's Sorrel	*Rumex acetosella*
Great Water-dock	*Rumex hydrolapathum*
Curled Dock	*Rumex crispus*
Broad-leaved Dock	*Rumex obtusifolius*
Clustered Dock	*Rumex conglomeratus*
Stinging Nettle	*Urtica dioica*
Water Forget-me-not	*Myosotis scorpioides*
Comfrey	*Symphytum officinale*
Bindweed	*Convolvulus arvensis*
Hedge Bindweed	*Calystegia sepium*
Large Bindweed	*Calystegia sylvatica*
Woody Nightshade	*Solanum dulcamara*
Water Figwort	*Scrophularia auriculata*
Monkey Flower	*Mimulus guttatus*[1]
Brooklime	*Veronica beccabunga*
Blue Water Speedwell	*Veronica anagallis-aquatica*
Germander Speedwell	*Veronica chamaedrys*
Thyme-leaved Speedwell	*Veronica serpyllifolia*
Wall Speedwell	*Veronica arvensis*
Water Mint	*Mentha aquatica*
Gypsywort	*Lycopus europaeus*
Selfheal	*Prunella vulgaris*
Hedge Woundwort	*Stachys sylvatica*
Black Horehound	*Ballota nigra*
White Dead-nettle	*Lamium album*
Skullcap	*Scutellaria galericulata*
Common Hemp-nettle	*Galeopsis bifida*
Bugle	*Ajuga reptans*
Great Plantain	*Plantago major*
Ribwort Plantain	*Plantago lanceolata*
Hedge Bedstraw	*Galium mollugo*
Lady's Bedstraw	*Gallium verum*
Goosegrass	*Gallium aparine*
Marsh Valerian	*Valeriana dioica*[2]
Devil's-bit Scabious	*Succisa pratensis*
Bur-marigold	*Bidens tripartita*
Ragwort	*Senecio jacobaea*
Groundsel	*Senecio vulgaris*
Coltsfoot	*Tussilago farfara*
Daisy	*Bellis perennis*
Yarrow	*Achillea millefolium*
Pineapple Weed	*Matracaria matricarioides*
Slender Thistle	*Carduus tenuiflorus*[1]
Spear Thistle	*Cirsium vulgare*
Marsh Thistle	*Cirsium palustre*
Creeping Thistle	*Cirsium arvense*
Welted Thistle	*Carduus acanthoides*
Ox-eye Daisy	*Leucanthemum vulgare*
Knapweed	*Centaurea nigra*
Nipplewort	*Lapsana communis*
Common Cat's-ear	*Hypochoeris radicata*
Autumnal Hawkbit	*Leontodon autumnalis*
Goat's Beard	*Tragopogon pratensis*
Dandelion	*Taraxacum officinale*
Beaked Hawksbeard	*Crepis vesicaria*
Smooth Hawksbeard	*Crepis capillaris*
Toad Rush	*Juncus bufonius*
Hard Rush	*Juncus inflexus*
Soft Rush	*Juncus effusus*
Jointed Rush	*Juncus articulatus*
Field Woodrush	*Luzula campestris*
Crow Garlic	*Alium vineale*
Yellow Flag	*Iris pseudacorus*
Southern Marsh-orchid	*Dactylorhiza praetermissa*[1]
Duckweed	*Lemna minor*
Branched Bur-reed	*Sparganium erectum*
Small Bur-reed	*Sparganium emersum*
Bristle Club-rush	*Isolepis setacea*[1]
Flat Sedge	*Blysmus compressus*[1 & 3]

SEDGES

Pond Sedge	*Carex acutiformis*
Carnation Sedge	*Carex panicea*[1]
Glaucous Sedge	*Carex flacca*
Hairy Sedge	*Carex hirta*
Common Sedge	*Carex nigra*[1]
Fox Sedge	*Carex otrubae*
Brown Sedge	*Carex disticha*[1]
Spiked Sedge	*Carex spicata*
Oval Sedge	*Carex ovalis*

GRASSES

Sweet-Grass	*Glyceria fluitans*
Plicate Sweet-grass	*Glyceria plicata*
Reed Sweet-grass	*Glyceria maxima*
Meadow Fescue	*Festuca pratensis*
Red Fescue	*Festuca rubra*
Perennial Rye-grass	*Lolium perenne*
Annual Meadow-grass	*Poa annua*
Smooth Meadow-grass	*Poa pratensis*
Rough Meadow-grass	*Poa tivialis*
Water Whorl-grass	*Catabrosa aquatica*[1]
Cock's-foot	*Dactylis glomerata*
Crested Dog's tail	*Cynosurus cristatus*
Quaking Grass	*Briza media*
Wall Barley	*Hordeum murinum*
Barren Brome	*Bromus sterilis*
Soft Brome	*Bromus hordeaceus*
Smooth Brome	*Bromus racemosus*[1]
Downy Oat-grass	*Helictotrichon pubescens*
Common Couch	*Elytrigia repens*
Yellow Oat-grass	*Trisetum flavescens*
False Oat-grass	*Arrhenatherum elatius*
Yorkshire Fog	*Holcus lunatus*
Tufted Hair-grass	*Deschampsia cespitosa*
Common Bent	*Agrostis capillaris*
Creeping Bent	*Agrostis stolonifera*
Timothy Grass	*Phleum pratensis*
Smaller Cat's-tail	*Phleum bertolonii*
Meadow Fox-tail	*Alopecurus pratensis*
Marsh Fox-tail	*Alopecurus geniculatus*
Sweet Vernal-grass	*Anthoxanthum oderatum*
Reed Canary-grass	*Phalaris arundinacea*

TREES

Hawthorn	*Crataegus monogyna*
Alder	*Alnus glutinosa*
White Willow	*Salix alba*
Crack Willow	*Salix fragilis*
Common Osier	*Salix viminalis*

[1] Plants of special interest or uncommon in Herts.

[2] One patch was recorded in 1995, but not seen since.

[3] This is the only recent record for Hertfordshire.

APPENDIX 9B

PLANTS OF ROUGHDOWN COMMON, 1999–2000

Recorded by Gerald Salisbury and Jill Saunders.

The former chalk pit on this land has been designated as a Site of Special Scientific Interest (SSSI).

Common name	Botanical name
Old Man's Beard	*Clematis vitalba*
Meadow Buttercup	*Ranunculus acris*
Creeping Buttercup	*Ranunculus repens*
Bulbous Buttercup	*Ranunculus bulbosus*
Lesser Celandine	*Ranunculus ficaria*
Garlic Mustard	*Alliaria petiolata*
Wild Mignonette	*Reseda lutea*
Hairy Violet	*Viola hirta*
St John's Wort	*Hypericum perforatum*
Rockrose	*Helianthemum nummularium*[1]
Bladder Campion	*Silene vulgaris*
Mouse-ear Chickweed	*Cerastium fontanum*
Fairy Flax	*Linum catharticum*
Herb Robert	*Geranium robertianum*
Black Medick	*Medicago lupulina*
Common Melilot	*Melilotus officinalis*
Red Clover	*Trifolium pratense*
White Clover	*Trifolium repens*
Common Yellow Trefoil	*Trifolium dubium*
Bird's-foot Trefoil	*Lotus corniculatus*
Tufted Vetch	*Vicia cracca*
Bush Vetch	*Vicia sepium*
Meadow Vetchling	*Lathyrus pratensis*
Raspberry	*Rubus idaeus*
Bramble	*Rubus fruiticosus*
Creeping Cinquefoil	*Potentilla reptans*
Herb Bennet	*Geum urbanum*
Agrimony	*Agrimonia eupatoria*
Salad Burnet	*Sanguisorba minor*
Enchanter's Nightshade	*Circaea lutetiana*
Rough Chervil	*Chaerophyllum temulentum*
Cow Parsley	*Anthriscus sylvestris*
Hedge Parsley	*Torillis japonica*
Burnet Saxifrage	*Pimpinella saxifraga*
Ground Elder	*Aegopodium podagraria*
Hogweed	*Heracleum sphondylium*
Wild Carrot	*Daucus carota*
White Bryony	*Bryonia dioica*
Dog's Mercury	*Mercurialis perennis*
Wood Dock	*Rumex sanguineus*
Stinging Nettle	*Urtica dioica*
Cowslip	*Primula veris*
Centaury	*Centaurium erythraea*
Autumn Gentian	*Gentianella amarella*[1]
Field Forget-me-not	*Myosotis arvensis*
Woody Nightshade	*Solanum dulcamara*
Common Toadflax	*Linaria vulgaris*
Germander Speedwell	*Veronica chamaedrys*
Yellow Rattle	*Rhinanthus minor*
Eyebright	*Euphrasia pseudokerneri*[1]
Red Bartsia	*Odontites verna*
Marjoram	*Origanum vulgare*
Thyme	*Thymus pulegioides*[1]
Wild Basil	*Clinopodium vulgare*
Self-heal	*Prunella vulgaris*
Hedge Woundwort	*Stachys sylvatica*

White Dead-nettle	*Lamium album*
Ground Ivy	*Glechoma hederacea*
Great Plantain	*Plantago major*
Hoary Plantain	*Plantago media*
Ribwort Plantain	*Plantago lanceolata*
Harebell	*Campanula rotundiflora*
Bedstraw	*Galium mollugo*
Lady's Bedstraw	*Galium verum*
Goosegrass	*Galium aparine*
Honeysuckle	*Lonicera periclymenum*
Field Scabious	*Knautia arvensis*
Small Scabious	*Scabiosa columbaria*[1]
Ragwort	*Senecio jacobaea*
Coltsfoot	*Tussilago farfara*
Daisy	*Bellis perennis*
Yarrow	*Achillea millefolium*
Ox-eye Daisy	*Leucanthemum vulgare*
Mugwort	*Artemisia vulgaris*
Carline Thistle	*Carlina vulgaris*[1]
Spear Thistle	*Cirsium vulgare*
Creeping Thistle	*Cirsium arvense*
Dwarf Thistle	*Cirsium acaulon*
Greater Knapweed	*Centaurea scabiosa*
Hardheads	*Centaurea nigra*
Common Cat's-ear	*Hypochoeris radicata*
Autumnal Hawkbit	*Leontodon autumnalis*
Rough Hawkbit	*Leontodon hispidus*
Smooth Hawkbit	*Leontodon saxatilis*
Rough Ox-tongue	*Picris hieracioides*
Goat's Beard	*Tragopogon pratensis*
Wall Lettuce	*Mycelis muralis*
Corn Sow-thistle	*Sonchus arvensis*
Dandelion	*Taraxum officinale*
Beaked Hawksbeard	*Crepis vesicaria*
Smooth Hawksbeard	*Crepis capillaris*
Field Woodrush	*Luzula campestris*
Black Bryony	*Tamus communis*
Twayblade	*Listera ovata*
Spotted Orchid	*Dactylorhiza fuchsii*
Southern Marsh Orchid	*Dactylorhiza praetermissa*[1]
Hybrid Orchid	*Dactylorhiza fuchsii x D. praetermissa = D. grandis*[1]
Pyramidal Orchid	*Anacamptis pyramidalis*[1]

SEDGES

Wood Sedge	*Carex sylvatica*
Glaucous Sedge	*Carex flacca*
Spring Sedge	*Carex caryophylea*[1]

GRASSES

Giant Fescue	*Fescue gigantea*
Sheep's Fescue	*Festuca ovina*
Red Fescue	*Festuca rubra*
Perennial Rye Grass	*Lolium perenne*
Annual Meadow-grass	*Poa annua*
Smooth Meadow-grass	*Poa pratensis*
Rough Meadow-grass	*Poa trivialis*
Cock's Foot	*Dactylis glomerata*
Crested Dog's-tail	*Cynosurus cristatus*
Quaking Grass	*Briza media*[1]
Upright Brome	*Bromus erectus*
Hairy Brome	*Bromus ramosus*
Wood False-brome	*Brachypodium sylvaticum*
Crested Hair-grass	*Koeleria macrantha*[1]
Yellow Oat-grass	*Trisetum flavescens*
Downy Oat-grass	*Avenula pubescens*
Meadow Oat-grass	*Avenula pratense*[1]
False Oat-grass	*Arrhenatherum elatius*
Yorkshire Fog	*Holcus lunatus*

Creeping Bent	*Agrostis stolonifera*
Cat's Tail	*Phleum bertolonii*
Meadow Fox-tail	*Alopecurus pratensis*
Sweet Vernal-grass	*Anthoxanthum odoratum*

TREES and SHRUBS

Juniper	*Juniperus communis*[1]
Sycamore	*Acer pseudoplatanus*
Field Maple	*Acer campestre*
Norway Maple	*Acer platanoides*
Horse Chestnut	*Aesculus hippocastanum*
Holly	*Ilex aquifolium*
Buckthorn	*Rhamnus cathartica*[1]
Dog Rose	*Rosa canina*
Blackthorn	*Prunus spinosa*
Wild Cherry	*Prunus avium*
Hawthorn	*Crataegus monogyna*
Rowan	*Sorbus aucuparia*
White Beam	*Sorbus aria*[1]
Apple	*Malus domestica*
Dogwood	*Cornus sanguinea*
Ivy	*Hedera helix*
Silver Birch	*Betula pendula*
Hornbeam	*Carpinus betulus*
Hazel	*Corylus avellana*
Beech	*Fagus sylvatica*
Common Oak	*Quercus robur*
Ash	*Fraxinus excelsior*
Elder	*Sambucus nigra*
Wayfaring Tree	*Viburnum lantana*

[1] Plants of special interest or uncommon in Herts.

APPENDIX 9C

PLANTS OF SHEETHANGER COMMON, 1999–2000

Recorded by Gerald Salisbury and Jill Saunders.

This land has been designated by Hertfordshire County Council as a Heritage Site. It has lost its SSSI designation.

Common name	Botanical name
Hart's Tongue Fern	*Phyllitis scolopendrium*
Male Fern	*Dryopteris filix-mas*
Broad Buckler Fern	*Dryopteris dilitata*
Old Man's Beard	*Clematis vitalba*
Meadow Buttercup	*Ranunculus acris*
Creeping Buttercup	*Ranunculus repens*
Bulbous Buttercup	*Ranunculus bulbosus*
Goldilocks	*Ranunculus auricomus*
Celandine	*Ranunculus ficaria*
Hairy Violet	*Viola hirta*
Common Milkwort	*Polygala vulgaris*[1]
Hairy St John's-wort	*Hypericum hirsutum*
Rockrose	*Helianthemum nummularium*[1]
Mouse-ear Chickweed	*Cerastium fontanum*
Lesser Stitchwort	*Stellaria graminea*
Fairy Flax	*Linum catharticum*
Herb Robert	*Geranium robertianum*
Black Meddick	*Medicago lupulina*
Red Clover	*Trifolium pratense*
White Clover	*Trifolium repens*
Yellow Trefoil	*Trifolium dubium*

Birdsfoot Trefoil	*Lotus corniculatus*	Annual Meadow-grass	*Poa annua*
Raspberry	*Rubus idaeus*	Wood Meadow-grass	*Poa memoralis*
Bramble	*Rubus fruticosus*	Smooth Meadow-grass	*Poa pratensis*
Silver Weed	*Potentilla anserina*	Rough Meadow-grass	*Poa trivialis*
Creeping Cinquefoil	*Potentilla reptans*	Cocksfoot	*Dactylis glomerata*
Wild Strawberry	*Fragaria vesca*	Crested Dog's tail	*Cynosurus cristatus*
Herb Bennet	*Geum urbanum*	Quaking Grass	*Briza media*[1]
Agrimony	*Agrimonia eupatoria*	Upright Brome	*Bromus erectus*
Salad Burnet	*Sanguisorba minor*[1]	Hairy Brome	*Bromus ramosus*
Dog Rose	*Rosa canina*	Wood False Brome	*Brachypodium sylvaticum*
Wood Sanicle	*Sanicula europaea*	Crested Hair-Grass	*Koeleria macrantha*[1]
Rough Chervil	*Chaerophyllum temulentum*	Yellow Oat-Grass	*Trisetum flavescens*
Cow Parsley	*Anthriscus sylvestris*	Hairy Oat-grass	*Helictotrichon pubescens*
Hedge Parsley	*Torillis japonica*	Meadow Oat-grass	*Helictotrichon pratense*[1]
Burnet Saxifrage	*Pimpinella saxifraga*	False Oat-Grass	*Arrhenatherum elatius*
Dog's Mercury	*Mercurialis perennis*	Yorkshire Fog	*Holcus lanatus*
Common Sorrel	*Rumex acetosa*	Creeping Bent	*Agrostis stolonifera*
Wood Dock	*Rumex sanguineus*	Meadow Foxtail	*Alopecurus pratensis*
Stinging Nettle	*Urtica dioica*	Sweet Vernal Grass	*Anthoxanthum odoratum*
Cowslip	*Primula veris*		
Autumn Gentian	*Gentianella amarella*[1]	TREES and SHRUBS	
Woody Nightshade	*Solanum dulcamara*	Juniper	*Juniperus communis*[1]
Germander Speedwell	*Veronica chamaedrys*	Yew	*Taxus baccata*
Slender Speedwell	*Veronica filiformis*	Scots Pine	*Pinus sylvestris*
Yellow Rattle	*Rhinanthus minor*[1]	Mahonia	*Mahonia aquifolium*
Eyebright	*Euphrasia nemerosa*[1]	Sycamore	*Acer pseudoplatanus*
Thyme	*Thymus pulegioides*	Field Maple	*Acer campestre*
Wild Basil	*Clinopodium vulgare*	Norway Maple	*Acer platanoides*
Selfheal	*Prunella vulgaris*	Holly	*Ilex aquifolium*
Hoary Plantain	*Plantago media*	Spindle	*Euonymus europaeus*
Ribwort Plantain	*Plantago lanceolata*	Buckthorn	*Rhamnus catharticus*
Harebell	*Campanula rotundifolia*	Wild Cherry	*Prunus avium*
Hedge Bedstraw	*Galium mollugo*	Blackthorn	*Prunus spinosa*
Lady's Bedstraw	*Galium verum*	Hawthorn	*Crataegus monogyna*
Small Scabious	*Scabiosa columbaria*[1]	Ivy	*Hedera helix*
Ragwort	*Senecio jacobaea*	Silver Birch	*Betula pendula*
Coltsfoot	*Tussilago farfara*	Hornbeam	*Carpinus betulus*
Daisy	*Bellis perennis*	Hazel	*Corylus avellana*
Yarrow	*Achillea millefolium*	Beech	*Fagus sylvatica*
Mugwort	*Artemesia vulgaris*	Oak	*Quercus robur*
Carline Thistle	*Carlina vulgaris*[1]	Goat Willow	*Salix caprea*
Field Thistle	*Cirsium arvensis*	Ash	*Fraxinus excelsior*
Dwarf Thistle	*Cirsium acaulon*[1]	Elder	*Sambucus nigra*
Hardheads	*Centaurea nigra*	Wayfaring Tree	*Viburnum lantana*
Cat's Ear	*Hypochoeris radicata*	Guelder Rose	*Viburnum opulus*
Autumnal Hawkbit	*Leontodon autumnalis*		
Rough Hawkbit	*Leontodon hispidus*		
Smooth Hawkbit	*Leontodon saxatilis*		
Goat's Beard	*Tragopogon pratensis*		
Wall Lettuce	*Mycelis muralis*		
Mouse-ear Hawkweed	*Hieracium pilosella*		
Dandelion	*Taraxacum officinale*		
Beaked Hawksbeard	*Crepis vesicaria*		
Black Bryony	*Tamus communis*		
Twayblade	*Listera ovata*		
Frog Orchid	*Coeloglossom viride*[1]		
Bee Orchid	*Ophrys apifera*[1]		
Spotted Orchid	*Dactylorhiza fuchsii*		
Pyramidal Orchid	*Anacamptis pyramidalis*[1]		
Cuckoo Pint	*Arum maculatum*		

[1] Plants of special interest or uncommon in Herts.

SEDGES

Glaucous Sedge	*Carex flacca*
Spring Sedge	*Carex caryophyllea*[1]

APPENDIX 9D

PLANTS OF FURTHER ROUGHDOWN, 1999–2000

Recorded by Gerald Salisbury and Jill Saunders.

The Box Moor Trust acquired this land as Exchange Land for the A41 By-pass and it was sown with wildflower seeds after removing arable soil.

GRASSES

Red Fescue	*Festuca rubra*
Sheeps Fescue	*Festuca ovina*
Perrenial Rye-grass	*Lolium perenne*

Common name	Botanical name
Juniper	*Juniperus communis*[1 & 3]
Meadow Buttercup	*Ranunculus acris*
Creeping Buttercup	*Ranunculus repens*
Mignonette	*Reseda lutea*[2]
Bladder Campion	*Silene vulgaris*
Mouse-ear Chickweed	*Cerastium fontanum*
Hop Trefoil	*Trifolium campestre*

Yellow Trefoil	*Trifolium dubium*[2]
White Clover	*Trifolium repens*[2]
Red Clover	*Trifolium pratense*[2]
Bird's Foot Clover	*Lotus corniculatus*[2]
Salad Burnet	*Sanguisorba minor*[1 & 2]
Wild Carrot	*Daucus carota*[2]
Cowslip	*Primula veris*[2 & 4]
Centaury	*Centaurium erythraea*
Bindweed	*Convolvulus arvensis*
Common Toadflax	*Linaria vulgaris*
Thyme-leaved Speedwell	*Veronica serpyllifolia*
Yellow Rattle	*Rhinanthus minor*[2]
Red Bartsia	*Odontites verna*
Marjoram	*Origanum vulgare*[1 & 2]
Wild Basil	*Clinopodium vulgare*[2]
Self Heal	*Prunella vulgaris*[2]
Great Plantain	*Plantago major*
Hoary Plantain	*Plantago media*[2]
Ribwort Plantain	*Plantago lanceolata*
Hedge Bedstraw	*Galium mollugo*
Lady's Bedstraw	*Galium verum*[2]
Small Scabious	*Scabiosa columbaria*[1 & 2]
Ragwort	*Senecio jacobaea*
Yarrow	*Achillea millefolium*
Ox-eye Daisy	*Leucanthemum vulgare*[2]
Spear Thistle	*Cirsium vulgare*
Field Thistle	*Cirsium arvense*
Lesser Knapweed	*Centaurea nigra*
Common Cat's ear	*Hypochoeris radicata*
Autumnal Hawkbit	*Leontodon autumnalis*
Rough Hawkbit	*Leontodon hispidus*
Smooth Hawkbit	*Leontodon saxatilis*
Goat's-beard	*Tragopogon pratensis*
Dandelion	*Taraxacum officinale*
Beaked Hawk's-beard	*Crepis vesicaria*
Pyramidal Orchid	*Anacamptis pyramidalis*[1]
Glaucous Sedge	*Carex flacca*

GRASSES

Red Fescue	*Festuca rubra*
Annual Meadow-grass	*Poa annua*
Rough Meadow-grass	*Poa trivialis*
Smooth Meadow-grass	*Poa pratensis*
Cock's Foot	*Dactyllis glomerata*
Crested Dog's Tail	*Cynosurus cristatus*
Quaking Grass	*Briza media*[1]
Yellow Oat-grass	*Trisetum flavescens*
False Oat-grass	*Arrhenatherum elatius*
Yorkshire Fog	*Holcus lanatus*
Creeping Bent	*Agrostis stolonifera*
Smaller Cat's Tail	*Phleum bertelonii*
Meadow Rox-tail	*Alopecurus pratensis*
Perennial rye-grass	*Lolium perenne*

[1] Plants of special interest or uncommon in Herts.

[2] These species were in the seed mixture sown after acquisition of this land.

[3] This species was planted.

[4] The Cowslip has exploded from the original sowing, it is estimated that there must now be over half a million plants.

APPENDIX 9E

PLANTS OF BOVINGDON BRICKWORKS, 1999–2000

Recorded by Gerald Salisbury and Jill Saunders.

Common name	Botanical name
Common Horsetail	*Equisetum arvense*
Bracken	*Pteridium aquilinum*
Male Fern	*Dryopteris filix-mas*
Broad Buckler Fern	*Dryopteris dilitata*
Meadow Buttercup	*Ranunculus acris*
Creeping Buttercup	*Ranunculus repens*
Lesser Celandine	*Ranunculus ficaria*
Lesser Swine's Cress	*Coronopus didymus*
Shepherds Purse	*Capsella bursa-pastoris*
Horse Radish	*Armoracia rusticana*
Hairy Bitter-cress	*Cardamine hirsuta*
Winter-cress	*Barbarea vulgaris*
Garlic Mustard	*Alliaria petiolata*
Hedge Mustard	*Sisymbrium officinale*
Weld	*Reseda luteola*
Perforate St. John's Wort	*Hypericum perforatum*
White Campion	*Silene alba*
Mouse-ear Chickweed	*Cerastium fontanum*
Sticky Mouse-ear Chickweed	*Cerastium glomeratum*
Chickweed	*Stellaria media*
Lesser Stitchwort	*Stellaria graminea*
Common Pearlwort	*Sagina apetela ssp. erecta*
Procumbent Pearlwort	*Sagina procumbens*
Many-seeded Goosefoot	*Chenopodium polyspermum*
Musk Mallow	*Malva moschata*
Fairy Flax	*Linum catharticum*
Cut-leaved Cranesbill	*Geranium dissectum*
Dove's-foot Cranesbill	*Geranium molle*
Herb Robert	*Geranium robertianum*
Common Mellilot	*Melilotus officinalis*
Red Clover	*Trifolium pratense*
White Clover	*Trifolium repens*
Yellow Trefoil	*Trifolium dubium*
Bird's-foot Trefoil	*Lotus corniculatus*
Goat's Rue	*Galega officinalis*[1]
Tufted Vetch	*Vicia cracca*
Bush Vetch	*Vicia sepium*
Common Vetch	*Vicia sativa ssp. segetalis*
Meadow Vetchling	*Lathyrus pratensis*
Grass Pea	*Lathyrus nissolia*[1]
Creeping Cinquefoil	*Potentilla reptans*
Silver Weed	*Potentilla anserina*
Herb Bennet	*Geum urbanum*
Agrimony	*Agrimonia eupatoria*
Parsley Piert	*Aphanes arvensis*
Gt. Hairy Willow Herb	*Epilobium hirsutum*
Hoary Willow Herb	*Epilobium parviflorum*
Sq. Stalked Willow Herb	*Epilobium tetragonum*
Rosebay Willow-herb	*Chamerion angustifolium*
Cow Parsley	*Anthriscus sylvestris*
Hedge Parsley	*Torillis japonica*
Hemlock	*Conium maculatum*
Hogweed	*Heracleum sphondylium*
Wild Carrot	*Daucus carota*
Dog's Mercury	*Mercurialis perennis*
Knotgrass	*Polygonum aviculare*
Redshank	*Polygonum maculosa*
Black Bindweed	*Fallopia convolvulus*
Japanese Knotweed	*Fallopia japonica*

Sheep's Sorrel	*Rumex acetosella*
Common Sorrel	*Rumex acetosa*
Wood Dock	*Rumex sanguineus*
Curled Dock	*Rumex crispus*
Broad-leaved Dock	*Rumex obtusifolius*
Stinging Nettle	*Urtica dioica*
Scarlet Pimpernel	*Anagallis arvensis*
Common Centaury	*Centaureum erythraea*
Field Forget-me-not	*Myosotis arvensis*
Russian Comfrey	*Symphytum x uplandicum*
Bindweed	*Convolvulus arvensis*
Large Bindweed	*Calystegia silvatica*
Hedge Bindweed	*Calystegia sepium*
Woody Nightshade	*Solanum dulcamara*
Mullein	*Verbascum thapsus*
Dark Mullein	*Verbascum nigrum*
Sharp-leaved Fluellen	*Kickxia elatine*[1]
Common Figwort	*Scrophularia nodosa*
Heath Speedwell	*Veronica officinalis*
Wood Speedwell	*Veronica montana*
Germander Speedwell	*Veronica chamaedrys*
Thyme-leaved Speedwell	*Veronica serpyllifolia*
Wall Speedwell	*Veronica arvensis*
Field Speedwell	*Veronica persica*
Yellow Rattle	*Rhinanthus minor*
Eyebright	*Euphrasia nemerosa*[1]
Red Bartsia	*Odontites verna*
Field Mint	*Mentha arvensis*[1]
Self-heal	*Prunella vulgaris*
Hedge Woundwort	*Stachys sylvatica*
White Dead-nettle	*Lamium album*
Common Hemp-nettle	*Galeopsis tetrahit*
Ground Ivy	*Glechoma hederacea*
Bugle	*Ajuga reptans*
Greater Plantain	*Plantago major*
Ribswort Plantain	*Plantago lanceolata*
Goosegrass	*Galium aparine*
Teasel	*Dipsacus fullonum*
Field Scabious	*Knautia arvensis*
Common Ragwort	*Senecio jacobaea*
Coltsfoot	*Tussilago farfara*
Canadian Fleabane	*Conyza canadensis*
Daisy	*Bellis perennis*
Yarrow	*Achillea millefolium*
Scentless Mayweed	*Tripleurospermum inodorum*
Ox-eye Daisy	*Leucanthemum vulgare*
Mugwort	*Artemesia vulgaris*
Burdock	*Arctium minus ssp. minus*
Spear Thistle	*Cirsium vulgare*
Creeping Thistle	*Cirsium arvense*
Common Knapweed	*Centaurea nigra*
Autumnal Hawkbit	*Leontodon autumnalis*
Bristly Ox-tongue	*Picris echioides*
Corn Sow-thistle	*Sonchus arvensis*
Prickly Sow-thistle	*Sonchus asper*
Dandelion	*Taraxacum officinale*
Beaked Hawksbeard	*Crepis vesicaria*
Smooth Hawksbeard	*Crepis capillaris*
Bluebell	*Hyacinthoides non-scripta*
Common Spotted Orchid	*Dactylorhiza fuchsia*[1]

TREES and SHRUBS

Large Leaved Lime	*Tilia platyphyllos*
Field Maple	*Acer campestris*
Sycamore	*Acer pseudoplatanus*
Holly	*Ilex aquifolium*
Spindle	*Euonymus europaeus*
Bramble	*Rubus fruticosus*
Field Rose	*Rosa arvensis*

Dog Rose	*Rosa canina*
Wild Cherry	*Prunus avium*
Blackthorn	*Prunus spinosa*
Apple	*Malus domestica*
Ivy	*Hedera helix*
Silver Birch	*Betula pendula*
Hornbeam	*Carpinus betulus*
Hazel	*Corylus avellana*
Beech	*Fagus sylvatica*
Pedunculate Oak	*Quercus robur*
Goat Willow	*Salix caprea*
Grey Willow	*Salix cinerea*
Ash	*Fraxinus excelsior*
Elder	*Sambucus nigra*
Butterfly Bush	*Buddleia davidii*
Aspen	*Populus tremula*
Hawthorn	*Crataegus monogyna*

RUSHES

Hard Rush	*Juncus inflexus*
Soft Rush	*Juncus effusus*
Clustered Rush	*Juncus conglomeratus*
Toad Rush	*Juncus bufonius*

SEDGES

Wood Sedge	*Carex sylvatica*
Hairy Sedge	*Carex hirta*

GRASSES

Red Fescue	*Festuca rubra*
Annual Meadow-grass	*Poa annua*
Wood Meadow-grass	*Poa nemoralis*
Rough Meadow-grass	*Poa trivialis*
Cocksfoot	*Dactylis glomerata*
Crested Dog's Tail	*Cynosurus cristatus*
Soft Brome	*Bromus hordeaceus*
Barren Brome	*Bromus sterilis*
False Oat-grass	*Arrhenatherum elatius*
Yorkshire Fog	*Holcus lanatus*
Common Bent	*Agrostis capillaris*
Black Bent	*Agrostis gigantea*
Creeping Bent	*Agrostis stolonifera*
Smaller Cat's Tail	*Phleum bertolonii*
Meadow Foxtail	*Alopecurus pratensis*
Sweet Vernal-grass	*Anthoxanthum odoratum*

This area is very much in a state of change, and some things listed here, i.e. annuals, casuals of disturbed ground etc. may well disappear, whilst others may come in.

[1] Plants of special interest or uncommon in Herts.

Sketch by Dennis Furnell, Chalkhill blue on horseshoe vetch, from The Country Book of the Year.

APPENDIX 9F

WATER SURVEY OF THE RIVER BULBOURNE AND OLD FISHERY

John Leonhardt has been undertaking surveys of the river Bulbourne and Old Fishery Cress Beds since 1988 and advising the Box Moor Trust of his findings. These were mostly in the company of 'A' Level Biology students, (associated with the Hudnall Park Outdoor Centre), who were studying the distribution of aquatic invertebrates and incidentally recording the small fish that were caught in the same nets.

John reported: 'In the winter of 1996–7 the river channel was reconstructed alongside Chaulden Meadows to improve the flow and diversity of habitats. At first there was a thorough dredging to deepen the channel, then wicker frames were made to retain banks of mud on one side or the other to force the water to run faster in a narrow channel, weaving from side to side or down the centre. Our aim here was to monitor the changes, which we did from 1997–2001.

There were slow improvements in the variety of animal life, with the first shrimps in 1998, along with three extra fish species (minnow, stone loach and bullhead), some water beetles and a few other insects. In 1999 we found the first caddis larva, but none in the next two years. A few mayflies were found in 2000 and more in 2001. We then decided that the water quality could be described as moderately good, but the actual numbers of indicator species were low. The general situation was that true worms, leeches of several species, water lice, midge larvae, water mites, many species of snails and two or three species of small fish were always to be found somewhere. Freshwater shrimps and mayflies had begun to appear in small numbers; bugs (such as water boatmen), alderflies and water beetles were scarce; caddis flies and flatworms were very rare. Our final visit to this site was in June 2001.

The strip of wetland between the railway embankment and the Grand Union Canal was once a watercress bed. The canal is raised above the level of the surrounding land at this point. The area of the survey started about 500 metres upstream from Old Fishery Lane and ended about 50 metres downstream from the roadway, in the corner of Fishery Moor.

Waterside Cottage stood in the middle of the upstream section, which looked promising since it had a stream flowing through its entire length. There was gravel beneath, which was exposed where the water flowed quickly, but large areas of it were mud, some very deep. The vegetation still included some watercress but consisted mostly of tall, reed-like plants. The patches of submerged plants were mostly Water Starwort. In July 1989 freshwater shrimps, true worms and water lice were commonly found, besides flatworms, leeches, midge larvae, water beetles, water mites, snails and both species of sticklebacks, but no mayfly nymphs or caddis larvae.

In March–April 2003, ten different sites were checked. The results showed that the variety of animal life varied considerably from place to place without much correlation with the water flow, substrate or vegetation. The richest site was the gravelly stream running past Waterside Cottage. About forty-two species of animals were recorded in all, including sixteen which had not been seen earlier.

In the small triangular lagoon in the corner of Fishery Moor, the water came from two culverts under the road. Some water was also collected from land drains, as well as surface water from the A41 By-pass. A small area of Reed (*Phragmites communis*) was planted there before the 1997 visits, in the hope that it might develop into a larger bed with the ability to remove pollutants.

Mayflies were found just once from 1997–2001; one Signal crayfish was discovered, the North American species, which is replacing the native White-clawed variety.

By 2003 there had been a small but distinct improvement. Stonefly nymphs, mayflies and caddis larvae were noted; all of these are indications of water quality.

To sum up, the river Bulbourne at Chaulden Meadows and Old Fishery wetlands are a habitat for a wide variety of aquatic invertebrates, several species of small fish, a limited range of submerged water plants and a modest range of emergent reed-like species. The area has the potential for a greater diversity in both plant and invertebrate life, probably dependent on improving the cleanliness of the water. This would be difficult in the case of the river because it flows through the canal before reaching the site. The other wetland can be isolated from the canal, but if the mud harbours pollutants from the past, these may cause problems for a long time. The present situation, however, is really quite promising.'

John Leonhardt

February 2004

Appendix 10

Box Moor Right of Pasture Plaques

List of individually numbered Grazing Plaques with the properties in existence at the time of the 1809 Act of Parliament to which they had been affixed in 1834. These have often also been referred to as 'share irons', 'plates' or 'marks'. All properties were in Hemel Hempstead unless stated otherwise, as listed in 1976.

1–11	Cherry Bounce	136	1 High Street	253	78 High Street
12	Plate in Trust's custody	137	Marlowes Nursery	254	80 High Street
13–15	Cherry Bounce	138	Hartridge and Rose	255	82 High Street
16	Plate in Trust's custody	139	Old Marlowes House	256	84 High Street
17	Cherry Bounce	140	Bury Road	257	96 High Street
18	The Royal Oak	141	Plate in Trust's custody	258–259	88 High Street
19–21	High Street	142–146	Bury Road	260–261	Walker's Alley
22	3 Bailey's Yard	147	Nag's Head	262	Pulled down. Plate in Trust's
23–25	High Street	148	Bury Road		custody.
26–29	91 High Street	149	86 Bury Road	263–265	High Street
30–31	High Street	150–152	84 Bury Road	266–267	Pulled down. Plate in Trust's
32–35	Plate in Trust's custody	153	Bricklayers Arms		custody.
36–39	Armstrong Yard	154–170	Bury Road	268	High Street
40–41	High Street	171	Six Bells	269	Pulled down. Plate in Trust's
42	Sun Inn	172	Star Brewery		custody.
43–46	High Street	173	Bury Hill	270–275	Pulled down. Harvey Place.
47	71 High Street,	174–175	Plate in Trust's custody	276–278	106 High Street
	(Late International Tea Stores)	176	Bury Hill	279–280	Marchmont Cottage
48–49	69 High Street	177	Pulled down. Plate in Trust's	281	Marchmont Farm, Piccotts End
50–52	67 High Street		custody	282	1 Piccotts End Lane
53	65 High Street	178	8 Bury Hill	283	42 Piccotts End
54	61 High Street	179	Bouncefield	284	44 Piccotts End
55–56	63 High Street	180	Plate in Trust's custody	285	46 Piccotts End
57–60	Austins Yard, 65 High Street	181	82 Bury Road	286	48 Piccotts End
61	High Street	182	8 Bury Hill	287	50 Piccotts End
62	Bell Inn	183–200	Bury Hill	288	52 Piccotts End
63	49 High Street	201	174 Anchor Lane	289	54 Piccotts End
64	High Street	202	Lockers	290	56 Piccotts End
65	Kings Arms Inn	203	Wards End Farm	291–293	Pulled down. Plate in Trust's
66	Kings Arms Yard	204–206	Bury Hill		custody.
67	Plate in Trust's custody	207	Anchor Lane	294	Two Houses, 60 Piccotts End
68	Kings Arms Yard	208–210	Bury Hill		(Late Crown Public House)
69	Kings Arms Yard	211	Police Station	295–296	Piccotts End
	(Converted into Warehouse)	212	Anchor Brewery	297	31 Piccotts Lane
70	High Street	213	Bury Mill House	298–299	62 Piccotts End
71	High Street	214	The Bury	300	Boar's Head
72	Late Home & Colonial Stores	215–225	High Street	301–313	Corner Hall
73–76	High Street	226	Westminster Bank	314	Pulled down. The Hall
77	1 Swan Yard	227	White Hart Inn	315	Corner Hall
78	Swan Inn	228–230	High Street	316	The Lawn
79–82	High Street	231	The Vicarage	317	Mill Street
83	Rose & Crown	232–237	High Street	318	Frogmore Cottage, Mill Street,
84–86	High Street	238	Late Red Lion		Apsley
87	Plate in Trust's custody	239	High Street	319	Frogmore Cottage, Mill Street,
88	High Street	240	Flower Box		Apsley
89	Late Boot Inn	241	High Street	320	28a Mill Street, Apsley End Mill,
90–91	Lloyds Bank	242	68 High Street		Apsley
92–111	Queen Street	243–244	Plate in Trust's custody	321	28 Mill Street
112	Swan & Trout	245	Pulled down. Plate in Trust's	322–323	Frogmore Hill House
113	Queen Street		custody.	324	Manor Farm
114–118	Old Queen's Head	246	2 Keen's Place	325	1 Storey Street, Apsley
119–123	Queen Street	247	3 Keen's Place	326	3 Storey Street, Apsley
124	(Late Gazette's Office, shop only)	248	Keen's Yard	327–330	Featherbed Lane
125–128	Plate in Trust's custody	249	9 Keen's Yard	331–332	Two Waters
129–130	High Street	250	Keen's Yard	333	Bell Inn, Two Waters
131–134	Plate in Trust's custody	251	74 High Street	334	Two Waters
135	Pulled down. Hempstead House	252	86 High Street	335	Two Waters Farm

336–341	Two Waters	445	Bourne Lane, Pix Farm	561	Moor End Cottage, London Road
342–348	London Road	446	Railway Tavern	562–565	Old Pastures, London Road
349	319 London Road,	447–448	2 Featherbed Lane	566	Swan Inn, London Road
	Two Waters School House	449	Moor End House	567	The Lodge, London Road
350–352	Two Waters	450–451	Marlowes	568	Box Lane
353	Paper Makers Arms	452	Felden Lane	569	Boxmoor House
354	Two Waters	453	Felden House	570	Box Lane
355–356	London Road	454	Town Farm, Felden	571	The Old House, 15 Box Lane
357	Pulled down. Mill House	455	Pulled down. (Late Bailey)	572–573	Dew Green, Felden
	Plate in Trust's custody	456	Henry VIII	574	Felden
358	Plate in Trust's custody	457	Cotterells	575–577	Felden Farm, Felden
359	355 London Road	458	Marlowes	578	Felden Lodge, Felden
360	257 London Road	459	Wood Farm	579	Farm converted into 3 cottages
361	359 London Road, Three Crowns	460	Two Waters	580	Lane Farm, Bovingdon
362–366	London Road	461–462	Plate in Trust's custody	581	Yew Tree Farm, Bovingdon
367	5 Stratford Way	463	Heath Park Hotel	582–583	Forge Cottage,
368–370	London Road	464–466	Moor End		27 Chipperfield Road, Bovingdon
371	Heath Farm	467–486	Pulled down.	584	12 Chipperfield Road, Bovingdon
372–375	St John's Road		Plate in Trust's custody.	585	7 Chipperfield Rod, Bovingdon
376–377	128/130 St John's Road	487	Gardener's Cottage	586	46 Chipperfield Road, Bovingdon
378	Pear Tree Cottage,	488–490	Pulled down.	587	The White Cottage, Bovingdon
	154 St John's Road		Plate in Trust's custody.	588	Rent Street Farm, Bovingdon
379	Pulled down. Elm House	491	Bourne Lane, Winkwell	589	Rent Street Cottage, Bovingdon
380–383	St John's Road	492	Old Cottage, Bourne End	590	Park Farm
384–385	23 St John's Road, Boxmoor	493–495	3 Winkwell	591	Bovingdon
386	19 St John's Road, Boxmoor	496	Three Horseshoes Public House	592	Street Farm
387–389	25/27 St John's Road, Boxmoor	497	Pulled down	593	Cross Farm, Bovingdon
390	212 St John's Road, Boxmoor	498	12 Anchor Lane	594–595	Bovingdon Cross
391	17 St John's Road, Boxmoor	499	Green End House	596	3 Bulstrode Cottages, Chipperfield
392–393	15 St John's Road, Boxmoor	500	Wilton Lodge, Felden Lane	597–599	4 Bulstrode Cottages, Tower Hill,
394–397	115 Anchor Lane, Boxmoor	501–502	101 Piccotts End		Chipperfield
398	Pulled down.	503–506	105 Piccotts End	600–601	Cottingham Farm,
	Plate in Trust's custody.	507	Plate in Trust's custody		Flaunden Lane, Bovingdon
399–400	Corner Hall	508–510	Piccotts End	602	Hollow Hedge, Holly Hedge Lane,
401–403	Anchor Lane, Boxmoor	511	107 Piccotts End		Bovingdon
404	92 Anchor Lane, Boxmoor	512	100 Piccotts End	603	Water Lane
405	88 Anchor Lane, Boxmoor	513	102 Piccotts End	604	Acorn Public House, Bovingdon
406	Bargrove Lodge	514	104 Piccotts End	605	Bovingdon
407–408	Green End Cottages,	515	Gadespring, 109 Piccotts End	606	Stagg Farm, Flaunden
	Green End Road	516–521	Plate in Trust's custody	607	Venus Hill Farm, Bovingdon
409	Plate in Trust's custody	522	Piccotts End House	608–610	Austins Hall, Venus Hill,
410–412	Green End	523	Piccotts End Farm		Bovingdon
413	The Firs, Green End	524–529	Piccotts End	611	Venus Hill, Dairy Farm,
414	Green End	530–531	The Windmill, Piccotts End		Bovingdon
415–416	Green End Cottages,	532–534	Piccotts End	612–613	Mauldens Farm, Venus Hill,
	Green End Road	535	Piccotts End Mill,		Bovingdon
417	Fair View, Green End Road		119a Piccotts End	614	Mauldens Cottage, Venus Hill,
418	The Bye, Green End Road	536	Water End		Bovingdon
419	178 Green End Lane,	537	Red Lion, Water End	615	Shantock Hall, Bovingdon
	Northridge Lodge	538	Piccotts End	616	Home Farm, Shantock, Bovingdon
420	The Hollies	539	Wood Wells Farm	617	Few Onions, Game Farm
421	Northridge	540	Gadebridge Farm	618	Marchants Farm, Pudds Cross,
422	Northridge Farm	541	Corner Hall		Bovingdon
423–426	Chaulden House	542	Anchor Hall	619	Southview, Pudds Cross,
427	Bennetts End Farm House	543	Bourne End Farm		Bovingdon
428–429	10 Bennetts End	544	The School House, Bourne End	620	Fernlea, Pudds Cross, Bovingdon
430	Tile Kiln	545–546	The Hermitage, Bourne End	621	Woodside, Pudds Cross,
431–433	Boxted Farm	547–548	Bourne End		Bovingdon
434	6 Boxted	549–550	7 London Road, Bourne End	622	Three Horse Shoes, Pudds Cross
435	Fields End	551	The Old Cottage, Bourne End	623	1 Pudds Cross, Bovingdon
436	Warners End Farm		(Late Coffee Tavern)	624	2 Pudds Cross Cottages
437–438	Pulled down. Bods End	552	Moor End Farm, Bourne End	625	3 Pudds Cross Cottages
	Plates in Trust's custody	553	Lock House	626	Little Colliers Farm,
439	Pouchen End Farm	554	Elder Cottage, 545 London Road		(Pockets Dell)
440	Cangles	555	London Road	627–628	Whelpley Ash Farm, Bovingdon
441	Fishery House	556	541 London Road	629–631	Whelpley Cottage, Bovingdon
442	161 Chaulden Lane, Boxmoor	557	543 London Road	632	4 & 5 Long Lane Cottage,
443	163 Chaulden Lane, Boxmoor	558	Plate in Trust's custody		Bovingdon (The Nest)
444	Pouchen End Hall, Winkwell,	559–560	London Road		

Moor End Farm, *sketch by Miss Ethel Salisbury*, c.1950.

GRAZING

Detailed records of grazing tickets and graziers are held by the Box Moor Trust for every year since 1834 with the exception of 1845–7 and 1856. Unfortunately, constraints of space do not allow for the full record to be included. The focus is therefore on the years 1834–41, in order to provide an insight into the earlier demand for grazing by the local inhabitants. It was in 1834 that the Trustees decided to identify the houses in existence at the time of the 1809 Act of Parliament in order to affix Right of Pasture Plaques. Clearly, grazing was an important factor in the minds of Trustees at that time; a comparison is made for the grazing demand at the end of the Millennium.

Date	Cows	Horses	Hogs	Total (excluding hogs)	Graziers
1834	132	35	19	167	82
1835	126	43	15	169	85
1846	111	39	18	150	78
1837	122	37	17	159	63
1838	114	50	14	164	68
1839	123	37	18	160	66
1840	84	39	16	123	64
1841	127	40	14	167	72

During these years the acreage under grazing was broadly comparable to the acreage being grazed in recent times. Elizabeth Kinder placed one hog on the Moor every year from 1834–1841. William White grazed 37 cows in 1839, the first year he was listed, twelve in 1840, but none in 1841. In that year there were sixty-four empty houses on the plaque list, a high percentage of the total in the Area of Benefit. In 1834, the comprehensive records name eighty-two graziers and, as their support was a crucial factor in the affairs and social history of the Trust, they are listed below:

Austin, John
Austin, Thomas
Axtell, John
Bates, Samuel
Beckett, John
Belch, Thomas
Blacknell, Charles
Breed, William
Buckingham, George
Catling, Mary
Cheshire, James
Child, George
Collins, Francis
Cooper, John
Coupland, Dennis
Crawley, Thomas
Davison, George
Deacon, T.E.
East, William
Eggleton, George
Field, George

Field, James
Field, William
Floyd, William
Fordham, Eden
Garrett, Mary
Godsden, John
Golding, John
Golding, Thomas
Green, Charles
Hall, James
Harding, John
Harris, Jackson
Headesby, William
Hobbs, James
Holloway, James
How, William
Howard, Daniel
Jennings, Mrs Elizabeth
Jennings, William
Jordan, William
Kinder, Elizabeth

Lavender, Nathaniel
Liddall, James
Lines, John
Lovett, Martha
Mead, Edward
Monk, John
Norris, Henry
Oakley, Richard
Oliver, Sarah
Orchard, John
Pedley, Henry
Pickton, James
Puddephat, Moses
Rawson, William
Reynolds, Samuel
Rickett, James
Saunders, Thomas
Saunders, William
Sedwell, Thomas
Sells, Charles
Smith, James

Smith, John (Brazier)
Smith, John (Two Waters)
Smith, Joseph
Stanes, Henry
Stephens, John
Steward, James
Suffolk, Edward
Tomlin, John
Vize, George
Vize, Thomas
Waller, John
Waller, Joseph
Ware, Mary
Warren, John
Webb, Thomas
Wilmin, John
Winchfield, Joseph
Winter, Issac
Young, William

	Graziers				Trust			
Year	Cattle	Horses	Foals	Total	Cattle	Calves	Total	Grand
			(not incl. in Total)			& Followers		Total
1973	136	22	7	158	0	0	0	158
1974	137	38	9	175	0	0	0	175
1975	94	47	9	141	0	0	0	141
1976	73	30	5	103	0	0	0	103
1977	79	18	9	97	6	3	9	106
1978	104	13	7	117	9	5	14	131
1979	90	10	2	100	14	4	18	118
1980	82	16	2	98	13	5	18	116
1981	96	12	2	108	14	5	19	127
1982	128	17	5	145	17	8	25	170
1983	67	17	5	84	14	9	23	107
1984	74	19	6	93	15	9	24	117
1985	58	18	9	76	21 (+10 Stores)	11	42	118
1986	47	24	11	71	17	7	24	95
1987	69	15	7	84	14	9	23	107
1988	63	14	0	77	14	9	23	100
1989	60	21	0	81	13	12	25	106
1990	45	13	0	58	18	15	33	91
1991	26	22	4	48	13	25	38	86
1992	17	21	0	38	15	30	45	83
1993	14	23	6	37	15	42	57	94
1994	30	23	0	53	17	42	59	112
1995	27	24	2	51	19	45	64	115
1996	20	25	3	45	22	54	76	121
1997	14	22	4	36	17	61	78	114
1998	12	13	5	25	14	49	63	88
1999	2	13	2	15	21	43	64	79
2000	14	17	4	31	15	33	48	79
2001	20	19	5	39	16	46	62	101
2002	19	28	4	47	15	21	36	83
2003	6	23	4	29	17	23	40	69
2004	23	17	3	40	19	still to calve	?	?

'Followers' include bulls, heifers, steers and barren cows.
'Stores' are stock in their final season of fattening for market.

Box Moor Trust Graziers 2004:

Elaine Bone, horses; Martha Brown, horses (sadly Mrs Brown, Charlie's widow, died during this grazing season); Elizabeth Edmunds, horses; Derek Falkener, cattle; Frances Hunt, horses; Martin Hunt, cattle; Chris Price, horses; Mary Sturgees, horses; George Tite, horses.

Box Moor Trust Bulls:

By Artificial Insemination: Firth King Henry, Burnside David, Shiralee Moonshine, Burnside Meteor 2nd, Broadmeadows Lennie.

Box Moor Trust Bulls from 1991: Broadmeadows Picasso, Bolbec Dun Conductor, Mochrum Braveheart, Boxmoor Dante, Merrick Geronimo.

Appendix 11a

Bye Laws of the Box Moor Trust 1763

'As also their heirs and assigns which at any time thereafter forever successively shall and ought to have and enjoy the said Meadowe and premises in manner and form aforesaid shall and will so long as they and every each of them shall be inhabitants and dwellers there maintain keep observe perform and fulfil all such and so many orders and bylaws as now are or hereafter shall be made at any time forever by twelve of the best of the inhabitants of Hemel Hempstead and Bovingdon aforesaid concerning the using enjoying and possessing of the said Meadowe and Fishing to the best commodity and benefit of all and every of the said inhabitants their heirs and assigns being inhabitants there.' Conveyance of Box Moor 26 April 1594.

'At a Meeting of the Trustees appointed for the Ancient Meadow now called Boxmoor lying within the Parish of Hemel Hempsted and Hamlett of Bovingdon in the County of Hertford had at the Kings Arms in Hemelhempsted aforesaid on Tuesday the 5th day of July 1763 pursuant to publick notice given for that purpose.

It is agreed that the twelve persons hereafter named (to wit) Hugh Smith, Michael Lea, Jeremiah Puddephatt of the Wood, Shadrach Godwin the Younger, Thomas Kellam, William Tiverton, Daniel Avis, Robert Perry, Samuel Lawrence, John Smith of Shantock, Richard Clark of Felden and John Batcheldor be a Committee to make such Orders Bylaws and Regulations concerning the using enjoying and Possessing the said Meadow called Boxmoor and Fishing for the Benefit and Advantage of the Inhabitants of Hemel Hempstead and Bovingdon and for the felling cutting down and converting of the Trees Bushes Furzes and other things now growing or being upon the said Meadow and Premises to be converted used and disposed of for the Benefit of the Trustees and Inhabitants of the said parish and Hamlett.

And it is further agreed that Joseph Smith of Cangles be Herdsman for the said Moor for one year in Case he will accept ye same and that he shall keep a book in which he shall enter the names of such Inhabitants of Hemel Hempsted and Bovingdon as shall put Cattle on the said meadow called Boxmoore with the Marks of the cattle and for every head of cattle the owner shall pay Sixpence at ye time such Cattle shall be put on the said Moor , and that an entry be made immediately, and so every year afterwards on or after the first day of February, And, if any Cattle be found upon Boxmoor not entered in the Herdsman's Book to be brought to the Common Pound of Hemel Hempstead; And for every head of Cattle so impounded every Inhabitant, for his refusing or neglecting to enter shall pay one shilling to the Herdsman and every person not having Right to put Cattle there to pay two Shillings and Sixpence for each head and the charges of impounding.

And it is further agreed that no sheep be suffered to feed upon Boxmoor from the first day of February to the 1st day of November and if any shall be found there to be put into the pound and for every Parcel or Flock belonging to one person each person owning said sheep shall pay to ye Herdsman two Shillings and Sixpence.

And it is further agreed no person be permitted to dig and carry away Turf or Earth from the said Moor on any Account whatsoever.

And it is further agreed that for every Load of Gravel taken away or used by any Inhabitant of the said Parish or Hamlett sixpence shall be paid and for every Load of Moor Earth one Shilling and no person not being an Inhabitant of Hemel Hempsted or Bovingdon shall have any Gravel or Moor Earth without paying five Shillings for every Load, which Money is to be received by ye Herdsman and be applied by the Committee in erecting Gates Rails and Posts to Fence ye Passages to ye said Moor.

And it is further agreed that Notice be immediately given to the several persons now having sheep upon Boxmoor to remove them in fourteen days from ye Day of the Date hereof and in default they will be sent to the Pound.'

Austin, John	Cole, Nicholas	Lea, Michael	Smith, John
Avis, Daniel	Collett, Joseph	Lovell, John	Smith, Thomas
Batcheldor, John	Crawley, John	Moore, Henry	Smith, William
Bedford, John jun.	Deacon, Elisha	Newman, John	Tiverton, William
Brickland, Matthew	Eaton, Charles	Perry, Robert	Warren, Richard
Brooks, John	Ginger, William	Puddefoot, Mary	Weedon, William
Bryant, John	Godwin, Shadrach	Puddephatt, Jeremiah	
Canfield, Joseph	Kellam, Thomas	Ramsey, Thomas	
Cater, William	Lawrence, Samuel	Smith, Hugh	

Appendix 11b

Bye Laws of the Box Moor Trust 1969

Notice is Hereby Given that the Minister of Housing and Local Government, on the application of the Boxmoor Trust, has made an Order under Section 193 of the Law of Property Act 1925 imposing limitations on and conditions as to the rights of access to Boxmoor Common, Shothanger Common, Dew Green, Roughdown Common and Chaulden Meadows, for air and exercise conferred on the public by that Section. A copy of the Order (with plan) has been deposited with the Hemel Hempstead Borough Council at the Town Hall, Hemel Hempstead, Hertfordshire.

The Following are the limitations and conditions imposed by the Order:–

Schedule

Without Lawful Authority no person shall in or upon the land:–

    (a)   Remove gravel, sand, soil or turf.

    (b)   Discharge firearms or throw or discharge missiles.

    (c)   Wilfully destroy, chase, or take or set traps or nests or lay snares or any wild animals.

    (d)   Permit dogs to chase game or other birds or animals or otherwise fail to keep dogs under proper control.

    (e)   Permit horses, cattle, sheep or other animals to graze or stray.

    (f)   Bathe in any pond or stream.

    (g)   Post or paint bills, advertisements, placards or notices.

    (h)   Train, break-in, exercise or ride horses except (i) on the tracks shown by brown lines on the said plan and or notice displayed at intervals at or near the said tracks bearing the words "Horse Ride" and (ii) on public bridleways not shown as aforesaid.

    (i)   Hold any show, exhibition or fair or place any swing, roundabout or other like thing.

    (j)   Erect or place any building, tent, booth, stall, fence, post, railing or other similar structure for any purpose.

    (k)   Sell, vend or expose for sale any goods or merchandise whatsoever.

Anyone who fails to observe any of the above limitations or conditions will be liable on summary conviction to a Fine not exceeding twenty pounds for each offence.

Note

The public are reminded that the commission of such acts as are listed in the left-hand column below may be an infringement of the corresponding enactment listed in the right-hand column.

Damage or destroy trees, saplings, shrubs, gorse or underwood or set fire to heath, gorse or fern.	Malicious Damage Act, 1861 and Section 14 of the Criminal Justice Administration Act, 1914
Injure notice boards, seats or receptacles for rubbish.	Malicious Damage Act, 1861 and Section 14 of the Criminal Justice Administration Act 1914.
Injure or disfigure any ancient monument or earthwork or object of historical, scientific or antiquarian interest.	Malicious Damage Act, 1861 and Section 14 of the Criminal Justice Administration Act, 1914.
Drive vehicles or camp or light fires without lawful authority.	Section 193 of the Law of Property Act 1925.
Create any nuisance or disturbance, use obscene language or behave in an indecent or disorderly manner to the annoyance of any person.	Section 5 of the Public Order Act, 1936.
Kill, injure or take any protected wild bird; take, damage or destroy the nest of any protected wild bird while that nest is in use; take or destroy an egg from any nest of a protected wild bird.	Section 1 of the Protection of Birds Act, 1954.
Deposit anything causing or tending to cause defacement by litter.	Litter Act, 1958.
Abandon motor vehicles or dismantle parts of motor vehicles or other things on the common.	Section 19 of the Civic Amenities Act 1967.

R. W. H. Raikes
(Clerk)
For and on behalf of the Boxmoor Trust, 10, Queensway, Hemel Hempstead.   Dated 1st October, 1969.

APPENDIX 12

PETITION TO THE BOX MOOR TRUSTEES 1835

Copy of the MEMORIAL presented to the Trustees of Box Moor, by the Inhabitants of Hemel Hempsted and Bovingdon, in October 1835.

TO THE TRUSTEES OF BOX MOOR.

We the undersigned Inhabitants of the Parishes of Hemel Hempsted and Bovingdon, (being the parties entitled to the benefits arising from Box Moor) viewing with extreme concern and regret that you have been called upon by the Legislature to part with so much of the Moor for the purpose of the Birmingham Railway (in addition to upwards of Sixty Acres which have been previously taken from us for the purposes of the Grand Junction Canal, and for Leases as presently noticed), beg to express our earnest hope that you will be extremely careful in your Sale of the Land to the Company, in order that they may not obtain from you one particle more, than by their Act of Parliament they can strictly claim of you.

The great object of this Memorial is to express our hope that you will use your utmost exertions in securing an investment of the Money about to be received from the Railway Company, in the purchase of Land as contiguous to the Moor and as nearly calculated to answer the objects of the Trust of it, as possible.

In presenting this Memorial to you, we cannot neglect the opportunity of noticing our regret that you should let so much of the Moor for building and other purposes, in contravention of the 11th September Act of Parliament; and we must hope that you will in your future disposition of the benefits arising from the Moor, entirely rely upon the guide which the 8th Sec. of the Act charges you with.

John Turner	Henry Eggleton	George Field	Elizabeth Simmonds
John Jones?	John Reeve	John Gilmore	John Fountain
Philys Brownlow	Charles Ellis	Mrs Oliver & Son	William Carver? X
James Mansfield	Isaac Pitkin	Thomas Read	Joseph Werriman
Edmun Gurney	William Briden	Henry Gleniste	Thomas Foster
Henry Thanes	Joseph Attsey	Mrs Flowers	James Aidsett X
Thomas Saunders	Thomas Rickett	James Hill May	Joseph King
Moses Pudephat	Joseph Pudenfatt	Mathew Hobbs X	John Hill X
Harry Reeve	James Hobbs	Samuel Phillips	John Read
John Letterby?	William Whatson?	Thomas Grace? X	Joseph Ware?
James Times	John Siddall	Thomas Brise?	William Honour
Edward Saunders	George Brise? X	John Halbin	Joseph Smith
Thomas Harris X	William Final	Thanius Drafter?	Henry Henting?
Jonathan Beckley	Frances Glennister	James Bull	Francis Scott
James Finn	Thomas Greener X	Joseph Pudeyphat in Horton	William Austin
Hibbicar How? X	Colline Beeson?	Daniel Skinner	James Calyhew X
John Hill X	Benjamin Edge	George Thorpe X	John Sear
Joseph Mead	James Homans X	Thomas Foster X	William Thackley
Jesse Tannaylass? X	Samuel Clarke	Ephraim Thoobs?	Samuel Collings X
William Radwell	Mary Dorsett?	Ralph Lewin X	William Blackwell
William Thickett	Thomas Tompkins X	William Gales	James Butler X
William Steward X	Charles Gunn	Abraham Deller	Thomas Clarke X
William Newton	Peter Short	William Durrant X	Thomas Putnham
E. Ball X	Daniel Water? X	John Dyer	William Timmins X
John Water? X	Joseph Fountain	James Preston X	Mary Seabrook X
Stephen Barnes	William Preston X	Samuel Belcher	Daniel Thorn
Michael Morton X	James Watkins?	Esther Edge	John Burgin X
Edward Ives	John Baldwin	Richard Byhouse? X	James Alun?
Charles Ellis	James Kemp X	Jonathan Beckley	William Breed
William Honour	John Palmer	John Meridon	Ann Baldwin

X = their mark   ? = name uncertain

BIBLIOGRAPHY

Barden, Ruth *A History of Lockers Park School* R. J. D. Barden (1999)

Barry, Jonathan and Brooks, Christopher (eds.) *The Middling Sort of People* Macmillan (1994)

Bell, Vicars *Little Gaddesden* Faber and Faber (1949)

Bell, Vicars *To Meet Mr. Ellis* Faber and Faber (1956)

Birtchnell, Percy C. *A Short History of Berkhamsted* P. Birtchnell (1972)

Box Moor Trust *This is your heritage* (1986)

Brereton, Lt. Col. F. S. *Hemel Hempstead Through the Ages* Herts. Newspapers Ltd

Brown, Sarah C. M. *Bovingdon* Bovingdon Parish Council (2002)

Bryant, V. J. M. *A History of Potten End* Broxbourne Press (1986)

Buteux, Elizabeth *Time's Highway* Dacorum Heritage Trust (1998)

Cannon, James and Hedley *The Nicky Line* Barracuda Books Ltd (1977)

Chauncy, Sir H. *The Historical Antiquities of Hertfordshire* (1700)

Cobb, Revd J. *History and Antiquities of Berkhamsted* The Book Stack (1883, reprinted 1988)

Coult, Douglas *A Prospect of Ashridge* Phillimore (1980)

Cussans, J. E. *History of Hertfordshire; Volume III* Stephen Austin and Sons (1879–81); (reprinted by E. P. Publishing Ltd, in collaboration with Hertfordshire County Library, 1972)

Dacorum Museum Advisory Committee *Dacorum at War* Dacorum Heritage Trust (1987, reprinted 1995)

Dacorum Museum Advisory Committee *Highways and Byways of Dacorum* Dacorum Heritage Trust (1985)

Davis, Eve *Around Hemel Hempstead in Camera* Quotes Ltd (1990)

Davis, Eve *Hemel Hempstead in Camera* Quotes Ltd (1987)

Davis, Jean *Straw Plait* Shire Publications Ltd (1981)

Evans, Joan *The Endless Web* Jonathan Cape (1955)

Fraser, Susan *Living on the Land* Welwyn Hatfield Museum Service (1979)

Furnell, Dennis L. *The Country Book of the Year* David and Charles (1980)

Hands, J. *ABC of Street Names in Dacorum* Dacorum Heritage Trust (1985)

Hands, J. (ed.) *Miss Salisbury's Notes on the History of Bourne End* Dacorum Heritage Trust (1985)

Hands, J. *Paper and Papermaking, An A–Z of People, Places and Terms* Dacorum Heritage Trust (2004)

Hands, R. & J. *Boxmoor in Camera* Quotes Ltd (1993)

Hands, R. & J. and Davis E. *The Book of Boxmoor* Barracuda Books Ltd (1989)

Hastie, Scott and Fletcher, Lynne *Hemel Hempstead; The story of New Town Development* Dacorum Borough Council (1997)

Hastie, Scott and Spain, David *Berkhamsted* Berkhamsted & District Local History Society/Alpine Press Ltd (1999)

Hastie, Scott and Spain, David *A Hertfordshire Valley* Alpine Press Ltd (1996)

Hertfordshire Environmental Forum *Quality of Life* HCC (2002)

Hertfordshire Environmental Forum *The State of Biodiversity in Hertfordshire 1992–2002* HCC (2003)

Holinshed, Ralph *Chronicle of England* (1577)

Jarman, A. H. *The Memoirs of Alderman Jarman* The Clunbury Press (c.1956)

Johns, Revd Charles Alexander *Flowers of the Field* SPCK (1853, reprinted 1919)

Legh, John *The Story of Ewelme Watercress* The Friends of Ewelme Watercress Beds (1999)

Matthews, A. and E. M. *Chenies Manor House and Gardens* Heritage House Group Ltd (2002)

Maurer, F. *Local Home Guard Experiences of Ernest Maurer* Dacorum Heritage Trust (1987)

McDonald, Tom *The Archaeology of the A41 Berkhamsted and Kings Langley By-passes* Dacorum Heritage Trust (1996)

Miles, D. and Hands, R. (eds.) *Railways of Dacorum* Dacorum Heritage Trust (1983, reprinted 2000)

Miles, D. and Nobbs, Mary *Canal Memories through Dacorum* Dacorum Heritage Trust (1999)

Morris, John (ed.) *Domesday Book: Hertfordshire* Phillimore (1976)

Morrison, Kathryn *Royal Commission on the Historical Monuments of England* English Heritage

Munby, Lionel M. *The Hertfordshire Landscape* Hodder and Stoughton (1977)

Nash, H. *Reminiscences of Berkhamsted* The Book Stack (1890, reprinted 1988)

Neal, David S. *Three Roman Buildings in the Bulbourne Valley* Hertfordshire Archaeology (1974–6)

People of Flaunden *Flaunden, The Past, Present and Future* (2000)

Pilkington, A. *Frogmore and the First Fourdrinier* Laurence Viney Ltd. for the British Paper Co. (1990)

Post Office Directories of Hertfordshire

Potter, Ray *Bovingdon Airfield* Dacorum Heritage Trust (1995, revised 1997)

Robinson, Gwennah *The Book of Hemel Hempstead and Berkhamsted* Barracuda Books Ltd (1975)

Sainsbury, J. D. *The Hertfordshire Regiment* Castlemead Publications (1988)

Sanecki, K.N. *Ashridge: A Living History* Phillimore & Co. (1996)

Senar, Howard *Little Gaddesden and Ashridge* Phillimore & Co. (1983)

Shipman, Cathy and Jackson, Don *Dacorum – Within Living Memory* Dacorum Borough Council/Pageprint (Watford) Ltd (1988)

Thompson, Robert *The Gardener's Assistant* (1859, reprinted 1925)

Tomlinson, Tom D. *Querns, Millstones and Gritstones* Hathersage Church Council (1981)

Victoria County History Volume II (1908)

Walker, Leonard *Background to Domesday* L.G. Walker (1988)

Ward, Peter and Lacey, Ray *The Canal: Tring – Rickmansworth in Camera* Quotes Ltd (1992)

Ward, A.J. (Peter) *The Early History of Machine Paper-making* Dacorum Heritage Trust (1984, revised 2003)

Ward, Peter and Lacey Ray *Apsley and Nash Mills* Quotes Ltd (1989)

Williams, B.H. Garnons *A History of Berkhamsted School 1541–1972* Berkhamsted School (1980)

Williams, Margaret Harcourt and Stevenson, John *Observations of Weather, the Weather Diary of Sir John Wittewronge of Rothamsted 1684–1689* Hertfordshire Record Society (1999)

Woodward, Sue and Geoff *The Harpenden to Hemel Hempstead Railway: The Nickey Line* The Oakwood Press (1996)

Yaxley, Susan (ed.) *History of Hemel Hempstead* Borough of Hemel Hempstead (1973)

GLOSSARY

Agger A low bank or causeway which allowed drainage into ditches at either side; the base of most Roman roads, especially over wet ground. Even though the road itself may have long disappeared, it is sometimes possible to trace the agger.

Alderman Until 1974, a senior member of a local council in England and Wales; elected by other members of the council.

Apsley A clearing by aspen trees: OE *aespe* and *leah*.

Appurtenance(s) Belonging(s); appendage(s).

Ashridge The monastery of the College of Bonhommes (Good Men) was founded at Ashridge on the borders of the present-day Berkhamsted Common, by Edmund, Earl of Cornwall, in 1283. The monastic buildings were completed by 1285.

Bailiff An official with judicial powers, mostly over minor cases and the affairs of the market. William Stephyn was the first Bailiff in Hemel Hempstead, elected by Henry VIII himself. Otherwise elected by the inhabitants in the Court Loft of the Market House on St Andrew's Day (30 November). The term 'High Bailiff' was used in the town from the early 1850s, but without any clear-cut reason for this addition to the title.

Bailiwick Area over which a bailiff has jurisdiction. Hemel Hempstead was a Bailiwick from 1539 until 13 July 1898, when it became a Borough with a Mayor, Aldermen and Corporation.

Beerhouse Premises with a licence to sell beer but not spirits.

Bonhommes Edmund, Earl of Cornwall, brought a portion of a sacred relic believed to be the blood of Christ back to England from Germany. He divided it and assigned two parts to his newly founded College at Ashridge under the care of the Bonhommes. They followed the rule of St Augustine until Henry VIII finally dissolved the monastery in 1539. A link with this Order and the Cathars or Albigensians of SW France has been suggested, but without any conclusive evidence.

Bourne End A district near a spring or stream; le Bournend in 1357 Rental. OE *burna* and *ende*. The Bourne 'Brook' Gutter flows into the river Bulbourne at Bourne End.

Bovingdon Derived from OE *bufan* and *dune* meaning above the downs; it is sometimes recorded as Bovington.

Box Moor A marshy wasteland by box trees; OE *mor* meaning marsh.

Chapel-of-Ease A chapel built to accommodate parishioners living at some distance from the parish church.

Cherry Bounce Probably a unique name for an English street; its derivation is uncertain, but may be from the long association with cherry growing in the Dacorum area. 'Bounce' may describe the action suffered by the rider from the poor state of the road; it was also a term for a fruit cordial. It was re-named Cross Street but has now reverted to its original name.

Chiltern Gap The valley of the river Bulbourne forms a gap through the Chiltern hills. Over the centuries, trackways, roads, canals and railways have made use of this natural transport corridor.

Churchill The name of the house once known as The Heath, St John's Road, Boxmoor. It was built on part of the estate of the old manor of Haybarns. The house stood near to the former Heath Park Hotel, on the site of the present Hemel Hempstead Sports Centre.

Clunch stone A soft limestone made from the hard chalk of the lower strata which reaches the surface at Totternhoe near Dunstable. Clunch can be carved into delicate and intricate shapes but is only suitable for interior work; if used externally it erodes badly through weathering.

College of Bonhommes See Bonhommes

Commission for the New Towns The transfer of assets to this body from the Development Corporation was achieved by 1 April 1962 and the main responsibility of carrying out the second development 'master plan' then fell to the Commission.

Common land Land belonging to a community, especially unenclosed waste land. The commons in England date from Anglo-Saxon times when villagers had to grow their own food. They often had certain 'rights of common', such as estovers, herbage, pannage, piscary and turbary.

Conventual Associated with or belonging to a convent; similar to the term collegiate, belonging to a college. St Mary's Church, Hemel Hempstead, had collegiate status until the dissolution of the monastery at Ashridge. The last collegiate rector was Thomas Waterhouse.

Coppicing The 'farming' by cutting down of trees to a height sufficient for them to grow again, usually in rotation. Up to the middle of the 1700s there were two typical kinds of English woodland: wood-pasture and coppice. Thin coppice wood was often woven into wattle fencing, whilst larger timber was used for building.

Copyhold Tenure in accordance with a transcript of manorial records.

Corpus Christi Day 29 May, the date of the annual fair in Hemel Hempstead.

Court Baron The Lord of the Manor exercised jurisdiction over his tenants in this court.

Court of Piepowder See Piepowder Court

Crouchfield The name for the settlement on the north side of St John's Road in what is now Boxmoor village. OE *crouche* meant cross, so probably referred to the cross roads; Crowchefeld in the Court Roll, 1487.

Dacorum Originally an Anglo-Saxon term for a larger area of land than the present Dacorum, believed to be from the Latin *Daneis* or 'of the Danes'. The use of the name Dacorum Hundred had been maintained for the magistrates' courts but was renewed for a new administrative area established in 1972. In April 1974 Dacorum District Council came into being, comprising Berkhamsted, Hemel Hempstead, Kings

Langley and Tring, as well as outlying villages and hamlets. The other towns and villages have Town or Parish Councils, but Apsley, Boxmoor and Hemel Hempstead do not have any separate representation. In 1984 a new charter created Dacorum Borough Council with its Mayor. (There are also separate Mayors for Berkhamsted and Tring, but not for Hemel Hempstead.)

Development Corporation In 1946 Hemel Hempstead was chosen as a site for one of the proposed New Towns and a Corporation formed with Lord Reith as its Chairman. Building work did not really get under way until 1949. The Hemel Hempstead Development Corporation was replaced by the Commission for the New Towns in 1962, after the first building phase was virtually completed. The Corporation was only a planning and building organisation and did not replace Hemel Hempstead Borough Council, with which it worked closely.

Domesday Register Records or registers made for William I in 1086 of most, if not all, of the land ownership in England; often known as the Domesday Book.

Enzootic Bovine Lucosis (EBL) A transferable, leukaemia-type cow disease.

Esparto grass A coarse grass from North Africa or Spain used for paper-making, suitable because of its short, smooth fibres.

Felden A valley with cultivated land. OE *feld* meant open land; Feldende in 1200 was the settlement on the edge of the cultivated land.

Feoffe/Feoffee Person to whom freehold land is conveyed by feoffement. (A fief was a person who held duty of arms to his lord.)

Feoffement A formal transfer of possessions. In medieval times, the act of the lord in granting a benefice to his man.

Feudal System Medieval European form of government based on the relation of vassal and superior, arising from holding lands 'in feud', i.e. inherited estate held in return for service.

Firemark Identification of properties insured against the risk of fire was needed as towns expanded. Company firemarks helped both the firemen and insurers in cases of fire damage. They were also an early form of advertising and were often displayed in bright colours. Some towns even had insurance company fire brigades and engines, as in Hemel Hempstead.

Fulling Mill A mill used for the working of wool.

Half stuff Partially broken or beaten fibres in the paper-making process.

Heath Park See Churchill

Hemel Hempstead Most of Hemel Hempstead belonged to Ashridge monastery until its dissolution in 1539. In the same year Henry VIII granted the town a charter for a market and fair, also allowing it to elect a Bailiff and Court of Piepowder for the Bailiwick. In 1898 Hemel Hempstead became a Borough with a 'Mayor and Bailiff', a title which continued until the formation of Dacorum District Council in 1974.

Heraditament Property that can be inherited; inheritance.

High Bailiff See Bailiff

Impropriation The transfer of ecclesiastical property or revenue to laymen.

Indenture A sealed deed, agreement or contract. Formerly, a duplicated document, each half having similarly indented edges for identification and security purposes.

Knickpoint A break in the slope of a river; a change in levels. Mills were often sited at such points.

Lady of Shalott The title of a poem by Alfred, Lord Tennyson, set in the time of King Arthur. The lady fell in love with Sir Launcelot of the Lake and died of unrequited love. (A shallot is a small onion, also known as a scallion.)

Lollardism The teachings of John Wycliffe, the fourteenth century English religious reformer; his followers were called Lollards.

Manor A landholding unit in medieval England. The demesne land was cultivated for the direct profit of the lord and the tenants' holdings were lands granted in exchange for rent or service. The manorial system existed from late Anglo-Saxon times.

Mechanics' Institutes Educational establishments first formed in the late eighteenth century to provide adult education, particularly in technical subjects, to working people.

Moor A watery waste; OE *mor* meaning marsh. Box Moor was a marshy wasteland by box trees.

Motte-and-bailey The mound, either natural or man-made, on which a castle was often built; its outermost wall or court.

Navvy Artisans who helped in many of the major construction works of the Industrial Revolution. These men were so called because their predecessors had built the canals i.e. navigated the waterways across the country.

Oakum The loose fibre obtained by unravelling old ropes, which was often used for caulking seams in wooden ships.

Old House Club See Mechanics' Institutes

Oratory A small chapel or place for private worship.

Peppercorn Small dried berry of the pepper plant; used to describe nominal or insignificant rent.

Piepowder/Piepoudre Court (From the French, *pieds poudre* or dusty feet). A court convened to act when immediate justice was required, 'while the subjects still had dust on their feet.' The Bailiff was required by the Borough Charter to preside over as many local inhabitants as necessary to constitute a reasonable jury for sorting out disputes on the spot for fairs, markets etc. where those in dispute may have been moving on shortly. The last such court in the country was held in Hemel Hempstead in 1898.

Plate A horizontal timber joist that supports rafters in buildings.

Pollarding The cutting back of branches to encourage a more bushy growth. The beautiful beeches at Frithsden near Ashridge were once pollards. Trees on common land were often pollarded.

Posting-house or Post-house Horses were stationed at post-houses, usually inns, along the routes taken by the post-boys to receive and deliver mail.

Pound An enclosure or fenced compound for holding stray cattle or animals which have to be officially kept apart.

Puddingstone Hertfordshire puddingstone is a naturally

occuring conglomerate rock, formed by the cementation of coloured flint pebbles (probably first laid down in the Reading Beds about sixty million years ago) with silica. It is extremely hard to work and was mainly used for hand querns; unworked blocks have been found in old walls and as boundary markers. It is a fairly unique geological feature and has many associated myths.

Quern   Hand millstones, in use for thousands of years. The Neolithic peoples used saddle querns and the Romans rotary querns, with the base held firmly and the upper stone rotated by a stick or lever, the grain being fed through a hole. Hard materials such as obsidian, millstone grit and even puddingstone were used in different locations.

Quit Rent   A rent paid by a freeholder or copyholder in lieu of service.

Rental   A list of tenants who were liable to pay rent as above. Roughdown   A rough hill; OE *ruh* and *dun*. Rowdown in 1497 Court Roll.

St Leonard's Day   6 November; a French saint associated with the town of Noblac near Limoges.

St Mary's Parish   Originally in the Archdeaconry of Huntingdon and the Diocese of Lincoln; from 1845 in the Archdeaconry of St Albans and the Dioceses of Rochester, then in 1877 in the Archdeaconry and Diocese of St Albans.

Scrivener   A person who writes or copies documents.

Serf   See Villein

Set Aside   Land taken out of agricultural use and left uncultivated, either for replenishment of nutrients or to alleviate over-production.

Sheethanger/Shothanger   Derived from OE *sceat*, a corner or projecting piece of land, and OE *hangra*, a wood on the side of a steep slope; Shotehanger in 1544 Patent Roll, often recorded locally as Shothanger.

Speenhamland System   The procedure introduced by the magistrates of Speenhamland in Berkshire in 1795 which gave out-relief to the poor of the parish based on the price of bread. It proved expensive to maintain and open to abuse by employers who paid very low wages; it was eventually replaced in 1834 by the English Poor Law.

Stint   A fixed or allotted amount of something, e.g. number of animals allowed to graze the Moors.

Straw plaiting   The craft of plaiting suitable straw into intricate patterns which then became made up into hats and bonnets, fashionable from the seventeenth to the early twentieth centuries. A whole cottage industry grew up, principally in Hertfordshire, Bedfordshire, Buckinghamshire and Essex. Children as young as two to three years old were sent to plait schools to learn the skill and eventually help to subsidise the family income.

Trammel   A fishing net in three sections, the two outer nets having a larger mesh than the middle one.

Terrier   A register or survey of land.

Vestry meeting   A meeting of parishioners for parochial business, usually held in the Vestry, the room attached to the church where vestments were kept.

Videlicet   Medieval English term: 'That is to say; in other words; namely'.

Villein or Serf   A person whose service was attached to the soil. A tenant entirely subject to the Lord of the Manor.

Warren   The right to catch rabbits on another's land; also the right to keep small game animals, birds or fish in an enclosed area of land or a general term for a colony of rabbits.

Waste of the manor   Uncultivated land; unenclosed common land.

Way-leave   Permission to pass over another's ground or property.

Westbrook Hay   An enclosure west of the brook; the estate of that name today lies east of the Bourne Brook Gutter and south of the river Bulbourne.

Wicked Lady of Markyate   Markyate Cell was formerly a Benedictine Priory. Katherine Ferrers inherited the estate in 1634 when she was only a baby. She was fleeced of most of her fortune by her father-in-law and lived alone at Markyate Cell from the age of eighteen. Local legend then tells of her association with a farmer and highwayman, Ralph Chaplin. When he was killed, Katherine took over the robberies, secretly disguising herself and holding up long distance coaches. She was shot on Nomansland Common, near Wheathampstead, and her body found at the entrance to her hideaway. Her ghost is still reputed to haunt the Cell.

Yeoman   Well-to-do husbandman or farmer. The average worth of a yeoman in the sixteenth century was just over £53.

Comparisons

Throughout the book measurements of land and amounts of money are regularly featured. Comparisons between measurements relating to land can be precisely achieved, although those relating to monetary values are not so precise. We hope that the list below provides a simple guide of general comparative values.

Comparisons between Imperial and metric measures:

12 inches	= 1 foot (ft)
3 feet	= 1 yard (yd) = 0.9 metres approx.
	(yards x 0.9144 = metres)
5.5 yards	= 1 rod, pole or perch
22 yards	= 1 chain
220 yards	= 1 furlong
1,760 yards	= 1 mile
840 square yards	= 1 acre = 0.4 hectares approx.
	(acres x 0.404686 = hectares)
60 square rods	= 1 acre
3.3 feet	= 1 metre
	(metres x 3.28084 = feet)
1 acre	= 0.404686 hectare
	(hectares x 2.47105 = acres)
2.5 acres approx.	= 1 hectare

Pre-decimal currency and decimal equivalents:

Pre-decimal value	Decimal value from 1.9.71
Sixpence (6d)	two-and-a-half pence
Shilling (1/-)	five pence
Florin (2/-)	ten pence
Half-a-crown (2/6d)	twelve-and-a-half pence
Five shillings (5/-)	twenty-five pence
Ten shillings (10/-)	fifty pence
One pound (£1)	one pound
One guinea (£1 1s 0d)	one pound and five pence

Day wages of a husbandman:

Year	Wage
1568	4d
1620	4½ d
1632	6d
1647	10d
1662	6d
1688	8d
1698	8d
1716	9d
1740	10d
1760	1s 0d
1788	1s 4d

Table showing relative value of the pound since 1600AD:

Year	Value
1600	£100 0s 0d
1650	£183 1s 10d
1700	£146 8s 4d
1750	£128 13s 0d
1800	£341 16s 8d
1810	£364 3s 8d
1820	£295 2s 6d
1830	£249 17s 1d
1840	£280 10s 3d
1850	£211 3s 5d
1860	£286 10s 7d
1870	£270 9s 8d
1880	£255 17s 5d
1890	£206 11s 9d
1900	£216 12s 4d
1910	£216 12s 4d
1920	£565 0s 10d
1930	£277 18s 8d
1940	£343 5s 3d
1950	£687 19s 3d
1960	£971 6s 11d
1970	£1,421 4s 0d
1980	£5,126.07
1990	£9,673.35
2000	£13,114.61

(Courtesy of John J. McCusker, *Comparing the Purchasing Power of Money in Great Britain from 1600 to Any Other Year Including the Present,* Economic History Services, 2001)

[The recent inflation of property values does not equate with this table.]

Prices for a quartern loaf of bread:

[A quartern loaf is a type of loaf four inches square used especially for making sandwiches, or any loaf weighing 1600g when baked.]

Year	Price
1754	4d
1757	7½ d
1800	1s 5d
1801	1s 11d
1810	1s 5d
1823	10d

(From Colin R. Chapman *How Heavy, How Much and How Long?*, Lochin Publishing, 1995)

Index

Good Friday Fair, *59*
Grand Junction Canal, 1, 16, 24–5, *25–6*, 29, 41, *44*, 45, *46*, 47
Grand Junction Canal Company (GJCC), viii, 22, 25, 27, 29, 32, 37, 41, 48, 61, *63*, 68, 91, 168, 169
Grand Union Canal, *58*, 45, 73, 138, 154
grassland, environmental management, 149–50, *149–52*
gravel pits, 61, 124, 171
Gray, C.E., *125*
Graye, Peter, 5, 9
grazing rights, 50–2, *50–4*, 61
Great Gaddesden, 103, 105
Great Northern Railway, 37
A Green Oasis, 190
Greene, Anthony, 105
Greene, Mr, *64*
Greenhills Primary School, 79
Grey, Lady Jane, 3, 5, 14
Grey, Richard, 5
Grim's Ditch, 15
Grimwoods, 166
Grindecob, William, 11
Grover, Ann, 114
Grover, Charles Ehret, 16, 36, 94, 112, 114
Grover, Harry, 16, 25, 28, 114
Grover, John William, 36
Grover, Walter, 16, 114, 115
Grover and Smith, 16, 27, 28, 122
Gurney, Lois, 185, 191

H
Hagh, Robert de, 180
Half Moon Meadow, 169
Halfway House, 85
Hall, John, 21
Halsey, Sir Lionel, *133*
Halsey, T.F., 72
Halsey, Thomas, 9, 10
Halsey, Sir Thomas, 84
Halsey family, 9, *10*, 106
Hamilton, Revd D., 117
Handpost Farm, 137, 185
Hands, Roger, 194–5, *194*
Harding, Mr, 61
Harding, Thomas, 29
Harding's Moor, *63*, 162
Harvey Coombe, 33, *55*,
Harper, Mr, 63
Harrison, Joseph, 165, 166, 170, *171*
Harrison, Mrs, 166
Harrison Bros, 166
Harrison's Moor, 153, 166
Harry, A.J., 85
Hassell, J., 20
hat trade, 1, 37, *100*
Hawes, Frederick, 56
Hawkes, Jesse, 129
Hawkins, George, 56
Hawkins, Mr and Mrs, 87
Haxters End Farm, 64
Haybarns, 10, 103
Haybarns House, 102
Haybarns Meadow, 168–9
Haydon, George, 43
Haydon, Samuel, 43
Hayes, G.W., 22
Hayes and Co., 22
Hayton, William the younger, 16
Hay Wood, *160*, *184*
Head, Sir Francis, 169

The Heath, see Churchill
Heath Barn, *7*, *63*
Heath Farm, 16, 61
Heath Park, 10, 94, *134*, 136, *156*, 137, 162, *186*
Heath Park Bridge, *38*
Heath Park Halt, *36*, 37, *38*, 73
Heath Park Hotel, *36*, 37, 73, 84, 124, *147*
Heath Park Recreation Ground, 125, 126, 132, 140
Hemel Hempstead, 2
  censuses, 30
  commons, 8, 58
  corn market, 1, 99
  hat trade, 1
  High Street
  manors, 9–10, 11
  Mayor and Corporation, *123*, *124*
  Royal Charter, 13, *186*
  Surplus funds, 91–3
Hemel Hempstead Boy Scouts, 69
Hemel Hempstead (Camelot) Rugby Football Club, 84–5, *84–6*, 140
Hemel Hempstead Club, 93
Hemel Hempstead Corporation, 63, 70
Hemel Hempstead Development Corporation, 84, 138, 140, 182
Hemel Hempstead and District Swimming and Lifesaving Society (HHDSLS), 69
Hemel Hempstead Engineering Company, 69, *142*
Hemel Hempstead Fire Brigade, 105–6, *105–7*, 110
Hemel Hempstead Gas Light and Coke Company, 106
Hemel Hempstead Gazette, 39, 71, 76, 117, 118, 125, 128, 129, 131, 185
Hemel Hempstead Girl Guides, 69
Hemel Hempstead to Harpenden Railway, 36–7, *36–8*, 85, 110, *139*, 140
Hemel Hempstead Hockey Club, 76
Hemel Hempstead Home Guard, 135, *135*
Hemel Hempstead Institute, 93
Hemel Hempstead Local History and Records Society, 99
Hemel Hempstead and London and North Western Railway Company, 170
Hemel Hempstead Operatic and Dramatic Society, *172*
Hemel Hempstead Recreation Ground, 91
Hemel Hempstead School, *7*, *205*
Hemel Hempstead Sports Centre, 70, 112, 140
Hemel Hempstead Station, 165
Hemel Hempstead Teachers' Association, 108
Hemel Hempstead Tithe Map, 65
Hemel Hempstead Town Cricket Club (HHTCC), *49*, 71, 72–5, *72–5*, 79, 108, 119, 135, 137, *186*
Hemel Hempstead Town Football Club, 76
Hemel Hempstead United FC, 8
Hemel Lads FC, 88
Hemelite, 37
Hempstead, Long Island, New York, *189*
Hempstead House, 104
Henry, Prince of Wales, 9
Henry VIII, King, 3, 9, 11, 12, 13–14, 58, 185
Herdsman's cottage, *17*, *55*, 56, 57, 145, *146*, 168, 169, 173
Herdsman's Moor, 145
Herdsmen, 55–7, *56–7*, 61, 62, 64, 87
Heritage Site, *60*, *151*

Hertfordshire Biological Records Centre, 150
Hertfordshire County Council, 39, 145, 200
Hertfordshire Development Plan, 143
Hertfordshire Environmental Forum, 150, 191
Hertfordshire Environmental Records Centre, 200
Hertfordshire Football Association, 87
Hertfordshire Library Service, 204, *205*
Hertfordshire and Middlesex Bat Group, 155
Hertfordshire and Middlesex Trust for Nature Conservation, 150
Hertfordshire and Middlesex Wildlife Trust, 150
Hertfordshire Natural History Society, 150
Hertfordshire Orchard Project, 198
Hertfordshire Yeomanry, 133
Hewitt, Mr, 124
Hicks, Martin, *176*
High Bailiff, see Bailiff
Hight, Joseph, 25, 28, 117
Highway Surveyors, 61
highwaymen, 18–19
Highways Board, 164
Hinson, C., 122
Hitchcocks, William, 20
HM Prison, The Mount, Bovingdon, 135
Hobbs, Ann, *103*
Hobbs, J., 120
Hobday, Sidney, 87
Hobson, Anne, *167*
Hobson, Hannah, *167*
Hodder, R.T. 'Tarn', 116, *116*, 145
Hodgson, William, 119, 195, *195*
Holden, William, 135
Hollinshead, Don, 85
Holloway, George, 28, 169
Hollybush Row, 171
Holme, Capt. H.E., 128
Homans, James, 168
Home Guard, 135, *135*
Home Park Mill, 84, 87
Honor, Joseph, 55
Honorary Vet, 51
Hope, Bob, 135
Hope Cottages, 173, *173*
Hopkins, Len, *77*
Horn, Tom, 180
horses, grazing rights, 50, 51, *51*
House of Commons, 28, 31
House of Lords, 28, 31
Houseman, Revd, 87
How, Daniel, *111*, 112, 120
How, Harry, 112
How, Leonard Leno, 112
How, William Henry, 112
Howard, Charles, 42
Howard, George, 31, 41, 102, 168
Howard, William, 27, 41, 61, *112*, 168
Howard and Deacon, 41
Howard and Son, 41, 45
Howe, C.H., *178*, 185
Howe, Charles, 25
Howe family, 94
Howe's Pleasure Ground, *178*
Howe's Retreat, 52, 58, 93, 136, 162, *164*, *177–9*, 185
Huband, A.C., 77
Huggett, Keith, 190
Hughes, Claire, 195, *195*

The Box Moor Trust can trace its history from Elizabeth I to Elizabeth II. Her Majesty the Queen was greeted by Herbert Christopher, Mayor of Hemel Hempstead, who later became a Box Moor Trustee, on her visit to lay the foundation stone at St Barnabas Church, Adeyfield, on 20 July 1952.